BRUCE
THE AUTOBIOGRAPHY

Bruce Forsyth is known to millions as the face of such shows as *The Generation Game*, *Play Your Cards Right* and *Bruce's Price is Right*. But his is an amazing story that spans more than two-thirds of the twentieth century. He made his debut as 'Boy Bruce the Mighty Atom' at the age of fourteen in 1942 but it was his appearance as compére on *Sunday Night at the London Palladium* in 1958 that made him a star. Now in his seventies, and happily married to former Miss World Wilnelia Merced, Bruce has decided the time is right to pen this show-stopping autobiography. As warm, funny and honest as the man himself, Bruce is a triumphant account of a life lived to the full.

BRUCE
THE AUTOBIOGRAPHY

Bruce Forsyth

CHIVERS PRESS
BATH

First published 2001
by
Sidgwick & Jackson
This Large Print edition published by
Chivers Press
by arrangement with
Macmillan Publishers Limited
2002

ISBN 0 7540 1849 0

British Library Cataloguing in Publication Data available

Printed and bound in Great Britain by
BOOKCRAFT, Midsomer Norton, Somerset

To my darling wife Wilnelia
My daughters Debbie, Julie, Laura, Charlotte, Louisa
And my only son, JJ

CONTENTS

ACKNOWLEDGEMENTS

I'm sure anyone who has ever made a speech and wanted to thank a few people, as I have, will understand when I say that you always find you end up leaving someone out! You feel terrible afterwards, and it can take days for the embarrassment of having made the mistake to wear off. So I'd like to mention a few people who I either haven't said enough about in this book, or indeed about whom I haven't said anything at all.

First of all, Alastair Macmillan (*nothing* to do with my publishers, so I'm not obligated!). Over the years Alastair has been one of my favourite directors, and we've done so many shows together—including the recent Palladiums, TV specials and game shows. I can't thank him enough. And I know I didn't give enough praise to my nineties *Generation Game* team—David Taylor, Bill Morton and Jeff Thacker. Ian Wilson, my manager, *has* been mentioned, but I wanted to add how grateful I am to him for helping me remember things I'd half forgotten over the last twenty years, quite apart from getting all the boxes full of so many memories down from the loft. Jan Kennedy, my agent, has also been mentioned, but not nearly enough. Jan has always tried to negotiate fees for more than I'm worth, and she usually gets them. But much more than this, she is a sensitive person with a generous nature and has helped me so much. Jan recently married and is now Mrs Tony Ball. I'm so happy for them both. On the writing front, Wally Malston and Garry Chambers; we did so many shows together sitting round a table, thinking up funny lines—and shouting at one another, but it was fun. Wally passed away three years ago, and I miss him.

A big thank-you to Barbara Nash for putting such a long life into some sort of order—quite a task. Just as big a thank-you to Gordon Scott Wise for his patience and calmness while I've been going crazy over all the corrections and at times becoming word-blind—*draft after draft after draft.* People told me it would be hard work; why didn't I believe them?

To all the stage and television crews who are such an important part of show business but never get much recognition, as well as the musicians who have backed me and been such a support, especially in my one-man shows.

My regular golfing pals Don, Cliff, Ben, Keith and Norman. I won't give the second names in case they're wanted by the police! And not forgetting my security guard Karim, either. He can get me in or out of any building in the world! Also my golfing pals in Puerto Rico: Eddie (Dr Majic) Shelton, Jim Lambert and Jim Teale—the best eight handicap in the western hemisphere.

I'd also like to thank all the other publishers who came to the book auction. I held it in person in order to get it all over with in one go. I answered questions for an hour and twenty minutes, and I enjoyed it. Thank you for coming. One of the last questions was, 'Do you think you can manage eighty thousand words for your autobiography?' I said, 'I must have done fifty thousand words this morning!' In the end, it's turned out to be over 160,000, in case you count . . .

I do hope I haven't forgotten anyone, and if I have, please forgive me. Right now I feel the same as I usually do when I'm packing to go away for a long time: if I've left something out, I can't do much about it—and even if I remember once I'm on the plane, it's too late!

PREFACE

You may have noticed by the cover that I haven't actually called this book anything. I'm going to leave that to other people. I was going to call it 'The Man I Love', 'The Forsyth Saga' or 'Did I Do Well?' In the end though, I realized I'd come up with so many apt titles, mostly catch-phrases, that there wouldn't have been enough room to put my face on the cover. The publishers were all for it. But I reminded them that my face could actually be a selling point.

Anyway . . . never mind all that. But I would like to say, right up front, my wife has not left me, so that won't be in the book. I've never been to a drug rehabilitation centre, so that won't be in the book either. And I'm certainly not coming out—mind you, after the last couple of years, I don't think there's anyone left in there.

So, if those three things are not in this book, what is? Five hundred and forty-nine pages of my life, that's what! My loves, my heartaches, my ups, my downs, my triumphs, my failures, my vitality, my favourite dance steps, my secret of eternal youth, my idiosyncrasies, my faults, my philosophy of life, my golf swing, my jokes, my shows, my music, my fantasies—maybe that's going *too* far.

But anyway, I hope you enjoy it. Now, please turn to page one.

Bruce Forsyth
Wentworth and Puerto Rico, 2001

CHAPTER ONE

FIRST LAUGHS, FIRST TEARS . . .
AND THE TUPP'NY RUSH

There's an old show business song called 'It's Not How You Start . . . It's How You Finish'. That's true of so many things in life—and also of this book, my autobiography. But where you start and where you finish are both crucial. So . . . *how*—and *where*—shall I start?

I don't want to begin by just telling you I was born on 22 February 1928. In fact, I would rather tell you I was born on 22 February 1948! Why? Because the last twenty-odd years have been the happiest and the most contented of my life. Since I met Wilnelia in 1980, my life has been on fast-forward, and there have been many times since when I've wished I could rewind all the earlier years to make all the bad times go faster and the good ones pass much slower. Time seems to go so quickly now. How, I wonder as I start writing this book, can Winnie and I have been married for nineteen years already and have a fourteen-year-old son, JJ?

Anyway, never mind all that . . . which is something I always say when I want to change direction. The more I consider where to start this book, the more I find myself thinking of the biggest regret of my life—that my dear mother didn't live long enough to see me attain the great heights in show business she had always wanted for me. Yes—she was more ambitious for me than I've ever been

1

for myself. She was the one who stayed up late into the night sewing sequins on my stage outfits until her eyes ached so much she couldn't see the sequins, let alone the needle. She was the one who took me to all the dancing classes so I could learn to tap-dance like my idol Fred Astaire, who entered me for talent competitions, and who was responsible for my first-ever appearance on TV in 1939. She was the one who encouraged me to 'stay with it' when I was weeks and weeks without work. My father did more than his fair share, too, but he was always so busy in his garage business, working to keep our family of five.

Right . . . I'm now ready to start. I don't know whether I mentioned this before, but I *was* born on 22 February 1928! I began life as Bruce Forsyth-Johnson, not quite as grand as it may sound, because, in those days when somebody married into a family which had a bit of money, it was the fashion to hyphenate the two surnames. My paternal great-great-grandmother, who was Scottish, married into the Johnson family and the Forsyths became Forsyth-Johnsons. My maternal grandfather was a river pilot on the Thames. Both my grandparents—on my mother's and father's sides—lived in Edmonton, North London. In those days Edmonton was a comfortably off residential area, but it has become poorer in recent years.

My parents kept the hyphenated Forsyth-Johnson surname, but I dropped it because my full name, Bruce Joseph Forsyth-Johnson, is such a mouthful. And, when I started out in show business and was bottom-of-the-bill, there simply wasn't enough room for all those names. Sad, really, because once you're top-of-the-bill, you can have as many names as you like. Anyway, I got rid of two of mine. My first choice, 'Jack Johnson', was already the name of a heavyweight boxer (who, if I remember rightly, actually became world champion) and there wasn't room for another—especially one with my physique! So, I settled for the very Scottish-sounding Bruce Forsyth.

My father was called John and my mother Florence. It was a family tradition that every first-born son was called John—so he was obviously the eldest. My brother—my parents' first-born son—was also called John. My sister, Maisie, was the eldest child.

Like my grandparents we also lived in Edmonton. We had a house opposite Pymme's Park, which made us a bit more up-market, and my father had a garage business in a little alleyway alongside the house. A talented engineer, he bought and sold old cars, serviced and repaired others, and had three pumps for the sale of petrol. He also had thirty lock-up garages at the back of the house. This business made life very difficult for him because he 'lived over the shop', so to speak—was always on the premises. I remember him working terrifically long hours, starting very early in the morning and never stopping until seven or eight at night. In those days, lots of people finished work at five, but not my dad. He would still be trying to get a job finished—especially if he knew it would bring in more money, or if somebody was waiting for a desperately needed car. Also, when you have a garage with petrol pumps, people knock at your door all hours of the day and night, even when the place is closed. People would knock at eleven o'clock at night, saying they had run out of petrol down the road and could they borrow a can? I don't ever remember my father sending anybody away. He would curse them, and often say: 'Don't bring your tupp'ny-hap'ny jobs down here again,' but he'd never ever send anyone away. He always used to make me laugh when he cursed because he did it so well.

My parents were members of the Salvation Army, but I can't remember ever seeing them in uniform. They were very religious, good Salvationists who knew right from wrong. And if they ever thought a wrong was being done they would say so—would be prepared to 'stand up and be counted'. As we grew up, they taught us to be grateful for things and ensured we kept faith with God. On Sunday mornings, afternoons and sometimes in the evenings, we would all go to Salvation Army meetings. I particularly remember the brass band. My father loved this, and often went to brass-band contests. These were normally held in the Midlands, where most of the bands seemed to be based, but others would come from all over the country to take part in the contests.

My father played the euphonium and the cornet in our local Salvation Army corps and was also in charge of the boys' drum-and-fife band. My mother, who had a lovely voice, used to sing every Sunday morning on Edmonton Green—a beautiful green space then. People walking by would stop and listen to Florence Forsyth-Johnson singing these wonderful hymns.

The month before I was born, Britain's newspapers published figures in January showing that the birth rate in the previous year, 1927, was the lowest on record. So, we could say all babies born at the same time as me were very special! The year 1928 also marked the birth—or I suppose I should say launch—of the Morris Minor car; and the first £1 note and ten-shilling (fifty pence) notes entered circulation. Altogether an auspicious beginning!

The night my mother went into labour with me was very foggy. My father, worried about our GP, Dr Tugan—who always travelled around his practice on a motorbike—went out to look for him in the fog. Dad just managed to get to Dr Tugan in time to stop him driving his motorbike right into a ditch. So, for me and my mother, it was a very good thing they met up.

When Dr Tugan arrived at the house, I was in a bit of a mess. My mother had had a bad fall a few days before, and apparently when I entered the world at about three thirty in the morning, my head looked like an old trilby hat—it was full of indentations. Dr Tugan did his best, pushing and shoving my soft skull around, but then announced he'd done all he could. Having placed me at the bottom of the bed, he added: 'If anything happens during the early hours of the morning, there's nothing more I can do except admit the baby to hospital during the day.' Remember this was 1928—labour, birth and childcare were still at a primitive stage. Dr Tugan, though, was obviously concerned because, before leaving, he said gently to my mother: 'Don't hold your hopes up too high.'

By daybreak, however, I was still alive and kicking—especially kicking—and crying my eyes out. So when Dr Tugan came back later that morning he was quite surprised to see me looking so active, and pushed my skull back into shape a bit more. I don't think he did anything to my chin!

My early childhood is a trifle hazy now, but I have never forgotten the first laugh I got when I was about five years old. It was Sunday teatime and my mother and father had a house full of people who were sitting around swapping stories. My mother then began telling them about the night I was born: 'It was a very foggy night,' she began, 'and John just managed to stop Dr Tugan and his motorbike going into the ditch—which could have been the end of Dr Tugan.'

'Yes, dear,' my father interrupted, 'and it *could* also have been the end of you.'

'Why, Mum?' I chirped in. 'Were you sitting on the back of the motorbike?'

The thought of my heavily pregnant, now in-labour mother riding pillion on the back of the doctor's motorbike was the very first laugh I ever got. It was a lovely feeling—*so* significant. I had said something funny and produced an uproarious laugh.

*   *   *

The house we lived in was the end one of a row of terraced houses, which is why it had a passageway at the side going down to the garages. The fact that it was opposite the park was lucky for us kids because we could go and play on the football pitch, and have boat rides on the boating pool. It was a three-bedroomed house. My parents had the front room with the semi-bay window, John and I shared the back room, and Maisie had the small front bedroom. We had a coke fire in the living room, and I remember the coalman, who was always satisfyingly covered in coal dust and sooty black, coming round shouting: 'Who wants coal?' and carrying the bags on his shoulder into the house and emptying them in a cloud of dust into the cellar. We also had a man who came round the houses selling cat meat.

Like a lot of children who are the 'baby of the family' I was spoiled, took the usual liberties and got away with blue murder. Occasionally, though, I got a clout which I more than deserved. If my mother and father were going out for the evening, my poor sister, Maisie, had to look after me. Evidently, this was a horrendous job because I was a nightmare to control—a horrible, miserable, bossy child who always wanted my own way. My harassed mother had to smuggle her coat and handbag into the car so that I wouldn't guess their plans. She and Dad then had to creep out of the house, down the garden, hoping I wouldn't see them. If I did, I would create hell's fury. I was unbelievable. If I was playing with my soldiers and heard the car going up the driveway on to the main road, I would rush out to the front garden and run along the road screaming and yelling. My poor sister would then have to run after me and drag me forcibly back into the house kicking and screaming.

I first went to school at five years old, in Brettenham Road. But I didn't stay long the first day. I cried so much my mother had to take me home again. Several days passed before she could face taking me back again. But, this time, by some miracle, I lasted that day out and settled in.

At that school, a hyphenated name did not mean a thing. Eventually, I was allowed to play in its football team. In fact I was quite a good footballer.

They called me 'Spider Johnson' because of my very long legs and quick movements. I was quite a devil on the right wing, I can tell you. I was there from five to eleven years of age.

My real passion, though, even more important than football, was DANCING. Fred Astaire was my superstar, my role model, the reason why I wanted to become a dancer. Having seen him in films with Ginger Rogers, I was enraptured—fixated, obsessed. Dancing from then on was the *only* thing I wanted to do, the only thing that made me 'tick', the most important thing in my life.

I saw the Fred Astaire movies at the Regal cinema, Edmonton, and went to each one at least three or four times. Sometimes, to my shame, I used to 'bunk in' the side door. To do this, I would have to wait for somebody to come out and then, before the doors closed, nip in. If there were no usherettes around, I was safe. If the cinema was full and I couldn't immediately find a seat, I was in trouble. I would have to stand at the side, risking being spotted. On one occasion an usherette caught me and unceremoniously handed me over to the doorman, who then dragged me by my ear back to the street. This isn't mentioned on my criminal record!

On Saturday mornings, I would go to what we used to call the 'tupp'ny rush' at the Hippodrome, a real fleapit of a cinema in our area. It literally cost tuppence, two old pennies, to get in, and you needed to get there early because of the hundreds of kids who queued to see serials like *The Lone Ranger* and *Flash Gordon*. It was very dangerous to sit downstairs, because little ruffians would throw things from the balcony. I often got a really bad knock on the head from a bit of hard, half-chewed nougat or even coins. My mother used to say it was more dangerous going to the cinema than to football matches. I wonder if she'd still say that today!

Our other cinema was the Edmonton Empire, situated on top of a very steep hill. We had a different kind of fun there. What we used to do—much to the annoyance of the cinema commissionaire, who was always on the look-out for us—was, first, roller-skate down the hill at a terrifying speed. Then, to his fury, skate back up on the opposite side of the road, cross over at the top and then glide back down past the cinema to the Midland Bank at the bottom. People coming out of the bank were in serious jeopardy. So were we! The commissionaire, beside himself by now, would be chasing after us, trying to catch us, while we were skating at breakneck speed. On one occasion, in my haste to avoid being caught, I nearly passed right through his legs and out the other side.

I have *not* forgotten Fred Astaire. I just always go off on a tangent about cinemas when I think of him.

At home, we had made a through-room of our front room and dining room, which had floorboards covered with linoleum and a carpet on top. I would lift up the carpet and roll it back, so that I could imitate Fred and make a more authentic tap-dancing sound on the lino. I'd dance my feet off—dance till I dropped. I didn't know whether I was doing his steps right or wrong, I just wanted to make that noise he made with his feet. For the same reason, I also danced feverishly, and as noisily as I could, on the corrugated roofs of my father's lock-up garages—not much fun for the neighbours, I can tell you. Come to think of it, I was the tap-dancing Billy Elliot of the 1930s!

One day, when I was about nine, my mother said to me: 'Bru,'—a lot of the family shortened my name to that, and 'Boo-Boo', which was a bit silly, but they all loved it—'if we paid for lessons . . . if we could afford to send you to dancing classes, would you be really interested in them, and want to go?' 'Oh, *yes*, Mum,' I said. 'I'd love to learn how to dance like Fred Astaire in the films. I'd *love* to learn all that.' There's the difference—my family encouraged me from the start, poor Billy's didn't. But in the film he did have Julie Walters as his teacher. Wasn't she lovely?

Anyway, my parents checked their budget, which was always quite tight, and found they could spare a few shillings a week to send me to classes at a dancing school run by Tilly Vernon in Tottenham— a bus ride away from where we lived. And, just like Billy, I was the only boy in the class. That, then, was how IT all started.

*   *   *

I suppose we were a middle-class family. Compared to many, we were reasonably comfortably off—we had a car, and a television. But, although my father always worked to the limit of his strength, there was never much money to spare. My mother belonged to what was called a Christmas Club. A family would save between two and five shillings a week (ten to twenty-five pence in today's money), and the Club Man would come round to the door to collect whatever cash could be afforded. Then, by Christmas, parents would have enough money put by for presents and festive food. In those days, this was the only way that working-class and lower middle-class families could save.

My parents were also in a Holiday Club and usually, by July, had saved enough money to afford an annual holiday. So, although we were always watching the pennies, we were never, as so many families were then, really hard up or destitute. We managed. And later on when I was travelling all over the country in variety shows, and often had weeks and weeks out of work, I was lucky. I always had a roof over my head, and because of the garage my father was always able to fill my car up with petrol and would give me a few bob to ensure I was okay.

Talking about the Holiday Club has reminded me of another one of my earliest memories. From the age of about three until the Second World War—and even a couple of times during that—we would always go to Cornwall which was *the* place to go for holidays then. We stayed in Newquay, which had the most beautiful beaches; and next door was a lovely place called Fistral Bay—where surfing championships are held these days.

Some of the happiest days of my childhood were spent on those lovely Cornish beaches because, when the tide went out, there were so many rocks to clamber over and so many rock pools to explore. We always stayed in the same boarding house, run by a landlady who cooked the most wonderful roast potatoes—the best roast potatoes we had ever tasted. My mother always tried to cook them just like her and, in the end, she managed it. Roast potatoes have been a favourite food of mine ever

11

since. Something nobody could do as well as my mother was jelly and blancmange. She used to make this on Sunday mornings as 'afters' for that evening's supper of cold-meat sandwiches, made from the leftover Sunday roast. She always covered the meat with a damp cloth to keep it moist and fresh, and retain its lovely meaty colour. My great treat was being allowed to scrape the remaining morsels of the delicious blancmange from the sides of the saucepan.

Because my father had a garage business, he was always trying to upgrade the family car. So the five of us would travel to Cornwall in a different one every time. Before we set off, Dad would work for hours and hours on whatever car was going to be used. Having got the three of us ready for an early afternoon start, my mother would pace up and down impatiently. She was a very punctual person and I take after her. Whether it's business or pleasure, I hate to be late and always apologize if I am, which is something too few people do these days. My father, however, was always late—his meals forever in the saucepan waiting for him to come indoors and eat.

Anyway, on the day of our departure, it would get to five, six, seven o'clock and my father would still be under the bonnet, while we were becoming increasingly tired and restless. In the end, Mum would put us to bed, fully dressed, until Dad finished mucking about with the car, sometimes at one or two o'clock in the morning. Fast asleep by now, we would then be woken up to set off to Cornwall, a 300-mile drive from London.

Still barely awake, we would find ourselves on Bodmin Moor. This was when my dad would come

12

into his own again. He'd get his little primus·stove and paraffin out of the boot, and pump away until he got it going. If you've never had eggs and bacon on Bodmin Moor, you haven't lived! The smell of the cooking combined with fresh air, bread being warmed up and a pot of tea being made, is the most wonderful, tantalizing treat. Even now, I often think 'I'd love to be having breakfast on Bodmin Moor.' It was all so beautiful . . . so lovely . . . so family.

There would be quite a few unscheduled stops on the way. Despite all Dad's efforts, nine times out of ten the car would break down. I remember Maisie telling me that we once had such a bad puncture that Dad was reduced to packing grass in the tyre to keep it going until we arrived. How we ever managed to get to and from Cornwall, I do not know. My father, a very determined man, must also have been a really great and inspired mechanic.

*   *   *

Once I had progressed sufficiently in my dancing lessons, tap-dancing competitions entered my life. These were terribly embarrassing for me because my mother used to dress me in my dancing clothes in the same room as twelve or so little girls. I was always very self-conscious about being so thin. I was a skinny little runt, and, to ease my embarrassment, my mother used to have to hold her coat around me while I was changing. I wouldn't mind, but I had nothing to hide!

My dancing clothes consisted of satin suits which my mother made for me and on to which she would

13

sew sequins. On one occasion, I remember her doing this into the early hours of the morning so that I would have a new dancing suit for a competition. She had fantastic patience, and would always make sure that the blouses, which were tight at the cuffs and billowed out along the arms, were loose-fitting; and that the trousers, which were quite tight, fitted properly and had sequins sewn all along the seams, and sometimes even round the hems to make them more glittery and showbiz.

As a light relief from being called a 'sissy' by other boys—because I loved dancing, wore 'funny' clothes and was blessed with a 'funny' walk—I played football. After school I would rush home with my football boots still on, grab my dancing shoes, and rush off to my dancing lessons. One particularly vocal boy always managed to pass me on his bike when I was on my way: 'SISSY . . . SISSY . . . Only SISSIES go to dancing lessons,' he was forever yelling after me. On one occasion, sick to death of all this, I shouted back: 'Get off your bike and I'll show you what kind of a sissy I am.'

He obliged and I gave him a right pasting.

*   *   *

As well as playing football, I also loved going to football matches on Saturday afternoons. And as Arsenal and Tottenham, the closest clubs to our home, shared the same ground, because Arsenal's ground was being used as a searchlight base during the war, this meant that one Saturday I would cheer on Arsenal and the next cheer on Tottenham. To this day, I'm a somewhat unusual football-club supporter. I've been left with a split personality—I suffer from divided loyalties and still root for *both* clubs. I've learned never to mention this. Only recently, when I was with Warren Mitchell of television's *Till Death Us Do Part* fame, I made the mistake of telling him. An enthusiastic Spurs fan, he was very shocked—couldn't believe his ears. He and his schoolfriends always shouted for the teams that were playing against Arsenal!

*　　*　　*

One of my really big childhood thrills was appearing on television for the first time. I was eleven. I can't remember the exact date, but it was just before the Second World War began in September 1939, when television was just getting off the ground. Jasmine Bligh, a BBC presenter, had a morning show where would-be performers—grown-ups and children—could go along, meet her and, after a short interview, perform a bit of their act for her. Then, if she thought you were good enough, you could appear on her 'live' TV show. I suppose it was one of the first-ever talk shows intermingled with some light entertainment. Having heard about Jasmine Bligh, my mother said: 'Would you like to go along, Bruce?' '*Yes*,' I replied.

So, having worked out a song-and-dance routine, I went along and explained my music to the studio pianist. On the show, Jasmine asked me about my dancing, who I liked and what I wanted to be. Thinking of the two most important loves of my life, I replied: 'I want to be a famous dancer like Fred Astaire and buy my mother a fur coat.' Jasmine was obviously surprised by this answer.

15

But, to my childish mind, buying a fur coat for your mother was what being famous was all about. Having recovered from what she thought was a comical reply, Jasmine laughed and said: 'All right then, do your song and dance for us.'

The studio set was designed to look like the lounge of someone's home. So, for the performer and the viewers it was just like being in a family's front room—the 'parlour', as people used to call it then.

The television cameras were HUGE, quite terrifying. All I had ever done before was sing and dance on little stages in church halls. It was all such a different experience. There was no audience seated in front of me in rows of wooden chairs—and, somehow, I had to create my own atmosphere.

There was also no such thing then as a recording of a TV show. Videotapes didn't come in until much later. There were no monitors or screens to watch yourself on, either. I had no idea what I looked like, which was probably just as well. If I had been able to see . . . well, this could have been a very different life story! It also meant that as my mother was with me, my father was at work, and none of my friends had been told about the event, nobody saw my first performance on TV; and no one could come up to me afterwards and say: 'I saw you on the box!' So the moment passed ignominiously. But, for me, it was part of the history of TV—and me.

In even earlier days when television had first come into our home, it came on in the morning with a tuning-in card and demonstration films for the trade, which viewers, if they wished, could watch at home. In the afternoon, once again preceded by the tuning-in card, there were programmes between three and four o'clock. The programmes then came on again in the evening at eight o'clock. Then you would watch until the bright dot disappeared from the screen between ten thirty and eleven o'clock. There was no choice of channels because there was only *one*. Remember, we were a lucky family to have a television set in 1938.

By 1939—the time of my appearance on the Jasmine Bligh show—morning TV had come into being. Jasmine's show was obviously put out to promote television viewing among housewives and people who were not at work. Before those days, radio was the 'star'—the chief form of family entertainment. In my home, we used to sit around the wireless listening to our favourite shows, *Monday Night at 8* and *In Town Tonight*. The latter would start with the sound of a busy street in the middle of London's West End, and the announcer would say: 'Once again we stop the mighty roar of London's traffic to bring you another edition of *In Town Tonight.*' *A* voice would then boom '*STOP*'—and I really believed all the traffic in London had been stopped so that they could do the show!

*　　　*　　　*

The remainder of my childhood was destined to be spent in a country at war. In September, fifteen minutes after the deadline had passed for Germany 'to stop all aggressive action against Poland', we heard Neville Chamberlain, Britain's Prime Minister, announce on radio: 'This country is now

17

at war with Germany.' I was just about to start high school, but plans were made to evacuate me straight away to Clacton. Perhaps this would have been fine, but while many of the evacuees were billeted in twos, not me. I was evacuated all on my own to this old lady who lived by herself. My sister and brother, because of their age, were not part of this mass exodus from London. In fact, as soon as war was declared, all John wanted was to go into the RAF as a pilot, and he enlisted on the day he was eighteen. He couldn't wait to fly and all of us were so proud of him—so looking forward to his letters telling us about his adventures.

For me, the experience of being removed from my lovely family and being left with no one to talk to or play with, was devastating. I was desperately homesick and, when my mother and father came on a surprise visit to see if I was all right and what kind of house I was living in, I cried my eyes out the moment I saw them, ran to the car, climbed in and refused to get out again. I had only been in Clacton for three days and, although the old lady had been very kind to me, I wanted to go home. I also hated my new school. Not having had time to make new friends, I was feeling really lonely and sorry for myself. Distressed by my reaction, my parents drove round to the headmaster to inform him they were taking me home. What had really made up my father's mind was that when he and my mother were driving into Clacton, he had noticed a huge warship at the end of the pier. Turning to my mum, he said: 'Good God, he's nearer to the war than we are.'

Nobody, then, knew which way the war would go—what was in store for us all. Questions such as:

'Will Hitler send a fleet of ships over?', 'Will his troops land on our shores?', 'Will his planes drop paratroopers in our villages, towns and cities?', 'Will London be his first target?' were on everybody's lips. But, even though my parents—like everybody else—were in a panic about London being saturated with bombs, having seen the warship at Clacton, they decided to take me home.

During the second week of September 1939, we learned that four British Army divisions had crossed the Channel and were now deployed alongside their French allies. In October the battleship *Royal Oak* was sunk in a raid by a German U-boat on the Royal Navy base at Scapa Flow. And in France, in November, the first concert was given by the Entertainments National Service Association—ENSA. Using these initials, its slogan was 'Every Night Something 'appens'. But this was cheekily changed to 'Every Night Something Awful'. If this was the case, although I applied to join ENSA, I'm glad I didn't get the job!

Not surprisingly, my schooling during the next three years, 1939 to 1942, was practically non-existent. By New Year's Day 1940, we knew from radio and newspapers that two million men between the ages of twenty and twenty-seven had been called up. That same month food rationing, limiting the use of butter, sugar and bacon, was introduced. In February, government ministers launched a campaign under the slogan 'Careless talk costs lives'. In March, there was some good news to cheer us all up: Vivien Leigh had won an Oscar in Los Angeles for her performance alongside Clark Gable in *Gone with the Wind*. In August, Winston Churchill gave his now-famous speech, praising our RAF pilots, and saying 'never . . . was so much owed by so many to so few'. In November, though, our spirits dipped again—Coventry Cathedral and much of the city had been destroyed by German bombers, and 568 people had died in the air raid.

*   *   *

During these years, a very important boost for my dancing—and for my later showbiz career—was that my mother and a group of her friends formed an amateur variety club to put on wartime charity shows. For these, a whole group of 'performers' was rounded up—comedians, singers, dancers, accordion-players—anybody who could do any kind of entertaining 'act'. My mother was the secretary of the club and my father, helped by Alf, a chum of his, was the spotlight operator. My father made the spotlights in one of his garages. Having created these from 12-volt car batteries and two tripods with old car headlights placed on top, he carefully positioned them on both sides of the halls, so that the performers would have a spotlight on them while they were doing their turns.

We performed all over the place—in school halls, churches and factories. The takings were for the 'Buy a Spitfire Fund'. Sometimes we only raised £50 or £75, but everybody was happy knowing that this could help to build another Spitfire. Then, when we heard that Hitler was giving Russia hell and that Stalingrad was under fire and unlikely to survive another day, we put on concerts for 'Aid to Russia Fund'.

The running order for these variety concerts was

20

usually a group of dancing girls and boys, somebody singing, somebody playing the accordion, someone cracking jokes, someone doing magic tricks, and so on. One of our biggest and most popular numbers was a patriotic drum dance. Dressed in military uniforms, six of my dance troupe and myself would jump on top of some drums and do a really enthusiastic song-and-dance routine. It was a show-stopper. Britain would never be defeated—Churchill and us were doing a good job!

In addition to dancing in the group, I would also do a solo singing and dancing turn. I felt proud. I had a very strong voice and would do numbers like the then-popular song 'Franklin D. Roosevelt Jones'. This always went down well as America was helping us in the war. I would sing a chorus first, then tap-dance, using all the winging steps I had learned at the dancing school.

During these concerts I also discovered to my great satisfaction that I could make not only my family but also an audience laugh. This came about because invariably the lady pianist (they were always lady pianists) would play the wrong tempo—especially when it came to my dancing routine, which needed a very fast tempo. I would have to stop in the middle of some steps and go over to her. Normally, she would be wearing a funny straw hat. I don't know why lady pianists nearly always wore straw hats in those days, but they did. Young though I was, I would say in a very grown-up way: 'No, dear. *No*. It's got to be faster.' And I would rap out the rhythm, adding in the same vein: 'Okay, dear? *Do* try and get it right this time.' The audience would fall about laughing at my curiously adult choice of words and my frustration, especially when I kept looking at the pianist and then back at them. I had learned by now that when I got flustered or frustrated, the audience would love to laugh at young Bruce in trouble. This continued throughout my later professional career. Whenever I was in trouble, the audience loved it and I learned to take advantage of that.

*   *   *

My mother and father, bless them, could not have been better or more supportive parents. Everything was a hundred per cent with them. My mother always ensured that I got to my dancing lessons on time, even when these were spread out all over London. She was really wonderful. And my father was special, too, in practical matters, such as the spotlights. Also because the surface of the stages were so awful and because some of the church halls had such bumpy floors, with knots of wood sticking up, he made me a tap mat which meant I always had a smooth surface to dance on. He was a wonderful engineer. Although he had never made anything like a tap mat before, he got hold of some slats of wood, about an inch or so wide, and some canvas backing. Having cleared the dining-room table, which was about six feet long when its two leaves were out, he laid the wood on it, backed each of the slats with sacking, and glued the two surfaces together. It was slow work. He had to get the mat as symmetrical as possible and, as he finished gluing on each piece of backing, he would have to keep turning the individual slats over to rivet each end to the sacking for a really strong finish. He took endless time and trouble, and the smell of glue hung around the house for days.

Throughout the entire process, he kept saying: 'D'you want it a bit longer, boy? D'you want it a bit longer?' And I would keep replying: 'Well, you know, Dad, for some of the steps I do, the longer it is the better.' In the end, he made it about fourteen feet long, which proved to be too long for some of the stages I was dancing on! From then on, the mat used to travel with us everywhere we went. Fortunately, Dad had a Hackney Carriage licence, which under wartime rules he was allowed to use for the charity shows, and meant he was given a petrol allowance. He would strap the tap mat to the back of the car we had at that time, an old Model T Ford—a perfect vehicle for transporting all the stuff needed for the shows.

One night, however, there was a DISASTER. He obviously had not strapped the tap mat on tightly enough and the next morning we found that it was missing—it had obviously fallen off the back of the car. Dad went crazy. So did I when he told me. I was in despair, thinking: 'What are we going to do? I've got a show tomorrow night.' We went to the police station and a kindly policeman noted down our loss. Luckily, as the disaster had happened in Edmonton, where nobody would want a fourteen-foot tap mat, and anyway wouldn't know what it was for, it was soon returned. So, thanks to the finder and the police, that was the tap mat which, even when I became a pro, continued to travel everywhere with me.

*　　*　　*

One day my mother had to go into hospital, but I was not told why. What I do remember is that my father had to cope with the family all on his own. My sister Maisie helped, of course, but it was a terrible upheaval for all of us. While Mum was in hospital, she was befriended by one of the nurses, and passed the time telling her new friend that I was a dancer, particularly good at tap-dancing, and that one day I would be a professional dancer on the London stage. Having listened to all this, the nurse bought me a white bow tie to wear when I was dancing around the house. When I saw it, I was thrilled and thought: 'Oh, I can *really* be Fred Astaire now.' I couldn't wait to get home, put on the white bow tie and dance my feet off.

The more I look back in time, the more I can see that John, Maisie and I were truly fortunate in our parents. As children we never wanted for anything; Mum and Dad would go without themselves to make sure we got the birthday and Christmas presents we wanted. And Christmas was always such a lark. Never able to resist mischief, John was always working out how we could outwit our parents and get our own way about this or that. Christmas Eves were especially challenging and we always succeeded in opening our presents the moment they were tiptoed into our room. My father always caught us, gave us a good telling-off and sent us back to bed. But John was undefeated. Like his father, he was a very inventive engineer. Not daring to put the light on in the bedroom again, he simply rigged up a small battery with a bulb and placed this under the blankets. Then, a few hours before daylight, we would start the

Christmas preview of our presents all over again.

When I read other people's autobiographies and discover how tough their lives were, how awful it was when their parents were down to their last penny, I feel very fortunate to be able to say it was never like that for John, Maisie and me. We were so lucky to have such a wonderful childhood and, above all, to be blessed with such loving parents who would rather skimp themselves than disappoint us.

*   *   *

While I was more often absent than present at school, I used to spend a lot of time watching all the air raids and dogfights between the planes. Every night, when bombs were about to be dropped from German planes, we would hurry to air-raid shelters. We had our own Anderson shelter in the back garden but, because people doubted how much protection these would really give, special shelters were built in the park opposite our home and most local families chose to go there. It is awful to recall that during this period, on 3 March 1943, 178 people were killed by a direct hit on Bethnal Green tube station where families just like ours were taking shelter from a raid. Edmonton was badly bombed, too, but because the German bombers flew in from the south coast to get to London, I don't think we had quite as much bomb damage as South London.

The bombing was, however, intense at times, and I particularly remember one occasion when a bomb was dropped on the other side of our park. My mother, anxious about a friend of hers, whom I always called 'Auntie' even though she was no relation, asked me to go round to see if she was all right. I have never forgotten the shock of arriving in the street where she had always lived. There was an empty space—her house had gone. When I ran home and told my mother she was distraught—couldn't believe it. As it turned out, her friend was okay. This losing of homes and all their contents happened to so many people. They would be down in the air-raid shelter and when they emerged their houses would no longer be standing. But the community spirit between neighbours was absolutely fantastic; and the humour of those times so very British.

During this period the Germans were dropping huge land-mines about eight or nine feet tall and three feet wide—huge ugly things that would float down suspended by parachutes. One night during the Blitz one of these was dropped in our area and we heard that one of the Home Guard (the real Dad's Army), who'd seen a parachute floating down, had fixed his bayonet to his gun and made ready to challenge it when it came to earth. It landed in a leaning position by a house and he shouted out: 'Halt. Who goes there?' before suddenly realizing, as the air-raid wardens arrived on the scene, that he was prodding a land-mine. If Captain Mainwaring had been present, he'd have said: 'You *sssstupid* boy!'

We didn't know anything about this at the time but, when we got up in the morning, everybody within a 200-yard area had been evacuated. I went outside to find ropes cordoning off the road, and a group of people standing there watching the naval bomb-disposal unit at work. I had taken my father's old telescope with me to watch. Soon most of the naval group dispersed, leaving only one man to take the detonator out.

My mother suddenly came out and, very shocked, asked me what I thought I was doing in such a dangerous situation. At that precise moment somebody yelled at us to lie down while the detonator was removed. The quietness and stillness, I have realized since, was like being in a theatre during a very dramatic pause when everybody is waiting for something to happen. The bomb-disposal officer took the detonator out and then lifted it up in the air to let others of his group know that everything was all right. We all stood up and applauded. It takes a very brave and special person to be a bomb-disposal officer—and I have never forgotten that man. It was one of those memorable moments that was more than worth the clip round the ear my mother gave me when she got me back into the house.

Every morning I used to climb on my dad's garage roofs and collect all the shrapnel that had fallen from the sky the previous night. I would then go indoors with handfuls of the stuff. When you got something with numbers on it, that was considered a real find and all the kids would gather around each other, swapping stories and pieces of shrapnel. For us, it was all so exciting. We had no idea yet of how awful war really was—it was just another adventure. It never really hit home to us that this was something life-threateningly serious. We didn't read the newspapers, didn't dwell on headlines such as 'British cities "blitzed" by German air war'.

No, we simply read our children's books,

laughed and played on, did not realize the scale of the human tragedy we were living through. Such events bypassed us as we went through our high-school years—years in which rather than living in terror I dreamed of being a dancer who, one day, would be on the stage. There was never a time when I wanted any other kind of career. Dancing was a fixation—a total obsession.

Going back a bit, when I was twelve years old—and had had lots of Tilly Vernon lessons behind me—I'd even started my own tap-dancing school. This I ran from No. 5 of my father's lock-up garages, 'furnished' for the purpose with a tap mat and a wind-up gramophone. Even though I had only danced for two or three years, I had become quite good. I charged my pupils—a few girls and one or two boys—a shilling a lesson, but I had no patience with the fact that most of them could not follow an instruction and do a simple shuffle and a hop on one foot, and then a shuffle and a hop on the other. They seemed to have cloth ears and two left feet! And, of course, they didn't understand what I was talking about when I said 'do a flap'. Even when I showed them, they simply couldn't get it.

Well, do *you* know what a 'shuffle' or a 'flap' is? If you are *really* interested, stand up. I said, *stand up!* I'm talking to *YOU*, the reader! Now, a shuffle is two beats. Raise your right leg, brush your toe on the ground, making the first beat—with your toe going forward—and while it is still off the ground, brush your toe back, making the second beat. Now, that is a shuffle. Try a few of those: forward, back, forward, back. Now do the same thing on the left foot—and let's hope you're not right-footed! For a

28

flap, the first beat is the same as a shuffle, but for the second beat you put your foot flat on the ground. Do a few of those—on both feet. All done? Feeling giddy? You are now a fully qualified tap-dancer. Sit down again, or have a lie down, or resume the position you were in to read this book. Whatever you do, don't get in a flap!

But never mind all that. Getting back to my dancing troupe, I would shout at them quite a bit, but it wasn't until I heard professional choreographers shouting and reducing girls to tears that I realized what a hard taskmaster I was at twelve years old. My 'pupils' just put up with me.

Not long after this, I decided that Tilly Vernon, a lovely lady with a slim figure and blonde curly hair, who always wore baggy trousers, had taught me all she knew. Fortunately, my mother had heard of Douggie Ascot, quite a famous dancing teacher who had a daughter called Hazel who tap-danced in films. So, off we went to where he taught in Brixton, which was a long way away from where we lived. The journey involved a trolleybus from Edmonton to Manor House, a long tube journey under central London to Lambeth, and a long walk up the hill to his studio. My mother never once complained—she had such a belief in me.

Douggie Ascot was a very good teacher, but I only went to his classes for a little while. I realized that his kind of dancing was not the kind I wanted to do—*not* the kind I had seen Fred Astaire and other film stars doing. Douggie taught English tap-dancing, and there is a great deal of difference between this and American tap-dancing. English tap-dancing is very elevated—mostly done on the balls of the feet and the toes. You lift yourself up as you dance and the movements are rather exaggerated and stiff. In American tap-dancing you use your heels much more. It's altogether more relaxed and you can move more naturally. The way I heard it, when so many Irish went to America and took with them a lot of their musical traditions, this included clog-dancing. When the black Americans saw this, they developed a version of it, but with a more natural feel for them. This is what became American-style tap-dancing. I used to love watching the Nicholas Brothers in the movies, who not only tap-danced, but also performed jumping splits over one another. In this country, there was a tiny black dancer called Ellis Jackson, who was featured in Billy Cotton's Bandshow. It was always a highlight when he came out of the band and did one of his routines.

Anyway, by now, I had heard of a black American teacher called Buddy Bradley who taught in Denman Street, in London's West End. He had a studio right on the top floor of one of the buildings. When I went along and saw one of his classes in progress, I realized that this was exactly what I had been looking for. His was the kind of dancing I had seen in the movies. Now, at last, I was getting somewhere. I also met someone who was to become one of my oldest friends there, John Shackell. And since then, I've always kidded him that he's older than I am because he wore long trousers and I wore short.

The first lesson Buddy gave me, however, was very disappointing. It was entirely devoted to limbering-up exercises, and I didn't like him showing me such simple steps. By then—with pupils of my own, after all—I thought I was a pretty good dancer. But all he was trying to do was to get me to 'feel' the floor, 'feel' the rhythm of his style. And he kept me doing this for the first few lessons. I remember feeling very frustrated and saying to my mother: 'I'm *not* learning anything, Mum. All I'm doing is walking around doing all these *silly* little steps.'

'Well,' she replied. 'He must be doing it for a reason, Bruce.'

After that, he started to teach me different routines, including his Number One and Number Two routines. He still kept up his sleeve, though, a marvellous routine that he reserved for his top pupils. This was danced to 'In the Mood', the big big-band number at that time. Buddy played Glen Miller's wonderful arrangement of this—and all his steps fitted the music perfectly. So if, like me, you loved dancing, this was the routine to aim for.

One day when I was about thirteen and still in the studio after my group lesson, a man came in for a private lesson. It was Jack Buchanan. I was transfixed. Jack Buchanan was one of the people I admired and loved to watch in British films because he used American tap-dancing more often than English tap-dancing. I suddenly realized that Buddy Bradley was his teacher, too, and he was rehearsing something for a show he was in. It was a very pleasant surprise.

What was not so pleasant—but us being youngsters, also quite fun at times—was when in the middle of Bradley's classes the air-raid sirens would sound and we would all have to stop dancing and run from the top floor and take shelter in the basement. There we would stay confined until the all-clear had sounded.

By the time I left school at fourteen years old, I had been learning to dance for four years and was incredibly conscientious about practising the steps. I would practise until my feet ached—literally. It got to the point where everybody in the family was only too grateful when I took a short break. They were always looking forward to me stopping altogether for the day, but I would stay in that room, on that linoleum, and dance on and on. To their horror, I was equally obsessive about my piano practice a couple of years later.

As far as my education was concerned, there was never a point at which my parents decided: 'This is it, Bruce. You're not going to continue with an academic education, you're going to leave school and go on with your dancing and singing.' Leaving school at fourteen came about simply because of the way things—and the education laws—were at the time. It was normal then to leave school at fourteen because, at that age, you could go into a job in a factory and help with the war effort. That, however, never entered my head. The only way *I* wanted to help the war effort was by going into show business. I didn't ask Buddy Bradley if he thought I had a future as a dancer. It didn't even occur to me to do so. I simply took it for granted that I did have a future and that he knew I wanted to be a dancer. I did, though, tell my mother and father about my plans, and the support they gave me was fantastic. Knowing just how much I wanted this, they said: 'Okay. Go for it, Bru.'

As I soon learned, going into show business was

going to mean working in variety theatres all round the country. No problem. At this time every city in Britain had about three or four theatres that were functioning well because, as it was still wartime, there was nowhere else for people to go for entertainment.

So . . . I left school with no exam qualifications whatsoever. I had managed to attend more or less full-time during my last year, but had not attended very often and certainly not studied much during the previous two. On the day I was going to leave the headmaster called me into his room. 'Well, Forsyth-Johnson,' said Mr Davis, 'I'm afraid looking at your schooling puts me in a very difficult position . . . I can't give you anything like a good report on what you have done.'

'Don't worry about that, sir,' I said, full of confidence.

'What do you mean,' he said, " 'don't worry"?'

'I'm going into a business, sir, where they go more by what they can see you do—rather than what you've done.'

'What business is that, Forsyth-Johnson?' he asked, intrigued.

'Show business, sir.'

Laughing aloud, he said: 'Then you're going to need all the luck you can get. Off you go!'

He signed my school-leaver's form and that was the last time I ever saw Mr Davis.

I've got stronger schoolday memories of the gorgeous French teacher who took us for French and drama. She was really very nice—a sophisticated lady who used a head-turning perfume. Just like the commercials! I liked *her*. In fact, my biggest regret after I left school was that I missed her—and her perfume. I suppose I'd had a crush on her. As a result, I'd been getting quite good at French! And was sorry I couldn't keep that up.

*   *   *

In 1942, when I was fourteen, we had our first shocking family tragedy. My sister Maisie was married to Tom. She met him in the Salvation Army—he played in the band. He was a trombonist. He also worked in my father's garage business. He'd often take me over to the park to play football, or we'd kick around in the garage area.

At the time of the tragedy, Maisie was in hospital recovering after the birth of their third child, Lynn. A young garage assistant was syphoning petrol from a car's carburettor into a can, and Tom—my brother-in-law—went to look over his shoulder to check what he was doing. All of a sudden there was a short circuit, followed by an explosion of flames. If the young lad had thrown the can to his left, it would have been all right. But unfortunately he threw the can of flaming petrol to his right, where Tom was standing. Tom was taken to hospital with terrible burns and died a few days later. Imagine how Maisie felt, rushing from the maternity hospital to find Tom in such a terrible state, hanging on to life by a thread.

It was one of those moments from which nobody in a family ever truly recovers. It was a terrible time for Maisie, but a tragedy for us all. It scarred the end of my childhood. But at the time, I had no way of knowing that there was an even worse personal tragedy in store for us, just one year later, when I was fifteen.

CHAPTER TWO

ON THE ROAD ... ON THE WAY

As somebody who throughout his career has relied on his hands, legs, feet and voice to earn a living, I have been pretty lucky in avoiding near-death experiences and reasonably fortunate with my general health. But, like most people, I've had a couple of potentially life-threatening moments.

One day when I was a child, a gypsy knocked on the door of our house asking my mother to buy some lucky heather. My mother, not having any change in her purse, refused. But then, aware of the old superstition that refusing things from gypsies brings misfortune, she sent me to the corner shop to get some change. When I came back, I ran up the garden path to the house but, just before I reached the brass doorstep, I tripped. As bad luck would have it, there was a small piece of jagged brass sticking out of one of its corners and, as I landed face down on this, it penetrated the skin just above my eye.

Panicking at the sight of so much blood, my mother got the pushchair out, stuck me in it and made my sister Maisie run alongside holding my eyelid together, to stop the flow of blood. Half a mile later, we reached the North Middlesex Hospital, and my cut was stitched up. When we returned home, my mother said to my father: 'So

35

much for good luck! The next time a gypsy knocks at the door, I'm not going to answer it.'

As I mentioned earlier, we lived opposite Pymme's Park and one day, when I was about seven, I saw a little boy, his face covered with blood, coming out. 'Oh!' I said, astonished. 'What happened to him?' 'He's been hit in the face by a cricket ball,' I was told. Ever since then, I've been terrified of cricket balls. People simply do not realize how solid they are and what damage they can inflict. It's the same with golf balls. They might look as harmless as ping-pong balls, but they're lethal—they've killed people. Fortunately, I've never lost my interest in watching cricket—and have certainly never been put off playing golf—but I've never actually played cricket.

I also remember being in a car with my first wife, Penny. We'd been to a carol concert in London, and she was driving us home in the snow and ice. For some unknown reason—nothing to do with women drivers!—the car suddenly went out of control, skidded several times and hit a brick wall. Luckily, although it was very scary—with one's life flashing before one's eyes and all that stuff—Penny was uninjured and I only hurt my knee. Another driving incident was when a Royal Mail van suddenly—and without warning—slewed right across my path and hit the car I was driving. He was in the wrong but, in those days as I remember it, you couldn't sue one of the Queen's drivers. Paying for the repairs to my car was down to me.

During my childhood I often had a sharp pain in the small of the back near my kidney and my mother used to put hot-water bottles there to ease the discomfort. There came a time, however, when

I was about twenty-one, just out of the RAF and working at the Windmill Theatre for the second time—when one kidney, which had proved to be malformed, was playing up so much it had to be removed. When I was told this, I honestly thought it was the end of everything—certainly the end of my showbiz career. Although I was musical and could play various instruments, my act still consisted mainly of my first love—dancing like Fred Astaire. The surgeon, though, was a clever psychologist. After I had had the operation and was lying miserably in bed recuperating, he sent in loads of his former patients who had had the same operation. One of them was a rugby player. 'Have you had any post-op problems?' I asked him nervously.

'No,' he replied cheerfully. 'I was running around six weeks later, then went back to training. I've been playing rugby ever since.'

I was immensely reassured, really glad he'd called in. 'Rugby', I thought, 'is a really tough game, tougher than dancing with Windmill girls!'

That kidney operation took place in a local hospital fifty years ago—in pioneering-op times—and I was very fortunate to have such a good surgeon. At the time I had no idea how serious and potentially risky a kidney-removal operation was. But—on the bright side—at least I only lost an organ I had two of!

When I was forty—and twenty-six years into my career—I was told I had to have my tonsils out. Luckily, I didn't realize then that the older you are, the longer it takes to recover from this operation. At the time, I was working with Tom Jones and Tommy Cooper. Both of them being of a really cheerful disposition, they told me that I would feel absolutely *terrible* when I first woke up after the operation; would feel as if Jack the Ripper had slit my throat. 'Just like that . . .' Tommy said, helpfully demonstrating the action.

Because of what they told me, I didn't sleep for three days after the operation, even though I was given the maximum dose of sleeping pills. My subconscious mind was saying: 'Don't go to sleep because, if you do, you'll feel absolutely *awful* when you wake up.' Come to think of it, I forgot to thank Tom and Tommy for their support during this difficult time! When I did finally sleep and woke up again, I knew *exactly* what they'd been talking about. Applying some ice eased the pain. But I learned to be very careful when doing this. Ice, I discovered, can cling to the flesh and burn.

It took me eight long weeks to get over that operation. During the recovery time I was asked to referee a golf exhibition between Peter Alliss and Tony Lema, a really great American golfer who won the British Open the first year he came over, but who was later killed in a plane crash. I'd been really looking forward—*longing*—to go out with these two guys. But, when I did, I was still so weak the organizers had to give me a golf buggy to ride around the course in and do the refereeing. Even sitting in the buggy, I could only manage nine holes before I needed to go home.

Fortunately, having my tonsils out didn't affect my voice—don't be cheeky!—and, after eight weeks or so, I got back into the swing of things.

Then there was the time when I was in a summer season show at Blackpool and discovered I had caught something nasty off my two daughters,

Debbie and Julie. It was mumps, a particularly dangerous, scary infection for adult males because, apart from the usual discomforts, it can cause impotence and sterility. I was saved from that—but I missed the opening of the show. As I was doing at least five spots, they had to get Morecambe and Wise and Tommy Cooper, who were not as big names then as they proved to be later on, to fill in all the gaps for me.

When I'd noticed something was wrong with me, I'd phoned my doctor, Dr Ashken, our local GP in Totteridge where we lived, and said: 'I'm a bit worried . . . my daughters have had mumps and I'm just wondering if I might have caught it.'

'What are the symptoms?' he asked.

'Well . . .' I said, 'the left one *is* supposed to be larger than the right one, isn't it?'

'What?' he replied, puzzled.

'The left one', I said again, '*is* supposed to be larger than the right, isn't it?'

'Oh,' he said, falling in. 'I *see* what you mean! Yes, the left one should be larger.'

'Well,' I said, 'my right one is definitely larger than the left!'

I didn't want to say 'balls' or 'testicles' over the phone. It sounded *so* rude—and you can never be sure who's listening.

Dr Ashken flew up to Blackpool immediately, examined me, and was very firm about his instructions.

'You mustn't', he instructed, 'work or do anything physically strenuous and exhausting like your stage act.'

So, disappointed, indisposed and none too pleased, I was out of the show for a long five weeks.

39

From an early age—about ten onwards—I always suffered from swollen glands. No, not around there this time! The swelling would last for days and certain foods—especially sweet things—would make them even worse. Looking back, I can now see that this problem was probably related to dodgy tonsils. When I went into the Air Force and was once again troubled by this condition, the medics put me in an isolation ward, thinking that it could be mumps—again!—or glandular fever.

It wasn't until I came out of the service that a doctor, who X-rayed me, informed me that we have very tiny tubes running down the sides of our faces into our necks, and that all my tubes were unusually small and thin. 'Sometimes,' he told me, 'these tubes get blocked, and it's this that is causing the swelling.'

I had a marvellous idea—thought of a way in which I could possibly release the blockage in my lymph glands. Off my own bat, I decided to drink a couple of bottles of water, not eat anything that might aggravate the swelling, get into a bath of hot water, as hot as I could bear it, stay there for twenty minutes, make myself perspire, and continue to add more hot water as the bath cooled. Then I fasted for about eight hours. It worked! I was cured. Since then, tiny tubes or not, I've never had any more bother from swollen glands. I've since told several doctors about 'my miracle cure', and they've always replied: 'That was obviously a very good idea.' So, how's that for DIY?

*   *   *

From about twelve to fourteen, I became really

interested in music and, what a surprise, first learned to play . . . the Hawaiian guitar. This choice of instrument was inspired by hearing Roland Peachey and his Hawaiian Serenaders on radio, followed by a door-to-door salesman knocking on our door peddling the beauty. Invited in, he showed me and my parents how the guitar worked, and how simple it was to play. Charts showed you where to put your fingers to pluck the right notes, and how to hold a steel bar in your left hand to achieve the Hawaiian sound. A course of thirteen lessons was on offer for a certain sum. And, at the end of these, having mastered the instrument, you would also own the guitar.

As always, my parents reacted very generously to my sudden interest in the Hawaiian guitar. Musical themselves, they were only too happy to further my interest in music, including, later on, the piano accordion and the ukulele banjo. George Formby—whose films I adored—was the inspiration behind the latter. I wanted to sing like him to the ukulele banjo. From the point of view of playing, it was very similar to the guitar in the way that you had to stretch your fingers over it.

So, those were the musical instruments I loved. And, given what was soon to happen to me, they—along with my dancing—stood me in very good stead.

In thinking about all this I have also just recalled that of all the kinds of cars my father had, the one I remember best is that black Model T Ford—and that's the one in which he taught me how to drive. Traffic laws were not so strict then! Driving me home one day, he was busy talking away about how to drive, but I wasn't really listening—had my mind on other things like music and dancing. When we got to the top of our road, he suddenly said: 'Well, it's about time you had a try, son. You have been listening, haven't you?'

I could only reply with a meek, 'Yes.'

'Well, get into the driving seat.'

Not daring to own up or protest, I did as I was told. And he made me drive home. Fortunately, in those days, there were so few cars about, there was little danger. Somehow—I know not how—I must have done reasonably well because, from then on, he allowed me to move cars around in the lock-up garage area to get, he said, 'some experience'.

*   *   *

Luckily for me, a variety agent used to come to the charity shows in which I was doing my numbers. One day, when talking to my mother and father, he said he thought I had a future in show business. He was based in Tottenham, just along the road from where we lived, and he mentioned he was putting on a show in a few months' time, and could offer me a spot in it.

'In the meantime,' he added, 'would your son like to come and work for me in my office?'

Would I? Yes!

So I did. I became his office boy, making tea for anyone who came to see him, and answering the phone when he was out. My main function, however, was to keep him constantly supplied with whipped-up eggs in milk in a pint glass. He had a stomach ulcer—what agent doesn't!

When the time came for the show to go on tour, the top-of-the-bill—also the producer—was a man called 'The Great Marzo'. And *I*, by now, was rechristened—wait for it—'Boy Bruce, the Mighty Atom'. My parents and I had come up with this wonderful showbiz name because science was very much in the news then, and atoms were what everybody was talking about. We also thought it a particularly suitable name for somebody as young as I was. You see, in the programme notes you also had what was called 'bill-matter' printed underneath your name to describe the kind of act you were. The best I ever read was 'Spike Milligan—The Performing Man'!

About a week before we were due to set off to the Theatre Royal, Bilston, in the heart of the Midlands, the agent suddenly said to me: 'Bruce, would you ask your mum and dad to come and see me?' I was immediately anxious, wondering what this could possibly be about, searching my conscience for things that I may or may not have done. In due course, though, when my parents went to see him, it was they not me who were worried. He and the producer had a serious cash-flow problem—didn't have sufficient funds to open the show.

'Could you', my parents were asked, 'possibly contribute twenty-five pounds towards expenses?'

Twenty-five pounds was a great deal of money in those days—and a small fortune for my parents—but somehow, not wanting to disappoint me, they found it. How they managed to do this I will never know. But, even as young as I was then, I realized what a struggle it was for them, and I felt really miserable and uncomfortable about it.

My mother, who as I've said was never-endingly more ambitious for me than I was for myself, died in September 1957—exactly one year before I was to get my Big Break at the London Palladium. My father, though, lived long enough to enjoy a couple of years of my success. I've always said that when my mother reached Heaven, she immediately started to pull strings, and so was responsible for my success at the Palladium. Her favourite number in my song-and-dance repertoire was 'When You Wish Upon A Star' from Walt Disney's film *Pinocchio*. A really lovely lyric, the last two lines of the song are: 'When you wish upon a star, your dreams come true'. I know my mother did that for me—and my Big Break dreams did come true. When she was alive, we used to watch *Sunday Night at the London Palladium* together and she so wanted me to appear on the show one day. In addition to wishing on a star, I think she found the biggest agent up there and said: 'Come on, I want you to get my son booked into the Palladium. He's worked hard—he deserves it.'

Having endured taking me to all those dancing classes and talent competitions, she would have been so thrilled to see me on the stage of that great theatre. Also, I could have repaid the £25 she and my father had invested in my 'Boy Bruce, the Mighty Atom' days, and bought her the fur coat she always wanted. What a thrill that would have been for me. But . . .

*   *   *

With her and Dad's money duly invested in my first appearance at the Theatre Royal, Bilston, off I went by train, travelling with a trunk which had been in our loft for years. On board with me was my ukulele, my tap mat and my accordion. Imagine arriving at the cramped digs with all that stuff. As a growing lad, I recall the landlady dishing up three delicious square meals a day. At fourteen years old, I was feeling very grown up, happy and confident. I was in show business, about to work in a real theatre, what more could I ask of life? I was a pro!

It was almost impossible for me to believe that only a couple of years before, when I had been evacuated from London with hundreds of thousands of other children with labels pinned on their coats and home-made knapsacks on their backs, I had suffered from such dreadful homesickness that my parents had had to take me home three days later. Not now. No chance. I was up and dancing!

During those days, according to the facilities they provided, theatres were graded as One, Two or Three. The one in Bilston, it turned out, wasn't even good enough to be graded a Number Three. Okay, so it was a dreadful theatre, but was I downcast? *No.* I was in show business. That's all that mattered. I had my 'parts', *band* parts, sheet music to give to the band on the Monday morning. And on the first night, I did this awe-inspiringly awful act where, dressed up as a hotel pageboy, I walked on stage carrying as much luggage as I could. In the story-line, I was supposed to have been to the railway station to bring stuff back to the hotel for its newly arrived show guests. In my act, I had to open all the cases, looking nervously behind me to ensure the owners were not around, take an accordion out of one and play it. I then followed the same routine with a ukulele, and finished off with a tap-dance. What a truly dreadful

45

plot!

Things did not improve. Business was bad at the theatre, with hardly a 'bum' on the seats. Worse, some of my distant relatives came to see the show, and were so embarrassed by how ghastly it was they didn't even come backstage afterwards to see me. By the end of the week, the takings were so terrible, the management decided to split the money up between us, according to our billing. Well, The Great Marzo was top of the bill, and I was very much the bottom. In fact, my name, 'Boy Bruce, the Mighty Atom', was listed next to the wine and spirits the theatre sold. So my share was thirteen shillings and four pence—not even a pound!

On the Saturday night, I arrived back at my digs with only this amount in my pocket and, to my embarrassment, had to phone my parents to ask for some extra money to settle my digs and the train fare home. A friend of my parents said: 'Well . . . if that's his first week in show business, he'll either quit now or be in it for life.'

But, baptism by fire as it was, I hadn't lost any of my enthusiasm. I did want to be in it for life. My ambition was to get on a Number One Theatre Tour. I didn't think of stardom—dream of being a star. I simply wanted to get into top theatres all over the country—like the Empire Theatres in Glasgow, Leeds, Sheffield and all the big cities.

*   *   *

There was, fortunately, loads of work. It was 1942—still wartime. Most of the male population, unless they had something physically or mentally wrong with them, was in the Army. There were hardly any young men to be seen. And, given that every major English city had at least three or four variety theatres, all—other than the disaster in Bilston!—doing wonderful business, there were plenty of opportunities.

The newspapers, though, were full of the Second World War raging on. In January, they told us, the first US troops in Europe since the First World War had landed in Belfast. In March, at Westminster, MPs were informed that gas and electricity were to be rationed. In May, the RAF launched its first 1,000-bomber raid, with Cologne as its target. In July, to the horror of children everywhere, sweets were rationed. In December, in a joint statement with its allies, the British Government condemned the anti-Semite atrocities which it said were being perpetrated by Germany.

Air raids remained a serious hazard—not least to performing! The sirens would sound and people would either remain seated in the theatres, or start to go to the air-raid shelters. But I was still young and the fear of being bombed never particularly worried me. The nearest I ever came to real trouble was when I was at the Shepherd's Bush Empire. I was in the second half of a show called *Leonard Urry's Discoveries* and, in addition to doing my own little bit, I used to accompany all the other performers on the piano. The lovely singer and impressionist Diane Miller was singing away, and I was busy playing the piano, when a doodlebug came over. We paused, listening to the terrible noise it was making. It sounded like a clapped-out motorbike, but threateningly louder. We all knew that as long as we could hear that sound we were all right; but the moment the motor cut out and the sound ceased, we would need to worry about where the bomb was going to land.

Suddenly there was total silence. Everybody in the audience leapt up and dived under their seats. I jumped off the piano stool and grabbed hold of Diane. We then ducked under the piano and huddled there for what seemed an eternity until the bomb exploded nearby. The theatre shuddered dramatically, but remained standing. Slowly, Diane and I got up, dusted ourselves down, resumed our previous positions, and the audience burst into applause.

'Hold on . . .' I said. 'Hold on . . . we haven't finished yet,' and we went back into the number, starting again from the beginning. I was, without even thinking about it, demonstrating that old showbiz adage—'The show must go on'!

*   *   *

So during the next few years I was constantly on tour, working in revues. The train journeys were horrendous. It was nothing to travel thirteen or fourteen hours on a train and, skinny as I was, I would often wrap myself up in a blanket and stretch out on the luggage rack to get some sleep.

On one occasion I had a six-hour wait in Crewe—the place where you had to change trains. Remember the song: 'Oh, Mr Porter, what can I do? I want to go to Birmingham, but they're taking me on to Crewe . . .'? I remember fixing a gig—a Sunday concert in Redcar—while waiting there. I was still in my very early teens, doing all this travelling on my own, and thinking nothing of it. I wasn't frightened, wasn't worried, wasn't homesick. I was focused on my career and nothing could deflect me from that.

To while away the time on the trains, many of the other passengers would play poker. Initially I just watched but, as I got older, I used to join in. That's when I found out I was unlucky at cards. Can you believe it? I couldn't play my cards right! So I stopped playing. Later on in life, I was very grateful for this experience. By then, I was working with top-of-the-bill names. Some of these worked at night and had so much free time during the day that they used to go to the dog tracks or horse races in the afternoons. They thought nothing of travelling fifty miles or more to get to a meeting. These were top people—stars—who earned a great deal of money, and who lost so much of it gambling, they sometimes came a cropper. One of the most hazardous things—when you hit the Big Time and have money to play around with—is to be a gambler. It can be dangerous to be that lucky. I was very lucky to be unlucky! At cards, anyway.

*   *   *

When the time came for my parents to tell me the facts of life, like many parents of that period they totally dodged the issue. On reflection, I don't think my mother and father saw any danger in leaving me in ignorance around other performers. And I doubt that they even knew homosexuality existed. The first problem for me was that in those days gays were called 'queers'. And I had been brought up to believe that if somebody was described as 'queer', it was because he or she was feeling unwell. So, when I started to mix with show-business people, and somebody said to me, 'You do know so-and-so is queer,' I in all innocence responded: 'How long has he been queer?' 'Oh, about five or ten years,' they would reply. And I would be left baffled, thinking, 'How *can* he have been ill that long?' It took me a long time to understand what they meant by 'queer'. But I never blamed my parents for leaving me so vulnerable where such matters were concerned because that's how things were then. Sex of any variety was almost considered a 'dirty' subject, and certainly not one that was easy to explain to a child.

When I look back now—and remember how naive I was—I can see how very easy it would have been for me to have become confused about my own sexuality, and how that could have changed my entire way of life. I could so easily have got in with the wrong-for-me clique. Female impersonators and drag performers were in every show I was in—and, before I knew what was happening, I could have met a predatory person. But, ignorant though I was, I somehow always knew that I was sexually attracted to girls.

When I was about thirteen, for example, I had a big crush on a girl who lived four blocks away from me. I would often get on my bike and cycle round there in the hope of seeing her. I would hang around outside her house for ages, just hoping she might come out and I could say 'hallo'. These days, I suppose I would be called a stalker! But I was really infatuated with her. She was in the same form as me at school. I think her name was Joan Turner but, I hasten to add, not *the* Joan Turner, the singer-comedienne.

Anyway, I did eventually find out what male homosexuality was all about. A chap in the troupe explained it all to me. Some time later, I was in a show, where two girls were doing a nude posing act. We were all staying in the same digs and I couldn't help but notice how the two girls were behaving with each other—how very affectionate and lovey-dovey they were. I was *stunned*. Nobody had ever mentioned this aspect.

It wasn't until the end of the week that one of the chaps explained to me that they were lesbians. But even that was not much help. I hadn't a clue what being a lesbian meant. I couldn't sleep that night, trying to work out what-was-what, who-was-who, and what could possibly be going on between them. Life was so confusing! Even so, at the age of fourteen, on tour for the first time, I swear I knew more about sex—and the outside world—than my parents. I never told them about the sexually explicit matters I was encountering. Had I done so, I think it would have been too much of a shock for them and they would doubtless have ended my touring days there and then. Sex remained a taboo subject between us. I still wish things had been different though, because, in truth, I was left feeling like Dean Martin, when he parodied a song, singing: 'This is my first affair, so what goes where?'

Having kept 'mum'—and still knowing so little— I was left in a quandary. There was so much sexually explicit behaviour on the tours. The guys in the show were always picking up girls on Saturday nights and bringing them back to our digs. The next morning the girls always had huge bags under their eyes and looked totally drained—worn

51

out! Somehow, they always looked more exhausted than the guys. I wonder why! It was, believe me, all very bewildering most of the time.

Some male homosexuals—especially those in show business—are wonderfully extrovert and witty. Their phrasing and timing, bitchiness and squabbles can make them great fun to be around. Many are really wonderful company. But I soon realized that a pretty girl's face and a lovely female body was what I was fantasizing about. And with all those showgirls to get to know, I certainly felt I was in the right business. My chief problem was I was the youngest in the troupe. Love and sex were all around, but not for me, it seemed. And I hadn't got a clue how to change things. All the girls were older than me and, although I thought they were lovely, they simply saw me as a kid. And for what seemed like for ever, they treated me as the baby of the show. Yes, they were happy to sit with me, look after me, but only in a big sister way. I, of course, didn't want to be their little brother. In the tour coaches, I would cuddle up to them, put my head on their shoulder, but to no avail. I just remained 'the baby', 'the kid', 'the little brother'. They'd give me chocolate, but nothing else! And, just to cap matters, there was not a single 'Mrs Robinson' among them. She would have helped!

I remember the guys always loved working in Nottingham because there seemed to be more lovely girls there than in any other town. Once, when we were doing a week's cabaret there in a dance hall, I had my eye all week on one particular girl in the audience—and kept it on her during the before-and-after dances. She was quite tiny, but wore high heels, had a lovely walk and danced really well. I thought she was *stunning*.

After we had finished doing the last show on the Saturday night, I drummed up the courage to ask her for the last waltz, and then asked if I could see her home. She said yes! We got to her address, and all was still going well. She invited me in. But, then, while she was in a bedroom, taking off her coat, I had a very nasty shock. I discovered through photographs on the mantelpiece that, although she simply didn't look old enough, she had a baby boy. There was also a photograph of a guy in soldier's uniform—obviously her husband.

'Oh, God,' I thought, 'I *can't* . . . I shouldn't be here. I'll stay for a quick cup of tea, and then say I've got a headache.' That's what girls always say! Anything else, I decided, would be very wrong. Her husband was away fighting in the war and here I was in his wife's house. 'No,' I thought, 'this is *not* on.'

It was a testing situation that must have happened so many times during those years to so many people.

I was both lucky *and* unlucky the next time—the first time that anything *really* sexually exciting happened for me. This was about 1947, when I was about nineteen, and in a show in Carlisle. Before I joined this particular production company, not sure I would like the show or Carlisle, I arranged for a two-weeks' notice clause to be put in my contract. Denny Willis—a very good Scottish comic—was one of the acts. He had recently done an absolutely hilarious hunting song with three other guys at a Royal Variety Show, and was known to always go down well in summer season shows. Despite this, the business in Carlisle was not good.

The show was supposed to run for four months but, after eight weeks, the takings were so poor the management team decided to dismiss the people whose contract they could end most easily. Denny was one, I was one—and a couple of dancing girls shared the same fate. One of the girls was about the same age as me. I had always liked and fancied her, but never asked her out because I was too shy! Nowadays, when I think back to what some of the guys used to get up to, I can see how slow I was. But, at that time, I always seemed to need to get to know someone reasonably well before asking them out!

Anyway, on the day we were both dismissed, the girl and I finally got together for a few drinks. When I took her home that night in the car, we were both still very upset about being dismissed from the show, were very emotional and spent a long time comforting each other. When you are that upset, you become physically close very quickly, and things do tend to happen . . . They did. Okay . . . I agree . . . cars are not the best place for making love—especially when it's you yourself who are wearing the 'L' plates. But that's where it happened. Despite the uncomfortable, cramped circumstances, I christened my car and we did each other a bit of good! If by chance Doris reads this, I wonder if she'll agree with me.

*   *   *

In those now far-off wartime days, if you were doing well in show business and had a few weeks' work under your belt and a couple of months' bookings ahead, you'd enter the dates in pencil in your diary—not counting your chickens until you had the contract in your hand. Then, and only then, would you ink in the dates.

If you were doing *really* well, you would splash out and have a drink at a very swish bar in Leicester Square, called the Café Anglais, where all the in-work pros gathered. If you were doing *exceptionally* well, you'd buy a Crombie overcoat— the signal to everybody that you'd either arrived or were definitely on your way! To my great distress, when I eventually 'arrived' and bought my Crombie overcoat, it was stolen very soon afterwards. If you were *not* doing so well, if you'd been out of work for four to six weeks and were still looking, still hoping for something, then you would *not* be in the Café Anglais. You would be round the corner in Charing Cross Road, in the more humble Express Dairy. There you would remain for as long as you could, too frightened to leave in case an agent or producer came in offering work.

There was a terrible 'in' joke doing the rounds at this time. A comic, who had not worked for three months, had fainted in Charing Cross Road. A concerned crowd gathered round him and somebody shouted: 'Give him air . . . Give him air . . .' Hearing this, the comic sat up and said: 'Give me Aberdeen to follow.'

*   *   *

I'm no longer quite sure where I met Peter Crawford, but I think it was in the Express Dairy when I was about fifteen years old. He was my first double-act partner. Peter was a much better accordionist than I was so, for a lot of our act, I

55

accompanied him in the background, making sure I hit all the right chords for his clever twiddly stuff. He was also a very good drummer, so we featured that, too, included a little patter, and normally finished on my tap-dancing. Having succeeded in getting a few cabaret bookings, we then heard that the American Red Cross was looking for people to tour American air and army bases to entertain the troops being held in readiness for D-Day. These bases were all over southern England, so that when the offensive finally took place, the troops would be ready to move out. 'Why not', we thought, 'give this a try?'

Having prepared ourselves and rehearsed a lot, we arranged for an audition at the American Red Cross headquarters in Rutland Gate, near Hyde Park. On arrival, we were met by a Major Brill who had terrible trouble saying his 'r's. We did our audition. As we finished, the major looked at the secretary and a few other people gathered there and said: 'That was gwait . . . That was absolutely gwait. You kids were absolutely gwait. Would you mind coming upstairs? I'd like some other people to see this because you weally are absolutely gwait.'

So we went upstairs and did the act all over again. The major then got people from other offices to come in and see us working and watch Peter on his drums. 'Aren't they gwait, these kids?' he kept repeating. 'Have you ever seen kids so gwait? Would you mind coming upstairs?' In the end, we did the act *three* times, but we got ourselves the US bases' contract.

We thought Major Brill was an absolute scream, but also a very nice chap. The money was good and, of course, everything the Americans had at that time was better—food, clothes, chewing gum—everything.

To do the job, we had to be fitted with American uniforms. I was fifteen years old and tall for my age, so imagine how I felt being fitted for an officer's airforce-blue uniform that had patches on its epaulettes, plus a forage cap sporting a Red Cross badge. Having been told that if we were ever unfortunate enough to be captured by the Germans we would at least have the rank of major, I couldn't wait to be taken prisoner. And the uniform made me look so much older.

So, wearing these uniforms, we stayed in first-class hotels. I never forget that when I was first billeted in a twin-bedded room all to myself, I phoned my mother.

'Are you all right?' she asked anxiously.

'Fine,' I said. 'Fine. They've just checked us into this *beautiful* hotel. There's a dining room downstairs. It's all so *lovely*. I've got a bedroom all to myself . . . I've got a bathroom all to myself . . . and I'm calling you from a phone *in the bedroom!*'

At that time, no one had *two* telephones in a house, let alone one in the bedroom. The only phone you had then was in the hall.

'Well!' said my mother. 'That must be wonderful, Bruce.'

'This is the *Big* Time, Mum,' I said. 'They're treating us so well.'

It really was bliss—the most perfect experience.

We travelled from base to base in what we called a 'clubmobile'. This was a Green Line single-decker coach, which had been converted to hold three beds as well as seating in the back. We transported our own piano, a certain amount of

57

lighting, all the drums and the microphone equipment—everything we might need. We were a company of about eight people for the show and were completely self-contained. We could do a show anywhere, although sometimes our lighting was not quite up to scratch.

Once we went to a base where there was no hall or hangar where we could perform because the troops were practising for D-Day. So, on this occasion, we actually went out on manoeuvres with the men. When it came to the time for our performance, they lined up all the jeeps, switched on the headlights to act as spotlights, and created a kind of stage platform that we could stand on and do our bits and pieces. So we did our performance outdoors, under the stars.

An hour before the performance, we would always try to get to the enlisted men's mess. The food there was *so* good. We would also ask the mess sergeant if he had any spare tins of fruit we could take home. After all, this was Britain at war—1943—food was rationed. We hadn't seen a tin of pears or peaches for years, so any we succeeded in getting from the US bases were, as Major Brill would say, a gwait luxury.

It's difficult to explain to youngsters these days just how fortunate the US servicemen were. If we managed to get some tinned fruit or cigarettes to take home to Mother, it was absolutely marvellous. At one time, we got American PX cards, with which you could buy everything, even golf clubs. It was wonderful. To us, at the time, shopping in a US-base store was like being set loose in Harrods. There was so much their forces had that we had been deprived of, and it was all so cheap.

In particular, we were always trying to get our hands on pairs of nylon stockings to take home for the girls. The fashion at the time was to have stockings with seams up the back of the leg so, if you went home with some of those, you were well and truly in!

My two years with the American Red Cross was when I really got into jazz—still one of my great pleasures in life. After the shows the American musicians would come round, say 'Hi', and talk to our drummer, pianist, tenor saxophonist or clarinettist. And then they'd all get up and have a 'jam' session. I wasn't too familiar with this kind of music, but then I got into jazz in a big way. I used to think: 'How marvellous—they take a tune, improvise around the melody with a chord sequence and there it is.' I started to watch the pianist. Chords fascinated me and I began to get less and less interested in playing the accordion and the piano took over. My brother John also played the piano, but his tastes were very different from mine. He was much more interested in the classical side of music. From the American Red Cross days onwards, I just loved jazz and from that moment on I used to go and listen to the big bands whenever I could—bands like Ted Heath and all the others that were around then. I would travel miles—anywhere—to hear a big band and became a great fan of the Nat King Cole trio. I was so impressed by Nat's wonderful piano-playing.

The other thing I remember about our days with the American Red Cross is that, during the war, there was an American GI cartoon character called Sad Sack. A bit simple in the head, he was always getting into terrible scrapes with the sergeant. I dressed up in the fatigue uniform that the Americans wore and did a kind of impression of Jerry Lewis, but made Jerry Lewis into a recognizable version of Sad Sack. This was the first time I had done comedy for an audience—real comedy, with Peter as the straight man and me as Sad Sack. We did truly terrible jokes like, 'She was once a sergeant's girlfriend . . . but now she's an officer's mess', which the enlisted men loved. I wore the denim fatigue outfit with the army cap pulled down jauntily over my forehead, and managed a good imitation of Jerry Lewis's high-pitched American accent.

On occasions we used to go to what the Americans called a 'coloured' camp. Ghastly as that sounds now, in those days the US Army used to segregate blacks and whites and you would never see a black American in a white unit. If it was a battalion, then all the troops would be black, with white officers. When we were at a black camp, any black musicians who were in the audience would come round backstage after the show. It was wonderful. I would stay on for two or three hours while they played 'modern jazz', which was just coming in then. Also—being young guys—they would play bebop.

Stan Kenton was a very ahead of the times band at that time, and Glen Miller was *the* band that played regularly on AFN—the American Forces Network—a radio station just for the Americans that we also loved to listen to.

*   *   *

At one point in 1943, I was given a few days' leave

and decided to go home to see my parents. When I arrived, I could tell the very first moment I opened the front door that something really awful had happened. The house felt so empty.

My parents, I learned, had been informed that my brother, John, who was only twenty years old, had been killed while on an RAF training exercise at Turnberry—very close to Ayr—Scotland. What made this loss so much worse was that he had been posted as 'missing while on low-altitude practice'. In those days to hear that somebody was posted as 'missing' meant that there was still a possibility they were alive; that you could continue to live in hope, possibly for years. My mother was convinced that John had been rescued from the sea by a passing trawler, taken to South Africa or South America, was still alive and would come home one day. But it was not to be. John's body was never found.

Very recently, a Mrs Margaret Morrell, who had been doing some research into the many accidents that happened in that part of the country, wrote to me. I phoned her up and, at last, heard the true story of my brother's accident while he was serving as Flight Sergeant John Frederick Forsyth-Johnson in the Royal Air Force Volunteer Reserve. The story I had always been told until then was that on Friday, 21 May 1943, seven aircraft were lost on the same night while on training exercises to lay sea mines or torpedoes. But Margaret Morrell found out—and has now sent me the documentation—that three Wellington aircraft were lost that night. The first plane, 'doing low-level attacks on a target ship, misjudged the height and crashed into the sea'. This was subsequently recorded as the pilot's 'error of judgement and inexperience' while flying on a 'dark night' when 'the sea was glassy'.

Evidently when anything like this happened, the other planes with the squadron would stop the exercise, put on their lights and go to see if there were any survivors. But what happened on that particular night was that after the first Wellington bomber ditched into the sea, the other two Wellingtons—including my brother's aircraft—collided with each other while circling in the search for survivors. I'm grateful my parents didn't know this.

It was bad enough to accept that my brother was killed while only on a training exercise, but that it should have been an accident between two planes searching for survivors made the tragedy so much worse.

In the event, there were seven survivors picked up during that night and the next morning. The rest—eleven men, including my brother—were listed as missing. He is now, along with them, remembered with honour at the Air Force Memorial at Runnymede in Surrey. The words carved on the stone plinth are: Their name liveth for evermore.

Among the papers that Margaret Morrell sent me was the following report on the accident from Squadron Leader Tony Spooner DSO DFC AE:

> We did not have, but much needed, low-level radio altimeters. We only had the pressure-sensitive ones which were marked in hundreds of feet and lacked the detail we required. Low-flying, therefore, had to be judged solely by the pilot's eye. This was okay as long as the sea had visible ripples, waves, white-caps,

etc., but in a still calm sea it was deceptive. The sea could then look the same from 500 feet to 0 feet. This led to our only losses.

One night when I had left Norman Lightowler in charge, a rare, dead-flat calm persisted. Consequently one of the 'Wimpys' flown by a crew towards the end of a course, flew into the water. Trying to be helpful, when it became known that an aircraft was 'in the drink', the other crews put on their landing lights, flew low and looked for survivors. As a result, due to the flat and deceptively calm sea, providing no definition of height, two other aircraft flew into the sea. Of the eighteen men, only seven were picked up that night or next morning.

It speaks of the high morale, that the next morning the skipper of the aircraft which had initially flown into the sea, came to report. He had spent six hours in the freezing water, been fished out early that morning near the Mull of Kintyre, had found a flight back to Turnberry from Macrahanish, and after discussing the night's losses with the other survivors, had realized that between them they could make up a complete crew. 'Would it be all right, sir, if we formed up as a crew and finished the course?' He had already obtained the consent of the survivors from the other lost crews. What could I do in the face of such determination but say yes.

When John died I was fifteen—just five years younger than him. When I came home and heard the news, I realized that something really strange had happened to me at the time of his death. On what was the day of his fatal accident, I was on an American Red Cross base at St Neots, near Bedford, and we had the afternoon off. It was a nice sunny day and a group of us went down to a river and played around there for a while. Then we started a ball game. While we were playing, somebody threw the ball rather hard and, as I went to catch it, I bent my finger right back. It *really* hurt and, as I felt quite sick, somebody said: 'Why don't you go back to the clubmobile and sit in the shade for a bit? You will probably feel better there.' So I did. I went back and, while having a lie-down, had this very strange feeling that I was in an aeroplane and that it was flying low over the sea. I then jumped out of the plane and, as I did so, I half fell off the bunk I was lying on and woke up with a start.

'What a strange dream,' I'd thought at the time—and more so when later I discovered this had happened on the same day as my brother's accident. For many years I pondered and wondered about this. I do believe in the subtle spirit world. I have never delved into it, but I do think there is something other than this world which, in normal circumstances, we cannot see or hear. That dream is the only experience of this kind I have ever had, but I am not surprised it happened. We were a *very* close family and John's accidental death was exceedingly hard to come to terms with. Especially for my mother.

64

John, as I've said, played the piano beautifully and, strangely, it was about this time that I started to fall out of love with the piano accordion. It is now an instrument that I do not like much at all. John played classical piano—and was a really loveable lad. The day he was eighteen—as I mentioned in Chapter One—all he wanted to do was enlist. But that was what most young men then wanted to do when they were eighteen. They thought joining the services was not only patriotic, but an adventurous thing to do.

My father had taught John to be a very good mechanic, but he never wanted me to follow in his footsteps. If I ever went into the garage to oil my roller skates he'd tell me to get out and not touch anything. He always said: 'You're not going to have a filthy job like this,' and he'd show me his hands, and point out how the grease and dirt had ingrained itself into his skin. He'd say, 'No, boy, this is not for you.'

Before he died, John had done further training in the Air Force, then went to Pensacola, Florida, to get his wings. He loved it over there. After passing his training course, which was only a few weeks, he was allowed to pilot a Catalina flying boat all the way across the Atlantic because aircraft were so needed over here. Then of all bases he could have got posted to, Turnberry was his reward—a station which we heard had a high accident record.

I have often thought how incredibly lucky I was not to have been born a couple of years earlier and therefore been old enough to be called up, because in many cases, as soon as you went into any of the armed forces, your days, like John's, were numbered.

CHAPTER THREE

CAN YOU DO ANYTHING ELSE?

By the time my double-act partner, Peter Crawford, was called up and went into the Army, the war was actually at an end and the American Red Cross was being wound up. I decided to move into the variety circuit as another double act— Forsyth and Roy—with a guy called Les Roy. Les was a wonderful drummer and a 'big boot' dancer. Big Boot dated back to a man called Little Titch who was tremendously popular in the 1920s and 1930s. What these dancers did was wear shoes that were like big flaps—about two and a half feet long. To dance in this particular style, they flip-flopped their big boots on to the boards, hence the name 'big boot' dancing. So Les did a bit of this, and I played the piano and did some impressions. The two of us then finished the act with a tap-dance routine.

The VE (Victory in Europe) Day celebration on 8 May 1945 coincided with us performing at the Whitehall Theatre in the Phyllis Dixey Show. From what I can remember now, VE coincided with a lovely sunny spring day and, from the Whitehall Theatre, we had wonderful views of the dense crowds waiting in the streets for Prime Minister

Winston Churchill's three o'clock broadcast, declaring 'the German war is at an end', and that hostilities would end at midnight. I remember sirens and hooters sounding, flags and bunting everywhere, and a parade going down Whitehall, with the band playing for all its worth.

Everybody from the show—including Les and I—was up on the roof, watching. Some of us chaps, I must confess, had one eye on the parade and the jubilant crowds, and the other on the Phyllis Dixey showgirls who were sunbathing. Because strap marks looked very bad on stage, they sunbathed topless, apart from a couple of coins on their nipples. They usually used halfpennies for this purpose, but sometimes larger half-crowns were needed! Although I often said, 'Anybody got any change?' nobody ever took me up on it!

So . . . VE Day came and went. Bonfires were built all over the country, impromptu fancy-dress parties were organized for the children, and churches and pubs were filled to capacity. Winston Churchill appeared on a Whitehall balcony and told the waiting crowds: 'This is *your* victory. God bless you all.' Alongside him, Labour's Ernest Bevin led a rapturous round of 'For He's a Jolly Good Fellow'. Everybody was in party mood, and the streets were busting their seams with people singing and dancing, embracing each other, and forming human chains to do the 'Hokey-Cokey' and 'Knees Up, Mother Brown'. Then, when Big Ben sounded the 'official ceasefire' time at midnight, a deafening roar went up, followed by fireworks exploding and the pealing of the capital's bells. Yes, VE Day was enduringly memorable for all of us.

I didn't go into the Air Force until 1947, by which time of course the war was over. I was nineteen years old, and supposed to have gone in at eighteen, but my call-up was delayed because of my show-business contracts. The trouble about going in then was that it all felt so pointless. The war had been won, so why should I have to risk my career for two and a half years in the forces? To be out of circulation for that long—especially from a business where you needed to keep your name up-front—was agonizing. But I had no choice . . . Fortunately, it all worked out in the end, because just before I received my call-up papers in April 1947, something wonderful happened . . . something which meant that after I finished my conscription in the Air Force, I would not—unlike so many men returning from the war or post-war conscription—have to endure hard times trudging around looking for work. But I don't want to get too far ahead of myself.

*   *   *

After my sister Maisie had the terrible loss of Tom, her husband, and was left with three young children, Barbie, Terry and Lynn, to bring up alone, my parents suggested that she should work as the secretary for my father's garage business. But this created a new financial problem of its own, of course. When too many need to live off a family business, that's where all the profits go. So Dad's business never really made that much money.

As I mentioned in Chapter Two, my mother died on 19 September 1957, aged sixty-three. Three weeks before she had suffered a stroke while sitting in a chair at home. Although she remained alert in many ways, she didn't recognize us. People who have strokes seem to have a million questions hovering in their eyes, which they can't ask and we can't answer. We have no way of knowing if this is because they are in a state of limbo, where nothing makes sense any more. Perhaps it's the first stage of passing away? Some people get over strokes, make a reasonable recovery. My friend, Harry Secombe, proved in a brave film that he made after his stroke that this could be done. How cruel that after all that effort—which took months—he died shortly afterwards of prostate cancer. But my mother didn't recover from her stroke. She died within a month.

My dad was very lonely after she died. They'd been in love for so many years, and she had always done so much for him. I can't begin to imagine how difficult this time was for him. It must have been dreadful to be suddenly alone in the house. I was away so much, my brother was lost in the war, and Maisie had three young children to look after. I really wasn't that surprised when, three years later, my father married my mother's sister, who had lost her husband when she was in her forties. The marriage didn't come as a shock to me because my mother had always been very close to her sister— and Auntie Dolly, as I called her (although her real name was Britannia!), had always been a part of our family life, even joining us sometimes on holiday. She was a dear lady with a lovely sense of humour and she and I had been very close since I was a baby. I was very glad for my dad. He was a bit of a loner, wasn't one for going to a pub with mates or into sports like football. I can even remember taking him to the Spurs one Saturday afternoon and having to explain what a football match was all about! People couldn't believe this little boy telling his father the rules of football.

To run ahead of myself again, the marriage caused even more financial problems for Maisie when Dad died on 30 December 1961, aged sixty-nine. Father had made a stipulation in his will that Auntie Dolly should always be looked after, should have all her expenses paid, and should always have a car. Auntie Dolly lived until 24 December 1994, when she was ninety-three, and Maisie had to take this money, in addition to her own allowance—and wages for her son, Terry, and daughter, Barbie, who were also working for the business—from what small profits there were. As you can appreciate, such a number of people dependent on the business inevitably caused a great strain. Sometimes family businesses prosper, sometimes they don't; and when, from necessity, more is being taken out than is coming in, things can be very difficult.

I was working in Manchester when my father passed away. He had been ill for some time, had a heart attack and was sent to Chase Farm Hospital, Enfield, where he died. When Maisie telephoned me to break the news, she said: 'Don't cancel the show, Bruce. Dad wouldn't want you to do that. And it would cause so much disappointment to all the people who've booked to see you. Don't come home for the funeral. We'll be all right here.' I thought about it and realized that Maisie was right. Dad wouldn't have wanted to cause all that fuss— bless him. What really upset me, though, was the fact that I wasn't with him when he died.

One of the worst audiences Les Roy and I ever encountered was in Barnsley, Yorkshire—where, incidentally, Michael Parkinson comes from. Whether he had anything to do with this, I don't know! They were a *terrible* audience all week, as far as laughs went. In those days, it was customary to finish your act, bow, go offstage, and then come back for a second bow. And if you were a double act, as we were, you 'milked' it—by calling each other back to take another bow, and so on. But at Barnsley you'd finish your act to quite good applause, go offstage, come back for your second bow, and the applause would just stop immediately. You were just left there, feeling like a couple of plonkers—to borrow a phrase! And they did this *every* night!

On the Saturday, I said to Les: 'I'm so sick of this. We've never had an audience like this. Don't let's go back onstage. Let's do one double bow— bow to them, bow to each other—then go offstage and not return.' So, as agreed, we did just one double bow on Saturday night. It was marvellous, gave us great satisfaction because of course that way they couldn't humiliate us on the last night.

The show's top-of-the-bill was a ventriloquist. He came round afterwards and said: '*That* was a *very* untheatrical, unprofessional thing to do.' '*Why?*' we both protested. '*Why* should we stand there and be humiliated by these people?'

'Well,' he repeated, 'it's *unprofessional.*' 'Well,' I said, 'it may be *unprofessional*, but it made us feel good—and we can't wait to get out of this place.'

Hand on heart, I have always loved Yorkshire audiences in Leeds, Hull, Sheffield, Wakefield, and so on, but Barnsley was *dreadful—quite, quite* awful. What they're like nowadays, I do not know because I've never been back! Mind you, they've never asked me back!

*   *   *

One of my impressions during this time was of the lead singer in the Inkspots. And each time I went for one of his incredibly high notes, I used to pretend to take a pin from my lapel and jab myself in the bottom to help me get there! Another very popular piece during this time was my Claude Hulbert impression. A very famous comedy actor, he was such a very funny man who always made me laugh. In one of his films, *Sailors Three*, a favourite of mine, he was standing at a bar, obviously legless and holding himself up by the bar rail. He then, in his outrageously posh voice, said to the barman who was offering him a drink: 'No, thank you very much. Glass of milk, please.' An immortal line.

Les and I worked together on the variety circuit for quite a while until, at last, we succeeded in getting on to the stage of Number One theatres. That was quite a moment! Cissy Williams, a lady who ran the bookings for Moss Empires, had seen us and liked us. And if Cissy liked you, you were definitely in the running for Number One theatre bookings. By then, we also had an agent called Brian Roxbury. Things were looking up.

One of these bookings was for a Dundee venue with Tommy Morgan who, although unknown down South, was one of Scotland's biggest comics.

72

In those days, you could be a big name in Scotland, Yorkshire and Lancashire, even a big name in the Midlands, but down South that would not necessarily mean a thing. The same applied to comics who were big names in the South. They couldn't go any further than the Midlands.

So, there we were in Dundee for Christmas. By the way, *never* go there for Christmas—New Year's Eve, yes, but *not* Christmas. Then at least they worked all through it. When Les and I tried to wish everyone a 'Merry Christmas' nobody seemed to care. New Year's Eve, however, was a different story. I remember finishing this with half a bottle of rum in one pocket, half a bottle of Scotch in the other. And, as I walked down Dundee's main street, I was stopped so often by people wishing me—an English lad in Scotland—a 'Happy New Year', I never even found the party I was supposed to be heading for and couldn't even remember how I got home.

Following the Dundee show, there was a big revue called the *Mayfair Merry-Go-Round*, and our agent, Brian, said Cissy Williams would like us to be in this. We'd have to spend two weeks in every major city in the country. Marvellous. The only drawback about this show—a bit of a comedown for Les and me—was that we had to give up our billing as a double act and become additional solo members of Jack Jackson's Band. Jack was a very popular bandleader and I ended up playing the piano, while Les played drums. During the second half of the show, however, we were allowed to do a couple of bits from our own act.

For non-showbiz reasons, it actually turned out to be a good experience. The thing about playing

73

piano in a band-show is that you have plenty of time to look around the audience and spot any available 'talent'—that is, 'crumpet'. This last word, no longer politically correct, was in common usage then. As was 'rumpo', which I always found funny, but a bit crude. Anyway . . . having spotted a pretty girl, you would give her the glad eye and make it obvious you'd like her to come round to the stage door after the performance. Readers will have to take on board here that we were working nights in a different place every two weeks. And if we hadn't done this roving-eye trick, we wouldn't have had any female company at all. Unless, that is, we were lucky enough to meet a girl in a dance hall, which we did sometimes.

They were fun days, but not without their hazards. Some of the girls could look very promising and attractive when viewed from above the footlights. But when they came to the stage door, they could look dreadful. When this occurred—and it did more often than I care to remember—I would just take them out for a coffee then, with great relief, say: 'I've got to get back to my digs by ten thirty or my landlady will lock me out.'

When Les and I joined Jack Jackson's Band, we discovered that all the musicians played golf. Jack himself was a 'scratch' golfer with a lovely swing. I also recall now that when the truck delivered all the luggage and props for the show to the theatre, it also—given the number of golf fanatics among them—had on board at least twenty to twenty-four bags of golf clubs.

Now . . . there are many reasons why people take up the game, but mine came via a challenge during this period—and it was a challenge that changed my whole life. While Les and I were in Dundee for the two weeks at Christmas, we had very good digs but a landlord who thoroughly disapproved of us lying late in bed every morning. For young men, which of course we were, he thought this was a diabolical waste of youth. 'You ought to be out playing golf,' he kept saying indignantly. 'Golf!' we kept replying cheekily. 'That's an old man's game!'

Anyway . . . one night after the show, we had a couple of drinks, went back to the digs for supper and, once again, he challenged us about what time we would like breakfast. 'About eleven . . . eleven thirty,' we said. This was too much for him. He started carrying on about golf again. 'That's what you *should* be doing in the mornings,' he kept saying. And he went on and on. In the end, just to shut him up, we agreed to play the next day.

He woke us at seven which, to us, felt like the middle of the night. And, believe me, no sergeant major could have done a better job of making sure we got up. He then drove us to Carnoustie and, on the way, explained that, as it was a wee bit frosty, we would play with red balls. He also told us that he would give us two shots—I thought he meant whisky!—on every hole and that he would play our best ball. Les and I, full of confidence, agreed to all this, giving each other a wink and knowing look. You readers will not be surprised to learn that we did not win one hole and finished totally exhausted.

From that day on, I never believed that golf was an old man's game. It became one of my obsessions—almost my favourite pastime. Les was also hooked. To begin with, we used to tee off after the other members of the band, so we wouldn't get in their way. But sometimes one of them would kindly condescend to play with us and give us a few tips. Since then, I've had very few golf lessons. I've simply picked up my own technique along the way. Sometimes it works—most of the time it doesn't!

*　　*　　*

While Les and I were with the Jack Jackson Band, we met top-of-the-bill singer Monte Rey, and a quick-change impersonator named Owen McGivney. Owen, performing as Bill Sykes, Fagin, the Artful Dodger—and Nancy!—in his *Oliver Twist* act, impressed us enormously with his astonishingly quick costume changes. He would come out as one character, the lights would come up, and then he'd rush through a door to two guys in black suits who'd help him change into the next character in split seconds. It was so impressive. He would do the whole sketch in this manner in about eight minutes.

The other two tops-of-the-bill I became friends with were brothers, Syd and Max Harrison. They were comics, singers, dancers—and great golfers, not to mention characters. They obviously thought I was a kindred spirit because, even though they were much older than I was, they took me under their wings. And Syd's father-in-law, 'Pop', showed me how to tie my own bow tie out of a bit of straight material. People are still sometimes amazed that I manage this on my own.

All this period, then, was an exciting learning curve for me—a time when I discovered three ongoing 'loves': pretty girls, jazz and golf, almost at the same time.

Today, looking back on those days, I realize I wasn't really a good enough pianist then to be playing with the Jack Jackson Band. I *really* wish I had been better. Even at the time, I knew I was a bit lacking and felt very self-conscious about this. As a result, when the first tour ended—and the band was going on to a Number Two theatre tour and I was getting very close to going into the RAF, I decided to make a radical career change. It was, after all, a bit of a comedown to go from the Number Ones to the Number Two theatres. Also, as Les and I were no longer doing our double act in the show and he wanted to go on the second tour with the band, I decided we should split up and go our separate ways. This we did. As is so often the case in life, we just lost touch with each other. About ten years ago I was very sorry to hear that Les had passed away. He was a good partner and we shared some lovely growing-up times together.

Having taken such a radical decision and risk, I was very fortunate. Particularly lucky, considering that at that time you could go for weeks without any work between bookings. And even more lucky, given that a lot of performers were coming down South from up North, trying to find work in London. Many of these had no money. But I had a mother and father who always ensured I was never in want for a meal or the means to get around.

I spent most of my unemployed days going round agents, and eventually while doing this heard some good news. The Windmill Theatre was apparently looking for 'juveniles' who could do ballet, modern dancing or tap-dancing, and who could also sing. It seemed strange at nineteen years old to associate myself with the word

77

'juvenile', but beggars can't be choosers and I thought, 'Maybe . . . ?'

So I wrote off for an audition and was duly asked to go along, at nine in the morning. In those days, 1947, the Windmill opened its doors to the public and started its six-shows-a-day schedule at eleven thirty in the morning. On this occasion, so many 'hopefuls' had turned up for auditions that, by eleven fifteen, somebody announced: 'Anybody who hasn't yet done their audition can stay on, and we'll do the rest upstairs in the rehearsal room.' This particular room was on the top floor, next to the canteen. When I saw it, I was disappointed and worried. There's a world of difference in doing an audition in a bare-floored rehearsal room to being on a proper stage where you can present yourself well. However, given no choice, I waited another hour for my turn. By this time, I had been there four or five hours. Finally, my moment came. First, as usual, I went over to speak to the pianist. Her name was Molly and she was not, bless her heart, wearing a straw hat. 'Okay,' she said, after I told her what I was going to do. 'That's fine.'

Vivian Van Damm, the owner of the Windmill, and his casting director, Anne Mitelle, were present. I started singing my song, got halfway through and Van Damm stopped me: 'Okay. Do you do anything else?' 'Yes,' I said, 'I play the piano.' When he nodded his assent, I sat down at the piano, started playing and, halfway through, he said, 'Yes, okay. Do you do anything else?' 'Yes,' I replied, 'I do a few impressions.' Once again when he indicated, I did a few quick ones—Claude Hulbert, Edward G. Robinson, James Cagney . . . But only halfway through the other names on my

78

list, Van Damm said: 'Yes, okay. Do you do anything else?' 'Yes,' I answered. 'I tap-dance.' 'Oh, you do . . .? Okay, then tap-dance.' Over I went and started to do a tap-dance. But just as I got to the second chorus Molly got the tempo wrong. I went over to her and said: *'No, dear*, I want it quicker than that.' But Van Damm shouted across: 'I can see you can dance. Okay. That's all.' 'But . . .' I said emphatically, 'I want to do the last part of my act. That's when I do my winging.' Now 'winging' is when you elevate yourself, then flick your feet to either side. It's a *big* impressive finish. 'No,' he said, 'I've seen enough.' 'Will you let me finish?' I asked, by now really frustrated. 'No,' he replied, 'I've seen enough.'

I went over to Molly and said: 'Play my music.' 'No,' she replied, closing the piano lid firmly. 'Mr Van Damm said he's seen enough.' Angry by now, I protested: *'All right* . . . I'll do it without you.' So, off I went back to the middle of the floor and did this 'winging' chorus to no music. Then, having finished what I had been determined to do, I collected my music from Molly, grabbed my shoes and stormed out. I was *really* angry. I thought Van Damm was very wrong not to let me finish the dance properly. But the poor man had been taking auditions for six hours.

The next morning, at about half past ten—I always slept in during those days—my mother came into my room and said: 'Bru, there's a lady on the phone for you.' 'All right, Mum, take a message,' I said. 'No,' my mother said. 'It's the lady from the Windmill—Anne Mitelle.' 'Oh!' I said. *'Anne Mitelle?* I must have left something behind—must have dropped something as I stormed out.' 'Well

'. . . she wants to talk to you,' my mother said patiently.

I went downstairs, picked up the phone and the voice said: 'Hallo? Hallo, Mr Forsyth, Anne Mitelle here. I'm wondering . . . We wouldn't want you to be a solo act in the show . . . but would you consider being in the resident company? We have an "A" company and "B" company. Would you like to come along and discuss the possibility of joining us as a regular member of the Windmill team?' I was speechless, bewildered, *couldn't* believe it. 'Yes,' I said. 'But I am a *little* surprised.' 'Are you?' she replied. 'Why? You did a very good audition . . . Mr Van Damm was impressed, would like to have you. Come along and see me.'

By now, feeling very reassured and reasonably calm, I went along that same afternoon to meet Anne Mitelle, and we discussed money, which was about £25 a week. Compared to what I had been used to being paid, this was good money. 'We're beginning a new show in two weeks' time,' she said. 'Could you start rehearsals then?' 'Oh, *yes*,' I said. 'I can.' *Could I!* I'd taken a chance leaving the band and Les, and it had really paid off!

'There is one thing,' Anne Mitelle added soberly. 'You will be working with some *very* beautiful girls at the Windmill—probably more beautiful than any you have ever worked with before. They wear *very, very* little. And lots of the tops they wear are very scanty and see-through. And when the girls are posing, the Lord Chamberlain has said they must *not* move. And even the girls you will be dancing with—those who *are* allowed to move—will have *very, very* little on. So, please, you must understand that you are not

80

allowed to fraternize with them, and must not make it obvious, by staring at them, that you are aware they have very little on. I have to give you this word of warning because Mr Van Damm will not stand for any nonsense—and will step on that immediately.'

'Yes, of course . . .' I said, trying not to smile or look anxious. 'I understand. I've never danced with girls wearing see-through tops before. But I think I can cope with that.'

Funnily enough—and this may sound strange to readers—when I was working with them, it *was* in a very professional way. When I was first around the girls, I couldn't fail to notice how lovely and sexy they were. But I never stared—never embarrassed them or, come to that, myself. Alert and aware, *yes*—what chap wouldn't be?—but I kept my cool, remained very professional, never behaved improperly. Having said that, if a girl suddenly stood up and moved across the stage during rehearsals, and was in my line of vision, I couldn't resist sneaking a quick look. But this was never too obvious, never a lingering up-and-down look, and I certainly never made any rude remarks. We all knew, without needing to be told, that the girls appreciated respect from their fellow performers. They had more than enough ogling to cope with from guys in the audience. So, honestly, Anne Mitelle's warning did not worry me. Of course, all my male friends—the chaps I used to have a drink with back home in Edmonton—could not believe I was unfazed by all this. And when they found out I'd got a job at the Windmill, they had plenty to say about it. You can imagine the questions I was asked!

Anyway, having reassured Anne Mitelle, I joined the Windmill and attended all the rehearsals leading up to the first night of the show. Then came a truly bitter disappointment. I had only been at the Windmill for three blissful weeks when my call-up papers arrived. I was *devastated.* I explained to Anne Mitelle that I had already delayed my conscription for a year, and that this was my final summons.

There was, however, a really wonderful surprise in store for me. Anne Mitelle said the Windmill was *very* sorry to lose me. I had done the song-and-dance duets so well, they knew that these would always be one of my strong points. Then she delivered her lovely surprise: 'When you come out of the forces,' she added, 'we'll still be here, and if you feel like coming back to the Windmill, then Mr Van Damm will consider taking you on again.'

So . . . when I'd stormed out of the audition, I clearly had not burned my boats with him. But then Van Damm was *that* kind of person. If you did something he thought was wrong, he would dismiss you quicker than a click of his fingers. He was *very* authoritative. But if you were in the right and stood up for yourself, as I did when I defied him, he was impressed. Audition tantrums or no tantrums, maybe he would have employed me anyway . . . I will never know.

Despite all my good-behaviour reassurances to Anne Mitelle, I remember there was a vivacious red-haired Windmill girl who I thought was absolutely gorgeous but, as she was going out with a Polish flight lieutenant, I had no chance of blotting my copybook with her. On the night I was leaving, though, I bumped into her on the stairs as she was going to her dressing room. 'Oh! You're leaving tonight, aren't you?' 'Yes,' I said. She must have known I liked her because she added: 'Wouldn't you like a kiss for good luck?' I didn't have time to answer. She gave me a truly wonderful lingering kiss. As I watched her run up the stairs in her scanty costume, I thought: 'If Van Damm had seen that, I'd have been sacked on the spot! But, so what, I'm leaving anyway.'

The truth is I wasn't really there long enough to have a chance with any of the girls. And, having had the 'hands-off' warning, I didn't want to do anything too silly so early on. I did find out while I was there, though, that 'boys will be boys', threats or no threats, and a couple of the other guys had totally disregarded the warnings and were dating Windmill Girls. I also discovered that if Mr Van Datum thought it was 'a good match', he didn't protest.

*   *   *

In April 1947 I went into the RAF and was posted to a big base at Padgate, near Warrington. This was where all new recruits were sent to start off with, then we could be posted to other places to do our square-bashing, so called because of the bashing you did with your boots on the parade square!

I've never forgotten my first day in the RAF. I had been earning £25 a week at the Windmill, and feeling I was the cat's whiskers. Then I arrived at this *awful* place, with these Nissen huts all over the shop and was given some gear, a bed for the night, and told I could get a meal if I went over to the mess hall. So I went along and was dished up all this terrible food. I sat down at a table and hadn't been there ten seconds when this corporal came over, and said: 'What *do* you think you are doing?' 'I've just arrived and I'm having a meal,' I said indignantly. 'Not on *this* table, you don't,' he snapped back. 'This table is for corporals and non-commissioned officers. *Get off*. Or you'll be on a charge before you have time to eat a baked bean.'

So, this was my introduction to forces' discipline. Having said that, I can honestly say that the discipline I was subjected to in those first eight weeks in the RAF—and in the two and a half years that followed—did me no harm whatsoever. I know lots of people have said what I'm about to say, but I honestly do not think we would have the kind of hooliganism we have today in this and other countries if there was still some form of National Service conscription. When you're between seventeen and nineteen years of age, you *need* discipline. It's the best thing for you. Although I didn't want to go into the Air Force, it taught me an awful lot. And I loved drilling—*really*, I did. I suppose it was the rhythm and the sound of all those boots. I finished up being the right-hand marker, a very important position, which means you are considered the best at drill, and everybody lines up with you and takes the pace of the march from you. It is actually the easiest job in the world, because when you are the right-hand marker, everybody on your left—and even the people behind you—all mark off from you, so *you* can do no wrong. I was chuffed to get that job. It was a bit like show business with a huge cast of dancers alongside you. On the downside, though, they were not so beautiful or so scantily dressed!

I'm still friends with a guy I met at Padgate called Alan Poore. He came from Southgate in North London, so we had home locations in common. After the first couple of weeks there, I found out that he owned a little Austin Seven car, and I had an Austin Ten. To ingratiate ourselves—and make our lives a little easier—we used to give the corporals a ride into town to meet their girlfriends. Alan became a good friend—and still has a great sense of humour. We had so many laughs during those first eight weeks, especially when we managed to survive doing guard duty together one night. The sergeant picked me up from my post, marched me to Alan's post and ordered Alan to shoulder arms. He did, but accidentally stuck his bayonet in the sentry box. I started to laugh, but the sergeant said to Alan, 'You clumsy airman . . . *What are you?*' And Alan replied dutifully, 'I'm a clumsy airman, Sergeant.' How he said it without laughing and stayed standing at attention, I do not know. By this time my face was contorted with laughter, but I didn't make a sound.

At the end of every week or two, there would be this terrible event called a billet-and-kit inspection. During this, the officer-of-the-day would come round and inspect our boots. You had to polish these by spitting on them, then get the hot end of a spoon and rub it on the toe cap until it really shone and you could see your reflection in it. I *hated* that. It was *dreadful.* It really was. Then, again, your trouser legs had to have a wonderful crease in them, and all your kit had to be laid out in a certain way. Even the stove had to be blackened and polished, and the floor lino had to shine until it was dangerously slippery. Lethal for tap-dancing.

If your hut didn't get a good result from your kit inspection, your leave would be cancelled for that week—or maybe even two weeks. And you might even be put on 'punishment', where we had to go outside and cut the grass with a knife. Sooner or later, we all ended up cutting grass in this way. Then, eight weeks later, this part of our life in the RAF was over.

Alan knew I had worked at the Windmill Theatre, but I didn't tell the others. I had had enough teasing and bullying when I was a child. It was in the NAAFI that I would practise the piano. The pianos were mostly awful out-of-tune instruments, but at some bases there would be a good one. And I met a man called Harry Bence who was a wonderful alto sax player. He formed his own big band and I played in a group with him a few times, but I still had a lot to learn. I used to spend hours and hours playing the piano there. I also always smoked during this time, because I thought it was the thing to do. Everyone smoked in Hollywood movies; whenever there was anything dramatic going on, or a pause in the action, out came the cigarettes. I loved to have a cigarette, especially a Peter Stuyvesant because they were long and elegant, dangling from the corner of my mouth. This was what the pianist Hoagy Carmichael used to do in films, and I thought it looked really cool.

In the RAF, you also had to choose a trade that you could do—or wanted to do. I decided to become a teleprinter operator. 'This', I thought, 'will keep my fingers nimble for the piano.' I certainly didn't want to do anything too manual that might injure my hands.

Unfortunately for me it was Alan—who also wanted to become a teleprinter operator—who was posted to somewhere near Bournemouth to go on a training course and then posted to Singapore, which was a wonderful experience for him, and something I would have loved to have done, too.

After we were demobbed, Alan and I decided to go swimming at an open-air pool in Chingford, Essex. It was a scorching hot day, so we went quite early in the morning. By two o'clock, we were both done to a turn and decided to leave. We had driven there in my Austin Ten and, as we left the car park, the sky turned black. Within minutes, it was pouring with rain, followed by hail, thunder and lightning. I could hardly see through the windscreen and, with the engine spluttering, I had to keep pulling the choke out to keep us moving. As we crossed the lights by the Angel, Edmonton, we encountered severe flooding under the railway bridge. As three cars were already stuck there, with water almost covering the car roofs, I immediately turned into a road on my left and came out on to Edmonton High Road. No sooner had I done this, than the main drains burst. The water was getting higher until it got into the exhaust and the car came to a halt. As it rose still higher, Alan and I decided there was only one thing to do. We climbed into the back of the car, took off all our clothes, put on our swimming trunks again and climbed—this was not easy, we were both six feet tall—out of the back windows of the car, and started pushing it. By this time, there were stranded cars, buses and even trolley buses, everywhere. People couldn't believe their eyes when they saw these two young men in trunks pushing a car through the flood. Apart from

87

all the laughter, they just couldn't figure out how we happened to have swimming trunks on! But we got home and Dad fixed the car.

Anyway, to return to my career as a teleprinter operator, I was sent to Carlisle Headquarters of Maintenance Command, and placed in the signals section, with no real qualifications for the job. This meant that I and another guy had to learn as much as we could about the procedure, then practise on teleprinters, and learn how to send signals. Once we knew what we were doing, we would send signals all over the world, which was a fascinating thing to be doing. The amount of work we got through in the signals service was phenomenal.

While at the Headquarters of Maintenance Command, we had a flight sergeant for whom I acted as a taxi service, taking him into town in my Austin Ten to meet his girlfriend, and then picking him up again later. We also had a sergeant who was giving me and my signalling colleague a really hard time because we had never been on a teleprinter training course, and he thought we were useless and not worth teaching. But we continued to learn from others, picking up things wherever we could, and practising and practising. Then, when the right time came, we could if we wanted—and we did— ask to have a trade test. For the teleprinter operator test, you had to come down to London, then go to Chigwell, Essex. We filled in the form to do this, and the sergeant said: '*What?* You've filled in the form to take the test? What a waste of the RAF's time.'

So we came down to Chigwell, took the test— and passed. The chap who came with me became an AC1 Teleprinter Operator. I—because my typing was pretty good—became LAC Forsyth-Johnson. As an LAC (Leading Aircraftsman), you were given badges with a two-blade propeller on them to sew on to each arm of your uniform. When we got back to Carlisle Signals Section we made a point of walking past the sergeant who had been so uncomplimentary. I'm sure my two propellers cut him to pieces. He just couldn't believe his eyes.

One evening, my friendly flight sergeant said: 'I want to go into town tonight. Can you take me?' 'I am', I informed him, 'a bit short of petrol, short of money, and want to go home this weekend.' 'Well,' he said, 'you know this is 14 MU [Maintenance Unit], Carlisle?' 'Yes,' I said, wondering what he was implying, 'I'm quite aware of that, Flight.' 'Well,' he said, 'you know all those lorries lined up by the main gate . . .? Well, they've been here for as long as I have—four years. I imagine there's a lot of petrol in those tanks . . .' 'Yes, Flight,' I said, catching on quick. 'I think there must be.' 'Well,' he said, 'if I manage to stumble across some rubber tubing and an empty can, you might be able . . . when it's dark . . . But beware of the guard dogs . . .'

So, from then on, clutching the rubber tubing and a can, I would go up at night and syphon off gallons of freebie petrol. To do this, I had to put the tubing into the tank, making sure I was lower than the tank, suck on the tube to get the petrol flowing, put my finger over the tube to stop the petrol flowing out, and very quickly place the tube into the can to drain. To begin with, I got mouthfuls of petrol, but I soon became quite good at it.

As I mentioned, I used to smoke at this time but, fortunately, remembered not to do this after I'd been syphoning petrol. It was, however, *very* testing on my nerves. But, thank goodness, I never got mauled by the dogs. If I had, the flight sergeant, of course, would not have known anything about my activities, and *I* would have been the one on a charge, and sent to the 'glasshouse'—the RAF prison. So, I was very lucky—and, needless to say, never suffered from a fuel shortage again.

*   *   *

By this time, I had become a voluntary RAF musician and had been given a gold harp badge to pin on my sleeve. I used to go into Carlisle all the time to play the piano because there was a reasonably good one there. We formed a little group and used to play mostly jazz, but would also play for RAF dances—waltzes, foxtrots, quicksteps. Sometimes I would get up and sing, too.

Once I had got over the upset about going into the RAF, the music helped tremendously because I was so interested in it. I also quite enjoyed the teleprinting. I knew that if show business didn't go too well for me later in life, I would at least have a trade. The RAF was, though, a completely different life—a huge shock to the system to be in such a masculine environment after all those Windmill Girls. It was also very frustrating at times not to be in the business I loved. But, all in all, I spent quite a happy time in Carlisle. My pianist friend and I had a couple of lovely girlfriends, and we all used to go out together in the car. Yes, there was some really nice female company in good old Carlisle—and by then I had become used to cars doubling up as love nests.

On one occasion, when we were having the usual kit inspection, we were among some guys who had just returned from the Far East. When you were posted out there, you were allowed to wear shoes instead of boots. One of these guys—I think his name was Gilchrist—was a nice chap whom I became friends with. When he was laying out his kit, I noticed he had a lovely pair of shoes that had never been worn. 'What size are they?' I asked.

'Eight and a half,' he replied. My size! 'I'd *love* a pair like those,' I begged. As he was about to be demobbed, he gave them to me.

So, delighted to have shoes instead of boots, I laid out my kit. When the officer arrived to do the kit inspection, he stopped by my bed, looked at my kit, and then said accusingly: 'You've got shoes there.' 'Yes, sir.' '*Why*, Forsyth-Johnson, have you got shoes there?' 'I've swapped them, sir,' I said nervously. 'Swapped them?' he said. 'But they're Far East issue, aren't they?' 'Yes, sir.' 'So, what gives you the audacity to swap your boots for a pair of Far Eastern Air Force issue?' 'Well, sir,' I began tentatively, 'I'm a dancer and when I get out of the RAF, which will probably be a year from now, possibly a bit longer, I'm going back to being a dancer. And when you tap-dance, sir, which is what *I* do, sir, you need to have flexible ankles. But the boots, sir, that I'm having to wear all the time—and have had to wear for the last year—are killing my ankles and stiffening up my joints. And that, sir, is *why* I've swapped them.' 'Oh, really . . .? You're a dancer?' 'Yes, sir. I was a dancer at the Windmill

91

Theatre before I came here, and I'm hoping to go back there.' 'Really, Forsyth-Johnson? Well . . .' I held my breath. 'Carry on, then!' And he walked away. I don't know how I got away with it. He must have liked tap-dancing. My secret, though, was out. The rest of the boys, who could hardly believe my luck with the officer, now knew I was a tap-dancer, with potential access to Windmill Girls. More questions. More answers. More teasing. Later on, back in Civvy Street, I was always expecting that officer to come to the Windmill's stage door and ask me for a free ticket. He resisted.

Around this shoe-incident time, I became an acting corporal. I tried not to let this go to my head! But it did mean that on my shifts I was in charge of the signals section. The next thing I tried to 'pull', because I was stuck 300 miles from my home, was a posting to Bletchley, Buckinghamshire. I succeeded, was there for a while, then got moved to Chicksands Priory, quite near to London. Well, I was steadily getting nearer home. The priory was renowned for having a ghost in the officers' mess but, although I played the piano at a couple of dances there, it never came out and danced for me.

Then there was a miracle. Of all the luck, I requested a posting to Bush House, London, and I actually got it. I could *not* believe it. If you were at Bush House, you were allowed a living-out pass, rent and travel allowances, and could even go to work in civilian clothes! So I had my fares paid to and from my parents' house in Edmonton, which was a bus and tube ride away. I thought this was fantastic. I was as happy as a sandboy because it meant I could get on with my show-business plans.

When I had time off, I could go round the agents, just in case the return to the Windmill didn't happen, could keep in touch with the business, know what was going on, meet a few people, and go to see some West End shows.

Then came a whammy. I had only been at Bush House for about three weeks, was actually standing at the teleprinter, when a message came through that read: *Post with immediate effect, Acting Corporal Bruce Joseph Forsyth-Johnson to RAF Andover. Confirm that A/C Forsyth-Johnson will be here as soon as possible.* It was signed by an officer—I forget his name, but I know what I called him at the time! I was *stunned.* Should I tear it up, I thought, make out it had never arrived? I read it again and *again* and *again.* I even thought it might be a practical joke. But nobody in the section owned up. Finally, I controlled my twitching fingers and asked to see the Commanding Officer of Bush House. 'Sir,' I said, 'I've been in the Air Force for nearly two years. I've only got six months to go and I've just received this posting to Andover.' I then explained my situation. 'Well . . .' he said, noting my obvious distress, 'I probably can't do anything about it, but I will find out the reason for the posting. And, if I don't think it's a good enough reason, after what you've told me and what it means to you to be at home and, given you've tried for this for such a long time, then I'll make a couple of phone calls . . .'

So the next day, in fear and trembling, I waited for him to call me into his office. 'Well, Forsyth-Johnson,' he announced, 'I'm afraid I've got bad news. You've got to go there. You're a voluntary musician and they need a pianist for a pantomime.'

'*What!*' I said, agonized. 'Can't I *not* volunteer?'
'You've already *volunteered* as a musician,' he
reminded me, 'and they are in desperate straits for
a pianist.'

What could I do? I went off to RAF Andover as
miserable as sin. And it was quite a few days before
I could come down from the disappointment and
start rehearsals for the wretched pantomime. They
were all so pleased to meet me and sympathized
with what had happened—but it remained a big
low point in my life.

One of the guys I really admired at that time was
Ray Ellington and his Trio. Ray was always on the
bill with Ted Heath and his big band who did
wonderful Sunday concerts at the Palladium. I
really loved that theatre, but never dreamed that,
one day, I'd be top of the bill there. Anyway, at
Andover, I had an idea that the officer in charge
went along with. During the interval of the
pantomime, I suggested I could do a couple of Ray
Ellington numbers. And, as it was a pantomime, I
did Ray Ellington's 'The Three Bears'. I sang this
at the piano—which some people thought was the
best part of the pantomime—and had a very nice
drummer to help me. It worked really well—gave
me the feeling of being back in show business.

During this time, I also had a WRAF girlfriend
to cheer me up. I stayed at her parents' house in
Portsmouth a couple of times. The downside was
how upset my mother and father were, when for
the first time I didn't go home for Christmas. I've
never forgotten how hurt they were, and still feel
sorry about it. I suppose my son JJ will do the same
to Winnie and me one day.

*   *   *

When the time came for me to leave the RAF in the autumn of 1949, the first thing I wanted to do was to see if the Windmill would keep its 'promise' to take me back. So, two and a half years after leaving there, heart in mouth, I phoned Anne Mitelle.

'Oh, Bruce . . .' she said. Then, proving to be as good as her word, added: 'Mr Van Damm would *love* to have you back at the Windmill. Welcome home.'

This was what I'd hoped for. I'd lost touch with so many people in the business while I was out of circulation, and it would have been *very, very* difficult to start all over again. But I didn't have to because, there and then, I was given the chance to be re-employed at the Windmill, and earn good money again after the poor salary that His Majesty's Royal Air Force had been paying.

*   *   *

When there was a big nude scene at the Windmill, the girls would have to pose on a pedestal, sometimes holding only a bunch of grapes. Under the Lord Chamberlain's rules of that time, they were only allowed to pose naked as long as they did not move. Other scantily dressed dancers would be dancing around, but the naked ones had to stay absolutely still. If they moved Van Damm could have lost his licence—one reason why he made the rule that nobody waiting at the side of the stage should ever make them laugh. Also if one of the girls started to giggle and caused bodily 'parts' to

95

move, nobody could be sure what the men in the front row of the stalls would do. Heaven knows, they were in a bad enough state anyway. Sometimes I felt like throwing a bucket of water over them.

All this reminds me that when a nude scene finished at the Windmill, and you were the next act on, the first part of your act was a complete waste of time. This was because if anyone vacated a seat in the front row—and they might have been in the Windmill for four or five hours, since eleven thirty in the morning until four in the afternoon— everybody from the back rows would start jumping over the seats into the front row.

Honestly, it was like the Grand National. *Unbelievable.* A bookie could have made a fortune.

CHAPTER FOUR

GAY TIME?

On my return to the Windmill as a 'juvenile', I was allowed to sing and dance and do different bits in the various scenes. It was simply wonderful to be back in a *real* theatre which, unharmed by the Blitz, was still proudly standing and displaying, as it always had since 1931, its neo-Georgian style, all its art-deco embellishments still intact. For me this was a really lovely time because, although the shows changed every five or six weeks and we had to rehearse between performances, we also had plenty of time off. The 'A' company performers would work one day, the 'B' company the next.

Having made a bit of an impression the last time I was there, I was so proud when I was made responsible for arranging the song-and-dance duets. I really *loved* doing this. The rehearsal rooms had mirrors all around the walls so, when I was creating a new routine, I could see exactly what the dance looked like while I was rehearsing the steps. Mirrors are so important to dancers. They're your eyes, show you so much. There were also some really lovely popular numbers around during this time—like 'Baby, It's Cold Outside' and 'Take A Letter, Miss Smith'.

When Lionel Blair and his sister Joyce joined the Windmill, Lionel, a tap-dancer like me, would perform the duets I had arranged. So, how about that! I was Lionel Blair's choreographer—and not many people can say that! Thereafter, a favourite joke of mine was: 'Lionel and I worked at the Windmill together. I was on the pedestal on the left, he was on the pedestal on the right. But I was the one with the bunch of grapes!'

By now it was the beginning of the 1950s, a time when big Hollywood musicals, such as *An American in Paris, Singin' in the Rain, Oklahoma!* and *Carousel*, were either on or coming soon to our screens. All of us boys and girls at the Windmill *lived* for these musicals that brought us brilliant dancers, singers and actors, such as Gene Kelly, Donald O'Connor, Judy Garland, Debbie Reynolds, Cyd Charisse, Anne Miller and Mitzi Gaynor. Like Fred Astaire, Gene Kelly was one of my great screen idols. He and Donald O'Connor were fantastic dancers. Gene Kelly was brilliant at the balletic-type numbers in *Singin' in the Rain*— dancing on pavements and in, out and over puddles—and Donald, who had an even more relaxed style, was a superb hoofer. All these stars were doing what we wanted to do—living out our passion. To perform in such films was what we were all dreaming about, hoping for one day.

A gang of us would meet after rehearsals and go to the Empire, Leicester Square, where we'd see a variety show in the first half, followed by a Hollywood musical film in the second half. They called this Cine Variety. The Empire had a superb orchestra in its pit, and was famous for its stage shows. There were some really wonderful acts for us to watch and learn from. It was our equivalent of Radio City Music Hall in New York. But sadly Cine Variety stage shows weren't seen in our big cinemas much longer after that.

During this period, despite Mr Van Damm's rules, I had a few girlfriends at the Windmill. Penny Calvert was one. A great pal of mine, Jimmy Perry—the boy I had grown up with—used to come and see me a lot, and he particularly liked the look of Penny, who had a lovely personality, not to mention her singing and dancing. So, because I knew Penny didn't go out that often, I suggested a date for the two of them. Jimmy was thrilled and took Penny out. The next day, I asked him how they had got on. 'It would have been *very* good,' he replied, '*but* for one thing . . . *All* she did all evening was talk about *you*.'

Until then, I hadn't realized that Penny had any romantic feelings for me but, thanks to Jimmy, I did now! Penny and I started going out together regularly after that. I can't say it was love at first sight because, although I was very attracted to Penny, there were so many pretty girls at the

98

Windmill, it was all rather confusing for a chap! I did, though, always have a soft spot for Penny because, from our early chats, I knew she was having a hard time with her family, and didn't seem to have experienced much family love in her life. For somebody who had show-business ambitions— and Penny was very ambitious then—she was having a really tough time, looking after her mother, three brothers and sister.

When her elder sister, Hope, left home, having married a South African guy called Gordon Mullholland, Penny became the bread-winner for the entire family. I really admired her for doing this. Other Windmill Girls were always buying new outfits, but not Penny. She had too many financial responsibilities. Later—after Penny and I had fallen in love—I went to live with her and her mother for a while to make life easier for them. I never met her father, never knew anything about him.

Penny and I had lots of friends at the Windmill. John Shackell, whom I had first met at Buddy Bradley's dancing lessons, was there, with his wife, Joy Marlowe. John later worked with me in summer-season shows at Bournemouth, and we also danced together at the Palladium. Our other great friends were Diane—a Windmill Girl dancer—and her husband, Bernard Coral. We spent a lot of time together and our families grew very close.

So, Penny and I—now 'courting', as it was called then—worked our cotton socks off at the Windmill. But much as I was enjoying myself and good though my 'juvenile' job was, after a while I began to feel I wasn't *really* in show business . . . I was in the Windmill Theatre, in a girlie show. Yes, it was a wonderful experience and I was learning a lot but, in my heart, I was yearning to perform in something other than a showcase for a nude review.

Penny and I were getting closer and closer—so close she used to come and stay at my parents' house at weekends—and we had a long chat about my doubts and what I would really like to do. It was actually not until Penny came to stay with us that she knew what it was like to have a room of her own, birthday cards and presents at Christmas. She really did have a *very* hard childhood. Anyway, having talked, we came to a radical decision. We decided to grasp the nettle, give up our jobs at the Windmill, become a double act, and see if we could get into the kind of work I wanted to do—broader-based variety. We were young—and the young are renowned for throwing all caution to the wind.

It was also a new decade. The troublesome 1940s had given way to the 1950s. The country, despite the post-war austerities still affecting us, was coming alive again. The first package holiday had just been introduced, and families who could afford it were able to take up Horizon's offer to fly to Corsica for £32 10s. J. Sainsbury had opened its first self-service grocery shop. The BBC had proudly transmitted the first television pictures from overseas with a two-hour programme from Calais. To help dispel leftover wartime gloom, plans were being made for the Festival of Britain in May 1951. When it opened, King George VI would say encouragingly to all of us: 'This is no time for despondency.' So, it was perhaps along with many others who were being carried along on this new wave of optimism that we made our resolution.

Away from the protection of the Windmill, our first major handicap seemed to be that we were too versatile! We were a song-and-dance double act who, at that time, performed two Fred Astaire and Judy Garland numbers, 'We're a couple of swells' and 'How could you believe me when I said I loved you, when you know I've been a liar all my life?' *And we danced.* Unforgivable! This meant that when we went round the agents we found that, although we got a few cabaret bookings here and there—and although the Hollywood musical was the biggest thing you could go to see in the cinema—in variety you had to be *either* a singing act or a dancing act. You could *not* be both. If you were, you were very limited as to how many bills you would be booked for, and therefore in trouble.

So, lacking the variety bookings I had so hoped for, we accepted cabarets. But these proved to be quite hazardous. The dance floors were designed for ballroom dancing, which is what most people loved to do then, and were far too slippery for our kind of dancing. When we put on a pair of tap-shoes and tried to tap-dance, it was nigh on impossible. We found ourselves slithering around all over the floor and having to struggle to keep our balance. It was really terrible.

By way of relief, between these bookings, we had some success when we travelled to entertain American troops still billeted in Austria, Italy and Germany. Saved from injury and also seeing a bit of the world, we were happy. During one trip we were taken by a new friend, a German lady, to see the night-life of Hamburg which had, she said, 'quite a reputation'. We went all over the city, including what she called 'the red light district', where girls were displaying themselves in windows.

'You and Penny, Bruce,' she said, 'are perfectly safe walking around this area as a threesome with me. But it would be most inadvisable for just the two of you to walk around here. If you were with just one woman, that would suggest you were "voyeurs"—sight-seeing'!

'I won't', I reassured her, 'put Penny and me in any danger of being accosted for that.'

One of the places we went to was an 'All-Drag-Artists Club' which was currently enjoying the reputation of being '*the* haunt of very, very beautiful women'. Aged twenty-two, I was still very naive and found the evening absolutely mind-boggling. They were all so convincing, so beautiful. But they were not women! When the time came for us to leave, an incredibly attractive—and I thought rather flirtatious—girl handed us our coats. Outside the club, our guide, who had obviously noticed that I had responded to this girl's charms, said: 'You *do* realize, Bruce, that that girl was *not* a girl.' My mouth dropped open. I was astonished. 'Don't be shocked,' she added reassuringly. 'It really is *very* hard to detect who's a girl, and who's a transvestite or female impersonator.'

'I'll bear that in mind,' I replied, still shaken.

This has reminded me of an occasion in the 1970s, when I was working at the Theatre Club in Stockton. Diana Dors, whom I'd always loved and adored, and Kenny Earle, part of the double act Earl and Vaughan (Malcolm Vaughan), were also working in other clubs nearby. We were all staying at the Billingham Arms and, as we finished work at about the same time, we used to meet back at the hotel and go up to Diana's suite for a coffee, sandwiches and a chat. When you're working at clubs, away from your home environment, it's a very enjoyable experience to spend time with other pros, and this stops you from becoming a bit of a loner.

The Saturday night I'm writing about was our last night there. Diana had come back from her club with a female impersonator in tow, and when Kenny and I went up to the suite we were introduced to him. Having ordered some sandwiches from the night porter, we all settled down for a chat. The female impersonator, having come straight from the club, was still dressed in OTT women's clothes and still wearing a blonde wig. When the night porter, quite an old guy, came up with the sandwiches, he stumbled in with the food and drinks, saying 'Where shall I put the tray?' Having looked around, he then caught sight of the female impersonator and was obviously very struck by 'her'. So, for fun, over the next couple of hours we kept ordering something else so that he would have to keep coming back. How soon would he realize that 'she' was a 'he' was the name of the game! Every time he returned, the female impersonator would do something outrageous, like draping a leg over the arm of the chair to reveal very sexy fishnet tights. The last time the porter came up—by which time we had had so many laughs—the female impersonator suddenly whipped off the wig and, in a very deep, masculine voice, said, 'I fancy another cup of coffee, don't you?' The night porter's face was wonderful to behold. The dear old boy nearly dropped his tray. It was a marvellous moment and a really good laugh.

In store for me, however, was an upsetting variation of this story. When Diana's autobiography, *A to Z of Life and Loving*, appeared a few years later, I discovered that she had written that I was the one who had been fooled and that I had 'dated a drag queen'. In her version, Kenny had supposedly asked the 'lady' to knock on my door 'and just say goodnight'. Then, she said Kenny had called her and told her to complain to the night porter that I had a woman in my room.

> Needing no second bidding, I did just that . . . The porter came running up the stairs at the precise moment Bruce was saying goodnight to his somewhat bizarre date. And the scene, to the porter's eyes, was exactly what I had complained about so bitterly—particularly as the 'lady' in question was wearing transparent black underwear . . . In the mêlée, the drag queen's rubber boobs came off in the porter's hands and, hysterically tearing off his wig, he shrieked: 'I'm not a bloody woman anyway. I'm a man!' I do not know who looked more astounded and embarrassed, the porter or Bruce who bolted back into his room and was not seen by anyone for several days.

None of this was true. I suppose Diana did it to make the story more interesting for her readers. But if the day arrives when I can't tell the difference between an obvious female impersonator and a real woman, I will have long passed on to realms where such things do not matter! The first thing I always do is look at the Adam's apple—that is always a giveaway. And then the shoulders, arms and hands. Diana was usually such wonderful fun, but I found it very hard to forgive her for telling the story in this way. Especially as she had also said in her book that, 'over the years' she had been 'the victim of many scathing attacks in the press, and also the object of a few catty remarks from [her] fellow actresses'. For me to realize that someone in my own business was doing something like that to me was most hurtful, especially as she was a friend. I never said anything to her about this but, when we sat next to each other in make-up, getting ready for a tribute show, she knew, even though neither of us mentioned it, that I was upset. The same story also appeared in a book written by Mike Sullivan, who was married to Dany Robin the French film star. Mike, who was Irish, was a loveable rogue who was my agent for a while. But he also had a crazy Jekyll-and-Hyde side to him which wasn't so loveable. Shirley Bassey, though, achieved great career successes with him.

*   *   *

One day Penny and I met an agent named Jack Bontemps who booked us for a couple of venues, and then asked us if we would like to go on a four-month tour. The place he named took us completely by surprise. It was India. Once we had got over the initial shock, we looked at each other and I said: 'Well, it's work . . . We'll be together . . . It'll be an experience—and we'll be doing cabaret.'

105

So we said, 'yes'.

About two or three weeks before we were due to travel, Jack told us he was making a booking for us to sail on the *Stratheden* which would dock in Bombay. At Bombay, we would take the train to Calcutta then, after two or three weeks there, we would fly to Karachi in Pakistan, where we would be based at the Palace Hotel. It all sounded very exciting and exotic. Then he delivered a surprise. 'I can't get you a cabin together—you'll have to be split up.' Then, after a pause, he added, 'But if you were married, you could have a cabin together . . . D'you want to think about that?'

Penny and I thought this was a marvellous solution—much better than being separated every night and having to share a cabin with a complete stranger. So we talked it over and, since by then we both knew we wanted to get married, we decided to go for it. So, *yes*, in a way, Jack Bontemps proposed for me. But I *was* in love, too. Penny and I had already done so much and been through so much together.

Having made the decision, we then got married *very, very* quickly in 1953. You could call it a ship-gun marriage! (Sorry about that . . .) And, of course, nobody believed the explanation we gave them for going up the aisle in such a tearing hurry. Our wedding ceremony took place in the Methodist Central Hall, Fore Street, Edmonton, mainly because we couldn't get into any of the other churches in time. I was twenty-five, Penny was twenty-three.

What could have been better? We were young, married, in work and off on an adventure. We were able to honeymoon on board a lovely ship, and

106

were soon visiting places like the Suez Canal and Port Said. At this stop, loads of Arabs wanted to buy Penny because she was so blonde and so *very* attractive. It could have changed the course of my life. I could have moved over into the camel business!

*   *   *

When we arrived in Bombay we were completely overwhelmed by the sheer mass of its population and staggered by all the strange sights and sounds. We had just one show to do there. The venue was the roof garden of a hotel that proved to be a lovely place in which to perform. Even though India was under prohibition, the atmosphere was excellent, the guests were delighted with us and, personally, I think that was the best show Penny and I did on that trip.

I can't remember either of us being overcome by the heat—even when, two days after Bombay—feeling knocked for six by the sheer mass of its humanity—we had to set off on a train journey, with tickets for second class which would have been the equivalent of fourth class at home. The train was bursting its sides with passengers, had no air conditioning, and the entire journey was horrifically cramped. When we finally got off in Calcutta, there must have been 400 refugees, from I know not where, living in the station. I could hardly believe my eyes. The conditions they were having to endure were terrible, and the resulting stink was truly appalling. 'Breathe in, hold your breath, and *run*,' I said to Penny.

What really upset me about India was the

poverty. We could not walk anywhere without children, minus limbs, following us. And I was so shocked to hear that there were parents who would maim their children deliberately, because they would then hopefully arouse more compassion and earn more money. The begging completely put me off walking anywhere outside the hotel. When we did go outside, we were constantly accosted for money. It was one of the most awful experiences I have ever had and, to this day, I would find it very difficult to go back and risk seeing any of that again. But it was over forty years ago, and things may well have changed for the better. I do hope so. We all know that poverty exists, is distressingly prevalent throughout the world; we also know that the world is not fair—and may never be. But to see that level of deprivation at that age upset me greatly.

*　　　　*　　　　*

In Calcutta, we stayed at Singh's Hotel. Our audience was very cosmopolitan—the British who lived there and the well-off Indians who went to the hotel for a jolly night out and to see the cabaret. The cabaret room, thank goodness, was air-conditioned. But, even so, when we finished our act Penny and I would be steaming hot and perspiring. We would then walk to the lift and go up to the top floor to join the band and all the others in the show. The hotel's staff accommodation was prefab-type boxes, built on top of the roof, with no air conditioning. The temperature up there was about 110 degrees, and it was incredibly difficult to get any sleep at all. I spent most of the night armed with my slippers killing the cockroaches that were running up and down the walls and across the ceiling. It was a pretty unpleasant experience—the time could not go quickly enough for us, and it was pretty difficult to remember we were still on our honeymoon. We kept joking about this, saying we were very lucky not to have had cockroaches on board the ship.

There was another problem in store. One night Penny was suddenly taken very ill with flu-like symptoms. She was burning up so much, we knew she couldn't possibly work that night. At that precise moment, it dawned on me that I'd been in the business twelve years, yet I hadn't got a solo act. Yes, I could sing, dance, play the piano, do impressions, and make jokes with the audience, but I didn't have a bloody act! I had never planned anything that I could do alone, nor now without Penny, for eight or ten minutes. This was not really surprising. Ever since my amateur concert days finished, I had always been part of a double act. Even at the Windmill, all the feature spots I performed in included me dancing with a girl—sometimes the same one, sometimes a different one.

However, despite my sudden anxiety attack and confronted by necessity, I told the hotel's management that I *would* get an act together for that evening's cabaret. And that night, true to my word, I did my first solo act. It was all right. The audience was obviously happy. 'At least', I thought, 'I've proved to myself I can perform alone.' I was particularly pleased about this because I knew that when I left the Windmill to become a double act with Penny, Van Damm had said to her, 'Okay, it'll be good for the two of you to be a double act. But, sooner or later, you know, Bruce will have to go solo.'

Penny was a really good artiste—a lovely dancer and singer. She could easily have made a successful career for herself. And I think it was this that eventually created some of the difficulties that blighted our marriage. When you are a double act, married to your partner, sooner or later, as Van Damn had foreseen, one of you inevitably goes on while the other is left behind; one of you eventually gives up the business and sacrifices their talent to the other person. Sadly, whoever that is, is bound to find the situation very frustrating and difficult. Or you each go your own way.

But, as usual, I am jumping ahead of my story.

*   *   *

There is nothing more nerve-racking, I discovered on my first evening as a solo performer in Calcutta, than being totally responsible for entertaining an audience, and not knowing whether you will be a success or not, whether they will like you or hate you. When you are up there alone, suffering all the slings and arrows of misfortune, it is not the same as having somebody with you, sharing the credit if it goes well, the blame if it does not.

That first night I was very nervous on my own, very concerned about how I would go down. I was wise to be anxious. I knew that when anybody asked comics the ideal time for their act, they would usually reply: 'For twenty minutes to half an hour, I'm great—after that, I'm struggling.' This is because many comics rely on rapid-fire one-liners and, if left too long on stage, their jokes can become too similar. Part of the problem is that a lot of comedy does not have much depth. A raconteur, on the other hand, can last for much longer, can go into long, complicated, three-to-five-minute stories. Then, provided the last line is a 'belter', they can elicit laughs all the way through their act.

I have always been lucky. If people don't find my kind of comedy funny, they can say: 'Oh . . . *but* at least he does other things.' Nevertheless, throughout my career, I've always *wanted* to be thought 'funny'—needed this for myself! Since childhood, I've revelled in getting laughs. This has always been so important for me. *But*, having said that, I *can* do other things and this gives me a shoulder to lean on.

Fortunately, Penny's illness only lasted four nights and she made a quick recovery. We then left Calcutta and flew to Karachi for our next cabaret appearances. This time the hotel's accommodation was much nicer, but the audience left a great deal to be desired. Some evenings there was hardly an audience at all. And the food was dreadful. Because all the meat in Calcutta and Karachi looked so awful, we lived mostly on boiled eggs for about six weeks. We still suffered bouts of stomach cramps, but this did not succeed in putting me off curry. I *loved* it—and still do.

I had always been a skinny chap but, by the end of our Indian tour, I was even skinnier—had lost nearly two stone in weight. I was now *really* skeletal. In many, many ways, that tour proved to be an experience that would remain with me for ever.

＊　　　＊　　　＊

When we finally returned to England, I realized that if Penny had not been ill, it would have taken me much longer to appreciate that I *had* to do something about our lack of bookings—and go solo. Before India, although we 'couldn't get arrested', as they say, we hadn't really had a chance as a double act and had to keep relying on infrequent cabaret jobs. Cabaret, I must say, can be the very worst thing in which to work—especially when you are in a badly organized place, with hardly anyone present. Often Penny and I didn't even have a stage to give us some atmosphere. We were simply stuck out there on a floor with people talking all around us, rattling glasses and all that sort of thing. On a good night, a cabaret audience could be sixty or more people, on a bad night, just a couple of tables. Either way, we still had to go on. We were paid to work, and if we didn't, we were not paid.

As there was no work for us on our return to England, I decided this was the moment to launch out on my own. The first thing I did was to return to the Windmill in the hope of getting re-employed as a single act. I worked out a routine, rehearsed and rehearsed the various bits, and then arranged an audition with Vivian Van Damm who had always shown such confidence in me.

On the day, I finished doing the act for him and, feeling very pleased with my performance, I walked down the steps of the stage. Van Damm came to join me in the stalls. 'Yes, Bruce—definitely,' he said. 'Oh! *Definitely . . .!*' '*I'm in!*' I thought.

Then, taking the breath right out of my body, he added: 'Yes—you *definitely* need material.' I, of course, crashed from being prematurely up on high to almost flat on my face. I had worked *so* hard getting the act together, and I was now left downhearted, thinking, 'So . . . that's that.'

'Go away, Bruce,' Van Damm said, 'and come up with something else. I'll see you as many times as you like.'

As I left, I thought to myself. 'I wonder if he's teaching me a lesson for leaving the Windmill and his show which means everything to him to become a double act with Penny? I wonder if he really wanted to say: "Well . . . it wasn't *so* bad here, was it? It *was* regular work and you turned your back on it."' I will never know the answer. But I do know I started working on another act for him at once.

When I returned with the new material, Van Damm agreed to take me on as one of his single acts. By then, I was ready and willing to do anything. If I'd met somebody in a side street who said: 'Do that bit you do in your act with the phone,' I would have replied: 'All right,' and done it! I was so geed up, my brain so overactive, I would have responded on automatic pilot to any instruction.

During this time at the Windmill, Tommy Cooper was working there quite regularly. As he was quite popular with a group of our West End regulars, I thought I would finish my act with an impression of him. Nobody had done this before. He was still at his semi-star stage, not yet the wonderful name he became later on TV. I did the impression for Van Damm and he thought it was

113

marvellous.

I started this part of my act with a couple of Tommy Cooper jokes with cards and then concluded, in a good imitation of his voice, saying, 'And now, I'm going to disappear right in front of you. *Disappear—just like that. Disappear*, okay?' The Windmill had a glass stage that was arranged in squares. 'I'll now say the magic words "Hocus-Pocus . . . Fish-Bones . . . Choke-Us . . . *Sh-sh-shuuush . . . sh-sh-sheesh . . ."*' Having raised the audience's expectation, nothing would happen—I'd still be standing there. I would then look to the side of the stage and say in an audible, desperate-sounding stage whisper: 'Am I standing in the right place?' Having obviously received a nod, I would then repeat all the spells a number of times with increasing frustration. Then, at breaking point, I'd say to the stage manager through clenched teeth: *'Pull the lever . . . Pull the lever.'* The guy would then step out from behind the curtains and bark back furiously: *'Pull the bloody thing yourself,'* and then throw the lever on the stage. It always ended in a big, big laugh.

While I was at the Windmill—and doing my Tommy Cooper impression—I still used to go round the theatrical agencies at nine thirty every morning before I went to the theatre at eleven o'clock. I hadn't had an agent for quite a while. The agents' offices were all based around Shaftesbury Avenue, Charing Cross Road and the lower end of Regent Street. I was always asking one or another to walk just a few hundred yards to the Windmill to watch me perform. I desperately wanted a good agent, but nobody would make the effort to come and see me. Every time I left my

114

name with a receptionist, I could almost feel her crumpling up the piece of paper and throwing it into the wastepaper basket.

One agent, a chap called Miff Ferrie, *did* eventually come to see me. But, as I thought at the time, primarily because he was Tommy Cooper's agent and suspected I was pinching his client's act. I wasn't. That would have been a terrible thing to do. I was just doing an impression. Miff Ferrie, I discovered, was a trombone player and the bandleader at a West End nightclub called the Blue Lagoon—a club where Tommy often performed his act. While Miff was there he got to know a lot of the other performers and, one day, the owner of the club suggested that he should become an agent and book the acts. Thinking this was a good idea—a second string to his bow, so to speak—Miff agreed, booked Tommy and became his agent.

When he came to see me, he said he liked my act, didn't mention my Tommy Cooper impression and, after a couple of meetings, said he wanted to sign me up for a five-year contract. In all fairness—and this is relevant to later events—he did say that he wanted me to think carefully about the contract and make sure I was happy with it. Overeager, perhaps, I said I was happy and signed on with him. With the new contract in my hand, I decided to risk all once again, leave the Windmill and concentrate on the hoped-for variety bookings that Miff was confident he would find for me. He was true to his word for a while and everything seemed okay. But I soon realized that, essentially, he was a musician who, although he thought he was put on this earth to produce great comedians, knew nothing about comedy. So, within three or four years, Miff and I

115

were having serious differences of opinion about a lot of things.

Alec Pleon, a wonderful comic, was in *Strike a New Note*, the show that made Sid Fields a big name. Alec was the second comic and he did some wonderfully funny things. We worked together in a variety show televised from the Shepherd's Bush Empire. By then, I knew that Miff Ferne was also his agent. On the day of the show, Alec said to me: 'Miff's wonderful. I've never known anyone to take such an interest in me. He's worked really hard on my act . . . I hope it's okay . . . He's rehearsed me so much.'

Having already had a similar experience with Miff myself, I felt anxious for him, but could only say: 'Good luck, Alec. I hope it'll all work out fine for you.'

When I saw Alec's act at rehearsal, I thought it was *terrible*. But I just didn't have the heart to say to him, just three or four hours before a television show, that in my opinion it was a disaster; that I thought he shouldn't try to do it that way. I reckon Miff did him a lot of harm with his advice—and I actually heard that Alec had a breakdown afterwards, although who can say what was the cause?

*   *   *

One day, Miff got me a booking to perform my act at the Empress, Brixton, South London. It was built as a cinema, but it should have been a morgue. I hated that place and had the unhappiest week of my entire life there. It was so big and, as second-spot comic, I had the task of warming up

116

the audience. On the first night I went down like a stone, received nil response. Penny, realizing what a miserable time I had had, came with me every night after that. It didn't get any better. I was *so* embarrassed. I would walk in, go to my dressing room, make up, get dressed, do the act, go back to my dressing room and stay there. Penny even had to bring me a cup of tea because I wouldn't go to fetch one or enter the bar. The atmosphere was so awful, I couldn't face anybody. To make matters worse, a lot of out-of-work pros lived in Brixton, and would come along to see the show at the Empress, especially on Mondays when they were given a free pass. They would then lounge about and criticize the lucky people who were in work. So I felt I was up against them as well; that they would be sitting there thinking, 'Well . . .! How has *he* got a week's work when *I* haven't?'

I have never forgotten Miff phoning me during that week to say that the impresario Bernard Delfont was coming to the Empress to see me at work. Already a bag of nerves, I waited and waited, but Miff never got back to me to let me know what was happening. At the end of the week, I just had to phone him. 'I know it's been a *terrible* week for me,' I said, 'but did Delfont ever come in?'

'Oh, yes,' he said casually.

'Oh . . . So, what did he say?'

'He said your voice is too high, that you should get a tape recorder and learn to speak in a pseudo-American accent.'

At the time Dickie Henderson, a very slick performer and one of the best acts in the business, had adopted a slight American twang over his English accent. Perhaps knowing how successful

117

this had been for Dickie, Bernard Delfont had decided every up-and-coming performer should do the same.

'Really?' I said, full of doubts.

'Yes,' Miff instructed. 'Get a tape recorder, work on your voice—and pitch it lower.'

Overcoming my reluctance, I bought one of the earliest tape recorders. These were not at all like the wonderful miniature machines on sale today. My one was at least two feet high, about nine inches wide, with two big wheels—the size of a large bra. I had to keep clicking it on and off, and laboriously winding it back. Its mechanism also made quite a racket. Talking into it, I would try and try to do what I had been told. But in the end I thought, 'This just *isn't* me. I have a high voice—so what?—*that's me!*' One of the hardest things in our business is to go on stage and be yourself—not how you or others think you should be, but how you are.

There is, though, a sting in the tail of this story. Although I eventually decided to disregard what Bernard Delfont had said to Miff, when I was ordering from room service during my first time in America, I realized he had a point: 'Two eggs, sunny-side-up, crispy bacon, hashed brown potatoes, English muffins and a pot of tea,' I said down the hotel's in-house phone. 'Yes, madam,' the girl replied. Since then I've always ordered things an octave lower!

*   *   *

After that terrible week in Brixton, Miff got me a booking for the City Varieties, Leeds. Two hundred miles up country, performing the same act I had

118

used in Brixton, everything went so unexpectedly well. I was on the same bill as Dave King, and we had an absolutely marvellous time, getting loads of laughs. So, I went from having my worst ever week as a solo performer to feeling really successful. From Leeds I went to Hull, for another good week's work. Then I came back to London—to The Met, Edgware Road.

I had been to shows at The Met quite a few times, especially to see Max Miller whom I absolutely adored. Now performing there myself, I once again had a wonderful week. On the Saturday night, Albert Stevenson—second in command to Richard Afton, a BBC senior producer who did a show called *BBC Musical Hall* from the Shepherd's Bush Theatre, the old Empire—came round to my dressing room after the performance. 'I thought you were very good,' he said. 'Would you be available next Saturday to do a *BBC Music Hall*?' I couldn't believe it. 'Yes,' I said, 'for goodness sake, I'd *love* to, Albert.' 'Great,' he said, 'let's have a talk about it next week to sort out what you'd like to do on the show.'

I was amazed. Three weeks ago I had left the Empress, Brixton, thinking: 'If this is what it's going to be like, do I want to stay in this business?' And now a BBC television producer was offering me an appearance on a huge show. I was over the moon.

Having done the Saturday show, which went down very well, Richard Afton then asked me to do another. After that, Richard always claimed the credit for giving me my first big break but, in truth, it was Albert Stevenson. For the next of Richard's shows, I was planning, among other things, to do

119

my Tommy Cooper impression which he liked so much. But Miff Ferrie said to me, 'You *can't.* I'm his agent—and I'm saying you *can't* do that impression on the show.' 'But', I protested, 'Richard and Albert love that part of my act.' 'You don't want to be another Tommy Cooper,' Miff muttered. 'You should concentrate on developing your own individual style.' He would not give way and—even though it was only a small part of my act—remained deaf to all protestations. Then, to make matters worse, Richard said to me, 'If you don't do the Tommy Cooper impression, Bruce, you won't be in the show! Simple as that . . .'

So, completely deadlocked between the two of them, I didn't. I was so disappointed to miss this opportunity to be in another TV show—I felt devastated. But to be frank it was only one of *many* awful things that happened to me while Miff Ferrie was my agent. The man was a joke—unreal . . .! I'm sure he was a good trombone player, but he should have stayed with his music.

*　　　*　　　*

During this time Penny and I also went on a revue-type touring show, produced by Donald Clive, an ex-Windmill artiste. The show didn't do very well, but there was a very good comic in it, called Hal Blue. Because it was so much cheaper than rail fares and putting up at digs, Penny and I would travel around to my dates in a caravan, drawn by our Wolseley car. We journeyed through every kind of weather—even heavy snow and black ice. What we achieved in that mobile home was quite amazing. By the time it left our lives, we had been

120

all over England in it trying to get work.

In 1955 I worked in a cinema at Cleethorpes, in the North of England, when Harry Secombe was top of the bill. I had worked with him before, but didn't know him all that well. On the Monday, I went to the theatre to see what was going on and to organize my band parts. While there, I had a look at the dressing-room list. I was just a small act on this bill and, as I looked down the names, I saw that while Harry was duly in the Number One Dressing Room, I was way down the bottom in Number Eight. The list read 'Bruce Forsyth'—and what I thought for a moment was another person's name—'Duncan Collis'. What it *actually* read was 'Bruce Forsyth and Duncan's Collies'—one of the biggest dog acts in the country. I went immediately to the stage manager to complain, but he said, 'Sorry, Mr Forsyth, we're *very* short of dressing rooms at the moment, so you *have* to be in with the dogs.'

When I went to the dressing room with my case, the dogs were so pleased to see me that they were all over me. Pawing my trouser legs, sniffing. 'How', I thought, 'can I possibly get dressed like this?' So I walked out, went back to the caravan and said to Penny, 'I'm going to have to use the caravan as my dressing room this week. I'll get dressed here. And, because the car park's so muddy, I'll have to change my shoes at the stage door. I am *not*', I muttered miserably, 'sharing a dressing room with all those dogs. With a name like Bruce, *I* could finish up in their act—imagine doing twice-nightly for a few tins of Chum! How can I dress with all them running around me?'

So, having dressed and done all my make-up in

the caravan, there I was, ready for the first show on the Monday night, changing my shoes by the stage door. At that moment Harry Secombe came in.

'Hallo, Bruce,' he said. 'What *are* you doing?' 'Changing,' I said sulkily. 'Why here? Haven't you got a dressing room?' 'I know this will give you a laugh, Harry,' I replied, 'but they've put me in with Duncan's Collies.' I was right. He roared with laughter. 'So what are you going to do?' he asked. 'Well . . . I've got my caravan with me, so I'm dressing there and putting my shoes on here.' 'You *can't* do that for the whole week,' he said. 'Come in with me.' How many top-of-the-bills would have said that?

From that moment, I became Harry's guest. But, then, *that* was Harry—the kind of person he was— one of the nicest men in the business. Now, whenever people ask me about him, I always tell this story because he was very special and had a wonderful nature. And, no matter how many times I repeat it, I always remember how nice he was to me. Not because he was top-of-the-bill, but because he was that kind of person.

Talking about Harry has reminded me of an occasion when I was performing in Pwllheli, North Wales. Having arrived there, Penny and I couldn't find anywhere to park the van. Somebody then directed us to a farm. The owners turned out to be really lovely people who were happy to let us stay on their land for the week. On the Saturday morning, the farmer said he and some friends were going to take their horses out for a ride. Penny, who was used to riding regularly with some of the other showgirls, said she would like to go too. So, next day, out came all the horses. I explained that I had never ridden before, didn't know one end from the other. They said they would give me a horse that was not too frisky. *'Please,'* I reiterated several times, feeling very nervous. They put me on this so-called 'gentle, unfrisky' animal. Now, when you get on a horse, the animal knows straight away what it's got on its back. They can sense immediately if they've got an idiot who, as in my case, knows nothing about riding. The horse's ears immediately started to twitch and I thought, 'My God . . . he's uneasy.' Then he started walking back towards his stable with me on his back. 'Where's he going? What do I *do*?' I shouted in mortal terror. 'Pull on his reins,' they all called back. The horse, however, had other ideas. Intent on reaching his hay for a nice second breakfast, he changed into a trot. If he'd had time, he'd have gone into a canter and a gallop as well! Clinging on for dear life, I could see some really serious trouble ahead. The top of his stable door was closed, but the bottom was open. *He* could get in, *I* couldn't. It was a *very* close shave. But for the farmer's wife—bless her heart—I might not be here today. Seeing the danger, she ran in front of me, pulled open the top of the stable door and in we went. I half slid and half fell off the horse, and have never mounted one since. Indeed, I will *never* get on another horse for the rest of my life. It scared the living daylights out of me.

When Penny and the others returned from their adventurous two-hour ride, they were still laughing. Okay, I admit I was absolutely useless . . . but then, people have always loved proving I'm not good at everything and enjoy bursting my bubble!

All in all, those caravan days were quite

something. Readers may think they sound very romantic—like a free, roving, gypsy way of life—and, in part, they were. But when you have to rely on finding a tap in order to wash, or only sometimes have a dressing room where, if you are lucky, you could take a shower, it is not so romantic. You miss the simple things of life—*and*, of course, toilets!

Even though we were no longer a double act, Penny continued to travel with me. She kept caravan! When we were not travelling, we stayed with my parents and parked the vehicle down the side of the garage. It was always so reassuring to know that they were there and we would not be lacking a roof over our heads when we were not working. And, believe me, in those days, I *could* be weeks and weeks without work.

*   *   *

There are so many other things that come to mind when I think back on my touring days. For instance, there was the Grand Theatre, Byker, Newcastle. It was an *awful* place to perform. They didn't even employ a stage-door keeper. On the Saturday night, we always had to pack everything ready for the train call the next day. I was rushing up the stairs to do this when a guy came tearing down. We did one of those ridiculous side-to-side dances that you do, before somebody gives way, saying, 'After you.' He then went speeding off down the stairs—obviously in a panic. As I continued upstairs to my dressing room, all the girls ran by to their room. Suddenly they all started to scream. Convinced somebody had been murdered, I rushed to see what had happened. They had been robbed. Their salaries, jewellery, everything valuable was gone. The thief, I realized immediately, was the guy I had just 'danced' with on the stairs. But the robbery could not have happened if the miserly theatre had employed the customary stage-door keeper.

During this time, the only thing that saved us from serious hunger while I was so poorly paid or unemployed was my father's generosity. He let me do little things for him in the garage and gave me wages in one of the brown envelopes he used for his garage staff's pay-packets. I often had one of these, containing a ten-shilling note, tucked in my pocket—just enough to buy a good dinner.

Some of the digs I stayed in, when travelling alone, were *dreadful*. I remember sleeping in a bed that was so uncomfortable that, after the third night, I said to the landlady: 'That bed is dreadful.' 'Really? she said. 'Yes,' I said. 'I can't sleep . . . it's so uncomfortable.' 'Well,' she said, 'it was all right last week when Dudley's Midgets were here.' Suspicious, I went upstairs and looked at the bed again. It was a child's bed and she had put some beer crates at the end of it, to make it longer!

Some landladies were lovely and really looked after you, especially if you were in your twenties and reminded them of their sons. But when we came across a baddie—and some of them were really awful, dishing up ghastly food and expecting you to sleep in terrible conditions—we used to plot our revenge. At that time, we still had to have our ration books with us, and our way of getting our own back, on the morning of departure, was to buy a kipper. Then, with the help of a couple of drawing pins, we would stick it under a drawer in

125

the chest. We knew it wouldn't be discovered there and that, after a week or so, the smell would be unbelievably dreadful and the landlady would live to regret the way she had treated us.

I remember a terrible week in Bolton, the same theatre where Harry Secombe had had a bad experience. At this time, Harry used to do a shaving act, portraying all the different ways that men went about this. It didn't go down all that well with the audiences, and when the manager saw Harry having a drink between shows, he paid him off, saying, 'You're not going to shave on my time.' While there, I didn't personally have any trouble with the manager, but I did have problems with the musical director. I wanted to open my act dancing to the song, 'Just One of Those Things', played at a *very* fast tempo. At the first house, the tempo wasn't fast enough, so I looked down at the musical director, saying, 'Faster . . . *faster,*' but he didn't like me shouting at him from the stage. Now I think about it, it was rather rude, but I wanted the music to be right. Anyway, after the show, he said to me, 'I'd prefer it if you *didn't* shout at me in front of the audience.' 'Well,' I replied, 'I would prefer it if you played the music at the correct tempo for me, then there wouldn't be any need for me to shout at you.' 'Okay,' he muttered, adding with more of a threat than a promise, 'you want it *fast*, do you?' '*Yes,*' I challenged. 'In fact, you cannot play that music *too* fast for me.' 'Oh, *can't* I?' he said heatedly.

I *knew* I was on to a good thing. There was no way he could conduct that music too fast for me. So, there he was frantically waving his arms around, with me smiling sweetly and giving him the thumbs-up. It became a duel—a bit like the *Flight of the Bumble Bee.* In the end, he was furious that he couldn't conduct faster than my feet could move and, worse, that I was smiling throughout.

Don't forget that at this time, television was still in its infancy. To see how things were going to go, I had a little test. I would start my stage act with that dance, then suddenly stop and say to the audience: 'Would you say I was *too* sexy for television?' By their reaction—if they got my kind of humour—I could always tell if they were going to be a good audience, or not.

*   *   *

There were two occasions during the tours when I had things thrown at me on stage. One was at the Wood Green Empire. I had been going there—and to the Finsbury Park Empire—for years and years with my parents, so to finally get booked for Wood Green, a Number One theatre, doing my solo act was a *big* occasion for me. And it was near home.

I will never forget that Saturday night. I had only been on stage for about five minutes when, right from the upper circle, down came this packet of fish and chips, wrapped in newspaper. *Whack*, it went, as it landed. Some of the audience gasped, a few sniggered nervously. 'How do I get over this?' I asked myself. I walked over to the fish and chips, unwrapped the paper, and started to eat. 'Too much vinegar and not enough salt,' I muttered, throwing it off side-stage. The audience, realizing that it had actually been an upsetting incident, rose wonderfully well to this. Later on, I began to think that someone else on the bill, a chap who was a bit jealous of me, had got somebody to throw those fish and chips—he was responsible for the tricksy moment even if he hadn't actually thrown the fish and chips himself. But, lacking proof, I didn't challenge him.

Jumping ahead, the other occasion was in 1966 when I was in the lovely *Five-Past-Eight Show* at the beautiful Alhambra Theatre, Glasgow. During the interval this guy went to the stage-door keeper, demanding to see me. When the doorman came to tell me, I rushed to the door, saying: 'I'm sorry, I can't see anybody now. I've got to do a quick change for the second half, but I'll come and see you after the show.' 'Bruce,' the guy kept saying, 'I want to see you *right now*!' He was being impossible, but was sent back to his seat in the auditorium. Near the end of the show, I was playing the piano when a bottle was thrown, again from the upper circle, landing just in front of me and shattering a part of the stage that was itself made from glass. I was so shocked, I couldn't react—couldn't do anything for a moment. If the bottle had also shattered, it could have killed somebody in the front seat of the stalls; and a fragment could certainly have pierced my eye. I knew *who* had thrown it and, to calm us all, explained the stage-door event to the audience. While I was speaking, I could hear scuffling and knew the ushers were removing the man. He was taken to the police station where he was kept in custody overnight. The next day he appeared in court and was fined fifty pounds, and ordered to pay it at one pound a week, 'to keep it in your mind for a year'.

What amazed me was that, just before he appeared in court, a reporter, who had got on to

128

the story, said he would love a photograph of me shaking hands with the bloke outside the police station! 'Do you realize how *dangerous* this man is?' I said. 'Why are you trying to make out he is someone special?' The photograph was never taken.

Another bad audience experience—they can be an incredibly tough lot—was in Dewsbury. Again, as second-spot performer, I had to warm the house up. *Impossible* there, I can tell you. But what I remember most about Dewsbury was my gourmet landlady. When I arrived home one night, she said: 'I've got your supper all ready, Bruce, and would you like a cup of tea?' 'Yes,' I said, 'I'd love a cup of tea. What have we got tonight?' 'Cheese and tomatoes on toast,' she said. 'Oh?' I replied, intrigued. I had never had this snack before and *loved* it. To this day, if I ever ask myself in the evening, 'What do I fancy?' it's *always* that snack. It has to be grilled cheese, with tomatoes on top and a sprinkling of celery salt. Thank you, Dewsbury landlady, for introducing me to this treat.

By 1955, workers in the railway, docks, electrical and newspaper industries were on strike from March until July; then, in May, 'Teddy Boys'—lads dressed in a flamboyant Edwardian fashion, in long coats with velvet collars and drainpipe trousers, their hair slicked greasily back—were creating clashes with rival gangs in our cities. It was, looking back, a very eventful year: Winston Churchill resigned, Sir Anthony Eden succeeded him; Ruth Ellis was found guilty of the murder of her boyfriend, David Blakely, and hanged; Princess Margaret announced she would not marry Peter Townsend; and John Osborne's drama, *Look Back*

In Anger, was put on at the Royal Court Theatre, Sloane Square. Oh, yes, and this will upset many, traffic wardens were introduced!

As 'Teddy Boys' had entered our lives and I always liked to make my material topical, I added an impersonation of one of these youths to an existing routine about the different ways in which people would pick up a half-crown coin they had come across in the street. For the first character, a bookie, I sported a big cigar, picked up the coin, flicked it in the air, slapped it on the back of my hand, and said: 'I lost,' and then tossed it away. For the ballet dancer, I moved ever so gracefully, stretched one of my legs right out in a balletic fashion as I stooped down, picked up the coin, kissed it and leapt off the stage with a grand jeté. For the Teddy Boy, I wore one of their typical, velvet-collared black jackets that went down to my knees, the usual black drainpipe trousers, a 'string' tie, and slicked my hair back into a 'V' shape. Chewing gum, I moved in a 'groovy' way to the number, 'The Creep'. When I noticed the coin, I took the gum from my mouth, placed it on the sole of my shoe, and then put my foot over the coin. I then lifted up my foot, nonchalantly removed the coin, slipped it into my pocket, and then did the Teddy Boy walk off. It was one of those laughs that grew and grew, ending in applause.

On a personal level, 1955 was also a very eventful—and thrilling—year for Penny and me. Our first daughter, Debbie, was born on 24 June. At twenty-seven, I was a father. Sadly, I wasn't present at the birth—*not* for the usual 'work commitments', 'the show must go on' reasons—but simply because it was not the 'done thing' in those days. The 'New Man' syndrome had not quite arrived with the Teddy Boys! I was left pacing up and down the corridor, not knowing what was going on until I was informed I had a baby girl.

Debbie was a darling little girl, everything one could hope for—blonde curls, lovely face, absolutely beautiful. But then—jumping ahead yet again—I have been ever so lucky, all my daughters, all five of them, are beautiful. My only regret is that I was not with them as often as I wished, especially after my Big Break came along in 1958. But whenever I did have a week off, I tried to make up for it, and we did have some nice holidays abroad, too.

Until Debbie was born, Penny travelled with me but, once we had the baby and then our second daughter, Julie, on 4 April 1958, that was not always possible. Sadly, such prolonged absences eventually did put a great strain on our marriage.

*   *   *

During our caravan times, Penny and I had a lovely dog called Rusty—a Labrador cross that we had adopted when he was a puppy. A most beautiful animal, he travelled with us everywhere. But there was trouble ahead for him and us. He developed suppressed distemper, which paralysed his back legs. From then on, he could only drag himself around the caravan and, when I did take him for a walk, I had to help him along by holding him up by his tail. He *loved* going out and this didn't hurt him at all, but people used to think I was *terribly* cruel— even abusing him. Incensed, they used to shout threats after me, and if I tried to explain that he

131

was ill, that only made matters worse! Because every vet we visited—and it was a different one in every town—kept telling us it wasn't right to keep Rusty, that he should be put down, we were getting very close to thinking that maybe we should. But Penny, who was heartbroken and very reluctant to do this, started to spend hours and hours massaging Rusty's legs. She just wouldn't give up on him.

One day, as I walked in, Rusty knocked over his water bowl and there was a flood running everywhere. 'Oh, Rusty, you *bad* boy,' I said. But I didn't really mean it because he was always so obedient, so wonderful. 'You *bad* boy,' I repeated. 'Look at what you've done . . . *Come here.*' And a miracle happened. Rusty got up and walked— walked *very* shakily—but *walked.* He managed this because he so wanted to obey me. I always had that kind of voice—the one I use when I deal with contestants, or anybody I get to come up on stage. I almost bully people to get what I want. But, nevertheless, that moment when Rusty got up and walked was as though there'd been divine intervention.

He could also do tricks, like allowing a biscuit to be balanced on his nose before flicking it up and catching it. He did that one night on *Sunday Night at the London Palladium.* The audience loved him. He never quite managed to get his back legs moving in coordination with his front ones, but he lived for a few more happy years and I think genuinely loved doing his tricks for us. He died in 1962 and was buried in the cemetery of the People's Dispensary for Sick Animals in Essex. We were all so sad, especially our two little girls who loved him so much.

*   *   *

While performing in one of the variety shows, I met a young guy called Peter Dulay who was from a family of performers. One day, he said to me: 'You know, Bruce, you're very versatile and would be wonderful in Summer Season. Would you like me to ask Hedley Claxton, the guy I've been working for, to come and see you, with a view to booking you for a show?' It was a brilliant suggestion. Hedley Claxton came to see my variety act when I was working at the Hackney Empire, East London. Afterwards, he came backstage to meet me. Afflicted with a pronounced lisp, he said, 'I think you could do well in conthert party. Have you ever done Thummer Theathon?' 'No,' I replied. 'Well . . .' he said, 'leth talk about it.' Still lisping, he said, 'You'd have to be the principal comic all the way through the show. You'd have to learn four sketches for each programme, and we have six changes of programme. So, in all, you'd have to learn twenty-four sketches, and do six single acts of about six to eight minutes long at the end of each show, just before the finale.' By the way, I'm not taking the mickey here. As you may have noticed, I've got a bit of a lisp as well.

Anyway, the show he was talking about—wait for it—was called 'Gay Time'. Can you imagine calling any show that these days! These—hold your breath again—were the opening words of the performance:

Gay time . . . Let's have a gay time,

133

'cos this is playtime,
let's have some fun.
Say goodbye to worry and care,
let your troubles go like
bubbles up in the air.

And, to accompany the song, we would all have to stand there doing this ridiculous kicking movement. There was a cast of fourteen consisting of the orchestra of two pianos and drums, the three dancing girls, a soprano, a dancing duo, me, a comedienne, a baritone, an accordionist, and a straight man for the comedy sketches I did.

When Hedley Claxton asked me if I would like to join it, I thought the experience would be invaluable—absolutely phenomenal. So, he fixed it that Babbacombe, Devon, would be my opening venue and, as Peter Dulay had himself been there three years running, he was able to tell me all about it. 'I am sure', said Peter encouragingly, 'the people there will love you. You will be amazed. When the show has been running for two or three weeks and you walk down the High Street, they will treat you like a star. Everyone will know you, and will tell all the people who visit the town to go and see the show.'

* * *

My first Summer Season theatre at Babbacombe in 1955, the same summer Debbie was born, was a 600-seater perched right on the cliffs, overlooking the sea. And the experience I gained was, as I had thought it would be, quite incredible. There was so much work involved. I was very good at sketches—

and loved doing them. Working out the six acts, even though it was very hard work, was also fun. After the first couple of weeks, we also did a Sunday Show concert.

The running order and timing of the Sunday Show was very important because the Lord Chamberlain's laws governing Sunday entertainment in those days meant that a Sunday Show had to finish—no matter what was happening on stage—no later than ten o'clock. Even if you were in the middle of the last song, that was it. *Ten o'clock you were off.* You were also not allowed to wear any costumes on a Sunday other than a dinner suit for the men and a cocktail dress for the ladies—no funny hats and no props in sketches were allowed. The whole show had to be completely self-contained, with no production numbers, no dressing up in South American costumes or anything like that.

The other thing about the Sunday Show was that, to fill the time, I had to play games with the public—my first opportunity to try out audience-participation skills. This is another reason why it was such a very important period for me. Hedley Claxton showed me the games—stupid things like 'Bathing the Baby', where I had to get four guys up with a tin bath and they had to bath the baby while I talked to them; 'Name That Tune', which was a television show at the time; and a game that involved eating a sugary doughnut without licking your lips. All those kinds of silly things.

But in the instructions Hedley said: 'Whatever happens, Bruce, the curtain *has* to come down by ten o'clock. So, in the first half, you do this-and-that game, then finish the first half on that game

135

there; then, in the second half, you do this-and-that game there, and that should bring you to ten o'clock. Apart from all that,' he added, 'just go out on stage, relax and enjoy it. Audience participation is fun. If you are enjoying it, so will they.' 'Fine,' I said confidently, wondering what was going to happen. 'I always like talking to people. Okay . . . Good . . . I'll do that.'

So we started the first half promptly at eight o'clock, and—*what happened?* I got out there, relaxed, had fun with the people, and found that I loved *not* knowing what was going to happen next! The first half finished at nine forty, when there was a ten-minute interval. *Twenty minutes to ten!* I had had such fun with the audience, I had forgotten the Lord Chamberlain, Hedley's instructions and the time. Hedley came round and said, 'What *are* you doing?' I thought I was in for a rocket and the sack. But he added: 'It's marvellous. What you're doing *is* marvellous, Bruce . . . But we will have to rearrange the whole show next Sunday. We will have to take two of the games out, so you can have your kind of fun with the people. That's fine. But you *do* realize that all we have time for now this evening is a ten-minute second half.'

He was right. There was just time for the curtain to go up and do that funny old song: 'If I was not upon the stage'. Eight of us did this, then the soprano delivered one short number, and it was straight into the finale. It was a memorably crazy ending to my first taste of audience-participation skills. I learned a lot from Hedley Claxton, who had five or six other shows going on all over the country. He simply loved show business.

136

*   *   *

Between 1955 and 1958, I had four long years of Summer Season—and three of them were at Babbacombe. The very first year brought a surprise and a thrill. I won my first award—the Bucket and Spade Oscar—presented to me by Leslie Henson, famous for his West End revues. I was so chuffed and thought, '*This* is going to be the beginning of the Big Time for me.' The way the award worked was that Leslie Henson was engaged to tour all the Summer Season Shows in the country so that he could pick out who, in his opinion, was the best company, the best performer, the best this-and-that. And he chose me as 'the best performer in concert party in Summer Season'. As I said, I thought this was my gateway to everything. Was it? *No.* The award didn't mean anything to those outside the Summer Show business. Summer Season is like repertory theatre—semi-detached, a little unit doing something for a few weeks.

So I continued at Babbacombe without any of the anticipated Big-Time breaks, and without repeating any of the sketches. This meant devising twenty-four new sketches for the second year, and a further twenty-four for the third year. It was a *busy-busy* time. My dreams hadn't quite come true. But I had won my first award and had not, by any means, given up hope. And, above all, the experience was to help me so much in the years to come.

After I had done my first Palladium series on television, my Summer Season Shows got bigger and better. The first of these was at Weymouth. I was getting a bit fed up with being recognized every

137

time I arrived at or left the theatre. So, one day, I put on this hat and an old mac before walking out of the stage door. It was a hopeless disguise. As I walked down the street, a woman shouted after me: 'It's no good putting all that on, Bruce, I'd know you anywhere by your *funny* walk.'

So, there you are, if you are blessed with a funny walk *and* a funny face, you've had it.

CHAPTER FIVE

WHAT A YEAR!

Penny and I had come to a big decision. We would sell the caravan and use the money as a deposit on our first home. Betty Driver—a dear friend and a *very* special lady—had told us about the house after she had bought one on the same estate. For us this was both an exciting and worrying time. The house—a brand-new terraced one—was in Admiral's Walk, St Albans, Hertfordshire. It was lovely but, despite my optimism of the previous summer, the end of 1955 and the first five months of 1956 were not at all lovely.

From Christmas until June, the beginning of my next Summer Season Show at Babbacombe, I was having a *very* hard time professionally and, therefore, financially. Bookings were few and far between. Being out of work so often when the monthly payments for the house were due was a nightmare. I remember phoning every day in case something had come up, but that period, when things were looking *very* dicey for me and my show-business career, seemed to go on and on. Thank God for my parents who, as usual, were wonderful, and always saying: 'Are you all right, boy? Do you need anything?' But, because I had always tried so hard to be independent, I was very embarrassed about not being able to find work. I never, however, took the usual course while 'resting'— waiting at restaurant tables, and so on. Instead, I did a bit of driving for my father who had a taxi— picking up people from the station, and all that kind of thing.

Anyway . . . on a lighter note, let me tell you about Max Miller, a very funny and notoriously cheeky man. I only worked on one bill with him, at the Royal Theatre, Hanley, in the Midlands, but it proved to be quite an occasion. He was someone I had always admired, even when I was a kid. The most risqué, 'blue' comedian of the times, I didn't always know what his jokes were about, but I always appreciated his stage presence and the way he held an audience in the palm of his hand from his first entrance. He used to walk onstage in this outrageously funny suit made of chintz. It was loose fitting, with an overcoat to match. He also wore a white homburg hat. When he walked on, he'd say: 'He's here. *He's here.*' It didn't need to make sense. The hilarity was in the way he said it and looked at the audience, from the stalls to the upper circle. He always made a theatre so intimate—something I loved about his performance.

One day, he happened to see my golf clubs when passing my dressing room. 'D'ya play? D'ya play?' he asked. 'Yes,' I replied. 'Well, we'll have a game . . . Are you doing anything on Wednesday?' 'No,' I said. 'Fine,' he said, 'we'll use your car.'

As he had a reputation for being one of the meanest men in show business, I wasn't surprised at this. But, in truth, I don't really believe he was that mean. It was true he didn't tip any of the stage staff, a show-biz custom that most of us, including me, are only too happy to go along with. But he did do some wonderful charity work in Brighton where he lived. On the other hand, he was never known to buy anybody a drink in the bar. Everybody bought him drinks! Perhaps he thought, 'Why should I? I'm the one who's been out there working. Why shouldn't they buy me a drink?'

Anyway, he then said: 'Pick me up at the hotel, Bruce.'

'Where are your clubs?' I said on arrival.

'Oh, I didn't know I was going to play this week,' he replied. 'But don't worry, I'll borrow some at the club. I might be able to borrow some shoes, too.'

The only person at the golf club was a cleaning lady who informed us that no one else would be around until the bar opened a little later in the morning. So Max couldn't borrow any clubs or shoes.

'Well, we're here now,' he said, unfazed. 'You've got clubs. We'll both use the driver and, after that, I'll just use a five-iron for any other shots. I don't want to keep walking backwards and forwards to you with a club, or you coming to and from me, it'll be too messy. And we don't want to keep changing putters on the green, so I'll putt with a two-iron.'

'*What?*' I said, astonished.

'I'll putt with a two-iron,' he repeated, 'and play all my other shots with a five-iron. And I'll use your driver off the tee for the holes that are not short

140

holes.'

'Well . . .' I thought. '*Well . . .*'

Max then rolled up his trouser legs so that he wouldn't get mud on his turn-ups, took off his jacket, but kept on his waistcoat and homburg hat. 'What are you playing off?' he asked. 'I'm a sixteen handicap,' I said. 'Oh well,' he said, 'to make it easier for you I'll give you a shot a hole.' Quite an offer! 'How can he', I thought, 'give me a shot a hole?'

Anyway, we went round the golf course and I didn't win a single hole. I managed to halve a couple, but he was a tremendous golfer. When he was younger, I'm sure he would have been good enough to be a pro. He was absolutely magnificent— and under such adverse circumstances. He played throughout with clubs he didn't even know the weight of. When you think how most golfers have to have a specific weight and certain thicknesses of grips, it was truly amazing how well he played. In his hand, the clubs were like magic wands. He really was a marvellous character—somebody I am so glad I met. I always knew he was a wonderful performer, one of the best, but, thanks to that day, I now know he could have been a great professional golfer, too.

*   *   *

After my second Summer Season at Babbacombe, I once again decided to go back to the Windmill to see if I could get re-employed there. Fortunately Van Damm, ever patient with me, liked my new act so much he asked me to get another one ready for about six weeks' time. In the end, having been a resident comedian at the Windmill for by then twenty-three weeks, he wanted me to sign on for another year. Given how many times I had been in and out of the Windmill, this was very lovely of him, and would also have meant a salary of about a hundred pounds a week more—but, once again, I was in the same dilemma, asking myself 'Is this the side of the business I *really* want to settle for on a long-term basis?' Having decided yet again that it was not right for me to stay any longer, that my heart was still elsewhere in variety, I took another risk and didn't sign up for another year.

Van Damm was to pay me the most wonderful compliment. On a painted billboard, mounted on a wall at the back of the Windmill Theatre in Archer Street, he used to display the names of anybody who had appeared at his theatre and become famous. To my astonishment and delight—and it was the only time he ever did this for anyone—he had my name placed on the wall *before* I was famous. I am almost lost for words to say how I felt when I first saw my name there.

*   *   *

Time now for me to mention that by December 1957, a new musical craze was raging through our land, our record shops and over our airwaves. Rock 'n' roll had arrived here from America where in the mid-1950s, with the advent of Bill Haley and his 'Rock Around the Clock', followed by Elvis Presley and Chuck Berry, it became the heartbeat of teenage rebellion. Here Tommy Steele was discovered, strumming his guitar to the number 'Singing the Blues', in the Two Is coffee bar, Old Compton Street, Soho. This song, which became a

142

phenomenal hit for him, also demonstrated that the British could rock 'n' roll as good as any American. Recognizing the potential in all this new energy, BBC television decided to transmit *Six-Five Special*, those days' equivalent to our *Top of the Pops*. We were then treated to another new sound called 'skiffle', introduced by former jazzman Lonnie Donegan, using improvised instruments including tea chests and washboards. This type of music was usually accompanied by a singing guitarist. Cheap guitars and washboards—normally used for rubbing soap into dirty collars and cuffs—then appeared in the shops to encourage hundreds of other amateur hopefuls to jump on the bandwagon and form their own rock and skiffle groups.

During this time, like John Osborne's Jimmy Porter character in *Look Back In Anger*, I became a very angry young man—incensed by what was happening to music. I had grown up loving the big bands and, a little later, jazz. Now, all of a sudden, almost overnight, everything I loved seemed to have been pushed on to a back burner.

Although I had nothing against the rock 'n' roll beat, even liked some of it and danced to it, the overall sound was nothing like the music I really loved. And just because the youngsters looked good on TV and played 'live', it didn't mean they knew much about music or could even play their instruments well—if at all! Many of the popular groups' musicianship was so limited, so poor, that when they got recording contracts, real musicians had to be hired to play for them. Perhaps I was a little out of step with the times. But I still wanted a mainstream choice; wanted to listen to four trumpets, four trombones, five saxes, a great big rhythm section, bongos and so forth; wanted to listen to jazz trios—a pianist, a saxophonist and double-bass player.

When rock 'n' roll first came in I thought, 'This can't last. It's too ordinary—too basic—the groups have never studied or practised music, don't know enough about their instruments.' I was wrong. Fifty years later it's still going strong. I realize that if any youngsters read this, they'll probably think, 'What's the silly old . . . going on about?' But just imagine how they would feel if all their Top Ten favourites were suddenly completely cut off; banished to some small, difficult-to-locate radio station. And all they had to listen to was a classical string quartet or other chamber music!

Perhaps if I had been older than twenty-nine when rock 'n' roll first came here, I would not have had the same reaction. Perhaps I just needed another ten years to enjoy the kind of music and brilliant musicianship I loved then—and still love now. But, as it was, I was an angry young man. And now, as I write this, I'm an angry old man! But even having said all this, I must add that I did love the Beatles. Their songs had such great melodies and you could hear the words. This is why they're still acclaimed today.

The other thing about rock 'n' roll was that it was so boring to watch on television—just three guys strutting around, strumming guitars, accompanied by a drummer. To try to make it more interesting for the viewers, the cameramen were then instructed by the directors to shoot the groups from different high and low, all-over-the-place angles. This, I think, was the beginning of

144

television becoming overdirected by directors who simply became too powerful. They began to make their job too complicated—almost, it seemed to me, to justify being a director! This problem then spread throughout television, even in comedy programmes. To give an example, all that is needed in a comical situation is to see Tony Hancock and Sid James sitting at a table together, or Morecambe and Wise in bed together. It isn't necessary for a director to get a cameraman to shoot from here, there and everywhere! Some directors definitely overdo it. What I'm trying to say is, I don't want to see them shoot from the side or close up—as Fred Astaire always insisted, 'Shoot me from head to toe!'

*   *   *

But on with my shows! Female impersonation is often thought of as a British comedy staple, but the only time I appeared as a 'drag artist' was also in 1957, when I was in a pantomime with Charlie Drake at the Theatre Royal, Southsea. I wasn't actually involved in the storyline because my job was to do several variety spots in front of a cloth while the stagehands were clearing up the mess from the slapstick scenes created by Charlie, who was the star of the show. However, there was a scene where everybody in the panto had to come down a staircase, and I had to 'drag up' for a principal-boy number, which is usually played by a girl. This meant putting on an elaborate blonde curly wig and a three-cornered hat, and wearing a doublet that only reached as far as my thighs. My legs were clad in sexy fishnet tights, and I was wearing very high-heeled shoes. The number I walked down the staircase singing was 'Strolling down the Strand, with a banana in my hand, hey-ho, away-we-go . . .' It was chock-full of innuendo.

During this time I was staying in digs with a very nice landlady who cooked delicious food. When I got home there was always a lovely supper waiting for me. As the theatre's management had told us we could have a few complimentary tickets, I gave two of these to the landlady who said she'd like to come with the lady who lived next door. I forgot which evening she mentioned she was coming. One night when I came home and went into the dining room for my supper, she came rushing in saying: 'Oh, Mr Forsyth, I *did* enjoy the pantomime. It was marvellous. And haven't you got *lovely* legs!' '*What?*' I said, momentarily taken aback. 'What are you talking about?' 'Oh,' she said, 'when you came down those stairs I thought you had such *lovely* legs.'

I locked my door for the rest of the week—I didn't trust her after that! But she was really very sweet, paying me her compliments in a very nice way, after all.

*   *   *

When the summer of 1958 rolled around, it found me at the Hippodrome, Eastbourne. It was lovely to be closer to home for a Summer Show, but *that* was the only advantage. The Hippodrome then was a horrendous place. My dressing room was dark, with no windows. It was such a weird room I used to say to everybody who came to see me that I felt like the Prisoner of Zenda. The theatre was run down and, to add to our problems, the Fol-de-Rols, the number-one concert party in Britain, were at the rival theatre. Sometimes we would open our first house to an audience of about twenty or thirty people. It was really terrible. So my Summer Season at the Hippodrome was a time of working in a really nice company, with absolutely lovely people, in truly terrible surroundings. But, although it was not the best place to perform, it did lead on to something wonderful . . .

In my variety days, before going into Summer Shows, I had often worked on a bill with an act called François and Zandra. By that time my caravan days were over and, because François and Zandra became friends, I used to stay in the same digs as them.

When I first met them they were a dancing act in the first half of the variety shows, and I had the second-spot comic position. That, of all the luck, was the very worst spot to be; as I mentioned before, you were the one who had to warm everybody up, all the other acts who came on after you reaped the benefit of your efforts. After week after week of doing this, I was totally in despair. Every time I arrived in a new town and looked at the running order, the list would always mention a dancing act, followed by Bruce Forsyth in the second spot, and I knew I would never have a chance to make my name there. Occasionally there would be an audience on a Friday or Saturday night which I succeeded in getting in the mood for me, but that was very rare. Usually, it remained a soul-destroying experience. So much so, I gave myself five years, deciding that if I hadn't succeeded in getting a better variety billing before then I should pack it all in. I suppose the first person on in Comedy Clubs these days finds it just as difficult. Many years later—apart from the first series of *The Generation Game* when I had Bill Martin, a really nice guy and a wonderfully trustworthy warm-up man—I always did my own warm-ups. This was partly because other comics often do too-similar things to you, but also because if I'm going to be with a studio audience for a couple of hours, I think it's best to get them on my wavelength immediately and keep them there. A lot of performers disagree with me—they like having their own warm-up person—but it doesn't work for me.

Anyway, François and Zandra were very good pals to me during this miserable second-spot time and, before the shows, we would often talk backstage. They, it emerged, had a very dear friend, an agent called Billy Marsh, who was the right-hand man of Bernard Delfont in Delfont's agency. Every now and again Billy would come down to see François and Zandra who, by then, had seen me performing in the show at Babbacombe. Until that day, they had not been aware of all the things I could do. Very flatteringly, they thought I was marvellous. Then, after they had come to see me in the Babbacombe Sunday Show as well, and had seen me in action using audience-participation skills, they talked Billy Marsh into coming to watch me at work.

Thanks to them—and to Billy for having seen me in action and having faith in me—my wonderful Big Break occurred. In September 1958 I was booked by Brian Tesler, the director of television's *Sunday Night at the London Palladium*—and later the Chairman of London Weekend Television—to appear in another show he was constructing. This was for new young performers who, like me, were hungry for exposure. It consisted of singing, dancing, sketches, and other bits and pieces. Called *New Look*, Brian booked Roy Castle, Lionel and Joyce Blair, Joe Baker, Jack Douglas, Des O'Connor—and me!

*   *   *

Having made it into the side of the business I had always wanted to be in, I was beside myself with happiness. But there was something even bigger in store for me. One day when we were rehearsing for one of the *New Look* shows, Brian, obviously undeterred by all the cheeky references that the press had been making about my big chin, suddenly said to me, 'If a spot became available on *Sunday Night at the London Palladium*, would you like to do it? Think about it and let me know.' 'I've thought about it,' I said straightaway, 'and the answer's *Yes.*' Brian laughed, and replied: 'I think it will do you good.' So I was booked to do a spot.

Now, when you were the host—the compère—of the show you always worked from the prompt corner which was stage left. This meant you were near the stage manager if anything went wrong, and he—because he was always in touch with the producer and director—could tell you what the problem was and give you instructions. I was told to come on for my spot from the right-hand side of the stage and move towards the centre where Tommy Trinder, the host, would be introducing me. So I did. But instead of Tommy going offstage the way he had come on, he walked straight *at* me. 'Oh,' I thought, 'have you done this on purpose?'

I was left with no alternative but to react spontaneously—to ad-lib. I grabbed hold of him, looked him straight in the eye, spun him round, went to centre stage, looked towards where Tommy had gone, and said to the audience, 'Oooo, hasn't he got a big chin?' This got me a good laugh from the audience who probably thought it was all part of the act. But it was not. I have no way of knowing if Tommy had heard a rumour that I was being considered for his job when he left but, given that it was a tradition to always walk off the same side you came on, in order to avoid bumping into the next performer, it was a *very, very* strange thing for him to do. I don't like to think he did this deliberately, but it could easily have put me right off my stride.

I suppose this event also says something about my growing self-confidence at the time. I was learning to trust myself and react spontaneously. I had just done four years of Summer Season Shows—and was still so hyped up that if anybody, professional or otherwise, had said to me: 'Go down to the bottom of the garden . . . See that statue there . . . Well, sing a song to it,' I'd have done it. I had become *that* used to being onstage all the time, and constantly thinking up ideas. So, my reaction to Tommy walking straight at me was: 'Okay? *Fine.* What can I do about this?' It didn't, thank heavens, unnerve me.

Then, when an opportunity did come up for a new face to take over from Tommy Trinder, the departing host of *Sunday Night at the London Palladium*, during the summer of 1958, Billy Marsh once more championed me and put my name up for it.

The first question everybody asked when somebody new was being proposed for this job, was: 'What about "Beat the Clock"? Will he be able to do this?' In my case, Billy was able to say, 'This guy can do "Beat the Clock" standing on his head. I've seen him in Summer Season—that's the least of your worries.' Billy opened the door for me, and I'll always be grateful for his faith in me.

And that is how in September 1958, at the age of thirty, I left that dowdy old theatre at the Hippodrome, Eastbourne, where I worked sometimes to only forty or fifty people, to the London Palladium, which seated 2,500 people and had a 30-piece orchestra and everything that went with this. The contrast was *unbelievable*. And *scary*. Before I could enter the stage door the first time, I was so nervous I had to drive round the block several times, terrified the stage-door keeper wouldn't know who I was. As it happened, he greeted me with a cheery 'Hallo, Mr Forsyth' and within months, the Palladium was to become my whole life.

*   *   *

The show for *Sunday Night at the London Palladium* was in three parts, and 'Beat the Clock' was the middle part of the programme, before the top of the bill. Couples were introduced by Angela Bracewell, the hostess, and they then had to play a couple of physical games and a word game, all against the clock. The jackpot went up a hundred pounds every week if it wasn't won, and if it reached a thousand pounds the money went to charity. But that was just one part of the show.

Before I went onstage for my first appearance as compère, I had rehearsed and rehearsed 'Beat the Clock' and had kept telling myself, 'I'll be fine—it's *just* a game.' But, when the moment arrived to start the show, it was collywobbles. Standing there, I thought, 'This is *IT*. I've got to go on now and introduce all the stars.' *Sunday Night at the London Palladium* was the biggest show on television—and I'd got it. I now had to prove I was the man for the job.

On that first bill were Jewell and Warriss, who were the most successful double act of the day; Anne Shelton, a huge singing name with a really lovely voice; David Whitfield, another singer with a lovely voice; and, would you believe it, Peter Sellers, who was doing some variety then. They were all so nice to me. They knew this was my big chance and their encouragement was an enormous help.

That first time on *Sunday Night at the London Palladium* was a nail-biting but truly wonderful moment. As the seconds rolled by . . . I knew I was not only beating the clock but achieving my lifetime's ambition. I was now under contract to Bernard Delfont's agency and was being paid £85 a week for the show. I knew I was being exploited, but that didn't matter—I'd got my Big Break. Almost instantaneously, I was one of the biggest names on television, an 'overnight success' and, after six weeks, an established one. Fame had its price, though. Now, wherever I went in London, everybody recognized me. Lorry drivers and taxi drivers would shout out a catch-phrase I had used on the programme—particularly 'I'm in charge', which I had used when organizing 'Beat the Clock'.

This line had come about when I was trying to show a couple how to throw plates on to a table-tennis board balanced on a trestle. The plates had to be thrown first one way then another to avoid unbalancing the board. They were making a real hash of it, so I shouted, '*Stop the clock. Stop the clock.* What you have to do, is . . .' Then, as I turned round, I saw they had started *before* I started the clock. '*Wait a minute . . . wait a minute . . .*' I said. 'It's *my* game—*I'm in charge.*'

The following morning people phoned me to say, 'That was *very* funny, Bruce, when you pretended to be irate with the contestants, and said "I'm in charge".' '*Really?*' I said.

It was just an ad-lib moment that became my first catch-phrase—and, after that, you heard it everywhere. People even used to put it on the back of cars and lorries. A good catch-phrase just trips off the tongue. You can't really premeditate them—they just happen.

On another night, a wonderful lady called Beattie came on the show with her husband. She was so beside herself with excitement at meeting me and being at the Palladium, she was a terrible chatterbox and just couldn't stop talking. I was trying to show her how to win this television set, which was worth £300—a lot of money in those days. But each time I tried, she talked and talked. Then when she reached the 'jackpot' stage, and I was once again trying to show her how to do it, she still couldn't stop talking.

I knew we had hooked a great character—a godsend—and I was having great fun with her. Hardly able to get on with the game, I kept saying,

153

'*Will you shut up, Beattie* . . . *Will* you shut up, dear
. . . I'm *trying* to show you how to win the money,
and all you're doing is *talk-talk-talk, Beattie.* Let me
show you again.' I had no idea how fantastic the
public's response would be because, when I'm
working in a theatre, I'm inclined to think I'm
just playing to the audience there. But this
programme—the top-rating show at that time—
was being beamed into television sets all over
Britain.

The next day, on the Monday afternoon, I was
back in my 'day job', the Palladium's *Sleeping
Beauty*, and in one scene the witch flew in on her
broomstick and started ranting and raving about
everything. As usual, she went on and on. Just for
an 'in' joke with the boys in the band (it was the
same band which played for *Sunday Night at the
London Palladium*) I said, '*Doesn't* she go on? She's
worse than Beattie.' But I was in for a big surprise
. . . everybody laughed. After just one night on
television, every person in that audience knew who
Beattie was—and that moment became one of the
biggest laughs of the pantomime. The power of
television—and its mass audiences—really came
home to me then.

It was the same when I did a piece about drip-
dry shirts, which were perfect—and I certainly wore
them on tour. 'Aren't these drip-dry shirts
wonderful?' I said to the audience. 'D'you know, I
washed this one two hours ago and, *look at it*.
Perfect. The only trouble is my shoes are full of
water.' When I came into the Palladium on
Tuesday morning, I was in for another surprise. As
I walked in, George, the stage-door keeper, a
wonderful man—one of the *very* best—said: 'Oh,

Bruce . . . your mail's by your dressing-room door.'

'What's he smirking about?' I thought. I went to my dressing room and there were these two huge sackfuls of postcards and letters. People—about two thousand of them—were writing all kinds of things about drip-dry shirts, things like: 'If your shoes are getting full of water, Bruce, you should wear pumps!' or 'Why don't you have a tap on the knee?' or 'You should wear drainpipe trousers.'

That had only been a twenty-second joke on the programme, but the outcome went on for weeks. And with people like that looking in, who needed gag writers!

*   *   *

Another unexpected side of 'Beat the Clock' was skeletons being pulled out of family cupboards. I remember a newspaper cutting about a police superintendent in Liverpool who was watching the programme on an off-duty evening when he spotted something familiar about a man who had been brought on stage to play the game. When the superintendent 'clicked', he got straight on to Scotland Yard, to say: 'That man who was on "Beat the Clock" tonight has been on our wanted list for three years.'

The Yard swooped—and the man was later charged.

Likewise, I gleaned through the newspapers that Inland Revenue officials who watched the programme spotted three income-tax defaulters, who were tackled immediately after the show. But any prizes they had won were not, of course, subject to tax!

155

I also remember Val Parnell telling a wonderful story about how *SNAP* (although it had 'London' in the title, it was always 'SNAP' for short), affected people's lives. 'One Church of England vicar, the Revd D.P. Davies, of Holy Trinity Church, Woking, Surrey,' he told us, 'now starts his Sunday evening services half an hour earlier, so that his congregation can get home in time to see the show'!

*　　　*　　　*

After I started on *Sunday Night at the London Palladium*, other pros kept warning me to be *very* careful about becoming too overexposed on television because it could swallow me up and people wouldn't go to see me in theatre. So, after four or six weeks, when I'd got through nearly all the material I'd used in Summer Shows—and because I wanted to keep my variety material separate so I wouldn't be doing the same things on stage as on television—I said to Billy Marsh: 'I'm worried about being overexposed.'

'I know a lot of performers have this theory,' he replied. 'Would you like to go and see Val Parnell?' 'Yes,' I said, 'if you come with me.' So we went to meet Val Parnell in Cranborne Mansions where he had his office, on the corner of Charing Cross Road. He greeted us, saying, 'Hallo, Bruce . . . Hallo, Billy . . . Everything's going lovely, isn't it? Everything's wonderful, isn't it?'

'Yes, everything's fine, Val,' I replied, looking at Billy, as much as to say, 'you start it off'! 'Well, Val,' Billy said, 'Bruce is a bit worried. He's been doing the show for six weeks now and he's concerned he might be becoming overexposed . . .'

'What d'you mean, overexposed?' Val asked. 'Well,' Billy replied, 'Bruce has already used up so much of the material he has gathered over the years, and we are just wondering how long it will last. He doesn't want to be overexposed.'

'*Overexposed!*' Val exploded. 'What a load of nonsense. How can he be overexposed? He's a *new* face. Hardly anyone's seen him on television. Here we are in 1958, with a few new people coming along—nobody knows who *he* is yet. Yes, they're getting to know him, but he's not exactly *overexposed*. Don't worry about it . . . We've only done six, Bruce will go on till about June, so he's got another thirty-three live shows to do.'

'Thirty-three!' I exclaimed, stunned. Until this moment, all I had known was that I'd gone to the Palladium more or less on trial—that if I didn't hit it off in the first two to three shows, I'd be out, and someone else would replace me.

'Do each one as it comes along,' Val said. 'And as soon as you've done it, forget it and think about the next week. You're there for the run. *Don't worry . . .* If you haven't got a funny joke or bit to do, just go out and do a straight announcement. All the people like you. We know that already by the amount of mail you're getting.'

That was true. There was so much, Billy had had to employ somebody to take care of it.

'Just go out and enjoy it,' Val said. 'Everybody loves you. So, you're booked for another thirty-three weeks. We can get you some writers. Don't worry, it's going to be fine!'

That was that—Val's assurance had done me a lot of good. I was booked till June.

157

We did get some writers—Jimmy Grafton, who was excellent and who did a lot of stuff for Dickie Henderson. And then Sid Green and Dick Hills, who wrote for me for many years and became great friends of mine. They were very creative and did many shows for Morecambe and Wise as well. Sadly, they have both since passed away.

After another six weeks or so, Billy thought he would try me out as a second top-of-the-bill at a variety theatre in the Midlands. He put me out with David Hughes, a big singer at the time—and a friend of Penny's and mine. During that week, the theatre did wonderful business. And when checking the audience, the producers discovered that lots of the people had been coming to see *Bruce Forsyth*, not just David Hughes. It was a very satisfying experience for my first appearance as second top-of-the-bill, and particularly gratifying to get applause when I walked on—and not be second-spot comic any more. Billy then put me up for more shows as the *only* top-of-the-bill. This was thrilling enough. But then, to and behold, never having worked in a stage production at the Palladium, Val Parnell amazingly asked me to be in that Palladium pantomime, *Sleeping Beauty*.

What a year! Having started there in September, I did a couple of top-of-the-bill dates in variety during October and November, and then at the end of November three weeks of rehearsals for the Palladium pantomime.

This meant I was now going to be working with Robert Nesbitt, the biggest theatrical producer in the business. I'd heard so much about him—knew he was suave, sophisticated and so 'West End'—I was scared stiff. Rosalie, his very dear secretary,

158

greeted me and I waited to be summoned into his office. I was to play the part of Presto, the jester, and had written an opening song for my first appearance. So, after we had exchanged greetings and had a general talk about the production, I mentioned the song.

'Phil Park', Robert explained, 'is writing the music, but I'd like to hear your effort.'

So I sat down at the piano and sang it for him. As I finished, he said: 'It's ideal for the show—and I'm sure Phil won't mind.' I could hardly believe the meeting had been so rewarding—and that I had met someone who would be so instrumental to my career from then on.

Everybody in the panto soon realized that Robert and I had a special rapport, so one morning when the rehearsals had gone on late and we had all missed our coffee break, Thelma Ruby—who played the queen so beautifully—said: 'Bruce, tell him we haven't had our coffee break.'

'All right,' I said—and did.

Robert glanced at his watch and replied: 'It's too late for coffee—but you can have a Martini break if you like!'

A lot of people didn't think he had a sense of humour, but *I* knew he did. It was a dry sense of humour, like his Martini.

Robert also produced the Royal Variety Shows for years. He never liked the fact that these were televised because this spoiled his lighting—at which he was a master. During daytime rehearsals for one particular Royal Variety, Pinky and Perky were the next act on, but had not arrived. I should mention for younger readers that Pinky and Perky were a puppet act, two little pigs (way before Miss Piggy)

159

who were very popular on TV and stage. Anyway, having heard Jack Matthews, our stage manager, announce that Pinky and Perky were not present, Robert got up from his production desk halfway up the stalls, left Charlie Henry, his assistant, sitting there, buttoned his jacket (he always did this when he stood up) and walked up the steps to the stage: 'Well,' he said, '*where* are they? *Have* you asked their agent? *Have* you phoned their home? *Has* anyone seen them?'

'We've done all that, Mr Nesbitt,' Jack replied. 'But we can't find them anywhere!' Then, from the production desk, we all heard Charlie Henry say over the speakers, 'Have you tried Sainsbury's?'

It was a wonderful moment! Even Robert had a wry smile.

Also in the panto were Charlie Drake—one of the biggest comedy names in the country—and Bernard Bresslaw of *The Army Game* fame; Edmund Hockridge, a wonderful Canadian singer, was third top-of-the-bill; and I was the fourth top-of-the-bill, with my name up there in lights. It was all too incredible for words.

*   *   *

For the seven days a week at the Palladium, I received £190. I was certainly underpaid, but from the beginning of the year, when I had hardly known where the next week's work was coming from, I had moved on to this absolutely amazing situation. The first thing I bought was a new car. I'd always wanted an estate car, one big enough to carry all my stuff when I was travelling around the country. And another luxury was being able to go to—and being able to pay for—a nice meal in a good restaurant without worrying about the bill. Ironically, though, once I became known, I'd go to the restaurant dying to pay the bill, but head waiters would say: 'Have this with our compliments, Mr Forsyth.' If I'd gone in there a few months earlier, starving, begging for a roll and butter, they would probably have chucked me out.

During the early period of the Palladium, Penny and I were still living in St Albans, but we decided she should start looking for a new house that would be closer to where I was working. Given I had a Monday-to-Saturday, two-thirty pantomime performance, followed a couple of hours later by another starting at seven and not finishing until about ten, coupled with rehearsals for the Sunday television show, I was arriving home only in time to sleep, then getting up to return to work. Inevitably, I was beginning to lose touch with Penny and the family.

This reminds me: I have always been astonished at the stories that circulate about the houses *we* are supposed to have bought. There's always a press cutting that says Bruce Forsyth or Jimmy Tarbuck or Ronnie Corbett 'has bought a house in . . .' Who starts these stories? Personally, I think the estate agents are responsible! They do it to push up prices on this or that luxury apartment, and to make certain areas seem desirable. Or undesirable!

At that time, I hadn't lived in *so* many different places: my parents' house, 95 Victoria Road, Edmonton; the caravan; mine and Penny's first house in St Albans. Then, in 1959, because it was so exhausting commuting to and from the Palladium, the move to Mill Hill and later to

161

Totteridge. The Totteridge house was made out of a lovely old coach house and the stables of a huge mansion, and it was called The Paddocks, dating back to 1773. It was really cute and we were able to rent another three acres of land there. It was a perfectly lovely home for our daughters to grow up in, because it gave them so much freedom. I *loved* it, too, but I didn't have as many years there as I would like to have done. I will tell you why later.

*   *   *

From the middle of December, seven days a week, including a daily matinee, we continued in the pantomime right through to April. And every Sunday I performed on *Sunday Night at the London Palladium*.

As you know by now, I love jazz, especially when it's played on the piano. One of the best exponents of this style was Erroll Garner, who was fantastically talented and one of my favourite pianists. I was thrilled to introduce him on *Sunday Night at the Palladium*. However, just as I was about to finish my introduction and bring him on, I glanced to the side of the stage and, to my astonishment, saw Jack Matthews, the stage manager, making signs at me to stretch things out by saying something else. So I burbled on, prolonging the introduction until, to my relief, Jack gave me a thumbs-up to indicate everything was all right. Relieved, I then said: 'Here he is, my favourite pianist, Mr Erroll Garner.' The curtains opened and there, sitting at the piano, was Erroll Garner.

'What was that all about?' I asked Jack when I

joined him.

'Look at the front leg of the piano,' he replied.

'Yes . . . what's wrong with it?'

'It's a bloody beer box with some black velvet draped over it.'

'*No!* What on earth happened?'

'As we were wheeling the piano on,' Jack said, 'the front leg collapsed and the boys had to put a support under it. We had to do all this behind the curtain.'

Erroll fortunately didn't know anything about this when he walked on and sat down happily at the piano stool. There he was, playing away on a two-legged grand piano. Oh dear! When we told him about this afterwards, he was surprised, but not ruffled. But that's the kind of man he was.

Although Nat King Cole became one of the world's most popular singers, he actually started out in a jazz trio. He was brilliant, one of my early role models, the reason why I wanted to play the piano. When he came to the Palladium many years ago in the sixties, because the team knew I loved him, somebody phoned me at eleven o'clock in the morning to tell me he had arrived. 'We have two pianos,' they said, 'because we've had another one brought in. If you can manage to get here by twelve, you could arrange a number to do with Nat.' 'Well,' I said, 'that would be *the* ultimate as far as I am concerned.' So I got to the Palladium as quickly as I could. Having been introduced to Nat, who I instantly realized was one of the most gracious people in the world, we went backstage while everybody else was having lunch. 'What can we do together?' he asked. 'I know a lot of your numbers that we could do together,' I replied, 'but

"Paper Moon" would be good because we could split it up between us.' 'Yesssah,' Nat said. 'What key would it be?' 'I think you do it in F,' I said. 'Fine,' Nat replied.

He then decided that he should sing the first eight lines, I should do the second eight, and we would do the middle eight together. He'd also play a bit of jazz and I would, too. Within ten or fifteen minutes, we had it all arranged. Then, because he knew I was interested in his work, he told me he had just finished recording an album and asked if I would like to hear him play some of the numbers from it. Would I! Imagine the scene: not a soul in the Palladium except Nat King Cole and myself, with him singing and playing this new album just for me.

Some years later I also had the opportunity to sing a duet with his daughter, Natalie, who by that time was a very versatile artiste and enjoying a successful career. I could tell just by looking at her, and listening to her, whose daughter she was. She is really lovely—a chip off the old block.

*   *   *

Stardom—becoming a household name—I discovered, takes over your whole life. Having been in the business for sixteen tough years, when I did get the lucky breaks I grasped them with both hands. I was only too aware that it had all gone wrong for other up-and-coming performers and 'overnight successes' and that, after a year or two, they were once more out of the business. Knowing this, I felt I had to lay the foundations for a long career—a Summer Season here, a pantomime there, another Summer Season somewhere else, a television series . . . And that's how it all began to cascade. Nevertheless, I always made sure I took more short breaks and holidays than Morecambe and Wise. I remember chastising Eric, saying: 'You're going straight from one thing to another—try to take some breaks in between.' But they never did.

I found the Big Time hard, but exciting—and suddenly becoming so well known was wonderful. Pretty girls were now giving me an extra long look, and temptation was being thrown my way twenty-four hours a day. As a married, young, heterosexual male in his prime, it was not an easy situation to find myself in. I'd always been a flirt, but when I think back on some of the opportunities I passed up—especially when it was going on all around me—I don't think I was *too* awful. Promiscuity was, after all, common in our business—as indeed it now is everywhere!

To cap it all, in the late 1950s and early 1960s, things to do with sex were becoming much more open and acceptable. And, because I had achieved something—was now a 'somebody'—a lot of my shyness was beginning to disperse. Hitting the Big Time was a boost to my all-round confidence—business and sexual. It made me more aware of what was going on, and I began to take advantage of this. So I've got to admit to you that I was unfaithful to Penny. Looking back, I have more of an idea why all this happened. I've certainly shouldered my fair share of the blame, but I know that Penny would be the first to admit her faults, not forgetting her very fiery temper! Now national stardom had arrived, the Press began to take an

165

interest in my personal as well as professional life. An abundance of rumours began to do the rounds. I would always say to audiences: '*I* start my own rumours. Then I know where they come from . . .' This always got a laugh.

By now though, Penny and I were not getting on at all well. But, there again, I do think that as much as she always wanted things to be good for me, there was—and I certainly don't blame her for this—an ongoing sense that she was missing out on her own career. I realize now that she was very young to have given up so much for me and the children; and that it would have been wiser if we had allowed each other five years to develop our own careers. But we didn't think like that then. When relationships go wrong, it's practically never one person's fault. And stardom doesn't only affect the person who becomes the star—it can affect their partner as well, who invariably also gets caught in the spotlight.

In the early days—after I became a solo act— Penny did appear in pantomimes with me, such as *Turn Again*, *Whittington* at the Hippodrome, Bristol, when she played the Queen of Catland and I played Dick, and in Great Yarmouth where we both appeared in *Showtime* at the Wellington Pier Pavilion. And even after Debbie was born, she continued to come with me and perform in other Summer Season Shows. But by then I had become a top-of-the-bill name, and Penny hadn't— probably because she never had the chance.

This is why, looking back, although we had some fun and nice years working together, it would have been marvellous for her to have made her own way, to get into a few shows that would have fulfilled her

166

ambitions, rather than waiting for the Summer Season so that she could continue to work with me.

When I was working in another production of *Dick Whittington* in Liverpool, we had a wonderful family Christmas. We went to Manchester where Harry Secombe, Tommy Cooper, Gary Miller and Roy Castle were working. Roy wasn't married, but Harry and Tommy were, and we joined them all there for Christmas Day at a place called the Captain's Cabin. This was a kind of a club that also had a few luxury rooms upstairs for show-business people to stay in—especially if they were top-of-the-bill.

When we arrived Harry and his wife, Myra, were up and about, but Tommy and his wife, Dove, weren't. We saw their breakfast tray going up to his room. On it was a bottle of champagne, some toast and some caviar. The guy who ran the Captain's Cabin had invited us all to his beautiful house in the country, but before we went there we were going to a lovely old pub to tuck into a Christmas lunch.

When we had all met up, we followed each other in our cars to the pub. Roy was in front, fooling around. He had a hat which he kept holding out of the window to indicate when to turn left or right. On one occasion he put his leg out of the window. We were all in fits, but when I glanced in my mirror I saw a police car right behind us, watching all these antics. They then overtook us, saw it was me, moved on to Harry, then to Roy, recognizing them. We could see by the way Roy nodded his head that he was going to be good from then on. The police car pulled away. We were so glad Roy didn't have his Christmas dinner in a cell.

167

When we arrived at the pub, we had a really lovely lunch. Tommy was drinking white wine, red wine, beer and brandy! Then we all moved on to coffee and went back to the house. Everything was laid out ready for our entertainment. Our host had his own projection room, and had managed to get a copy of that marvellous movie, which had just come out, *Gunfight at the OK Corral*, to watch together as families. It was a wonderful film, which we had all looked forward to seeing all week. Later on Tommy, who had been drinking since about eleven in the morning—about nine hours non-stop—went to our host and said, 'Could I possibly have a glass of milk? I think my tummy's upset!'

It was one of the best Christmas Days I have ever had—a *wonderful, wonderful* time. We were all so close then. Now, when I think of those days, of Roy, Tommy, Harry and our families, and the laughs we had together, I remember them as *very, very* happy times. But there were troubled times ahead for Penny and me.

CHAPTER SIX

MEETING SAMMY

In 1959, in addition to being the compère on *Sunday Night at the London Palladium*, I decided to go into education and become a child's tutor. Not just any old child, a famous little boy called Archie Andrews. No, I wasn't giving up the day job or abandoning TV. As an enthusiastic fan of the hilarious radio programme called *Educating Archie*,

I was thrilled to be asked to replace Archie's current tutor, Bernard Bresslaw, who by then reckoned he'd tried to educate Archie for long enough. Archie, for those too young to remember, was ventriloquist Peter Brough's hot-tempered life-size child dummy. Since *Educating Archie*'s first broadcast in October 1953, this radio comedy had become a barometer of broadcasting success. Sooner or later Archie's supporting players included names like Tony Hancock, Harry Secombe, Max Bygraves, Julie Andrews and Hattie Jacques. Its greatest star, Peter Brough himself, was also a businessman who owned several woollen mills. He made more than three hundred shows, and delighted vast audiences every week. Yet he remained a humble man, never claiming to be the world's greatest ventriloquist. He was not in the least upset when Jimmy Wheeler said of him, 'Blimey, his mouth moves more than his dummy's does.'

Not due to start knocking Archie into shape until October 1959, I concentrated on the next series of SNAP, as we called it. The Palladium, where I now found myself spending much of my time, was a fantastic theatre in which to work. Not long ago the Radio Times ran a story under the heading 'Venue of infinite variety', which gives you an idea of the atmosphere and history of the place. 'The original building no longer stands,' wrote their journalist, Madeleine Kingsley.

> After housing in turn a Victorian wine cellar and bazaar, and Hengler's Grand Circus and a National Skating Ice Skating Palace, it was knocked down in 1908 to be

rebuilt at the fabulous cost of £250,000, behind a pillared classical facade. Then about 1910, it re-opened as the London Palladium, the first metropolitan theatre with tip-up seats, designed expressly to be the greatest variety venue. It was the birthplace of, among others, Bud Flanagan's Crazy Gang. Its stage—famed for the Busby Berkeley-style revolve with centre lift—has witnessed virtually every top act from Danny Kaye to Shirley Maclaine; from Max Miller to Bette Midler.

Louis Benjamin, the spry and startlingly funny Managing Director of Moss Empires—the Palladium's holding company—claims to have fallen in love with the Palladium when he started in the firm as a lowly messenger boy—and, despite three or four trips a year to Las Vegas clubland, never to have wavered in his view that it is the greatest show business stage in the world. 'There seems to be a special warmth built into the place,' he once said. 'The royal circle sweeps round almost reaching the stage and somehow enwraps the artist into the audience.'

I could not have expressed any of this better myself. I also agreed wholeheartedly with the Palladium's manager, John Avery, who once said: 'Ours is the best-kept theatre in town, and it may be the only one with all its original gilt and marble intact. You'll find no *plastic* here. And the brass—

including all the stair-rails—is polished every day.'

There are, of course, other beautiful theatres dotted around—but none that to me equals the Palladium. There are also some with terrible acoustics and badly designed stages that are a nightmare to dance on. Funnily enough, a really nice theatre in which I enjoyed performing my one-man show in later years was a kind of council theatre that belonged to the town of Christchurch, New Zealand. But I have to repeat that no theatre on this earth has ever superseded the Palladium in my affections. It is just so special. Even though it seats well over 2,500, it feels as intimate as a family's front room. And when it's full to capacity and the curtain goes up, and the band starts to play, you feel its warmth. The Radio City Music Hall, in New York, is its US equivalent—and even bigger. But really it's just a huge barn of a place. It has none of those lovely traditional boxes on the side. In my book, all theatres should have boxes. They are so important—they give artistes the feeling of being more intimately engaged with the audience—even when they're empty. When you just have stalls with a blank wall either side of you, it's never the same.

My all-time favourite television shot of the Palladium is the one that would come on screen at the start of the show. For a shot like this, the director gets his team to mount the camera in the dress circle. The music starts, and the camera sweeps all the way down on to the stalls and then on to the curtain. At that precise moment the curtain would open, and the dancing girls dance away. I also remember Val Parnell saying, 'The TV show might be called *Sunday Night at the London*

Palladium and, of course, the Palladium is in London, but we must always keep in mind that most of the people who watch are from all over Britain. Londoners are only a tiny percentage of the viewers, the majority are in the provinces.' He was also fond of saying that he wanted the television audiences to feel they were actually sitting in a front seat at the Palladium. So, when I came to do the video of my one-man show a few years later, I decided it should be filmed in this way. 'Let's capture the intimate feeling of the place,' I said to the producers. 'Let's film it as if the camera was a member of the audience. If we can't get this right, I don't want to release it.'

These days, I can hardly bear the thought that the great days of variety have passed, and the Palladium is now used as a theatre, mostly for musicals. I have a nostalgic twinge every time I go there for one of today's musical productions. I'm not saying I don't enjoy them. Simply that, for me, the Palladium will always be what it was built to be—a wonderful variety theatre. I just can't forget the days when, even before I ever walked on to its stage, I used to go there as one of the young pros who were let in free for the Wednesday matinee. Days when it was a wonder for us youngsters to see all the American artistes performing—not just the big stars—but people whose names we didn't even know then. American comics, like Alan King and Jackie Mason, who became hits here even before they became big names in America. And when I used to go there in those early days as a kid, just because I was given a free seat, not once did I ever think that I would be a top-of-the-bill one day, or putting on my own one-man show. It really is a wonderful theatre that's featured every great name in show business, starting with Greta Garbo. And I've been told Palladium archivist Chris Woodward can prove that for us in writing!

Anyway, never mind all that . . . The early 1960s were a wonderful time for *SNAP.* American stars were happy to come over to London for just a couple of weeks, to appear in three television programmes—*Sunday Night at the London Palladium, Chelsea at Nine,* a 'Saturday Spectacular'—and then go home. From 1958 to 1965, our lovely dancers consisted of the Tiller Girls one week, the George Carden Dancers the next. Four of the 'Beat the Clock' hostesses came from that gorgeous line-up. And Angela Bracewell, who later married Stubby Kay, the very talented American actor and singer, was the main hostess who would introduce the contestants.

Despite the visiting US 'greats', one of the really big acts on *SNAP* was home-grown in Liverpool. The Beatles—John Lennon, Paul McCartney, George Harrison and Ringo Starr, formed in 1960, and under the management of Brian Epstein— were coming to the Palladium. It was a big occasion for us, and Val Parnell, the show's producer, was *very* worried. He hated the thought of young girls coming into the theatre and screaming their heads off: 'People don't want to be sitting at home listening to hysterical girls driving everybody mad,' he said. And he set about doing all he could to keep them out. But . . . there are ways and means for determined fans to get tickets for special nights like that and, knowing we could be in trouble, I went with that week's director to the Apollo, Finsbury Park, where the Beatles were doing a one-night stand.

I'd been away for a few weeks and when I returned to London it was to full-blown Beatlemania. Songs like 'She Loves You' and 'I Want to Hold Your Hand' were at full tilt, with the Beatles consistently surpassing all previous figures for 'live' concert appearances and record sales. Pearl Carr, the singer, was the first person to fill in the details for me. Although, as mentioned in the previous chapter, I was not a fan of rock 'n' roll, skiffle or 'pop' music, I was only too happy to admit that the Beatles were different. John and Paul's early songs involved simple but effective harmonies, which had won wide acclaim even from serious musicians and critics. The pair, it was generally agreed, had shown a remarkable ability to assimilate various styles and their compositional technique, enhanced by their producer George Martin, had developed very quickly. This, plus their decision to record their own songs, had the effect in the UK of ending the dominance of Tin Pan Alley—the commercial world of popular-music publishers and composers. Their music 'ranged from the lyrically lovely "Yesterday" to the complex rhythms of "Paperback Writer", the nostalgia of "Penny Lane", and the surrealism of "Strawberry Fields"', as a much more intellectual critic than me has noted. From my point of view, unlike the rock 'n' rollers and many other 'pop' stars, they were a group who really did have some phrasing skills, who could play their instruments, and who could even write their own songs. What's more, some of their compositions, like 'Can't Buy Me Love', could be very successfully re-arranged as really great Big-Band numbers. Their obvious musical talent convinced me they were different from most other 'pop groups'—and I couldn't help but join the bandwagon, and admire and like them.

As there were no seats to be had at the Apollo, the director and I just walked through the stage door and stood, leaning against a wall, in the auditorium. When the Beatles came on, I genuinely approved of their neat haircuts, white shirts and smart suits. I've always believed that performers should make an effort to look the part—and it still bugs me when I see scruffy, sloppily dressed film stars and singers on talk shows. When you are in front of a camera or an audience, I think you should look clean and presentable, and your shoes should have a shine on them. Even if you're wearing something casual, you should at least wear *clean*, well-cut jeans. I thought the Beatles were lovely, fresh-faced, wholesome-looking lads. The screams, of course, were deafening. Girls were fainting from sheer hysteria, and we couldn't hear what they were playing or singing because the interminable screeching drowned it all out.

'What *are* we going to do?' the director asked. 'They can't do three songs on our show, one after the other, without us breaking up their act with something else.'

Suddenly I had an idea. 'Come outside,' I said. 'Come outside for a minute.'

Once away from the mayhem, I said: 'Supposing I come on after their second number to break the programme up. We can't let them go to the microphone and talk because, if they do, the girls will go into even more raptures. So, how would it be if I made conversation with the four of them, using idiot boards?'

I will digress for a moment. We used to call the cue cards 'idiot boards' because you needed to be an idiot to use one! They're called cue cards, which *are* useful for one-word running-order reminders or to cue you into another part of a show. Today, however, these have largely been replaced by the porta prompter, which means you can read off the camera screen you're looking into. I remember that when the US comedian, Bob Hope, played the Palladium, nobody was allowed to sit in the front row because he had between thirty and forty cue cards placed on all the seats so that he could read them from the stage. He worked from these throughout rehearsals and even had them in his dressing room. This was probably because he changed his 'patter', liked to make some jokes more topical. He was so professional. Nobody watching TV would ever have known that he had all these cards lined up—even the theatre audience couldn't see them.

Anyway, never mind all that . . . Back to the Beatles: 'Paul McCartney', I said to the director, 'could rush off to the side of the stage, come back with an idiot board, stand there and speak the words on the board. The viewer at home would be able to see the board and, as soon as he had finished, John, George, and Ringo could each rush off in turn and come back with another board, and so on.'

So, to break up the Beatles' music, we worked out a whole routine in this way, knowing it would also introduce a touch of comedy to the show. On the night, it turned out to be a marvellous success.

After the usual introductory *SNAP* fanfare and girls dancing, we did a special opening for the

Beatles. As the curtains were raised, the audience could see a silhouette of four people with some objects placed around them. Of course, when the girls saw the silhouette they went absolutely crazy and started to scream. But, as the lights came on, the silhouette was revealed to be *me* playing cards with three stagehands. You can imagine the initial surprise—and the laughs. I looked up from playing cards, glanced at my watch and said, 'Oh . . . the show's started. Get up, boys,' then walked forward and said to the audience: 'Don't worry, *they are* here, but you're not going to see them just yet. They're our top-of-the-bill and you'll see them all in good time.' It was a wonderful opening—a gem.

Unfortunately, I never met the Beatles again as a group—just George on one occasion in a recording studio. What happened to John Lennon was so tragic because he had so much to offer. It was a huge shock to hear that he had been shot outside his New York home—that his life had been ended in such a violent way. His music lives on— will, I believe, remain for ever.

Towards the end of 1960, my third year on *SNAP*, there was a shock to my system—literally. I was taken ill, suffering from a suspected duodenal ulcer, and on doctor's orders had to stop work for a number of weeks. This meant I could not do the next series of the show that had made me a star. Don Arrol, a Scottish comedian, replaced me as compère, and was kind enough to say when interviewed: 'Every time I did it, it was like working with a ghost behind me. Let's face it—it's Bruce's show.'

Once I had recovered, I returned.

In 1961, the same wretched illness also resulted

in what was to become the first of my 'lost film parts' disappointments. This one, a film entitled *I'm In Charge*, was a comedy about a travel courier, starring me. But it had to be abandoned after only four minutes of film had been shot. My illness cost the film production company £25,000, but Ron Wilson, one of the directors, told the press that the loss was fortunately covered by their insurance. As the script had been written for me and around my character, there was no point in the production company continuing on the MGM studio lot with any other artiste. Ron Wilson added: 'It's a great pity for Bruce. This was to be his first-ever film and, in my opinion, it would have been a hit.'

Another opportunity I lost out on was the chance to take over from Laurence Olivier in the stage production of *The Entertainer*. This came about because Miff Ferrie, my agent, had adopted the cocky habit of telling people, without consulting me, that 'Bruce is not available for at least a year'. He thought this was a good business strategy, and made me sound even more in demand! Laurence Olivier was having to give up his stage performance in order to make the film, which was subsequently released with the same title. I was not entertained by my agent's attitude, and seriously miffed with Miff!

I cheered up fractionally when I was described in the *Daily Mirror* as 'the most popular TV performer'. Then cheered up a great deal more when I compèred 1961's Royal Variety Show at the Prince of Wales Theatre, in the presence of Queen Elizabeth the Queen Mother, and the Duke and Duchess of Kent. It was my third Royal Variety. The cast of singers, dancers, jugglers, and

178

comedians for this show were assembled by Bernard Delfont who, wise man as he was, halved the usual number of performers to allow each star a decent amount of time in which to make an impact on stage. Another reason I was very happy was because the theme for that year's show was traditional jazz, featuring a revival of all those 1920s songs. The three bands who performed these were one of the evening's big hits. Bowler-hatted Acker Bilk played 'In a Persian Market', Kenny Ball and his Jazz Men gave us 'South Rampart Street Parade' and 'Samantha'. And the three members of the Temperance Seven, sporting beards at this time, scored a huge success with their 'Pasadena'.

The show opened with the company of the West End musical, *Do, Re Mi*, singing their number 'Juke Box Hop', followed by Ugo Garrido, the Spanish juggler, who performed brilliantly with his hands and even better with his feet. Next came Danish songsters Nina and Frederick, with 'Listen to the Ocean', 'Sucu Sucu' and 'Little Donkey', and then our very English Morecambe and Wise in a bullfighting sketch, which led very smoothly into the Ballet Trianus dancing quite beautifully to Lecuona's 'Malageña'. I donned large glasses and did my impersonation of Sammy Davis Jr which I'd been doing the year before in variety, and sang 'The Lady Is a Tramp', then introduced Andy Stewart, 'Scotland's new Harry Lauder'. Arthur Haynes did his very funny comedy routine, and the first half was closed with a 'belter' by Shirley Bassey.

In the second half—what a show to compère!— La Compagnie des Marottes introduced their puppets, the McGuire Sisters, three husky-voiced blondes from America, sang 'Danny Boy', George Burns, the American comedian, danced with Jack Benny—both in drag—to 'Tea for Two', Lionel Blair assisted Sammy Davis Jr (*yes*, my hero was actually there, it was his second Royal Variety Show) in a sketch set in a hat shop, and Frankie Vaughan, with top hat and cane, used his personality to brilliant effect singing a quiet, soothing number. For the finale, Maurice Chevalier sang three of his 'favourites', including 'You Must Have Been a Beautiful Baby' to the Queen Mother, which the audience loved. I thought Maurice Chevalier was marvellous in his films, especially *Gigi* when he sings 'Thank Heaven for Little Girls'—which, as the father of five daughters, is one of my all-time favourites.

To conclude the finale, I opened a scroll and, looking up at the Royal Box, proud as Punch, read a poem to the Queen Mother, written specially for her by A.P. Herbert. It was a fantastic night, to my mind the best Royal Variety I'd ever been in.

The next day's *Daily Sketch*, under the heading, 'Bruce rocks the royal box', said: 'Bruce Forsyth, that lantern-jawed patter-merchant from TV, had the Royal Box, the Queen Mother and the Duke and Duchess of Kent rocking in their seats last night. They loved him. They hugged him with their happiness. And so did we in the audience. For Bruce commanded the Royal Performance. His throw-away lines slaughtered the rest of the comics . . . With superb cheek and wonderful timing he had the audacity to have a go at "Mr Show Business" himself, Sammy Davis Jr.'

Before the rehearsals for this performance,

Sammy didn't know that I could impersonate him and, when he saw me do it at the dress rehearsal, he was blown out of his mind, just fell about. He laughed so much at me imitating his mannerisms that he ended up, helpless with laughter, on the floor, kicking his legs up in the air, crawling up and down the aisle, and brought the rehearsal to a halt. This part of my act, as predicted by a member of the press who was present at the rehearsal, also stopped the evening show! It was one of the biggest nights of my life ever. What more could a compère ask! But what really crowned the event for me was meeting Sammy Davis Jr for the *second time*. He was one of my favourite performers. I idolized him. A tiny, bony, livewire figure in brown silk shirt, his collection of gold jewellery must have weighed almost as much he did.

The first time I met Sammy was in 1960 when he came to London to do a week's cabaret at the Pigalle nightclub, Piccadilly, and during this time also appeared as a guest star on *Sunday Night at the London Palladium* and that year's Royal Variety Show at the Victoria Palace. I was so looking forward to him appearing on that royal occasion, *the first time the show was televised*, and none of us was disappointed. He came on stage and totally commanded it. All the performers were only supposed to take one bow to the audience and one to the Royal Box when they finished their acts, and as compère I could stop all the applause just by looking at the audience and going into the next announcement. But Sammy was such a hit I didn't do this. When the audience applauded madly, I called him to come back for a second bow to both the audience and the Royal Box. He looked a bit

181

bemused by this change in instruction, but truly deserved that wonderful ovation. I also remember that he was so nervous before the show he kept calling everyone 'sir'. But, then, it is rather intimidating to meet people of the status of Noël Coward, Laurence Olivier and John Mills for the first time. After the Royal Variety, along with other members of the cast, I went to see him do his cabaret at the Pigalle—and we saw even more of the Sammy Davis Jr magic. We all queued up to congratulate him and he asked just a few of us to go back to his hotel. While we were having drinks, Sammy went into his bedroom and, shortly afterwards, one of his minders came over to me and said, 'Mr Forsyth, would you mind coming with me?' He showed me into the room and there was Sammy on the phone to his father. When he saw me, he said, 'Dad, I want you to say "hallo" to somebody—you won't know him. But he did something for me tonight that was so unexpected and wonderful, and I would like you to thank him, too.' I think Sammy was genuinely surprised that one performer could do that for another.

I already knew, before meeting him, that when he was driving from Las Vegas to Hollywood in 1955 for a recording session, he had been involved in an appalling car crash. The police said it was a miracle he wasn't killed—and the crash could certainly have wrecked his life and career. While in hospital, he received a hundred thousand telegrams from well-wishers. He'd lost his left eye, suffered other injuries, and many people thought he was finished. Sammy, however, thought otherwise. His first words after the doctors broke the news that he'd lost an eye were: 'Thank God it wasn't my leg.'

Within weeks of the accident we heard he had bounced back, and was strutting about the stage, singing, dancing, doing impressions and playing drums. His fans so warmed to him that two went as far as offering him an eye! When speaking of his 'sawdust days', Sammy was very fond of saying: 'You ain't lived till you work for ten dollars a night.' He was also quoted as saying: 'Entertainment is my life. There was no way I was going to give it up. The best way to describe it is this: in 1954, before the accident, I was earning 7,500 dollars a week in clubs. In 1955, after the accident, I was earning 25,000 dollars. So, in 1955, things really started to cook. I started tasting the highs.'

He was a lovely, courageous man. It was only a year after the crash, in 1956, that he appeared in his first Broadway show, *Mr Wonderful.*

Another of my favourite Sammy stories is when Sammy was booked for a second guest appearance on *SNAP.* By now, Lionel Blair and I had had a long and marvellous association since our Windmill days. People generally know that Lionel is a singer and dancer, but not many know he's also a wonderful 'ideas' man, more than capable of coming up with brilliant comedy lines, comical sketches, and so on. The problem in television, though, is that ideas people never get a credit. I think they should—it's a creative job in itself. I haven't yet mentioned Lionel's choreography because, as readers now know, I'm his choreographer from the Windmill days! Anyway, when Sammy Davis came over for *SNAP*, he said to Lionel, 'Can Bruce and I do a song-and-dance routine together?' As I was up-country, doing a

183

variety week before coming back to the Palladium to do the show on the Sunday, Lionel had to give his ideas for this to Sammy in London, then get on a train to explain to me what had been arranged. Poor Lionel! He had to keep travelling backwards and forwards between the two of us because, if I didn't like a particular bit, I'd say: 'Ask Sammy if we can do that,' and Sammy would say: 'I'm not altogether happy with this, ask Bruce if we can do that'! Then we didn't actually try out the number together until we went on stage on the Sunday morning for the band call.

I met Sammy again at the 1963 Royal Command Performance. I've never forgotten Sammy's generosity when he said to the press: 'Bruce is so like me. And here's what we have going for us. We're both multi-talented. He's a singer, a musician, a dancer, a mover, a comedian. So am I. We've both worked hard to get where we are, and Bruce has worked hard to help me get started in Britain. He was there, thank God, with a show-business crowd who knew what I could do, even though nobody else in Britain knew me.' He was also kind enough to tell the journalists that he was convinced that his appearances in Britain had made him a superstar. In an interview for the *TV Times*, he said: 'Britain *really* did start me off as an international star after the Royal Shows. I never dreamt for one minute that, after these, I would become as well known internationally as I was in America.' Sammy and I became lifelong friends who drifted in and out of each other's lives. More on that later . . . I loved that man.

Another unexpected pleasure while I was compèring the Royal Command Performance in

1963 was meeting Denny Willis again, for the first time since we and others were all unceremoniously dismissed from the Carlisle revue some sixteen years earlier. Denny, who had between times been the principal comedian with the Fol-de-Rols, reappeared in an act called the Quorn Quartet for the Royal Command. I remember saying to him: 'Well, Denny, we're not doing so badly now, are we?'

One accolade I received in the sixties was unlike any other. The British Clothing Manufacturers Federation included me among its ten best-dressed men in Britain, describing my appearance as 'immaculate'. How about that! A fit reward, I felt, for my habit of always hand-washing my shirts myself and sewing on any missing buttons. It's a habit that amuses or even astonishes some people, but quiet moments like that can be very soothing for a chap. Anthea, my second wife, once said to a journalist: 'When we first got together, I was never allowed to wash Bruce's clothes in case I didn't do it right. He washed everything himself by hand. His shirts had to be drip-dried on special hangers with the top and third buttons done up. When he finally decided to show me how to do it, I remember thinking, "My God, what am I getting involved in?"' The reporter then added, 'But that is part of Bruce Forsyth's success. He has a mania for perfection, coupled with ambition, boundless energy and enthusiasm.'

So . . . ? Nothing wrong with that.

*   *   *

During my third year at the Palladium, Miff Ferrie,

with whom I was still unhappily landed as my agent, told me he was having terrible trouble with Leslie Grade, the youngest of the three Grade brothers, about my pay negotiations. But before I go into this, I should fill you in on the Grade brothers themselves. *What a family!* Lew was the eldest, Boris the middle one. Leslie had joined forces with Lew, and was joint managing director of their theatrical agency until 1955. Boris, having changed his name, became Bernard Delfont. Bernard and Lew then became impresarios as well as agents, and financed groups of acts and whole shows. Lew, an early entrant to commercial television, became managing director of ATV in 1962. He also headed several large film entertainment and communications companies, and was eventually made a life peer, Baron Grade of Elstree, in 1976. Bernard, having acquired control of more than thirty companies, embracing theatre, film and television, music and property, presented a record number of West End shows—not to mention the annual Royal Variety Shows from 1958 to 1978. In 1976 he, too, was made a life peer, Baron Delfont of Stepney.

Back to the pay negotiations. When I first compèred *SNAP* I was paid £85 a week, but there had been some raises in salary since then. During the current round of negotiations, I heard that Tommy Steele, the rock 'n' roll star, had achieved the magical sum of £1000 for one television show. Now, in the early 1960s, *that* was a tremendous amount of money—enough to attract newspaper headlines for Tommy. But Leslie Grade had told Miff that my money was going to be increased to £750 a week for the next series. In view of Tommy's fee, I was *not* happy with this offer, and told Miff so. While I was at the station, before returning to Torquay for a Summer Season Show after a weekend at home, I rang Miff from a phone box to see if he had made any progress. 'Leslie's been on to me again and has increased his offer to £850,' he said.

'Well . . . I want £1000,' I replied. 'And, given everything that's happened to me in the past two years—when, according to press cuttings, I seem to be pretty big in the business, and when I'm filling theatres everywhere I go—I think I should be on the *top* rate. If somebody else is getting that, I should get it, too.' Especially as I had been underpaid at the start!

'Is that your last word?' Miff asked.

'Yes.'

'Well . . . Leslie has said that's *his* last word . . . *His* top offer.'

'Okay,' I said, 'tell him it's *my* last word. And *that's that.*'

Feeling, needless to say, very tense, I ended the call. The journey to Torquay took about two and a half hours. On the train, I was thinking, 'Have I done the right thing? What will happen?' I *knew* I was 'big', the public reaction everywhere I went was marvellous. It was a time when every article about me, and there were plenty, seemed to suggest that I could do no wrong, but all of a sudden I was beginning to doubt all the hype.

Following my arrival in Torquay, I went straight to the theatre. I was putting on my make-up when there was a knock at the door. 'Bruce,' someone said, 'there's a phone call for you.'

'Ask who it is,' I replied. 'My mind's in a bit of a

whirl at the moment, and I don't want to speak to anyone unless it's absolutely necessary.'

'It's Val . . .' the messenger said on his return, 'Val Parnell, I think he said.'

'The Guv'nor!' I thought, astonished. 'Why's he phoning me in Torquay?' I didn't know what to expect when I went to the telephone.

'Hallo, Bruce,' Val said. 'How are you?'

'I'm all right,' I replied. 'How are you?'

'Are you *sure* you're all right?' he asked. 'What's going on?'

By now I had recalled that, as well as running the Palladium, he was also head of Moss Empires and the top man of Associated Television so, of course, he would have heard about my pay-negotiation problems.

'Well,' I said, 'my agent's having a bit of a thing . . .'

'Bruce,' he interrupted, 'is it *only* the money that's holding all this up?'

'Well, yes . . . it is,' I said.

'Well, if that's *all* . . . Well . . .? What do you want?'

'A thousand pounds a week,' I said.

'You've got it,' he replied on the instant. *'You've got it.* What is all this nonsense? If ever you have any more problems with things like this, *deal with me.* I don't want your agent talking to Leslie, and all this going on. You shouldn't have to go through all this. And I don't want to have to hear about it from anybody else. Deal with me in future. *Okay, son?* Enjoy the rest of your Summer Season. I'll see you in September. We'll do another forty shows together—and I'm looking forward to it. Good luck to you. *It's a deal.'*

I felt wonderful—was on cloud nine. I had established an important principle, faced up to the guy at the top. I don't remember doing my act that night—I hope the audience did!

We could do with people like Val Parnell today—could do with a good few of them. Val's word was his bond. He appreciated you if you worked hard, treated you like a friend, would come backstage and speak to you if you were in a theatre. He was always so good with creative people; liked, whenever he could, to indulge them and give them their own way. When Shirley Bassey's manager, Mike Sullivan, insisted on twinkly little stars being placed around her name in the credits, Val agreed—and told me, with a twinkle in his eye: 'Bruce, you'll have twinkly little stars, too.' Yes, I *know* people always say, 'Oh, the good old days . . .' But, believe me, they *were*. People like Val—and his right-hand man, Charlie Henry, and Robert Nesbitt—made the business a pleasure to be in.

*   *   *

Now back to Miff Ferrie, whom I would like to dispose of in this chapter! During what I thought was the last year of my contract with him, I decided it was impossible for me to continue with him as my agent. I wrote to say I could not work with him any more. In response, he sent me a letter, saying *he* was renewing the contract! I wrote back, saying he couldn't, I wanted to terminate it. He wrote back, saying it could not be terminated. So I went to the Variety Artists Federation, which looked at the contract, and then informed me that Miff Ferrie was right. He had me under a contract *he* could

189

renew every five years and, as my signature was on this, *I* had no say in the matter. In fact, both Tommy Cooper—the hysterical comedy magician, renowned for his red fez headgear—and I were in exactly the same position, signed up for life. I *couldn't* believe it. My other niggle was that, at the beginning of our association, Miff had asked me to pay fifteen per cent commission when, generally in those days, it was only ten. At the time, I thought, 'If he's a good agent, it's worth paying the extra five.'

By 1962 the situation was totally intolerable between us. In the end, I decided to take him to the High Court to try to end our contract. After the first two or three days in the Court, my firm of solicitors told me they thought the case was going against us. The only other case they could use as a precedent concerned an earl who had had a serf working for him who'd been signed up for life. On one of the days, the judge came out with a lovely remark: 'In these times,' he declared, 'it's much easier, it seems, to get rid of one's wife than one's agent.'

It was not so funny when my barrister said, 'I'm afraid Miff Ferrie has got us . . . You'll have to settle with him.'

'What sort of sum are we talking about?' I asked, downcast.

'Seven thousand pounds,' he replied.

In those days that was a lot of money—it still is! Not to mention my own legal bills on top. Worse, he also informed me that the contract could only be reduced to seven years—and *that* excluded the five years I had already been working with Miff. So I had no choice but to continue with him as my agent. And he still had the right to continue signing contracts on my behalf and, however unsuitable the place, I had to turn up.

To round off this tale of woe, let me give a clear example of the kind of person Miff was. One day he came round to the Palladium when I was rehearsing *SNAP*. I had worked out what I called a 'chiffon' routine for the show. Yes, I will explain! Female singers who don't have all that good a voice often take attention away from this by holding a bit of chiffon in their hand and wafting it around in the air. I'd done the routine in the morning and Val and Charlie had given me some suggestions which I'd taken on board for the four-thirty rehearsal. I knew I had the right music, and it was all coming together very nicely. After the rehearsal when I was in my dressing room, Miff came in.

'You've *got* to drop that act with the chiffon,' he announced. 'You've *got* to take that out of the show. You *can't* do it tonight.'

'But,' I protested, 'Val Parnell and Charlie Henry helped me with it.'

'I don't care,' Miff said, 'it *isn't* worthy of you—and it *certainly* isn't worthy of this theatre.'

'*Right* . . .' I said, coming to the boil. '*Get out* of this dressing room . . . *Get out now* . . . because if *I* can't throw you out, I'll get somebody who can. *And, remember this, don't ever come round again to any theatre I'm working in. Just stay away. Clear out.*' He did. But, after dealing with someone like that, I still had to simmer down somehow in order to be able to go on to do a live, hour's TV show.

This incident was bad enough. But the last straw came when I was working up North and telephoned Frankie Howerd. Frankie's sister answered the

191

phone. 'Hallo, dear,' she said. 'How are you?'

'Fine,' I said. 'How are you and Frankie?'

'Fine,' she said. 'Oh . . . By the way, *good luck* to you in the pantomime at the Wimbledon Theatre.'

'*Whaaaat?*' I said.

She repeated the words, and then added: 'Bruce, it's in the *Evening Standard*. You're there for *Aladdin* at Christmas.'

I could not believe it.

'Who else is in it?'

'Tommy Trinder,' she replied.

Of all people! After the first *SNAP* incident—and the fact that I *had* taken over his job as compère—I somehow knew I wasn't his favourite person. 'How can I be in a show with him?' I thought. I was furious with Miff. But, after the High Court case, I knew I couldn't just end my contract with him. I phoned my solicitor, summarized the latest incident, and then said: 'Okay. This is *IT* for me! Please find out what he wants to finish the contract—what it will cost me to get away from him! I *can't* work any more with a Svengali like him. I've *got* to know where I'm going and *who* I'm going with.'

A few days later, the solicitor came back to me: 'Miff Ferrie', he said, 'wants twenty thousand pounds, in addition to the seven thousand you've already paid him.'

'Okay,' I said, resigned.

In the meantime, I had a word with the producer of the pantomime, warned him of the Tommy Trinder situation and said I didn't want to be involved in any stage action where I may have to match him for ad-libs and so on. Believe me, Tommy was a great ad-libber as well as a fine performer. I think the two of us ad-libbing would have been fine for a few shows, but not for a long run. So the producer arranged for me to do five different spots in *Aladdin*, without my actually being in the storyline. In this way, I could work throughout the show confident that Tommy and I would never meet on stage. In the event, we never even said 'Hallo'. The *only* time we appeared together was for the finale line-up! Offstage, however, we did have friendly conversations.

I paid Miff the lump sum—and life was wonderful thereafter. Billy Marsh, who had first championed me and then got me the job at the Palladium, became my new agent. Also, instead of paying fifteen per cent agent's fees, I paid ten per cent from then on. This meant that, in just a couple of years, the five per cent I saved covered the cost of paying off Miff. It was the best deal I ever did. Miff no longer had any hold over me. Fortunately, too, because I had already done sufficient work and—funnily enough, as a result of the *Aladdin* pantomime, I was on larger bonuses than I had ever received before—I could also manage the £20,000. So, in the end, it all worked very much in my favour.

After the various contretemps with Miff, the only time I ever saw him again was at Tommy Cooper's funeral in 1984. Tommy had died during the transmission of the television show *Live from Her Majesty's*. Miff had retained this dear, much-loved man under the fifteen per cent, lifelong contract until then—despite the fact that I had heard that Miff was banned from being around his television shows because he caused so much trouble with the production teams. But Tommy was a very different character from me—I simply could not work with an agent who understood musicians but not performers.

In the end, I felt quite sorry for the man. He desperately wanted to be a show-business agent, but was not the kind of person who should have done that sort of work. He simply did not know enough about it—and even less about television than the stage.

* * *

Now, Norman Wisdom is a guy who always knew what he was doing. Long before I got my big break on *SNAP*, and met him, Norman was in films which people, including me, queued right around the block to see. He was as popular then as any film star could be in Britain. And nowadays his films are seen all over the world in places like Russia, Albania and Arab countries. It's simply wonderful how he has continued to attract people to the cinema whenever his films are shown abroad. But then, he is quite simply unique.

I worked with him on two occasions at the Palladium. I thought both the shows were very good, but the first was my personal favourite. We didn't have videotapes then, but Norman wanted this show filmed. This was a very costly process—five or six minutes of film cost between £500 and £600. To do a whole hour's show would have been very expensive, so they didn't do it. Norman was left seething about this and, when we did the second show for transmission on 3 December 1961, never a person to be thwarted, he brought the subject up again and again. This time they did film it and, since then, it's been on TV quite a few times and was even released on video.

Norman, as I discovered to my cost, was also very meticulous about scripts. He insisted on every line being delivered *exactly* as it was written, with no deviation whatsoever; it had to be 'on the nose' all the time. Now, I don't particularly like working like this. I like to rehearse a thing well but, if something happens along the way, I like to be able to be spontaneous, ad-lib, have a bit of fun with it. But Norman made it absolutely clear when we were rehearsing together that the written line was *the* line and it couldn't be changed in any way. I also had to look in a certain direction and had to do this and that in a specific way. It was hard work, I can tell you. But that's how Norman performed throughout his career—and, as far as I know, in all other aspects of his life! He was a perfectionist, who knew exactly what was right for him, and he was right to be like that.

While we were rehearsing for the second show, we had lunch at Verrey's in Regent Street, just around the corner from London Management, where my agent Billy Marsh was ensconced. This was a wonderful place for lunchtime meetings and a great favourite of showbiz people. So, as we were having a few problems with one of Norman's slapstick ideas, we arranged for the writer, director, producer, and their PAs to be there, all sitting round a big table. Norman's plan for the closing of the first half of the one-hour show was to include a wallpapering sketch where I would be the foreman and he would be my idiot assistant. This would finish with him covered in a bucket of slosh which I had just tipped over him. But as this sketch was to

195

be followed by 'Beat the Clock', there was a problem. The mess on stage! It would also involve a very quick change of clothes for me. I'd need to wear my dinner suit, except for the jacket, underneath a set of decorator's overalls, and then get out of these in record time. Meanwhile, the palladium's stagehands would have to get rid of the set, the wallpaper and the slosh ready for 'Beat the Clock'. Norman then intended to come on at the start of this game still clad in his messy overalls, start talking to the lady contestant, take her in his arms, look at the orchestra and then, as they started to play, dance with her.

Now, the 'behind-the-scenes' staff at the Palladium were wonderful and just as important to the show as the top-of-the-bill stars. They worked incredibly hard to keep *SNAP* looking like a 'live' TV show, and were renowned for doing their best, however mad the ideas. But, on this occasion, the producer, director, and I all told Norman: 'It's a very funny idea, Norman. But, over the years, Val Parnell has always refused people permission to appear in or do anything during "Beat the Clock". To Val, you see, "Beat the Clock" is sacred.' But Norman wouldn't listen, wouldn't back off, kept on and on about the sketch, while we kept repeating it wouldn't be allowed. We each told him this at least ten times during the lunch. At the end of the meal, Norman said: 'If I go and see Val, and Val agrees with the idea, will that be all right with you lot?'

'Look,' we all replied. 'Of course, it's up to Val, but we know what the answer will be.'

'Okay,' Norman said, 'I'll speak to Val.'

'You do that,' we said, only too grateful to be out of the hot seat—and left to nurse our indigestion.

196

Norman phoned Val and, as expected, went on, and on and . . . He'd doubtless done this so often to so many people that it didn't even occur to him he could lose the argument. The next day, he came in and said: 'I've spoken to Val and he thinks it's a good idea.'

We all looked at each other in amazement. But we couldn't help laughing. Nobody but Norman could have pulled that off. We arranged for the lady contestant to wear a new, paid-for dress, so hers would not be ruined. It proved to be very funny—and people still remember that wallpapering sketch today. Since it was all mimed, the only sound was the background music and the roars of laughter from the audience. They loved it and, judging by the number of letters we received afterwards, so did the millions of viewers. In his autobiography, Norman said of this show: 'Bruce is a real professional who has never shirked hard work. We took the bull [he should have said pasting brush!] by the horns, worked for hours, day after day, for the entire week leading up to the show . . . At the end, we took our place on the famous revolving stage and received a standing ovation. It was one of the most enjoyable things I have ever did—a tremendous challenge that could have gone wrong.'

So that was our Norman, a man who knew his own mind, who nearly always got his own way. And in the end, I have to say, his way was best for him. But he exhausted me!

*   *   *

On 19 November 1962, there was some very good

news. Penny gave birth to our third child, Laura. Whenever anybody asked me if I was disappointed to have another daughter, I always replied that I was simply relieved everything had gone so well . . . that mother and baby were safe, and no harm had come to any of us. By then, I'd heard such terrible things about what *could* go wrong in labour and childbirth that the sex of the child was the last thing on my mind—and *should*, in my view, *always* be a secondary consideration. After little Laura was born, the gynaecologist did say to me: 'You're *very* good at girls, Mr Forsyth'! 'So was Henry the Eighth,' I replied!

While on the subject of our family life, I should mention Brutus, the dog we brought into our lives after Rusty died. Brutus was a Great Dane, a beautiful giant of a dog. There are so many stories I could tell about him. One evening, Jimmy Tarbuck had come over to see us and was sitting, glass in hand, on our settee. He hadn't met Brutus and didn't know that he was so tall, and that no settee-back was too high for him to place his head over. As Brutus entered the room behind the settee and did this, Jimmy, suddenly sensing that somebody was there, turned round to see who it was. When he saw Brutus's huge, salivating face he nearly jumped clean out of his skin. It's not easy to surprise Jimmy!

Brutus was wonderful with children, and always in his element when there was a birthday party at the house for one of our daughters. Two of our very best friends from our Windmill days, Diane and Bernard Coral, lived in the same area, and their children and ours grew up together. Bernie was the kindest of uncles—like a second father to our girls. He was always taking them out and, whenever things weren't too good between Penny and me, would always be there for us. He really was—and is—a very nice guy. Anyway, on this occasion, a birthday party was going on and Bernie—being the kind of guy he is—was in charge of the games. For this particular game, he had lined the kids up so that they could each run to him, one by one, and leap in the air so that he could catch them under their armpits, twirl them around and put them back down. Well, dear Brutus was in a corner of the paddock, chewing on some grass and observing this going on. Having obviously thought to himself, 'That looks fun. That's a good game, I wouldn't mind joining in,' he then stood up, pricked up his ears and started to run towards Bernie. Now, when Brutus ran across the paddock, his large paws made the sound of a horse cantering! As he bounded across the grass, Bernie saw him from afar and thought, 'Oh, well, he's just enjoying a run.' The kids, meanwhile, kept squealing and racing to Bernie who, by now, had realized that Brutus was also running towards him. So he told the kids to get out of the way. Having read some animal advice somewhere, his reasoning was 'Stay where you are and the animal will turn, at the last minute, to avoid you.' By now Brutus was within ten or twenty yards of Bernie and, looking forward to his turn in the game. Bernie, now rethinking his strategy, was saying to himself, 'Shall I go to the right or to the left? Shall I stay where I am or move? No, I'll stay where I am.' But Brutus, having arrived by now, leaped straight at Bernie and, at full length, caught him right in the chest, flattened him on the grass and knocked him out. I know one shouldn't laugh, but it was so hilarious. All Brutus intended was to join in the game. But, as I always say, Great Danes think they're Yorkies, and Yorkies think they're Great Danes.

On another occasion the girls phoned me in Kensington, where I was living at the time. They were crying so much I could hardly make head or tail of what they were saying. 'Something's wrong with Brutus,' I finally gleaned. 'He's foaming at the mouth and lying down. His eyes are all bloodshot and, Daddy, he's in a terrible state. *Please* come and see him.'

'Phone the vet,' I instructed. 'And I'll leave straightaway and get there as soon as I can.'

'What do you think is wrong?' I asked the vet, whose arrival at the house had coincided with mine.

'I don't know,' he replied, 'he looks really unhappy.'

Unhappy! Brutus was in an *awful* state—looked at death's door. It was terrible to see him so ill. And the girls were sobbing their hearts out in the corner.

'Well . . .' the vet added, obviously nonplussed. 'Let's try to get him on his feet—that might help.'

I don't know how much Brutus weighed, but he was a very, very big fellow, and must have been between ten and twelve stone. After a huge struggle, we managed to move him a bit then, having heaved again and again, finally succeeded in getting him on his feet. As we did so, he gave a tremendous sneeze and a toothpick flew out of one of his nostrils like a dart. We just couldn't believe it. Much happier now, Brutus shook his head, moved around a bit, and then started galloping around the house and out into the garden. He was fine.

'What happened?' I asked the girls. '*How* did Brutus get hold of a toothpick?'

'There *was* a party here last night,' Debbie replied.

So that explained it. Whenever there was a party, Brutus just padded around hoovering everything up. There wasn't a table top he couldn't reach to see if there was anything worth stealing. Having found a finger-food item, he'd obviously got more than he bargained for. The toothpick had lodged up his nose, and caused the fit and the foaming mouth and bloodshot eyes. It was quite a morning, that morning.

Later on, he was to have a more serious mishap. One night, after he'd taken himself for a walk, he staggered back into the house on three legs. He must have been hit by a vehicle. The vet came to see him but, being such a large dog, Brutus had to have a steel rod inserted in his leg and was put in a hammock-like contraption to support his body while the leg healed. He was handicapped for many weeks like this but, cheerful enough, he still managed to hop around. And he refused to be defeated even when, every now and again, we had to push the steel rod back into place after it had become dislodged due to his exertions. He really was a wonderful dog who enjoyed life to the full. Like Rusty, he will always have a very special place in my family's memories.

* * *

In 1962, a very funny thing happened to me—no, not on the way to the theatre, but in the theatre!—while I was doing an *Every Night at the Palladium* summer review with Morecambe and Wise, singers Eve Boswell, Teddy Johnson and Pearl Carr, juggler Ugo Garrido and ventriloquist Fred Roby. A very big show, this was presented by Lesley Macdonnell and Bernard Delfont and produced by Robert Nesbitt. One day there was a great deal of excitement backstage because we had been told that Ed Sullivan, the American TV host, was in London looking for artistes to appear in his New York TV show, the USA's equivalent of *SNAP*. And he would be in the audience that evening. I'm honestly not in the habit of knocking people, but he must have been the strangest of hosts for any programme. He had these peculiar, penetrating eyes and a weird manner. Although he had the top variety show, he would very often get his guests' names wrong. Eric Morecambe told me he introduced them as 'MORE-CAM-BEE AND WIZ'! Anyway, during the first half of the programme he saw Eve Boswell, Morecambe and Wise, the wonderful Garrido, and booked all three for his *Ed Sullivan Show*. As a result, Eric and Ernie appeared on his show several times and became known in America.

I performed the whole second half of *Every Night at the Palladium*, and hoped that his presence would present me with an opportunity I had longed for—to appear in a New York show and break into the American scene. Because this meant so much to me, I was on tenterhooks. But, just before I was due to go on stage, the theatre manager came round and said, 'Ed Sullivan and his entourage send you their respects, Bruce, but they've had to go on somewhere else and are not stopping for the second half of the show.' I was *so* disappointed. '*Why?*' I thought. 'If he's over here looking for new artistes and I'm top-of-the-bill in this show, *why* isn't he coming to see me as well?' Had somebody—like my agent—told him I was booked for the next two or three years in Britain which, in reality, was half true? I asked Billy Marsh if he knew what had prevented Ed Sullivan from staying to watch my performance, but I never really got a satisfactory answer. So—and, believe me, this was not easy—I just had to grin and bear it.

There are, I discovered—but fortunately not while I was compèring the Royal Shows—so many things that can distract you while you're performing. The biggest distraction is the audience. If, for example, someone gets up and walks out, it catches your attention. Fortunately, in my TV shows I could score on that, could stop the person in their tracks, saying, '*Where* are you going?' I remember doing this in my one-man show, taped at the Palladium, with a guy I had previously coaxed up on the stage to dance a top-hat-and-cane routine with three other guys. When he left the stage, he somehow lost his way and finished up walking right along the first row in front of me as I was announcing the only straight song in the show. I pretended to be very annoyed and got some big laughs out of the situation. You can't rehearse moments like this, can't think them up or write them in—they just happen or don't. That chap was marvellous, a gift from God. I could have kissed him! Far from being a nuisance, such audience-participation moments proved wonderful for

203

SNAP, for Summer Season Shows, and later on for my one-man shows.

*   *   *

I remember Val Parnell booking Jimmy Tarbuck for a Palladium show in October 1963. During this, Jimmy told me that his performance at the first rehearsal was so diabolical he couldn't even speak properly. When he got a message that Val wanted to see him, he thought, 'The sack!' Jimmy, *why* are you so nervous?' asked the great man. 'After all, it's *me* who should be nervous, not you—I booked you.' On the actual night, Jimmy thought his first and second gags went down like a stone, and that his third only produced a little titter. But when he went into his bread routine—the one where he played cards with a loaf of bread—he felt *that* did it! He was away. After the show the *TV Times* printed very flatteringly what Jimmy had said about his performance and me: 'My success on the show was thanks in no short measure to a certain compère with a big chin and an even bigger heart— Bruce Forsyth. His build-up *really* got the audience on my side.' I was touched.

I was not so happy, though, on the night I was introducing Adele Leigh on *SNAP*. 'Adele will sing the gypsy song from—' I began, then my mind went completely blank. I just couldn't remember the title of the song. With the camera full on me, I looked helplessly at Cyril Ornadel, the conductor. '*Countess Maritza*,' mouthed Cyril. But lip-reading's not so easy. Thinking I'd picked up the cue in the nick of time, I announced 'Carissima!' with such a happy triumphant smile that it was a bitter

204

disappointment when I realized afterwards how wrong I'd been. But as Val Parnell very sweetly said to a journalist afterwards, 'Bruce restored goodwill at once by saying, with that disarming smile of his, "I made a proper mess of that, didn't I?" This instantly endeared him to the public—both in the theatre and at home—who prefer their compères to be human like themselves, rather than faultless supermen.' Maybe Ed Sullivan wasn't that bad after all!

Val was always telling wonderful stories about how he could always glean how the public felt about a show by the telephone calls that would come through his office after a particular act. Girls thought nothing of ringing up from Glasgow or Yorkshire just to say: 'Please ask Cliff Richard to sing "Living Doll" for me,' and one very upset old lady telephoned to say she'd lost her cat on Putney Common. Would he please tell Bruce Forsyth to alert viewers in the area.

Then there were his Tiller Girl anecdotes. Each Sunday after they had appeared on stage, a man used to ring Val's office and ask to speak to one of them. 'Any one'—he wasn't fussy. Val was always polite to viewers but, after two months, this chap was proving tiresome. So, with all the severity he could muster, he said: 'For Pete's sake, will you stop ringing up every time the Tiller Girls are on!' The man, slightly taken aback, said: 'Who are you?' Out of devilment, Val replied severely: 'John Tiller!' Val never heard from him again and, as he said at the time, 'I hope the guy doesn't discover that old man Tiller has been dead for more than thirty years.'

I also vividly remember a night when the

comedian Vic Oliver was the top of the bill. During the four o'clock tea break, I said to him: 'Vic, d'you remember the man who used to run a hire-car service and used to drive you from theatre to theatre when you were "doubling" the music halls . . . and always boring you with tales about his boy who wanted to go into show business . . .? Well, that was my father and I'm that boy!' He was so surprised, and remembered my father with such warmth. 'If I'd known he was your father,' he said, 'I'd have given him a bigger tip.'

Another memorable night—but not for such a happy reason—was when Teddy Johnson and Pearl Carr were on *SNAP*, the same year they were also, like me, in a Blackpool Summer Show. Unable to get a sleeper on the train, they hired a chauffeur-driven car and, with me on board, started the journey south immediately after the show. Just outside Wigan we nearly lost our careers, let alone our lives, when a lorry whose driver had fallen asleep at the wheel approached us head-on for about ten agonizing seconds. He was awakened by the prolonged sounding of our driver's motor horn just in time to swerve clear. Teddy, Pearl and I ended up on the verge. We were all very shaken, but unhurt. All this frantic rushing to and fro, of course, was due to the fact that *SNAP* was assembled, rehearsed and presented on a single day—and a Sunday at that. Despite our quivery knees and shaky hands, the show still went ahead that night. Times like that make you wish you had a different job.

CHAPTER SEVEN

QUICK CHANGES

By 1962, I was becoming seriously overworked and spoiled for choice. My career had burgeoned beyond my wildest dreams—and beyond what was humanly possible for any one performer to cope with. With so many new opportunities on offer, I had to make a decision for the sake of my health. I decided to pull out of television for a while and not compère the next two series of *Sunday Night at the London Palladium*. What I most wanted to do now was take up two new challenges and appear in a three-hour panto, *Dick Whittington* at Manchester, which involved two shows a day, six days a week, until March. Then follow this with a Summer Season revue of the stage show *Every Night at the Palladium*. During this time Norman Vaughan, a comedian who always talked in what the papers described as 'jerky telegrams', and who was married to an ex-Folies Bergère dancer, took over my job. And he did it very well. Older readers may remember he had his *own* catch-phrases: 'swinging' and 'dodgy'.

In Manchester, when a *Daily Herald* journalist caught up with me rehearsing the pantomime, I said, 'I vowed never again to work seven days a week. My health is more valuable to me than money.' The *Daily Mail*'s headline read, " 'I decided," he said, "to live a little longer . . .' ", and went on in a very complimentary mood: '*Sunday Night at the London Palladium*, already shorn of its

207

Tiller Girls, is now shorn of its compère, Bruce Forsyth. To some of the viewing millions this news will merit the same gravity as if the Government had fallen. He has decided to put *Dick Whittington* at Manchester first—an act that reveals quite a lot about Bruce Forsyth . . .' I suppose, looking back, it could have been, as it obviously was, considered a radical career decision, not dissimilar in some respects to those I had made in my Windmill days. But I have always believed that life entails taking risks and following your heart. And I have certainly never regretted following mine. Anyway, I did return to *SNAP* again in September 1963.

I suppose it was Glyn Jones, an American guy who used to look after Bernard Delfont's top-of-the-bill stars, who taught me how to relax during particularly tough work situations. We met at a time when I was touring, doing twelve shows a week in variety plus *Sunday Night at the London Palladium.* One night Glyn, having looked hard at me, said, 'Bruce, you're very very tired.' I had to admit I was whacked. 'Well,' he said, 'you have a couple of hours before the first house, you know. Why don't you get some rest? Haven't you got the *SNAP* mattress with you?' I nodded. The famous *SNAP* mattress was a prop in my current act. In the Palladium show, it was used for a game in which two people were asked to cram three days of their married life into a time limit of under sixty seconds. For this, they had to keep jumping on and off the mattress.

'Then wait there,' Glyn said, picking up the phone and asking two stagehands to bring the mattress up to my dressing room.

'Go into your room for half an hour,' he added,

'and we won't let anybody bother you.'

'I never do this,' I protested.

'Go on,' he said firmly. 'Just relax. Close your eyes and try to blot everything out. You're tired. Give your mind and body a rest.'

'I don't know,' I replied doubtfully, thinking this might make me feel worse.

'Go on . . . Do it just once for me.'

So I did. And he was right. It did help. Ever since then, whenever I am doing a television or stage show, I pin a 'Do Not Disturb' note on my door, and rest for at least thirty minutes or an hour. If my dressing room hasn't got a settee or an easy chair, I simply sit in an ordinary armchair and just let my limbs go and relax completely. Even if I don't fall asleep, at least I relax and allow my mind to clear. Then I always feel as if I've recharged my batteries and am ready to go. I've become very good at it. As I sit there, I've often thanked Glyn Jones for suggesting this. Maybe this also explains an incident when, before appearing in a new show, I had to have a medical test for insurance purposes. The nurse, having attached all those rubber sucker things to my chest, went into her cubicle and said: 'Okay, Mr Forsyth, just relax a moment.' After a long pause, she added: 'Oh, you *really* can relax, can't you?' 'How do you know?' I asked. 'Because it's all registered on my instruments,' she replied!

That's not to say I've sailed through every medical check-up I've had. Once when I was quite young and I'd been suffering some abdominal pain, my doctor sent me off for an X-ray. Anyone who's had this sort of test will know what I'm talking about when I mention the barium meal they make you have. It's a porridge-like drink that shows up on the X-ray, so that the doctors can see what's going on inside. Anyway, on this occasion I was given a glass of barium meal ready to drink when I was instructed to do so.

'OK, swallow a few mouthfuls,' said the operator from behind his screen. So I did.

'Go on, drink a little,' he said again.

'I have,' I replied.

'Well, have some more.' So I did.

'Have some more,' he repeated.

'I have!' I again replied.

'Really? Well, have some more then!'

'I can't,' I answered, 'it's all gone!'

'What?'

'It's all gone!'

There was a long pause, then he said, 'I know it's difficult with the machine against your chest, but would you bend forwards as far as you can, and dip your left shoulder?'

I did what I was asked. Finally, he shouted 'Ah! There it is!'

He explained that I had a condition that in layman's terms is called a 'cup and spill' stomach. It means that food can get lodged in the upper part of your stomach and only move when you bend forward and dip your left shoulder. I was advised from then on not to eat large meals, and that if ever I felt the same pains to do the same movement, which would ease them. I still have a check-up for this every year—but I'd rather have porridge than the barium!

I never eat before a show. If I do have a meal, it has to be at least three hours beforehand. But I always drink a glass of Complan in my dressing room. The good thing about *this* liquid food is that

210

it contains all the vitamins and nutrients you are supposed to get from a good meal. When I come offstage I am always very thirsty, and I have a drink. This doesn't have to be an alcoholic 'pick-me-up'. I'm very fond of Ribena, which I have either iced or hot, according to the weather. Having satisfied my thirst, I'm ready for a meal. I know some performers like to eat a doorstep-size sandwich before they go on, but I can't do that. It's probably because I move around so much when I'm working, or my cup and spill stomach.

When I'm on the golf course in Puerto Rico I always have a big bottle of Gatorade with me. This is very good if you're perspiring and risking dehydration, because it replaces all the salts you have used up. American footballers keep gallons of this stuff on the side of the pitch and, at the end of a game, if they've won, they pour a great big barrel of it all over their coach! I also take with me a banana and a tin of Ensure (a vitamin shake) when I'm playing golf and, halfway round, after nine holes, I eat and drink these. Come to think of it, I don't really play golf, I just have a picnic! Dr Eddy Shelton, a retired dentist, is a regular partner of mine at Dorado Beach. He's eighty-two, plays every day, and hits at least two buckets of balls before starting a game. After eighteen holes, he always says: 'D'you wanna play a few more holes?' This year he even got me to play thirty-six holes without a break, except for my little picnic. This took six and a half hours. He's amazing, but I couldn't play with him all the year round!

*　　　*　　　*

So it was that, in September 1963, I returned to *SNAP*. I really did meet some wonderful people during those years, and it was even better when a number of them actually became my friends and, icing on the cake, golfing partners. One was the film star, Stanley Baker, later to be internationally acclaimed for producing and starring with Michael Caine in the film *Zulu*. He was a wonderful character, one of a whole gang of us who regularly played golf together. And it was always such fun to be with him on golfing holidays in Spain or Ireland. On one particular occasion, as I came out of a Spanish clubhouse, there was Stanley with Sean Connery studying a map they had spread out over the bonnet of a car. It was obvious from their conversation that they were considering buying some land in Spain, and were taking the matter very seriously indeed. Stopping behind them, I peeked between them at the map. 'Well, Sean, I prefer this land on the east,' Stanley was saying at that moment, 'but if you don't agree, let's toss for it.'

'I think the land on the west might suit me better,' Sean was replying.

'Well . . .' said Stanley, 'to be honest, I think the whole strip is valuable—not for now, perhaps, but for later on.'

'But maybe the land on the west might be the best choice,' Sean replied thoughtfully.

'Well . . . I think . . .'

And so they continued, on and on, almost in the character of their film roles.

Still peeking at the map through the middle of them and with Stanley's star role in *Zulu* in mind, I interrupted and said, 'And if the Zulus decide to attack you from the north, over that hill, you'll all finish up in the bloody sea.' Before they could turn on me, I rushed into the car park and got away faster than 007 in his Aston Martin. Thank God I did! They'd have killed me. Neither was in the mood for seeing the funny side.

I often went to stay in Stanley's house at Gualdamina with Kenny Lynch and my friend Leslie Vowles, and we always ended up as Stanley's staff. I would be chauffeur and Kenny—because we had to have a nice log fire at night when it got chilly and we were playing cards or swopping stories—would be in charge of logs. Leslie, because he once ran a hotel and was very good in the kitchen, would be the cook. Stanley? Well, he just kept a low profile and let his staff get on with it! We were happy to, we were all having a marvellous time.

Jimmy Tarbuck is another chap who's not only great company but is blessed with a wonderfully quick brain. On certain occasions and at certain functions he is marvellously 'on the ball'. I've known him for many years. In fact, Dickie Henderson and I were responsible for him learning to play golf. And what did he do as soon as he was proficient? He became better than we were! It's something I, for one, have never forgiven him for, but we still manage a lot of laughs along the way. Jimmy knows only too well that I can be a bit of a 'Victor Meldrew' on the course. But that's not surprising, because I am the unluckiest golfer in the world. '*Look* at that . . . *Look* what's happened to my ball . . .', I carry on ad nauseam. On one occasion we were playing in Sotogrande, Spain, and before we started to play, Jimmy straight up-front, said: 'Okay, Bruce, we haven't played for a while, so *no* moaning. You moan so much, it drives us all mad.'

'Okay,' I said, suitably contrite. 'I *won't* moan. No matter what happens I *will not* moan.'

We reached the third hole, not a very long hole, all hit pretty good drives, and it was my turn to play. There were bunkers all around the green and one right in front of the flag. Behind this bunker, a rake had been stuck in the ground in an upright position. This was not 'par for the course' because people usually lay rakes down. 'Now look,' I said to Jimmy, 'I haven't moaned up till now, have I? Even though I shouldn't have gone in that bunker in the last hole, I didn't moan, did I?'

'No,' he said warily. 'You didn't moan, Bruce.'

'Well,' I said, 'I'm *not* going to moan now. But look . . . *if* I hit that rake and, let's face it, the handle of the rake is only about an inch wide, I'm going to have a moan.'

'Okay,' he said resigned, '*if* you hit the rake . . . But never mind the bloody rake, just hit the ball.'

I hit the ball with an 8-iron and up it went into the air. It was coming down beautifully, heading straight for the green, when, lo and behold, it hit the rake and bounced back into the bunker. Jimmy looked at me, I looked at him, and neither of us could believe it. Defeated, Jimmy said: 'Okay, Bruce, you can have a bloody good moan now.' Did I? What do you think!

Eric Sykes is another guy I've always been very fond of and greatly admired. When the Variety Club gave a luncheon in his honour a few years back, I presented him with a lovely box of cigars— his favourites. You see, over the years, Eric and I played a lot of golf with Sean, Jimmy, Kenny

Lynch, Ronnie Carroll and Glen Mason. And whenever dear Eric played with me, he was nearly always smoking. On the tee, he'd place the cigar very carefully on the ground before he teed off. After he'd done this, I'd invariably say things like, 'Good shot, Eric,' or 'That was a bit to the left,' or 'I've got it marked.' Then, nine times out of ten, as I walked on to the tee, wearing of course my spiked golf shoes, I would spike a hole right through one of his expensive cigars! This happened so often, it became a joke between us. Sometimes Eric would remember to take the precaution of putting his cigar about five yards from the tee, so that I couldn't possibly step on it. But then, from force of habit, he'd forget and, time and time again, would put the cigar down in the usual place, and I would duly spike it. Given this, it was only right and proper that I should have made the presentation at the Variety Club luncheon!

I really can't praise Eric enough. Born in Oldham in 1923, he performed in service shows in the RAF and, after his discharge, became a brilliant gag-writer before writing scripts for radio shows, such as *Bandbox* and *Educating Archie*. In his heyday, he was one of Britain's highest-paid scriptwriters, and was the creator of his own BBC series, *Sykes*. His humour was simple, innocent, devoid of malice or offence, and included some wonderful slapstick situations. He was also a very talented actor—all in all, one of show-business's funniest lovable men. Almost totally deaf, he also wrote and directed silent films, such as *The Plank*, one of my all-time favourites. Yes, I really should go and see him and present him with some more of his special cigars.

I could go on and on about all the special people I've met, but I'd better save some stories for later. I ought to keep the main story moving along. Now, Robert Nesbitt, who worked with Bernard Delfont at Moss Empires, had had a brilliant idea—one that was to prove a star-spangled cabaret success for many years. His plan was to turn Moss Empires' London Hippodrome Theatre, situated in London's Leicester Square, into a theatre-cum-nightclub-restaurant called The Talk of the Town. Able to seat about eight hundred people, the theatre's stalls were subsequently converted into a spacious, central, open area to house a raised stage, complete with orchestra, and dining tables surrounding the stage. There was also more dining space in the dress circle. Despite all the renovations, there was still a lovely feeling of theatre about the place and stars loved to perform there. In fact, Frankie Vaughan and I hold the record for the most performances there.

Part of Robert's plan had been to expand his Talk of the Town idea countrywide by converting at least ten more of Moss Empires' theatres. But, unfortunately, the management of Moss Empires didn't go for the idea. Had Robert succeeded, I'm sure Britain's highly successful cabaret scene would have survived for much longer. Many British artistes and, I'm sure, many American artistes too, would have been happy to tour these theatre-clubs. And the Talk of the Town productions, including all the showgirls and different sets, could have moved on to the other venues, and thus helped the individual shows to pay for themselves. They would also have provided lots more work for artistes and production teams. Robert had had the foresight to

216

say to Moss Empires, 'This is the coming scene. Let's do it all over the country.' But . . . as always, it seemed to me, people on the management side of show business, although very happy to take money out, are not always so happy to risk putting money in. Robert's idea would also have had the advantage of theatre management being able to keep the theatre-cum-restaurant scene under their own control. Such places, those days, were generally run by individual owners, and very few were built properly. There isn't really a nightclub circuit now.

Anyway . . . one of the Talk of the Town regulars was a favourite singer of mine, Dorothy Squires. In her day Dorothy was, in many people's view, and not least mine, one of show-business's all-time 'greats'. She had a truly force-to-be-reckoned-with voice and a dynamic way of putting songs across. I always judge a singer by whether they make you listen to the words, and when Dorothy sang every word penetrated your ear and hung around in there. She really was a great performer. I didn't know her very well, but I did work with her on a couple of variety bills. The first time was quite early on in my career when I was a second-spot and she was an excellent top-of-the-bill. Dorothy was happy, a bundle of fun in those days. She was married to the actor Roger Moore, a very handsome guy who was the star of the TV series *The Saint*, and later took over from Sean Connery as James Bond's 007. Her language could be a bit strong at times, but she was just great with all the lads and we shared loads of laughs with her. It was quite common then to be on a bill with stars who were not that friendly, but Dorothy always found time to say 'hallo', chat, and be amenable to the theatre staff.

The time I remember her best, though, was when she was booked for a season at The Talk of the Town. Her marriage to Roger, whom she loved so very, very much, had just broken up. I went along with Billy Marsh to the opening night. Because Dorothy was still so deeply affected by the break-up, she had included in her repertoire that evening every sad, heartbreaking love song ever written—'The Man Who Got Away . . .', 'Can't Help Loving that Man of Mine', 'It Had to be You', and so on. She sang these heart-rending tear jerkers for an hour or more before finishing, as she always did, with a great big belter of a number about not being able to face life without her man, which went on, and on, and on. Oh, dear! My heart bled for her. And, although everybody by now was feeling a trifle depressed themselves, they all responded by standing up and giving her a great ovation. Billy and I were sitting next to Evelyn Taylor, a wonderful character and one of the best women agents in British show business. A petite lady, Evie looked up at me and said: 'Oh, Bruce, wasn't she absolutely marvellous. This is what ******* show business is all about.' Billy and I had to look away because we couldn't help grinning at her choice of word; or believe that she thought show business was all about people going on to give such free vent to their personal emotions! *That*, we thought, was quite something for such an experienced agent. But I loved dear Dorothy a lot, thought she was wonderful. And I, for one, never minded her wearing her heart on her sleeve.

And so it was that the next big excitement in my

professional life was my own cabaret debut at The Talk of the Town on 4 May 1964. It was a nerve-racking 'mega-time' occasion for me, with a lot of showbiz stars in the audience including singers Frankie Vaughan, the Searchers, Tommy Steele, Alma Cogan, the King Brothers, my golfing friend Ronnie Carroll, Millicent Martin, the Beverly Sisters and Gary Miller; comedians Norman Wisdom, Harry Secombe, Morecambe and Wise, Max Bygraves, Roy Castle, Tommy Cooper, Frankie Howerd, Des O'Connor and Don Arrol. What a gathering for a debut! And what a different place from my early days with Penny in cabaret. This was a superb, sophisticated, glamorous, glitzy venue, there were plenty of opportunities for interchanges between performers and the audience, and I felt very much a part of them and the warm ambience of the place. Despite the presence of food, silver cutlery, champagne and glasses, The Talk of the Town attracted a nice crowd who looked forward every bit as much to the cabaret as the food and drink, and listened to the performers.

It was a great night, and the reviews were marvellous. I particularly liked what the *Musical Express* said: 'Bruce Forsyth proved a smash hit in his debut cabaret season at The Talk of the Town. He clowned, sung, danced and impersonated his way through fifty minutes of fine entertainment. There were impressions of Nat King Cole, Anthony Newley, Frank Sinatra (complete with hat and upturned coat collar), Frank Ifield and, as a finale, Sammy Davis Jr (talking, singing and dancing as, until now, this writer thought only Sammy could).'

219

What a great pity we no longer have The Talk of the Town. I would give anything to appear there again.

*   *   *

Back at *SNAP* once again, I was in a dilemma. The Palladium had made me a star and I loved the show. People knew and recognized me as part of it. But . . . around this time, *SNAP* was also demanding a bit more of me than I had to give. I had found myself at a bit of a crossroads: should I continue to travel to London each week from Totteridge for the Palladium—which, in addition to other things, would mean a seven-day working week for me? Or should I concentrate on new shows, such as *I'm In Charge* in Blackpool, and the pantomime which was to follow in Liverpool, and only make occasional guest appearances at the Palladium? In Blackpool—and later in Liverpool— I would be playing for six nights a week, plus matinees. If I then travelled to the Palladium each weekend, it would mean getting the night sleeper on Saturday night, doing a whole day's rehearsals on Sunday before my actual television performance in the evening, and then returning to wherever I was supposed to be on the Sunday-night sleeper. On this schedule, I would not have a single day off, and it clearly wasn't a sensible, healthy option. Should I settle for appearing every eight weeks—or possibly at briefer intervals—on *SNAP*, I wondered. This, I hoped, would be some consolation for the big gap that would be left in my life if I actually left the Palladium.

But, out of the blue, the situation was resolved

for me. Thanks to *SNAP* and its 'Beat the Clock' reaching twenty million viewers and changing me from an unknown comedian to a household name, Arthur Lewis, the American producer, who lived in London and produced musicals with Delfont, offered me the star role in what was to be a West End production of the Broadway musical *Little Me.* 'This musical', he said, 'is tailor-made for you, Bruce.' He even suggested I should go to the States to see it. So, in the end, never one to resist a challenge, I did decide to leave *SNAP* at the end of the 1964 series and branch out. *Little Me* would be a marvellous new challenge. By the following June the papers were full of the show's new host, Jimmy Tarbuck, landing my 'plum' old job as its compère. 'Is it', reporters kept asking me, 'the money-for-jam job that we think it is when we're relaxing in front of our TVs?'

I told them that the Palladium job was actually a great strain because you had to do it every week for a large slice of the year. Eventually you got to the stage where you'd used up all your material and had to try out new material live in front of twenty million people. And no matter who wrote it, there was no guarantee people would actually laugh. The show also went on for a long time, from September to the end of May—forty weeks a year—and as compère you were under the public eye every week during those months. The job was also a kind of in-between job—not enough on its own to keep you occupied for a whole week, but if you worked at something else, you risked overdoing it. The ideal for me, I suppose, was two nights at a club or cabaret, plus the Palladium.

I was very pleased when my mate Jimmy took

over my job as compère for the next series which began on 26 September 1965. But not so pleased when Lew Grade—and possibly Val Parnell—decided not to include 'Beat the Clock' any more. I think Jimmy would have made an excellent job of this game, which was such an important and popular part of show. The problem was that the television critics, who always seem to be so dismissive about games, were forever criticizing it, saying why do we have to put up with this in a good variety show? In the end, I suspect the producers bowed to their opinion and dumped it. A great shame, in my opinion, because the audience loved it and *SNAP*'s ratings never rose above the heyday figure of twenty million after that.

Much of the credit for the success of the show in those days should go to the four wonderful directors that I was fortunate enough to work with—Brian Tesler, Albert Locke, Francis Essex and Jon Scoffield. Each of these chaps was incredibly talented. I had great respect for Brian and was so pleased for him when he became a member of London Weekend Television's hierarchy, and then its chairman. Dear Albert was a delightfully enthusiastic man, a real 'workhorse', who always got the job done, whatever the difficulties. Francis Essex was simply a joy, and I was thrilled for him a few years back when the West End stage show he co-wrote, *Jolson*, was produced, based on the life of Al Jolson. And, last but by no means least Jon Scoffield was a marvellous guy who was always, whatever the stresses of the job, such fun to be around. I really was very lucky to work with directors for whom I had such respect, and whom I could trust to make the most of whatever talent I had. *SNAP* was a team effort which, in their hands, successfully faced down all its rivals and, thanks to them, remained the top show on ITV.

Little Me is probably the best thing I will ever do in theatre. I don't think anything else could come along that would prove so satisfying. I played seven characters and had twenty-nine costume changes—one every three or four minutes. My roles ranged from a 16-year-old boy in short trousers to the 88-year-old miserly, wheelchair-ridden Mr Pinchley. The plan was to do four weeks' rehearsal in London before opening in Bristol for a two-week run on 29 October. My only regret was that when the show transferred to London's West End on 18 November 1964, it went to the Cambridge Theatre. Having been built as a cinema, this was a horrible place—and I was heartbroken when I heard the musical was going to be put on there. It didn't have much in the way of boxes for a start, and was stone cold. Even when a theatre's empty, you can feel its atmosphere just by walking on the stage. You can tell immediately what it will be like when the audience is present. But, despite all the disadvantages of the Cambridge, *Little Me* became the 'smash hit of the season', and my reviews were wonderful. I was no longer pigeonholed as a 'game-show host' or just a 'variety performer'.

There were some wonderful songs in *Little Me*. 'I've Got Your Number' was a show-stopper which Swen Swenson, a great artist, did as a solo, and so was 'The Rich Kids Rags', which the dancers did as snooty, toffee-nosed kids, with their noses in the air. 'Deep Down Inside' was another beautiful number that I did as the Steptoe-like character,

223

Old Man Pinchley. I performed this in a wheelchair, being wheeled up and down the stage, backwards and forwards, sideways, everywhere! When the kids—the dancers—cavorted around me while
I was singing, their wonderful vitality and exuberance helped make it another show-stopper. The great Bob Fosse was the choreographer, and his contribution was absolutely wonderful. Later on in 1973, by which time he had deservedly become a director, he was the only person ever to win an Oscar, Tony and Emmy in the same year. The humour he brought to our show was so special.

At the beginning of June 1964, I had to go to Bournemouth to do another of my Summer Season Shows. While there, I rented an apartment. By now, I knew my marriage to Penny was over. Then, as if I didn't have enough on my mind with the Summer Show, *Little Me*, and my marital problems, I met Ann Sidney, a nineteen-year-old hairdresser, who had won Bournemouth's 'Miss Front Page' beauty contest, at a bistro. A friend of mine had arranged to meet her there, and suddenly couldn't make it—honest! So, in the end, Ann and I had dinner together, during which I told her that Penny and I were separated. Although this was entirely true, it must have sounded like an old line. We went on to see more of each other. Two weeks later, Ann had competed in and won the 'Miss United Kingdom' title in Blackpool and was suddenly in the limelight. As 'Miss UK' she was the lucky girl who would represent Britain in the 'Miss World' contest in a few weeks' time.

Ann, as readers can imagine from her success, was an exceptionally beautiful girl. We went out together whenever we could and I was forever sending her flowers and little gifts—and good-luck telegrams, of course, while she was competing in the 'Miss UK' competition. When she stepped off the plane from Blackpool, her mother, father, grandmother, and Matt Monro and the singing Dallas Boys were there to greet her. I was there, too, in the background, and eventually stepped forward to give her a peck on the cheek and whisper, 'Well done, darling.' Dozens of photographs were taken that day, but the one that was splashed all over the papers the next morning was of Ann and me. Alongside it was a story that suggested we were having an affair. Ann, realizing this press coverage might damage my career and her chances in the 'Miss World' contest, was upset. Her father was upset, too.

Very concerned for her with this story running in the papers, I arrived at her parents' home at one o'clock in the morning—not the time they were used to receiving visitors—and said: 'It's all *my* fault for being at the airport and getting Ann involved in this press coverage.' I also told them that my marriage had been in difficulties for some time, that Penny and I were separated. The story went on that after I left, Ann's father said to her: 'He's a real gentleman.' But Ann and I did continue to see each other in Bournemouth, and when she later took a flat in Putney, South London, with a girlfriend of hers.

Penny had also read the reports. The day after the photographs were published in the newspapers, she told reporters that our marriage was 'over' and that she was coming to Bournemouth for 'a showdown'. According to the papers, my image as a 'happily married family entertainer' was over, 'irrevocably tarnished'.

When Penny came to see me, we tried to talk over lunch in a hotel. I've never forgotten this occasion. Our marriage had really turned sour, and the conversation didn't get very far. Penny was up and gone from the table in a flash. It was one of *those* moments that married people are so familiar with. I decided that, for both our sakes, things could not go on as they were; that Penny and I should formally separate, and I should move out of our lovely house in Totteridge.

During my last month in Bournemouth, I was learning the script of *Little Me* with its writer, Neil Simon. He spent the four weeks with me because, as it was originally an American show, it had to be anglicized for British audiences. With music by Cy Coleman and lyrics by Carolyn Leigh, *Little Me*'s storyline was based on a book by Patrick Dennis (the author of *Auntie Mame*) about screen star Belle Poitrine's progress from working-class girl to rich Hollywood divorcee. The girl came from the wrong side of the tracks, and one of the characters I played was Noble Eggleston, who came from the right side. In the anglicized version, he lived in Hampstead, and the girl lived in Camden Town! Because of the class-distinction aspects, the show actually made more sense here than it did in America—with, perhaps, the exception of Boston.

To make it London-based, there were many things to alter in the script, so it was a *very* busy time for all of us. The show ran for about two and three-quarter hours and I was rarely off the stage. I had to memorize the whole script in three weeks and, when it came to the last Saturday of the

Summer Season run in Bournemouth, even though I had been doing that show twice nightly, I suddenly had a mental block, became word-bound, didn't even know *where* I was. Exhausted from working too hard in the middle of so many personal problems, I had pushed myself too far.

This was the *only* time I ever blanked—'lost it', as they say—onstage. All performers are vulnerable to such moments, but we usually manage to get ourselves out of trouble. It's the momentary panic, in fact, that helps us to remember what we're supposed to be doing. It's the fear of being up there and the audience thinking we don't know what we're doing that saves us. We learn to ask ourselves: 'What was the last thing I did before this . . .?' Retracing our steps jogs our memory, leads us into the next thing. The alternative—if it's not too important an omission—is to forget that bit and move on to what comes next on the running order.

When I went to see Barbra Streisand on her world tour opening night at Wembley, there was amazing press coverage about her using autocues. I thought she was *wonderful.* To later audiences, Barbra said: 'I've been criticized for using autocues. But I do this because, in a live television show three years ago, I forgot the words of a song I'd been singing since I was a child. I just froze completely. So when you see the autocues up there, you can watch them if you want to, but I'm performing *here* and I'd rather you look at me! The autocues are my comfort blanket. And because I have that comfort-blanket, I'm able to perform. If I didn't, I couldn't. I *have* to have that security.' The audience, I'm glad to say, gave her a big, well-

227

deserved round of applause.

Why, I have often wondered, don't *we* have the equivalent of US female stars like Barbra Streisand, Judy Garland and Liza Minnelli? And why don't we have attractive comedy performers like Lucille Ball, Mary Tyler Moore and Goldie Hawn? These are never found in the UK. We have the talent, but it's not used in that way.

Anyway, never mind all that . . .! In the original Broadway show of *Little Me*, 'my' part had been played by Sid Caesar, a very good sketch comedian who was one of the biggest names in American TV, but he was not a dancer. One character was called Val-du-Val, a French nightclub entertainer, who sang. I did this with a tall, beautiful girl who was called Colette in the show. It was a lovely number which Sid Caesar, who could not tap-dance, had had to mime to the sound-effects of a drum to make it appear that he was tap-dancing. When it came to me, however, I said to Arthur Lewis, the producer of our show, 'As I *am* a dancer, wouldn't it be better, Arthur, if I actually did a chorus of real tap-dancing to strengthen the number?' Arthur thought this was an excellent idea. So I worked out a routine for this part of the act.

In the show there were some *stunningly* beautiful girls—not only among the dancers but among the singers, too. But I was in love with Ann Sidney, thought that what we had was very special, and I never took another girl out during the whole ten months I was in the musical. What control!

*   *   *

When I returned to London to begin the rehearsals

for the West End production of *Little Me*, I moved into an apartment—the first I ever bought—called Lord's View. Strangely enough, Penny had found this apartment for herself when she had decided that she was going to be the one to leave home. In the end, however, and after I had met Ann, Penny changed her mind and said she didn't want Lord's View. So, on my return, I lived in the apartment I had bought for her. It was a tiny place that overlooked Lord's cricket ground, but it was all I needed. Although I'd never been a great cricket fan, I could watch the cricket from the window, and there was always something happening in the ground—a function being prepared, and so on. It was always interesting, even in winter. I remained at Lord's View most of the time I was doing *Little Me*.

As well as having wonderful audiences for the show, we had some very special star guests to entertain. Judy Garland, Rudolph Nureyev—the magnificent ballet dancer—and the deaf singer, Johnny Ray, of 'Cry' fame, all came to see it. Nureyev actually came three times. I think he was trying to pinch some of my steps!

When Bob Fosse came to see the show, he was held in such high regard by all of us, who knew his name would go down as one of the all-time great choreographers, that we excelled ourselves. We were all on our toes for this performance. After all, he might be captivated by one of us, take us to Broadway. At the end of the show, we were all told to wait backstage so that Bob could come round, meet the cast and tell us what he thought of the production—whether he was pleased or not, whether he thought it was up to the standard of the

Broadway production. He complimented us all on our vitality, said the routines were all absolutely marvellous and that, although the show had been on for a couple of weeks already, our performance had been as fresh as a first night. He then turned to me and said: 'Oh, Bruce . . . *thanks* for the Val-du-Val sequence.' I was thrilled. He'd appreciated that I had made changes to his Broadway number, had done my own choreography, and was giving it his blessing. I should have replied: 'Can I have a choreographer's credit in the programme?' but I didn't. Why is it that I can always think of the best lines after an event! I was so happy that such a brilliant choreographer had praised me for what I'd done.

As well as singing and dancing, I also had the chance to do some serious acting in *Little Me*, which meant a great deal to me, especially as the show was being so well praised by the critics. I remember saying: 'I've proved to myself I can act, that I'm not just a compère-comedian man. *Now* I want to star in a film—and I'm just longing for the right script to come along so I can realize that dream.' But when a journalist asked me: 'Do you—like lots of comedians—want to play Hamlet?' I laughingly replied, 'I don't think that's *really* for me—my legs are too *thin* for tights.' Although my landlady in Southsea did like them.

Lord's View, 1964, was the first of a number of moves. Shortly after, I moved to Queensmead, St John's Wood, which I loved because the Horse Guards paraded in that area. At seven thirty every morning I'd hear the clip-clop of the horses' hooves and always knew the time without looking at a clock. Then I moved to a third-floor flat in

St Mary Abbotts Terrace, Kensington—which, coincidentally was once Tony Hancock's apartment—where I spent quite a few years. When I was living in Kensington, I had a most unexpected encounter with one of Ireland's most mercurial actors—Richard Harris, whom I'd met several times previously at showbiz do's. I had just had dinner with my tailor, Robbie Stanford, and he was driving me in his Rolls-Royce back to my flat, just off Kensington High Street. We'd just turned into the street and were slowing down to park when we saw this man, wearing a dressing gown, with his hair all over the shop. He staggered towards the Rolls, gripped hold of its angel mascot, and stood looking at the two of us sitting in the front seats. 'Good gracious!' I thought. 'It's Richard Harris.' He looked in a very strange mood.

'What shall I do?' Robbie asked nervously, thinking we were about to have trouble with a drunk.

'Don't worry,' I said, climbing out of the car.

'Hallo, Richard,' I said. 'Who's a naughty boy then? What are you up to? Where are you going in your dressing gown?'

'Ah, Bruce . . . ah, Bruce,' he replied in his lovely King Arthur of *Camelot* voice. 'It's lovely to see you . . . lovely to see you.'

'Richard,' I said, indicating towards Robert, 'this man is just driving me back to my flat. Is that all right with you?'

'Of course,' Richard said, 'of course. Away you go . . . but I'm going to have some fun tonight!'

I can imagine, I thought, taking one last look at his dishevelled hair and dressing gown. So . . . Robbie dropped me off at my flat and went on his way. I hadn't been indoors for more than half an hour when Robbie phoned me. 'What's the matter now, Robbie?' I asked.

'Well,' he said, 'I got back into Kensington High Street and Richard stopped me again. He grabbed hold of the statuette again, and I couldn't drive forward. So I got out and said, "I'm with Bruce." "Ah," he said, "Bruce's friend. Fine . . . On your way . . . on your way."'

When I picked up my newspaper the next day, I saw that Richard was about to start filming *Cromwell* that day! I think he was probably even more wicked than Cromwell at times. But there we are! I've *always* admired Richard, not just as an actor, but for the way he performs certain songs—especially 'How to Handle a Woman' from the Alan Jay Lerner and Frederick Loewe musical *Camelot*, which then, of course, became a blockbuster film, starring Richard, Vanessa Redgrave as Guinevere and Franco Nero as Lancelot. What a wonderful song 'How to Handle a Woman' is—one, we men, would be wise to listen to and learn from!

*   *   *

While back in London, and stuck into rehearsals proper for *Little Me*, Ann Sidney was competing in the 1964 'Miss World' beauty contest at the Lyceum Ballroom. For the dress rehearsals, I had a guy looking after me—a wonderful chap named Jimmy Lee—who was more than my dresser, more a personal assistant, companion and minder, and one of the funniest men I've ever met. He made sure everything was all right and that I wasn't

232

bothered by anybody. Late one evening, on the day of Ann's contest, I was rehearsing the scene where I was a mid-European prince who had lost all his money at roulette, and who had all these demanding women running after him and life was just too much. It was a *dying* scene! It had a wonderfully effective set. It looked as though I was in bed, but I was actually sitting in a chair which, because of its angle, looked like a bed. I was clad in a nightshirt, with all these people saying their final farewells to me, and singing the 'Goodbye' number, when Jimmy stuck his head round the set and said: *'She's won! She's won! She's "Miss World".'*

I couldn't believe it. It was the last thing I needed. There had already been more than enough publicity about our love affair, with stories headlined 'How Bruce Laughed the Beauty Queen into His Bed'—and now her success would generate more. I really *did* feel like dying at that moment! That evening, I went back alone to my apartment in Lord's View, telling myself that it must be marvellous for Ann . . . an absolutely wonderful night for a twenty-year-old. I knew there would be no chance of seeing her that night because Mecca, the sponsors, had told all the contestants that if they were crowned 'Miss World' and disobeyed their strict rules—or were involved in a scandal—they would automatically be 'out'. The winner would be kept under lock and key at London's Waldorf Hotel until the Coronation Breakfast the next morning—and for the next week.

About one o'clock in the morning, there I was in the apartment, drinking a glass of champagne by myself and toasting her success, when there was a tap on the door. There she was in her wonderful ball gown, but without the crown. If she *had* come with the crown, I'd have turned her away, telling her to try Buckingham Palace! She stayed for a couple of hours, then sneaked back to her hotel room undetected. With all the chaperones and security, I will never know how she did it.

Despite this wonderful achievement for her, I knew the time ahead was not going to be an easy period for us. Once crowned at the Coronation Breakfast, Ann would sign a £30,000 contract with the International Wool Secretariat to act as its worldwide ambassadress. And there was a clause in this contract that said any 'misconduct' on her part would mean instant sacking. It was obvious, for both our sakes, that we would have to keep our romance secret. So, while still appearing in *Little Me*, whenever I went to see Ann at her Putney flat, I dressed up in a selection of weird disguises. One night I appeared like Columbo, the TV detective, in a dirty old mac, on another as *The Pink Panther*'s Inspector Clouseau. I would put on wigs, hats, glasses—and even a funny little moustache. Once inside, Ann and I would fall about laughing. And, *before* anybody asks, I was very careful about my '*funny*' walk—and succeeded in avoiding detection!

This was not to last. Despite our secrecy, the story that I was having a love affair with Ann, 'reigning Miss World', would not go away. And soon the fun we had shared together began to wane . . . At Christmas 1965, when I had to go South Africa to appear in a variety show, Ann, who was with me, made me realize how much she hated the secret life we were living in England. But I honestly do not remember—what she subsequently told the press after we'd broken up—that she had asked me in the hotel room if I had any intention of marrying her. I'm sure she did not ask me this. She knew that I was having a hard time getting a divorce from Penny; and also knew that, when I was free, it was very likely that we would get married. I realize this was a particularly difficult time for Ann because that Christmas coincided with the end of her year as Miss World and, after all the attention she had been receiving, she was understandably feeling restless. So things could easily have become a bit muddled or, perhaps, even misreported. Either way, I also do not remember saying, as I was quoted as saying, that I wanted our relationship to go on as it had started, to remain as it was. It was later said that, in our hotel room one night, Ann drank too much alcohol and swallowed a lot of sleeping pills in an attempt to take her own life. There was a hurtful and inaccurate suggestion that she'd done this because I had refused to marry her. Ann may have had other reasons for drinking so much alcohol and taking the pills. And it might have been a mistake.

Thank God, Ann wasn't harmed by the alcohol and the pills, and she was very ashamed later. She flew home followed by loving cards, cables and letters from me. But this time things were not right between us and there was no going back. She was quoted in the press as saying her father was furious and that, unknown to her, had contacted me and said: 'If you *really* love my daughter, Bruce, you should leave her alone.' But her father didn't telephone me—I phoned him! I told him I thought Ann was so mixed up she should go home to Bournemouth for a while. Whether she did or not,

235

I've no idea.

The last time we spoke was when she telephoned me soon after I had met Wilnelia and shortly after a series of articles had run discussing our relationship of fifteen years before. I told her that after the articles, which contained so much that was untrue, I had nothing to say to her. We have lost touch since then.

CHAPTER EIGHT

CASTING DOUBTS

On 25 June 1965, *Little Me* had its 250th performance at the Cambridge Theatre and the ticket sales were still going strong. But in August, by which time most of theatreland had started to go through a bad patch, there was a shock in store. Bernard Delfont made an announcement to the press: 'We've had', he said, 'superb notices from the critics for *Little Me*—the best since *Annie Get Your Gun.* It's very sad, therefore, that we have to close *Little Me* on 4 September, after a ten-month run, but there has been a fall in the number of people going out midweek to restaurants, clubs and theatres.' I was heartbroken—the show was still doing so well.

The *Sun* ran a curious story headlined: 'How *Little Me* turned into a little flop without anyone really knowing why . . .' accompanied by a photo of me captioned: 'Bruce Forsyth last night outside the theatre where the glowing tributes on the billboards have suddenly acquired a hollow ring.'

236

The picture they had used was one of me walking by the theatre's billboards, with bullets that said, '• "A Great Big Winner", *Daily Mirror* • *"Little Me,* I suspect, will be at the Cambridge for a long time", *Evening Standard* • "Oh, what a night of triumph for Bruce", *Evening News'.*

About two weeks before the show was due to fold, something further happened that I found very hard to understand or take lying down. Something that, before this event, I hadn't even realized could happen. Late one afternoon, my sister Maisie phoned me and said: 'Bruce, a group of us would love to come along for the last night of *Little Me,* but it's proving impossible to get tickets.'

'Really?' I said surprised. 'I'll check up when I get to the theatre this evening.'

'Yes, *do,*' she said, 'because there are about fifty of us who'd like to come along.'

When I made enquiries at the box office, which Maisie had told me was not answering its telephones, I discovered that only a third of the seats were booked for the last night. So the next day I phoned several ticket agencies, which all said: 'The performance is sold out.' Knowing otherwise, I was baffled. Having personally arranged seats for my sister, I then rang her and said: 'Do me a favour, Maisie, keep phoning all the agencies and see if you can find out what's going on.' I then confronted Bernard Delfont who was, with others, responsible for a clutch of about five shows, including *Our Man Crichton,* starring Kenneth More and Millicent Martin, and *How to Succeed in Business Without Trying*—all of which I heard were running at a loss. *Little Me* was the only one that had had a successful opening and run, and I felt it

237

could still go on for years.

Delfont pre-empted my conversation: 'I hear you're saying that the last night is not fully booked. That's very strange . . . We should look into that.' And then he more or less dismissed my concern and moved on to other matters. But I remembered that Val Parnell had tried to talk me out of doing the musical—was he trying to tell me something? Just before I was going to America to see the show, he'd said: '*I've* seen it, Bruce. I don't think it has a chance in hell of being a success here. If you take my advice, you won't do it.' 'Well . . .' I replied at the time, 'I at least want to see it for myself.' It was then that I'd gone to see it, in Detroit. Sid Caesar was in the star role, and I could see that he didn't seem to be trying hard enough. Maybe, given that he also had this strange habit of coughing at the end of every line, he wasn't feeling very well. Nevertheless, I could still see that it was a wonderful production, and I thought with somebody out there *trying*—and if the show was anglicized as indeed it was, under Neil Simon's personal supervision—it could be a success.

But subsequently, everybody from management seemed amazed at how successful our show was at making money and how long it was running. It's true that when I was ill in the middle of the run with a flu-type virus that affected my throat, this didn't help, and caused us to lose a lot of audiences. But this is inevitable when the star of a show is replaced by an understudy. The success of any West End show's ticket sales largely depends on word of mouth. The people who go one week tell the people who go the next, and so on. So, two weeks of the show not being what it should be

238

can affect bookings for some weeks ahead. Nevertheless, I couldn't understand why nobody from the management seemed interested in investigating the London ticket agencies' claim that the house was full on the last night when it was not. When I confronted them with this, I expected somebody to come back to me with an explanation, saying 'so and so happened . . .' or 'the ticket agencies are pushing seats for other shows'. But there was no comeback—no feedback.

As I am a Pisces, I am always suspicious. When I saw that wonderful movie *The Producers*, I realized producers *could* build something up to be a flop so that it could be written off against tax. Was that why the *Little Me* box office was not answering its phones for ticket sales? Maybe I was clutching at straws in my disappointment. I will never know, but it was a wretched situation.

In any event, the last night was both wonderful and a *full house*—mainly, I think, because the management took enough steps to mean that I didn't have any more ammunition to take matters further. It was a hard lesson to learn but, in a way, it softened me up for even harder times that were to come.

So *Little Me* closed. I put all the last-night events behind me, realizing that, after all those wonderful reviews and tributes from fellow performers, I could be proud of myself. I remained sad about it finishing, but thrilled at the opportunity it had given me—and certainly had no regrets about performing in it. And it had done my morale all the good in the world.

*   *   *

Having realized while I was in *Little Me* that I could broaden my field and do other things, I accepted the part of the ghost in ABC TV's production of *The Canterville Ghost*. This was marvellous. A comedy, with a touch of pathos, I had to perform all kinds of feats and learn to walk through doors—as ghosts do! In August—to newspaper headlines that picked up on *Canterville*, such as: 'Forsooth! If it isn't Forsyth'—I also appeared as guest star on the first of a new six-part weekly ATV series, *The Frankie Vaughan Show*. At that time, Frankie's best-known number was 'Give me the moonlight, give me the girl, and leave the rest to me'. We were even known then as 'two of the best grins in TV'!

After that, I went to America. This was the first proper holiday I had had for three years, and I spent a wonderful time there playing golf with the singer Ronnie Carroll. How I have got this far without being sidetracked about golf again, I cannot imagine. Golfing readers, let me ask *you* a question: when you play golf—or talk about it—how many times have you seen people shrug their shoulders and say: 'It's *only* a game,' when they're really thinking, '*Is* it *only* a game?' Here, in my view, is what it probably is for them and me: an obsession, a religion, a way of life, a character-builder, a mental torture, a business lever, a business-breaker, a marriage-maker (if both play), a home-wrecker (if they don't), a relaxation (for only a few), a drug, a time-taker, a humbling experience, a humiliating experience, a walk into the sunset . . . or a walk into oblivion!

There are probably a few more, but I'm sure you'll have recognized at least two and, if they're

240

mostly on the 'down' side, can I suggest you just stand on the eighteenth green of your home club and watch the faces of the golfers when it's all over? How many of them walk off the eighteenth green with a smile on their face? But golf can be fun, too. If you have the right four-ball and a sense of humour, the dialogue and ad-lib lines are often worthy of the finest comedy. I certainly find it great fun—sometimes! Either way, from the moment I first became obsessed with it when I was a lad, I wanted to live next door to a golf course.

On my return from the holiday with Ronnie, I was very busy with more television work, rehearsing and recording shows. Besides a thirteen-week BBC TV series with musical guests, I signed a contract with ABC TV, which was based at Teddington and later became Thames Television, to make six hour-long spectaculars. And, according to press reports, the total cost of around £70,000 for this series made them the most expensive variety shows that ITV had ever produced. Philip Jones was the producer/director. I loved working with him because he enjoyed the shows so much himself. He was a real light-entertainment man; we were quite a team.

My first guest stars were Ronnie Carroll, with whom I had just been on holiday, the singer Kathy Kirby and Douglas Fairbanks Jr. Douglas was one of the most gentlemanly men I've ever met. We did a very funny sketch together called 'The Corsican Brothers'. He was so nice at rehearsals and he loved doing magic. He'd come in every morning and we'd all be looking forward to him performing another trick. He'd gather all the girls around him, show us his trick of the day—making something disappear, a card trick, or whatever. I've always regretted that I only did this one show with him.

Another of the early specials starred Cilla Black, Tommy Cooper and Frankie Howerd. Imagine Philip having to direct four people like us! But doing it was enormous fun. Frankie had been my favourite comedian since my RAF days, when I used to listen to him on *Variety Bandbox*. His timing was superb. One of our skits was based on the radio and TV programme, *University Challenge*. This featured just Frankie and Tommy. It began, as the real programmes did, with the two of them introducing themselves to the audience. Frankie, in a posh voice, said: 'I am from the University of [so and so], reading physics.' Tommy, in an equally posh voice, followed with, 'My name is Thomas Cooper from Oxford University, and I am reading pornography'! It really was a wonderful send-up of a serious programme. Frankie was a bit worried at first about being cast alongside Tommy who could be funny without even trying. Halfway through the day, poor old Frankie even got a bit green around the gills and said he didn't feel very well! But, believe me, when it came to the show they were both as funny as each other. We all got on wonderfully well and, in those kinds of situations, I often ended up as the 'straight' man. Well, somebody had to do it. In another part of the show I was allowed to be funny with the then up-and-coming Cilla, who not long before had been riding high in the charts with 'Anyone Who Had a Heart'. We sang and did some comedy together. She was a natural and, although she hadn't done any scripted dialogue before, Lionel and I went to see her and Bobby and persuaded them that she could do it. I

242

still wish I had a tape of that particular show so that I could watch it again.

Tom Jones was another of my guests. A very sexy singer—and what a mover!—he still, even as a grandfather, manages to set more hearts aflutter than anybody else I've ever known. And he has certainly had more knickers thrown at him than I have! We appeared in many shows together. But I particularly remember performing in a series he did for American TV, in which I played the part of the devil. Typecasting! During filming, Tom and I had lunch together every day in the Elstree Studio canteen. D'you know what he ate every single day for lunch? Braised hearts, washed down with champagne. Oh, how the other half lives!

Another of my ABC specials, scheduled for the Christmas period, included Miriam Carlin, who was renowned for her appearances in *The Rag Trade*, a popular television series about women working in a clothing factory. Miriam, a lovely lady and a wonderful sketch comedienne, played the shop steward and became a very big name. We did a very funny sketch together on owners who physically resemble their dogs. Believe me, many do! One woman came on with a poodle. She walked like her pet and had her hair coiffed in exactly the same way. Having featured several like this, Miriam, sporting a new blonde look, then came on with an amazing-looking Afghan hound, with the incredible name of Shangri La Simba II of Singapore. Afghan hounds, as you doubtless know, have a very long face. As I knelt down beside it, she said to the audience, 'Who could possibly look like an Afghan hound?' Everybody creased up with laughter, knowing that, if I'd been born a dog, I

243

would certainly have been an Afghan hound!

The singer Engelbert Humperdinck, Max Bygraves and Jack Douglas were others of my ABC specials' stars—and all wonderful guys to work with. Jack and I did a concert piece in which he was the conductor and I was the pianist. It finished up in total chaos, as you can imagine. It was one of those sketches that, no matter how many times Jack and I did it, we always ended up in hysterics ourselves. And I'm pretty certain that was the very first time I said what was to become another of my catch-phrases: 'Nice to see you . . . to see you, nice'.

I enjoyed doing those specials, which then continued for about three years. It's such a pity that programmes like these are never made now; that we are never given the chance to watch big stars performing sketches and songs with each other on television unless it's a 'special occasion' like Comic Relief. The fact that the Morecambe and Wise shows can be repeated time and time again and still achieve wonderful ratings proves that there is still an audience out there, hungry for this kind of light entertainment. Even in that heyday, I remember the *Evening News*'s 'Talking TV' column by James Green, noting: 'The BBC has tried storyline comedy in 57 different varieties. And in doing so has allowed variety to wither. Their handling of this has been inept and pathetic. Transfer to them Bruce Forsyth, Norman Vaughan and Dickie Henderson from ITV and they wouldn't know what to do with them.' So even then some critics were complaining about the lack of light entertainment. But it's nearly all gone now. Why? It's a crying shame for television and its viewers.

During November 1965, Eric Sykes gave the

world of TV a shock by deciding to quit his successful half-hour series. As I could understand only too well, he then flew off to Spain to his villa in Malaga for a golfing holiday. Eric had been complaining that *Sykes*, his BBC sitcom series with Hattie Jacques, was being put out against *Emergency Ward 10* on the rival channel. 'Why *should* artists have to compete against each other?' he asked. 'Why *should* they have to be worried about the ratings war?' In a further angry aside, he added that, apart from making appearances as a guest star or doing an occasional 'spectacular', he was quitting TV because it had become a matter of 'The bluer the joke, the louder the laugh' and 'There's now too much smut on TV'. Stars, he said, either love or hate the ratings-mania rat race, but he, for one, had had enough, thank you very much.

One thing that Harry Worth, Charlie Drake, Max Bygraves, I and others agreed on was that Eric had taken on the ultimate challenge by writing and performing in a weekly series. When interviewed by the *Evening News*, Harry Worth said: 'The rat race doesn't worry me unduly. It would be nice to find your show put up against a talk from the Stamp Collectors' Guild, but it's no good worrying about something you can't do anything about.' Commenting on Eric's announcement, I said: 'I only do single spots and specials these days, but I can see how tough it is for a performer and writer like Eric. But, then, I think you get this kind of rat race in every walk of life.' As I read this again today, it's obvious that the ratings war is going to get more severe. The more channels, the more competition. And in the end, who suffers? The audience, of course.

Because everything I do on stage is quick, on the double, I am always aware of everything and everybody when talking to an audience. That is why, when the lighting is dazzling, I don't like not being able to see anybody—the auditorium is just a black, empty space and it feels as if there's nobody there. I get lonely! So, whenever I can, I get the electrician to illuminate the audience, even if this is only possible for the first twelve rows. Then, if somebody does something, I can pounce on them—ask, 'What's going on?' Working with audience participation probably stems from my Summer Season days but, even as a child, I was always aware of the audience. My function is to get up on the stage and do something, the audience's function is to sit there, listen, look—and try to enjoy! And if they don't, I will tell them so! Even in my early days of variety, and when I worked at the Windmill, it was not unusual to see somebody reading a newspaper three or four rows back, or somebody who just decided to walk out. I knew this was because they didn't like me, and *I* had to suffer that. I knew they were thinking, 'Oh, this guy is going to be on for another five or six minutes. I don't want to waste my time listening to him. I'll go and get a drink.' All this is part of being a performer. I learned a long time ago that if you can please half your audience, you're doing well. It's the same today—especially on TV. It's impossible for everybody to like you.

Likewise, there were sometimes a couple in the third or fourth row kissing and cuddling each other.

On top of this I would look to see if there was a pretty girl in the audience who was enjoying my act. If there was, being of a flirtatious nature, I would check often to see if *she* was looking at *me*! Or when I played the piano, was she enjoying it— smiling? I picked out people like that. Also, in the old days, if I knew there was an agent out there, watching me, I'd certainly keep an eye on them.

So all these things went on while I was performing and, once I'd become a top-of-the-bill in theatres, I'd also check to see how good the 'house' was. This is called 'checking the house' because the manager comes round in the interval with what are called 'front-of-house receipts', to show you how much money is in from the evening's takings. Having judged in advance what the potential capacity of a theatre was, on the opening night, I could look at the stalls, circle and gods and do a quick mental estimate of how many people were present—how many 'bums on seats'. Then, when I got the receipts, I could gauge whether a manager was letting more people in for free than he should! You see, this sort of thing can affect your fee. Although many people think we work for a flat fee only, tops-of-the-bill—and even some second 'tops' if they are a big name—work for a basic wage plus a percentage of the takings.

Financial advantages aside, however much I may have longed to be successful at what I did, fame— being recognized everywhere—is a profound shock to the system, and has its problems. For example, I get requests for my ties, golf bags and golf hats to be auctioned for charity. People stop you in the street when you're trying to go somewhere or get something done. The most annoying members of the public, however, are those who just gawp at me, look me right in the face and then just laugh very loudly. They don't say anything, just react in a maniacal way. Thank goodness there are not too many of those. Most people are very kind.

After the second stage of thinking, 'How am I going to live with this?' I thought, 'Well . . . I've *got* to learn . . . Otherwise, it will get on my nerves so much I will have to become a recluse, or disguise myself whenever I go anywhere, or constantly avoid people when I go out.' When there's a big crowd, though, I've learned over the years to move very quickly. The alternative is to face up to the moment, revise your thinking and say, 'I won't let this drive me crazy. I'll accept it for what it is—very complimentary. Take it as that and enjoy it. It's part of your business and public relations!'

There are, of course, pluses as well as minuses in being recognized. If, for example, I want something that it's difficult to find, I make a couple of phone calls and can get through to the person I need to speak to and usually get what I want. And I can get into places I probably wouldn't if I was not who I am. I never have a problem when arriving at big get-togethers because my face is my ticket—but with more lines on it! The people on the door don't check to see if I have a pass or invitation. And if someone is with me, they let them in as well! So fame does have its perks—and most of the time people are very, very nice to you.

In restaurants—in order to be able to eat!—I always try to sit at a tucked-away table with my back to other diners, but this does depend, of course, on what kind of restaurant it is. What I don't like is when people, having recognized me,

248

wait until I've started to eat then come up for an autograph. I've learned to say, 'Could you just let me finish and then I'll give you an autograph with pleasure.' (Speaking of this, nine times out of ten when I'm at home and just about to start my meal, at that split second I'm wanted on the phone. This drives me crazy. It's quite a joke in the family.)

The most awkward time for signing autographs is when I'm playing in celebrity golf matches for charities. It's very difficult to concentrate when people keep coming up all the time. Having learned that I could expect hundreds of autograph-hunters on the last green, I now offset this *and* get some wonderful laughs out of the situation. What I do is sign about a hundred autographs on little pads *before* I go out, and keep these ready in my hip pocket or golf bag. I then line the waiting people up—mostly children—and hand the pages out like sweeties. Some people think I'm giving them a boring old stamped autograph, but every one, believe me, is handwritten. And this does mean I can get away more speedily to my car, or get a drink quicker in the clubhouse. I think this is one of my best ideas.

Now, it's about time I told you a bit about some of my famous catch-phrases. Like fame itself, they seem to hang around me, not always wanted—and often more amusing to others than they are to myself! As I've said, you'll notice that I avoided using one as the title of this book . . . The only one I did premeditate became, perhaps, the most famous: '*Nice* to see you, to see you, *nice*'. I got the audience to rehearse it with me before that series of six ABC 'specials'. But it wasn't until I did a *TV Times* commercial that it really caught on. In the storyline for the commercial, I was in a pub reading the *TV Times* when this guy came up to me and said: 'It *is* you, isn't it? It *is* you? Yes . . . with a straight-cut waistcoat . . . And what is it—"*Nice* to see you, to see you . . . *nice*". 'And *he*—*not* me—did the catch-phrase line. At the end of the ad, I then said straight to camera, 'I didn't know Harry Secombe was a Virgo.' The fact that this commercial was beamed into millions of homes got this catch-phrase moving. I was amazed at the effect it had. Immediately after that, when I was walking down a street workmen started shouting: '*Nice* to see you, to see you . . . *nice*.' I thought, '*Well* . . . isn't that marvellous. I haven't even promoted this one.' It was incredible that it had caught on like that. Catch-phrases can also, of course, drive you round the bend at times. After the initial, 'Isn't it marvellous? . . . everybody knows me—and my act', you sometimes think, 'Oh dear . . . have I got to live with *this* for the rest of my life? Is *this* what it is going to be like wherever I go?'

*   *   *

I mentioned that while I was appearing in *Little Me* I was very ill with a flu-type virus infection and that I had to take a couple of weeks off. It was one of the few times I was offstage during a run. The family doctor—the one I had used in Totteridge— came up to see me at the Lord's View apartment, and said that I needed twenty-four-hour care. 'You're in a bad way,' he said. 'Go home, stay there and rest.' Unaware of my marital situation, and certainly not knowing that I had now been

250

separated from Penny for seven months, he telephoned her and arranged for me to return to The Paddocks. Later, this homecoming was misrepresented in a *Woman's Weekly* interview, which quoted Penny as saying that I had phoned her and asked for a reconciliation! But this was untrue. Ann—who, at this time, was travelling all over the world because it was her 'Miss World' year—even rang me a couple of times while I was at Totteridge. Penny knew this—and I was very grateful to her for her care during my illness.

By way of some light relief, in August 1965 I was booked to do the voice-over commentary for the now-famous Brooke Bond PG Tips commercial with its star chimps. I wonder why they thought of me for this job? I may have a prominent jaw, but I don't jabber! Anyway, as a result of public demand—for the chimps, not me—the adorable chaps and chapesses were recalled from their three-year retirement to drink cups of tea and continue to charm us with their antics.

This brings me to my business manager, Ian Wilson—but no connection whatsoever with the above, honest! The star sign of both Ian—who has now been with me for twenty-five years—and me is Pisces. Ian first came into my life via John Davis, a golfing friend, who said to me one day, 'If you're ever looking for someone to help you—a kind of PA to go with you on the road—I know a young man who might be suitable.' When I said I was interested, he suggested that Ian, who was only twenty-one at the time, should come to one of my shows at the New London Theatre before meeting me. I learned later that Ian sat in the front row terrified I might pick on him—get him to come up

251

onstage. He was also terrified the first time he drove me. He'd never taken the wheel of a Rolls-Royce Corniche before, and began by having terrible trouble getting it out of the garage, then drove it like a hearse all the way to Thames Television: 'It does go over ten miles an hour!' I remember saying. Since that day, I've often had cause to regret that remark. Now, I'm forever saying: 'Slow down!' So, young Ian became my PA—stage manager, lighting director—and, in due course, my business manager. I'd better watch out—he may be after my job!

I think I'm very much a Pisces character, capable of seeing both sides of an argument but easily led—especially up the wrong path! I'm fairly even-tempered but, when I do lose my temper, watch out! Incompetence or unfairness is usually the trigger. The other curious thing about Pisces folk is that they're fine if they're a success, *but*—and this is *so* true of me—they're the worst sign of the zodiac to deal with when they're frustrated. They simply have to achieve something in life—be successful, or at least engage in something that gives them pleasure. I would have been terrible if I'd been a frustrated old pro, jealous of other people's successes. I'd have had sour grapes coming out of my ears. This reminds me of one particular occasion when something had gone wrong business-wise with a hoped-for film part, and Ian was with me in the kitchen. I was obviously moping, doing my Victor Meldrew, and said: 'I'm so unlucky.'

'*God, yes*,' Ian replied, 'you are *really* unlucky . . . Look at your career . . . this house . . . that Rolls-Royce out there . . . Your life's all crap, isn't it?'

He had a point!

*   *   *

I had always known that lots of famous stars had come to see *Little Me*; what I didn't know until I received an astonishing out-of-the-blue phone call from Lionel Bart was that he, too, had come to the musical—and had *loved* my performance. *Oliver!*, Lionel told me, having completed its highly successful stage run in the West End, was about to be made into a film—and there was some contractual difficulty with Ron Moody, who had played the stage part of Fagin so wonderfully well. Whether Ron did not fancy doing the film, which I find hard to believe, or whether it was a matter of him not being offered the kind of billing or money he thought he should get, I do not know. What I did discover from Lionel was that there was a problem. Having seen me play Old Man Pinchley, who was a sort of Fagin character in *Little Me*, Lionel said: 'Something's going on that I can't really explain right now, Bruce, but the producers are having some difficulties with Ron. This is just a tentative request to you, but *if* they can't come to an arrangement with Ron's management—and I really can't go into the ins and outs—would *you* be interested in playing Fagin?'

'*Lionel*,' I said, completely taken aback, 'I'd *love* to play Fagin. To do this film would be absolutely marvellous—the ultimate as far as I'm concerned.'

'Okay,' he said. 'I'll phone you again when I have more news.'

He did—a couple of days later—saying: 'The position is still the same. How d'you feel about it?

253

Could you be available?'

'Lionel,' I said, '*I will make myself available.*'

When I put down the phone, I was walking on air.

The third time Lionel rang, he said: 'Bruce, I haven't been looking forward to this call, but the situation's been resolved. Ron's going to do the film. I'm *so* sorry to have done this to you because it sounded as if you *really* wanted to play Fagin.'

I was winded—*so* disappointed. That part could have been the 'in' to a film career that I'd always hoped for, but never quite believed would happen.

This disappointment was one of the biggest 'downs' of my career. The possibility had only existed for a week, but I had built my hopes so high it took much longer than that for me to overcome the setback.

In the event, when the film was released in 1968, Ron was nominated for an Oscar.

Some years later, I had a similar experience with the film *Candleshoe*, which starred David Niven and Jodie Foster. Jodie was only about thirteen at the time—one of very few people who succeeded in going from being a big-big child star to a fully grown-up mega star. I was in Spain on a golfing holiday when I received a phone call from my agent, saying that *Candleshoe*'s casting director had been on to him, and that it was more or less certain that I had got the David Niven part in the film because David had turned it down, saying he wanted to spend time that summer in Gstaad with his family. For me, this was another breathtaking, walking-on-air moment. The casting director, I was told, had seen television footage of me, and it was now just a matter of meeting him the following week to talk things over.

Throughout the next week there were several telephone conversations about the meeting, and it was finally agreed that he would speak to me on the Sunday evening when I got back. On the plane home, the stewards came round with the newspapers. These were the days when the *Sunday Express* was a broadsheet, the most awkward type of newspaper to read on a plane. I was flicking through the pages, reading all the showbiz tittle-tattle, when I saw the following report: 'David Niven to play opposite Jodie Foster in *Candleshoe* . . . a wonderful opportunity for David who will play cameo roles of five different characters—handyman, gardener, footman, chauffeur and a colonel.'

My heart stopped—I could not believe it! The moment I arrived home, I telephoned my agent Billy Marsh who, very disappointed himself, said that he too had read the news in the *Sunday Express.* When I eventually spoke to the casting director, he said that David had changed his mind two days earlier. Evidently, once David heard that Jodie Foster had definitely accepted the part, he thought this would make *Candleshoe* a much bigger film and the whole project much more worthwhile from his point of view.

I was gutted—couldn't get it out of my mind for days, especially as it had come so soon after losing *Oliver!* Once again, it was like being offered—then losing—the Crown jewels. Both of those parts, which had come about because of *Little Me*, would have been ideal for me, would have placed me in an altogether different league, something I so wanted—and needed—at the time. But they were not to be. Ever since then, when anybody suggests the possibility of me doing something really special, I always approach the situation with extreme caution—and anticipate a negative. I've never again allowed myself to build my hopes so high only to risk having them dashed.

Looking back, one reason why I didn't do much in the way of film work was because Miff Ferrie had this daft habit of telling anybody who phoned that I was booked up for a year in advance! He thought that this made me sound good, but it was a disastrous strategy. Much better to make out that you are available even if you are very busy! I know, for example, that Dudley Moore only got the part in the film *10* because George Segal—who was originally cast for it—decided not to do the part, so Dudley got the role and it made him a megastar. If, like Miff Ferrie, Dudley's agent had said to the producers: 'I'm sorry, Dudley's not available for at least a year,' Dudley would have lost that chance. *Anything* can happen in the film business. Stars suddenly get ill, or don't sign their contracts, and the moment a producer says: 'Let's get someone else,' you need an agent who understands the business and says: 'Yes, he's available. When would you like him to start?'

As it is, I'll never get over the loss of all those films. To this day, I sometimes find myself thinking how different things would have been if I had played Fagin—Fagin more than any of the other parts because he was such a principal character and *Oliver!* would have given me a unique opportunity to play an in-depth film role which, having performed in *Little Me*, I knew I could have managed.

A film I *did* achieve a part in was *Can Hieronymous Merkin Ever Forget Mercy Humppe and Find True Happiness?*, based on the life story of Anthony Newley. I played the part of Uncle Limelight, a man who had been a very important influence in Tony's life. And Joan Collins—who was then married to Tony—was also in it. But, because the film had such an unusual, incredibly long title, there was no room—either above or below it—for anyone's name to appear in the credits!

What I love about Joan is that she is in real life exactly how she is in TV interviews—a lovely, warm-hearted extrovert who's always laughing at herself. During the shooting of *Hieronymous*, all of us were taken on location to Malta. And what I particularly remember about our time there, was the day we were ferried by speedboat to Gozo, a little island about half an hour from Malta. The schedule for that day's shoot included a scene of Tony standing on a mountain against a background of sea and clouds. For this, he was clad in a white robe, singing 'I'm All I Need . . . If I've Got Me Who Needs People?'—a wonderful number that he and Leslie Bricusse had composed together. Later that same day, I was to be filmed performing a musical number on a small stage that had been specially erected on the beach, and then—because all the cast were present—the finale was to be shot.

By lunchtime, however, those of us waiting on the beach—including Joan and me—received a message from on high, saying that Tony's scene was taking longer than anticipated and that the rest of us should return to Malta. On hearing this, Joan had other ideas: 'Let's make the most of being

here,' she said. *'Let's* have some fun . . . *Let's* party!'
In a flash, she had organized all the jeeps to go
down to a little village close by and load up with as
much food and wine as they could carry. In the
end, the drivers made three trips to and from the
shops and, thanks to Joan, we had a really
wonderful, memorable, impromptu party on the
beach. It was marvellous. But that's the kind of
person Joan is. Others, hearing they were not
needed that day, would simply have said, 'Okay'—
but *not* Joan! The return journey to Malta,
however, was not so much fun—it was a somewhat
groggy trip! As soon as we touched land, we all
took off to our beds. And nobody—and I mean
nobody—came down to dinner!

Another film I had a part in was *Star!*, the life
story of the revue artist Gertrude Lawrence. It
portrayed her rise from poverty to international
stardom. The film's director, Robert Wise, had also
seen me in *Little Me* and gave me the part of
Gertrude's father. Julie Andrews played Gertrude,
Beryl Reid played Gertrude's mother, Daniel
Massey, I remember, was Noël Coward, and Jenny
Agutter also appeared. Julie, Beryl and I had to
do an old-time musical number. Now old-time
dancing—like old-time tap-dancing—is done
mainly on the balls of the feet and, although it
always looks effortlessly graceful when watched on
screen, it's hard work and places quite a strain on
the calf muscles, even for a dancer like me. In
order to learn and rehearse the routine with
Michael Kidd, a great choreographer, I arrived in
Hollywood a week before Beryl. When she arrived
on the set during the second week of rehearsals, I
said to her before she started: 'Take it a bit easy,

Beryl. You'll find the routine rather a strain on the muscles.'

'Don't be so silly, Bruce,' she replied tartly. 'I've been dancing since I was five years old. What are you talking about? I'll be fine.'

'Beryl, darling, I'm just warning you,' I added. 'Take it easy.'

Anyway, next morning I thought I would give her a call to remind her what time we should go to the rehearsal. I phoned her room at the hotel, heard her say, 'Hallo,' and then the phone was dropped. I could hear her crawling about the floor, trying to retrieve it. I was getting really worried, wondering if I should call the police or an ambulance. Then I heard a weak voice say: 'Oh, hallo, Bruce.'

'Hallo, Beryl. Are you all right, dear?'

'Oh, my legs,' she groaned. 'I can't move, Bruce. I can't possibly rehearse today.'

'I did warn you, dear,' I said gently. 'But you were so headstrong.'

Beryl got there in the end, and our dance routine with Julie, a true star who never displayed any pretensions, was a big success. The set was a wonderful replica of Brixton Music Hall, circa 1916. Beryl also survived, as did I, having everything done for real in it, including the 'extras' in the audience throwing real tomatoes and cabbage at her and me as Gertrude Lawrence's parents doing their stage act. This response was in the script! We also sang the number, 'Piccadilly'. Robert Wise, of course, was a very influential film director and I couldn't help wondering if I had met him earlier on whether I would have had more film parts from him.

Dear Beryl, she was such a character, such fun. She once told me about the time Noël Coward had come to see her on Broadway when she was playing in *The Killing of Sister George*. After the show, they talked for a long time backstage, only to find when they finally emerged that everyone else had gone. On the way out, Beryl dropped her dressing-room key off at the stage door. 'Goodnight, Fireman,' she said. Noël, in that famously clipped voice, said to the fireman: 'Isn't she wonderful? She knows *everybody's* name!'

Back to near misses: apparently I was considered for a role in *Chitty Chitty Bang Bang*, which would have been another perfect part for me. When I met the film's producer, Cubby Broccoli, some time later at a showbiz function, he referred to the film and said that his production team had tried to get hold of me. But, again, Miff Ferrie was still my agent then and, as before, would probably have told anybody who enquired whether I was free: 'He's not available till a year's time.' Much as I like Dick Van Dyke as a performer, I have to say I think my English accent in the part he played would have been a little better.

I also had a small part in *Bedknobs and Broomsticks*, Disney's 'British' follow-up to *Mary Poppins*. The story was set in 1940 and concerned three evacuee children, riding above the rooftops on a magic bedstead, who team up with a kindly witch to defeat the Nazis' attempted invasion of England. It starred some wonderful people, including Angela Lansbury, Tessie O'Shea and David Tomlinson. I played the part of a spiv, with a very thin moustache—a sort of 'Arthur English' type of spiv, with watches hung inside my coat, all that kind of thing. It was a very tiny part, but it was great fun doing it. These days it seems to be shown regularly on Sky Television and I get a fee every year of about £15 for my appearance. So if nothing else, that will keep me in my retirement!

While I was doing one of the *Play Your Cards Right* series, I was asked to appear in a Russian film, of all things, about the life of Pavlova, the world-famous ballerina. The night before filming, I didn't get home from the television studio until about eleven o'clock. Not only did I have to be at the film studio at six in the morning for make-up and to don my elegant tail suit, I'd only just been given my lines. I stayed up until two in the morning to learn four pages of dialogue. The next morning, however, when I was met by the Russian director's French PA (who could speak Russian and a little English), she explained to me that the director didn't like the scene the way it had been written, so would I please ad-lib? After working so late to learn the script the night before, you can imagine how I felt.

In the film, I was the impresario Alfred Butt, who had booked Pavlova into London's Palace Theatre on Cambridge Circus, to appear in a variety show. (In those days it was quite permissible to have straight actors reading prose or doing a theme from a famous play or, as in Pavlova's case, to do a short ballet sequence, all as part of a variety line-up.) In the story, Pavlova had been such a hit at Alfred Butt's theatre, he was begging her to stay. She needed the money, but she was worried about her lover who was exiled in St Petersburg . . . Anyway, the cameras were ready to roll, and I was seated in my office when Pavlova came in—who, by

261

the way, was played by an absolutely beautiful Russian girl—dressed in a little tutu. I jumped up, put on my jacket, and started to ad-lib as requested, walking around the room and reading out imaginary press cuttings. I went on and on for as long as I thought the director needed, finishing up on bended knee. My final words were, 'I beg you, Pavlova, *please* stay.' She then just looked at me for what seemed a lifetime and finally said: 'No.' The director shouted 'Cut!' After all that, the actress hadn't understood one word that I'd said—and 'no' was probably the only English she knew anyway! It was one of the craziest mornings I've ever spent in show business.

So, how do I feel now, when I look back on my lost film parts? Gutted!

CHAPTER NINE

GOOD GAME, GOOD GAME—AND CRUMPET NIGHT?

By the end of the sixties, my career was actually at a bit of a low, with only spasmodic appearances on ITV. So, to fill in the gaps, I spent a lot of time travelling around Britain's club circuit, doing cabaret. Some of these clubs, in Newcastle, Liverpool, Manchester, Wakefield, and Leeds, were very good venues which attracted top-of-the-bill names. Others were really dreadful, with very heavy drinkers in the audience who were not the slightest bit interested in the show. The occasion that stands out most in my mind was when I was booked for a week's work in a club just outside Manchester. Having started on the Monday, the first four nights went down really well. But on Friday I woke up early with a really bad sore throat, which did not look good for a radio spot I had been booked for in which I would be singing with an orchestra, nor for that night's show.

As Friday morning wore on, I began to feel increasingly ill, knew that the sore throat was developing into flu, and knew I shouldn't work that evening. I phoned Don Hunt, my musical director, and told him that it was most unlikely I would be in a fit state to perform. But I was in a quandary. It had been such a good week, I really didn't want to let the audience down on the last two nights of my booking. So, changing my mind, I called Don back and said: 'I've decided to go ahead. Please meet me at the club.' That night my temperature was 103 degrees and I felt really dreadful, but I went ahead with the show. I really shouldn't have bothered. They were the worst audience I had ever experienced. From the moment I walked on to the moment I finished, I could hardly believe my eyes or ears. It was the rowdiest mob I'd ever tried to perform for. When Don came into my dressing room and exclaimed: 'My God, that was a tough evening,' I replied, 'Wasn't it *awful*. I felt terrible before we went on, but now I not only feel worse, I'm also very upset because they didn't give us a chance.' At this moment, the manager popped his head round the door and said cheerily: 'Hallo, Bruce, you all right?'

'Come in a minute, will you?' I said, adding, 'I nearly didn't work tonight because I've got the flu and I feel terrible.'

'Really, Bruce,' he said, concerned. 'That's a shame because normally we don't put the comic on, on a Friday night.'

'Then why did you put me on?' I asked indignantly.

'Well,' he said, 'you also sing and dance, and play the piano, and all that . . . But normally, we don't put the comic on.'

'Why?' I asked, bewildered.

'Because Friday night is crumpet night,' he replied.

'What?' I gasped.

'Friday night here is always crumpet night.'

'What do you mean, crumpet night?'

'Well,' he said, 'on Fridays all the married men come on their own, and all the women come on their own. So they all talk to each other from table to table, trying to pull each other.'

At that moment, I thought to myself, 'I wish I didn't have the flu. I just wish I was dead!'

The interesting thing about these club cabarets was that when you were top-of-the-bill, you were expected to be onstage for an hour, and this gave me the chance to develop a long act. Up until then, I'd only done four or five spots in Summer Season Shows or ten-minute spots in variety, but not a full hour on my own. In the clubs, I proved to myself I could do it successfully. I didn't know it at the time but, one day soon, this would hold me in very good stead.

Its perils aside, it's sad that the club cabaret scene was eventually killed by people who primarily went there to drink and were not interested in the performers. When people get drunk they quickly become disorderly and start shouting out and not

264

paying attention to the artistes onstage. It spoils the atmosphere for everyone. People who came to see me in the theatre would come to a club if I was billed to appear, not necessarily knowing what the club scene was like. And if they couldn't see or hear me because there was too much noise, they wouldn't go to a club again. It didn't put me off cabaret work at The Talk of the Town, though. That was a completely different experience.

In 1967, big television news was that *Sunday Night at the London Palladium*, by now compèred by Bob Monkhouse, was coming to an end. 'But it's still a hit,' Bob protested to his agent and manager, Peter Pritchard. 'Yes, love,' Peter replied, 'but Lew Grade wants to take it off while it's back at the top—have it remembered as a success. It was his baby, after all, his and Val Parnell's.' For the final show Bob Monkhouse invited three of *SNAP*'s previous hosts—Norman Vaughan, Jimmy Tarbuck and me—to join him onstage. The four of us then sang a parody of 'Dearie, Do You Remember When . . .', listing some of the most outstanding events in the history of the show since its launch by Tommy Trinder in 1955. Tommy wasn't well enough to appear on the last night, but Bob used his recorded voice as though he was phoning the programme, with some of his then still familiar catch-phrases: 'Trinder's the name! T.R.I.N.D.E.R., pronounced Chumley! I'm gonna sing to you—ha, ha—you lucky people!' The show then went off the air to the roar of cheers and applause of the audience.

After this nostalgic occasion, I found myself thinking about Billy Marsh, who had championed me for *SNAP*. Billy was a showbiz legend, an agent who cared about his stars and was thrilled when things were going right for them. A very tough negotiator when making deals, you knew he would stand firm whenever contracts were being discussed. Once, when he came to Canada with Anthea and me, he was very supportive during what was a difficult time for us and, thanks to him being there, we had a great time. *The* smoker of all smokers, there was a joke about him which went: 'I nearly saw Billy Marsh the other day.'

'What do you mean you nearly saw him?'

'I couldn't see him through the ash.'

Dear Billy, bless his heart, always had ash all over his lapels and down his suit jacket. When you went into his office he always had a packet of Players on his desk and would chain-smoke throughout the meeting. On one occasion when I went to see him, there had just been news coverage about smoking being bad for people's health. When I walked into the office, Billy had a packet of peppermints on the desk and was sucking away on one after another of these. Suddenly, he said: 'Oh, I can't stand this any longer,' and he threw the remaining peppermints into the wastepaper bin, opened his drawer, and out came a packet of cigarettes. Although this was funny in one way, it was tragic in another because there is no doubt that smoking is harmful to health. But Billy just did not look the same without a cigarette burning when he was talking to you or making a deal. They were so much a part of him.

Billy and I had many ups and downs, as clients and agents do. But in the main I was always so grateful to him for the Palladium job and his guidance in so many ways. He was held in very high regard in the business, and did a tremendous amount of work for charities, including the Prince of Wales's Prince's Trust and the Royal Air Force Benevolent Fund and the Guinea Pigs, the charity that helped its servicemen who were burned or disfigured during the Second World War. He never got an OBE or an MBE, or any sort of honour, but he should have done. He deserved this recognition, helped so many without ever making a fuss or noise about what he was doing. I was very sad when Billy suffered his stroke and had to give up his work as an agent. And even sadder when he died at seventy-eight. He was the kind of person you thought would go on for ever.

This is where Jan Kennedy, my agent, comes into the story. She had been working very closely with Billy for years and cared for him enormously during his long illness. When Billy died, she took over the agency, and even kept the company in his name. To this day, it is still called Billy Marsh Associates. She also had the wonderful idea of interring Billy's ashes under the stage of the London Palladium, and arranged for just a few of us to be part of the ceremony. There was no more fitting place to lay him to rest.

Lew Grade was also somebody I thought of that last night of *SNAP*. I so admired the way he loved show business and put his heart and soul into his work. It was wonderful how he went to America to do television deals, and played the Americans at their own game. And he was always a man of his word. One occasion I shall never forget is when Stanley Baker, Roger Moore and I were in Cannes for the film festival and sunning ourselves on the beach with all the other stars. Lew hated being in the sun, but he came down to join us, smoking a huge cigar and wearing long shorts and a ten-gallon brimmed hat, just to talk to us about the business.

His wife, Kathy, bless her dear heart, had the devil's own job to get him away from his office and used to have to force him to go on holiday to the South of France. He was in his office on the dot of six every morning to organize his day before anyone else arrived. He was a workaholic, but he loved it. Even on holiday the thing he enjoyed most was leaving the hotel to spend hours talking to people, and doing what he loved best—wheeling and dealing and clinching deals. He was a real bit of show business.

Speaking of Lew and America has reminded me of the strange way in which I met Dick Martin, and the beginning of our long friendship. The US comedy show *Rowan and Martin's Laugh-In* ran from 1968 to 1971 on BBC 2, and was a big hit in the UK. I enjoyed it enormously and thought the two performers were first class. When I was in Las Vegas, having noticed that they were in a show, I thought I would try to go and see it. On this particular night I was on my own which, believe it or not, wasn't often the case. By the time I got to the theatre, the show had started and there were no seats to be had. I told the manager I was from England and returning to London the following day, and asked him if I could possibly stand. 'I'd love to see these two guys,' I said, 'because their TV show is such a big hit in England.' Perhaps because he knew I was in show business, he said: 'Okay, just stand in this little passageway. You'll be able to see the show from there.' It was, indeed, a very good viewing place and I stood there enjoying

Rowan and Martin's act, loving every moment of it. Just then, a beautiful girl came in and stood opposite me. Between looking and laughing at the show, she looked at me and I looked at her, then she smiled. It was a lovely warm smile, no holding back. 'She's very friendly,' I thought. 'This could be the start of something big!' So we carried on thus all the way through the act, laughing at the jokes, and then looking at each other, to share our appreciation. Her smiles were getting bigger and bigger and she was becoming warmer and friendlier. At the end of the show, just as we were about to leave, she said, 'Aren't you Bruce Forsyth?'

'Yes,' I said, 'I am.'

'Well,' she said, 'my name is Dolly. I'm a very dear friend of Dick Martin's. (Actually, she was his girlfriend.) Would you like to go round to his dressing room and meet them?'

'Yes,' I said, 'I'd love to. But I'm a bit disappointed because I thought you and me were hitting it off pretty good.' This made her laugh, and I added, 'I thought it was going to be a different end to the evening, but I'll settle for meeting Dick and his partner.' So she took me round and introduced me, and a friendship blossomed between us. After that, every time I went to Los Angeles I played golf with Dick and always saw Dolly during the visit. I liked her so much, not just because she was beautiful, but because she had a great sense of humour and a very sweet nature.

*　　　*　　　*

On 21 October 1969 I appeared in a new West End

farce, *Birds on the Wing*, written by the Australian Peter Yeldham. With actresses Julia Lockwood and June Barry as my accomplices, I headed a trio of confidence tricksters who flitted from one international hotel to another from New York to Tokyo, via Paris and London, double-crossing our partners and duping everybody with irresistible aplomb. A reviewer said I 'played it with brilliant speed of attack', and the show was 'saved' by my 'genial comic's presence'. Another reviewer mentioned that I had 'turned down a lucrative Las Vegas contract' to do this show. This wasn't true—I wouldn't have been so stupid!

A few weeks later, in December, a one-act Noël Coward play in which I co-starred with Dora Bryan was aired on BBC 1. Entitled *Red Peppers*, this was originally written for the show *Tonight at 8.30.* The reviewers said that Dora and I were 'wholly incisive and authentic as the struggling pair of vaudeville comedians' and that my 'clever parody' of my 'normal stage manner to suggest failure rather than success was very impressive'. Some other very famous names decorated this lively little production—Anthony Quayle, Cyril Cusack and Dame Edith Evans all played cameo roles. Dame Edith was so funny. I remember her saying in that wonderful way of hers, 'One always dresses up a bit on the first day of rehearsals, in case one falls in love with the leading man.'

So, to a new decade—a decade in which Margaret Thatcher became the first woman leader of the Conservative Party and later Britain's first woman Prime Minister. Tony Jacklin entered golfing history by becoming the third player to hold the British and US Open Championships at the same time. The Queen celebrated her Jubilee; and Louise Brown, the first test-tube baby, was born. Oh, yes, my mates Morecambe and Wise pulled in an audience of over twenty-five million for one of their shows; Ian Botham achieved the finest all-round performance ever recorded by an English cricketer; James Hunt became world racing champion by one point; Trevor Francis joined Nottingham Forest as the first-ever one-million-pound footballer; and, not to be forgotten, McDonald's opened the first of their UK hamburger joints. Quite a decade for politicians, sports and junk food!

Anyway, enough of all that . . . In the spring of 1971, Billy Marsh arranged for me to go to see Bill Cotton, who was then BBC's Head of Light Entertainment. At an earlier meeting, I had talked to Bill about doing a chat show—something I really wanted to do—rather like *Wogan* was to be, or ex-newscaster Michael Aspel's show, and *Parkinson*, but with more entertainment included. I'd been thinking about this for a very long time, way before Terry and the two Michaels had got a foot in the door. I not only wanted to chat to the guests, but also to do some comedy bits and musical items with them. This, I thought, would make it a talk show with a difference—and set me off in a new direction. At the present meeting, however, Bill said: 'There's a videotape I'd like you to see.' Crossing to a television, he put on a tape of a variety-type game show from Holland, called *One Out of Eight*, presented by a lady called Miece Bauman. In this programme, professional people came on to do something that was a normal part of their job and then the contestants were asked to imitate what they had just done. The contestants were teams of two from the same family, but a generation apart. It was a two-hour show in which variety acts were interspersed between games. Bill, having spooled to and from different parts of the video, with one beady eye on me, said: 'D'you think *we* could do that in forty-five minutes, Bruce?'

'Not forty-five minutes,' I replied, 'maybe fifty, fifty-five minutes. It would be a very difficult show to do in less time than that.'

'Would it work better, d'you think, if we had fewer acts, and maybe a singer before the final game?'

'You could do that,' I said. 'Yes, I think that would work well.'

So we spoke about it—and spoke about it.

'Well . . .' Bill said, coming to the point. 'Are you up for it, Bruce? I'd like to make a pilot of it.'

'Yes,' I said, realizing he was in no mood to discuss my chat-show idea. 'It's different. I think it's in with a very good chance. It uses people on the screen in a way that hasn't been done before—gets them up on their feet doing things. I particularly like the idea of the contestants trying to imitate professionals. That could be *very* funny. What's the show going to be called?'

'*The Generation Game*,' Bill said.

I ran this title around my tongue. *The Generation Game*. It sounded different. As we were parting, I said: 'There's just one thing, Bill—I noticed the Dutch presenter wears a very slinky black dress. *I* won't be expected to imitate *her*, will I?'

'*That*, Bruce,' Bill said drolly, 'is something even I would never ask of you.'

And—to some people's disappointment!—he

remained true to his word when we set about organizing the pilot for my new *Gen Game*. The producers were James (Jim) Moir and Colin Charman (who, to our great sadness, died three years later in 1974). Jim and Colin were a wonderful team, and we all so enjoyed thrashing out ideas and putting the show together. But when we watched the finished product in May, we felt the pilot wasn't quite good enough, not as slick as we'd hoped. The show simply wasn't smooth enough and moved at too slow a pace when changing from one item to the next. It did, however, succeed in getting across the idea of what the *Gen Game* was all about. But none of us was really satisfied with our first effort. Feeling a trifle disappointed with the show so far, I went off to do my Summer Season Show in Bournemouth.

When I returned, we moved on from the pilot to recording the first episode of the *Gen Game*. To help it along, I even wrote the opening song: 'Life is the name of the game—and I wanna play the game with you'. The song worked okay but, as I had feared, the first programme didn't. In fact, it was a disaster. The production team, from pure overenthusiasm, had made it all too complicated. There were too many stops. Games that should have been zipped in and out of quick as a flash were too slow. For maximum enjoyment, the whole thing needed tightening up, needed to be simplified. I was *very* unhappy about it, Bill Cotton was unhappy and Paul Fox, the then Controller of BBC 1, was more than unhappy. Bill, James, Colin, Paul, Billy Marsh and I watched the tape once and then watched it again. Everybody, of course, had different views about what was wrong. 'What do you think, Bruce?' Paul Fox asked after the team had had its say. 'I agree with all of you,' I replied. 'And, what's more, I think we should forget this recording altogether and put out the pilot instead. Although, from a production point of view, that's not a particularly good show, it's still better than this one and it does give a good idea of what *The Generation Game*'s all about.'

This was Thursday night. The first programme was to be transmitted in two days' time on Saturday, 2 October 1971. The pilot had not been edited for transmission—and my suggestion had certainly put the cat among the pigeons. 'Let's have a look at the pilot,' the team said wearily. So we did. And, after everybody had agreed that at least it had the kind of atmosphere and content we were looking for, we decided to kick off the series with that. I felt very sorry for the people who had to complete the editing by the Saturday deadline, but it had to be done. We'd all learned a lesson and, I'm glad to say, we never made the same mistakes again—kept everything simple. And who would have believed then what a tremendous show it was going to be.

The secret of *The Generation Game*'s success was that we made it look like a 'live' show. Once past the pilot stage, we never stop-started too often, even though television production in those days was very much a stop-start affair—a frustrating matter of 'Wait here . . . Change this . . . Do that . . . Get this in here', and so forth. And all the time these shenanigans were going on, the studio audience would have to wait while, as host, I was fidgeting around, saying to the team: *'Come on . . . Let's move things along. Let's keep the pace* going.' In fact, whenever the stage crew was changed at the beginning of a series, I always used to gather them together and say: 'Forget TV—think of it as a stage show.' As so many of them also had stage experience, this helped a lot. It also helped to let them know that they were just as important to the show as us, the performers.

After the autopsy on the first show, we all went out for a Chinese meal. This was Bill Cotton's favourite food, something he always ate when stressed. With most of us still feeling dissatisfied with the show—and not yet knowing how it would be received in viewers' homes—it was a very 'down' night. But we needn't have worried. Although we didn't know it while we were eating our rice and noodles and splashing soy sauce about, success was soon to be ours. The pilot went out with only minutes to spare after editing and, after that, the show improved every week.

Never having been on television at six o'clock in the evening before, I remember saying to Jim Moir: 'What kind of ratings would be considered acceptable at this time of the day?'

'We'd be more than delighted with six million,' he replied.

We started off—and I like to think this was because I was hosting the show!—with seven million, then watched the ratings grow and grow until, within a couple of months, we had soared to fourteen million. We were then, of course, rescheduled to do eight or nine more and, even before we had completed these, the powers that be were asking for more. '*No* . . . No,' Jim Moir and I kept saying. 'Where are we going to get so many new games?' But somehow we found them.

Then I had the idea of including little plays, where the viewers could watch professional actors performing a couple of roles, followed by the contestants copying the pros. This idea, however, began badly. The scriptwriter, Tony Hawes, got hold of the wrong idea. He wrote some sketches, but I wasn't in them! *'No, no, no, no, no,'* I said. (I always say no five times when I want to make a point—like Oliver Hardy!) *'I've* got to be among the contestants, so I can pounce on them when things go wrong. And then, when they completely screw up, I can force them to do it all over again. That's half the fun.' So Tony retreated, tail between his legs, to rewrite the sketches. And, when he returned, they were so good we decided to include these as often as possible. As amateur actors, the contestants were so bad at times—and *so* funny. It was exactly what I had wanted, and was marvellous for the show.

As far as the games were concerned, in the end every member of the production and research teams were frantically thinking up ideas and looking for new ones. We made such progress with this, we were actually able to send games to the Dutch producers from whom we had bought the original ones. They were delighted to receive our ideas.

The Generation Game became so popular we had hundreds of applicants, which were screened by Jim Moir, who was described by the press as our 'amiable roly-poly producer'. For once, I totally agreed with them! A week before recording, the ideas for the games were kicked around at a meeting consisting of me, Jim and the back-up team of production assistants, researchers, designers and graphic artists. Tuesdays were devoted to work on the designs for the games and the sets. On Wednesdays, the action switched to BBC Television Theatre, Shepherd's Bush, where the show was recorded. First, the games were run through with a team of eight 'extras', who used the actual components or gadgets. And a security guard would stand by all day, guarding the prizes seen in the show's final conveyor-belt sequence.

I usually arrived around midday. Over lunch at a nearby restaurant, we would go through the names and background details of the contestants with a research assistant and look for likely leads to good gags about their lives. Barry Cryer and, later, with Garry Chambers, my writers (and close friends), helped me with all this. By four o'clock, the extras had played the games long enough to achieve near-perfect scores. Once the dress rehearsal was over, I'd go off to the make-up department. At six-thirty, the contestants would arrive and be taken off for tea. The researchers would then make sure that none of them had a medical problem. We didn't want someone who'd had a heart attack and who might have another while we were recording the show! Jim Moir would then give the chosen 'Magnificent Eight' a pep talk: 'You eight—and we seventy—are going to take on millions waiting to be entertained,' he would drum into them. 'We'll give you an opportunity to twinkle'—and his pep talk would finish outside the loos.

One day during a rehearsal for the *Gen Game*, Jim said to me: 'Bruce, you need to say something to link the moment when the contestants finish remembering all the prizes on the conveyor belt to when you walk in.' 'Okay,' I said, but promptly forgot about it. Just before the show, Jim came to my dressing room and asked me again.

'All right,' I replied, trying to think, 'I'll just say, "Didn't he do well?" It's not the greatest line in the world, but it'll do.'

From then on, I said this every week and, before we knew where we were, another catch-phrase had been born. It was being used everywhere—and still is in today's newspapers. The secret of a really good catch-phrase, it seems, is to give people something they can have fun with themselves.

Talking of catch-phrases, *The Generation Game* was the first time the world saw my famous 'pose'. Then again, I suppose I have always been a bit of a poser. Jim Moir had told me that when the show opened, I would be discovered silhouetted at the back of stage on a podium. I can't just *stand* there, I thought to myself. So the first time we did it, I just found myself going into Rodin's *Thinker* position—except standing up. Come to think of it, I do most of my thinking standing up! Anyway, it just became part of me, and it's better than a catch-phrase, because you don't have to say anything.

Week after week *The Generation Game* bounded along, going from strength to strength. It was simply amazing how the ratings continued to escalate. In November 1976 we topped twenty million for the first time; for the 1977 series we achieved this remarkable figure regularly. It really did become very popular.

An important addition to *The Generation Game* was, of course, its hostess—Anthea Redfern. She and I had first met, independently of the *Gen Game*, at a 'Lovely Legs' competition in a London nightclub. *No*, I wasn't one of the competitors, I

278

was one of the judges and Anthea was helping to host the contest. In the middle of this, a girlfriend I was with noticed Anthea first. 'Oh, Bruce,' she said, 'what a *beautiful* girl.' I looked round, saw Anthea and agreed she was stunning. She was wearing a two-piece lavender outfit with an eye-catching miniskirt. If she had entered the contest, the other girls would have been wise to stay at home!

During the evening, Anthea joined us at our table and showed me some photographs that her boyfriend, Louis Brown, had taken of her on holiday in the South of France. These explained why she was sporting such a marvellous suntan. We chatted for a while and—honest—that was that. I made no arrangements to see her again, so it wasn't a case of love at first sight. In fact, I thought no more about her until several months later when the BBC was looking for a hostess for *The Generation Game*.

By then, we had auditioned about fifty girls and compiled a shortlist of 'possibles' who had appeared on other shows. But really we wanted a new face that viewers had not seen before. Then I remembered Anthea. I recalled how professional she had been that night and asked a friend to suggest that she should come along for an audition. She did—and captivated the producers without any need for me to exert any influence on her selection. They just knew instinctively that she was the right girl, and gave her the job within ten minutes of her arrival.

During the subsequent rehearsals she was *very* nervous, and I carefully nursed her through these and the early programmes, reminding her to raise her voice, helping her with her lines. With her past modelling experience, though, her walk was always better than mine! Soon I was happy to bring her more up front in the show and we worked out routines that we could do together. Despite the difference in our ages—Anthea was twenty-one—the viewers seemed happy to accept us as a television partnership. They thought we looked right together.

Anthea's outfits soon became an important part of *The Generation Game.* In the first series there was a strict budget and her dresses came off the peg. Anthea would go off on an afternoon shopping spree accompanied by a dresser, and come back with gorgeous new gowns. Later, of course, the BBC had dresses specially created for her by the wonderful designer Linda Martin. Every week her entrance on stage would bring gasps from the audience, and a tremendous reaction in the postbag. One night, when she was looking particularly lovely, I blurted out: 'Oh, Anthea, *that's lovely.* Let the viewers see the back of your dress. Come on, *give us a twirl.*' Those unplanned words stuck—'Come on, give us a twirl' became another of my catch-phrases, one that's still used in shows to this day.

During breaks in rehearsals, Anthea and I used to go across the road to a little café called Oddies and talk about the show. Gradually our conversation broadened, and she began to confide in me about her relationship with Louis Brown and the problems she was experiencing. Louis had helped her to get started in modelling, and looked after her in many ways. She certainly felt a great loyalty towards him, but he was obviously exerting too strong an influence over her; was always watching her, never far away. His maroon, chauffeur-driven Rolls-Royce—in which she had made such a spectacular entrance at the Shepherd's Bush studios on the day of her audition—was always waiting to meet her at the studio door. He would also come to the recording of the shows and be very critical of her performance. I knew that when he was sitting in the audience, Anthea would be very on edge.

So, slowly, I came to realize that she was very unhappy living with Louis, and that her nervous state of mind was because she'd discovered he was running around with other girls. I became very concerned for her—even tried to patch things up between them. 'Louis,' I said one day, 'why don't you play the game with Anthea? Leave the other girls alone.' But it did no good. My rendezvous with Anthea in Oddies became more frequent. In the romantic setting of that little café, she continued to pour out her heart to me. We held hands, our knees touched under the table . . . and gradually we fell in love. Anthea always says that the moment she fell in love with me was the day I came into her dressing room when she was sitting there in Carmen rollers, wearing no make-up, and I kissed her for the very first time. She later said she wanted to be 'glamorous' when I first kissed her!

My marriage to Penny, despite two attempted reconciliations, was certainly long over. For Anthea, there was now the agonizing choice to be made: Louis or Bruce? She wavered and wavered. One day she would say she was leaving him, the next day doubts would creep in again. Oddies apart, there were very few opportunities for us to meet outside the studios. Mostly we chatted in one or the other's dressing room. My grotty little flat, off Kensington High Street, was not the most romantic of settings but, when Anthea found herself with a free evening, I invited her round for a meal. On that winter evening we discovered how much we had come to care for one another—and that was the night we fell deeply in love. I now desperately wanted us to be together, and gave her a lover's ultimatum: 'It has to be Louis or me.' To give her the space she needed, I took myself off—to a health farm. I needed all the help I could get! 'Look,' I told her before I left, 'I'm not going to contact you. Just telephone me if you are going to leave him.'

That Christmas Anthea made her choice. I was spending Christmas Day with Penny and the children—more on that later—when she rang to say: 'Yes, I want to be with you.' And it was the end of bachelorhood for me. She moved in with me at my flat, and joined me on a tour of Northern nightclubs. The public still suspected nothing—it seemed quite natural that the star of *The Generation Game* should be seen with his TV hostess. But our secret was not to remain safe for long.

After the first series of *The Generation Game* I went to Canada. I was starring in a touring version of the London Palladium show and had naturally asked Anthea to join me. Unluckily for us, a Fleet Street showbiz writer was travelling with the show. He saw us together and wasn't slow to sense he had a good story. We realized we could no longer hide our love for each other. When the reporter asked me if Anthea was the kind of girl I would like to marry, I said: 'Yes. If things work out right, I *will* marry her.' Anthea was thrilled at this public declaration of my love for her—and we shared a marvellous carefree few weeks away together.

I had taken the precaution of telling Penny about Anthea before we left for Canada—actually phoned her, to say: 'I'm off to Canada next week for the winter tour, taking Anthea with me. So, just in case we get spotted there, I want you to remember that I've told you myself.' When the story broke, however, there was an interview in which Penny was complaining bitterly. I must add here that, although the newspapers persisted in headlining our story 'Bruce's 20-year Marriage is Over', that was a fabrication. Penny and I had actually only lived together for ten years. For the remaining ten, we were, without the journalists' knowledge, living apart, but not divorced. The fact that the truth never came out was not done with any deliberate intention on our part, it just happened that way. I now realize, of course, that Penny could have been misquoted in the article and might not have said half the things that the journalists printed. But the way they reported it was that Penny had said bitterly, 'I thought he'd take a bird with him.' And naturally, now that our romance was public, Anthea and I were also front-page news. Among others, I can still remember a *Daily Express* headline: 'Forsyth walked off with Anthea (didn't he do well?).'

The BBC immediately suggested that Anthea should not be in the show. My reply was: 'I understand your feelings, but if you think our love affair is going to damage the programme I feel it would be wrong of me to stay while Anthea goes. After all, she has been a great success in the first series, and has not done anything wrong. I've been separated from my wife for ten years. It is not as if I'm leaving Penny for Anthea—or Anthea is a marriage-breaker.' For me it was a matter of principle—one that I was prepared to stand or fall by: 'I don't want to be awkward about this,' I added, 'but if Anthea's not to be in the show—then I won't be in it either. That's that.' They came back to me, saying: 'We understand how you feel, Bruce. Let's see how it goes.' But what they did was to bring in four more hostesses for the next show. Former beauty queens, these girls were dressed in gorgeous gowns with halter necks. Anthea, however, was put in the frumpiest grey dress, with a frill under her chin. She looked like a choirboy. They wanted to push her into the background. But so many people wrote in saying they hadn't seen enough of her, they had to give in. After that, there was no problem. Anthea stayed with the show.

*   *   *

During the part of the year when I was not working on *The Generation Game*, which we recorded in a thirteen-week run between September and Christmas, I continued with endless club dates. But I had to work a full year between the series, doing club and cabaret dates all over the country because the divorce settlement from Penny, which was finalized in July 1973, was going through and proving to be *very* expensive. It exasperated me. In fact, when Penny and I were sorting out this settlement, I walked out of one meeting at the High Court.

I did this because I had learned that the Queen's

Counsel's next in command (known as the leading counsel) is allowed to put his fee on his brief. This means the other side can see what he is being paid. My solicitor then said to me, 'His leading counsellor is getting more than yours.' I thought, 'What's going on here?' The solicitor then said to me that they wanted to know what the leading counsel's revised fee would be. 'I wouldn't do this in my job,' I replied angrily. 'If I'd arranged to do a show for, say, a thousand pounds, I wouldn't ask for fifteen hundred just before I was going on and threaten not to perform. To my mind, that's blackmail. So why are they allowed to display their fees on their briefs, so that the other side can barter? This is absolutely beyond all reason.' And I walked out of the meeting. After I had cooled down, I went back, knowing that one way or another the divorce had to be settled.

There were other unpleasantnesses. In those days, my fees were paid either by cheque or cash. And as part of her suit, Penny had reported that I may not have declared all my cash payments. She even drew attention to a recent shop opening I had done. Luckily, my very competent accountant, Malcolm Melbourne, was at the meeting in question and was able to check the payments in his file. 'Yes, Mr Forsyth was paid £250 for opening that shop,' he replied, showing the entry in the book. Before this, Penny's QC had said: 'I suggest, Mr Forsyth, the money received for these shop openings just goes into your pocket.' I said, 'You can be as suggestive as you like . . .' This shut him up. He didn't try to banter words with me after that. He knew that, like lawyers, part of my business is to banter and to extract double

285

meanings out of words. He knew that if he got into a cross-examination with me, he might not have been as successful as he would have liked. Perhaps he would have lost his silk, or maybe his silk would have faded! If only I'd been doing that Courts furniture stores commercial at the time, when I was dressed in a judge's gown and wig, saying 'See you in Courts', I could have judged for myself!

*   *   *

By the end of 1973 everything was sorted out. Like most people, Anthea and I wanted our wedding day to be *very* special—*our day*. No crowds, no press photographers, no ballyhoo. We planned the occasion meticulously, deciding the wedding would be on Christmas Eve because that was the last day anyone would expect a couple to marry. We invited about a dozen guests to the ceremony at the Windsor Register Office. The reception was then a quiet affair at a nearby hotel and, afterwards, our guests headed home sworn to secrecy. We thought we had got away with it—had married without all the usual showbiz trappings. But we had reckoned without Tony Fisher, a photographer friend of my sister Maisie, whom we had invited along to take a few snaps for our personal album.

I had arranged to take my daughters, Debbie, Julie, and Laura, to lunch on Boxing Day. My plan was to tell them that Anthea and I had married. I was terrified of what Penny's reaction might be if I broke the news before the holidays—and was determined that nothing would spoil my girls' Christmas. What I didn't know was that our so-called friend, Tony the photographer, had sold his

286

pictures to a national newspaper—and that other newspapers had got on to the story, too. A reporter telephoned Penny, asking if it was true that I had married Anthea. Naturally, my daughters were shaken rigid. Debbie rang me, very upset. I denied it. I still thought nobody had any hard facts on the wedding, that it was only rumour-mongering. And I still remember so clearly my words on the telephone to Debbie: 'No, darling . . . *No, darling.* It could be a rumour. They're always saying we've got married. Would I lie to you? *Of course I wouldn't.*'

I was still putting it off, knowing I was going to see the girls on Boxing Day, when I was going to tell them all at once, and in person. I thought that was the best way to do it. So you can imagine how I felt—absolutely poleaxed—and, more important, how my daughters felt—when they saw the photographs in the newspaper on Boxing Day morning. I explained things to Debbie as best I could on the phone, but she was in tears and we had to cancel our lunch and the trip to the cinema to see *The Sting*, starring Robert Redford, Paul Newman, Robert Shaw and Eileen Brennan. Fortunately, when Debbie looks back now, she always says: 'Daddy's plan was to tell us to our faces—the nice way. He admits that if he had to repeat the whole episode he would do the same again. All he wanted was to spare our feelings. But it backfired because of one man's dreadful behaviour.'

I am so grateful to Debbie for that understanding.

Sadly, things were not so easily resolved between Maisie and me. She was quite close to the photographer who had betrayed our trust, and we had a serious falling-out about the distress he had caused. It was very upsetting because Maisie and I had always been very close and had never had a serious quarrel before then. People always say that love is blind. Maisie didn't want to admit that Tony had done anything wrong, went on the defensive, and was very protective about him. Perhaps she knew that he was already sorry about what he had done. Whatever the reason, I was furious with him and her, and the fact that he made money out of the photographs increased my anger even more. Thankfully, in time, Maisie and I overcame all the bad feelings that he had created between us. Forgiveness is such an important part of family life.

*   *   *

Now—for light relief!—what some people may call a shaggy dog story: '*Anthea,*' I said. 'It's Bothwell or Brucie! *Him or me!*'

No, Bothwell wasn't another man in Anthea's life. He was a bossy Yorkshire terrier I had bought for her as a present, who was later joined by our mischievous other dog, Monty. Within a few days of getting Bothwell, I had to set off on a club tour. Anthea came with me and we took Bothwell along, too. He even accompanied us to the nightclubs. But it was a strange life for him, and he just wouldn't eat his food. Anthea, who has always been such a caring person for animals—in fact, she's often said she prefers animals to humans!—began to panic. I tried to calm her down, told her not to worry: 'The dog's whole system has been upset by all this travelling,' I said. 'He's got to adapt to a new way of life—he's in show business now.' But Anthea

288

continued to work herself up into such a state that I found myself adding: '*Look*, I *can't* stand all this aggravation over a dog. Take him to your mother's and sort him out. I'll meet you next week. It's either Bothwell or me.' Thankfully, since then Anthea and I have often laughed about my outburst. I can hardly believe I actually said it. But, at the time, I *really* meant it.

Bothwell proved to be a very intelligent dog and I trained him myself. But he was also a Jekyll-and-Hyde character. On the golf course I was his god, he obeyed my every word—but not everybody knew that. If I was playing with somebody I hadn't played with before, I always knew they were thinking, 'Oh, my God, *fancy* bringing a dog on a golf course!' But Bothwell would always wait until everybody had driven off and then, when we'd all putted, he'd run to the next tee and sit down. He was amazing. He never moved when he was not supposed to, never ran through a bunker, always sat quietly at the side of the green, and wouldn't have dreamed of picking up a golf ball. On our way back from the Wentworth Golf Course—by 1973, Anthea and I were living in an apartment at Ascot Towers—Bothwell would sit on my lap while I drove our cream Rolls-Royce. Going along, I would sing: 'We're going *hoooome*,' and I would howl the word 'hoooome'. He would then throw back his head, join in, and howl with me. When we stopped at traffic lights, people's jaws just dropped open. They just couldn't believe this grown-up man with this tiny dog on his lap, singing away! It was absolutely marvellous. What a duet!

On reaching home, however, Bothwell and I had more of a love/hate relationship. He was totally

Anthea's. 'You're the boss when we're out,' was his attitude, 'but only when Mummy's not around. When she's around, I'm Mummy's boy.' If I told him to come, he walked the other way with a disdainful air. He used to enter the dining room just to get my attention, then rush back to the kitchen to guard his bowl of food, growling and daring me to follow and go near it. Because he largely ignored me at home, I used to tease him quite a bit—get down on all fours and creep around, growling at him and making him growl back. I've never forgotten this because when we were in Manchester, staying at the Excelsior Hotel while I was playing at the Golden Garter, I was teasing Bothwell one night before the show. Clad in a loose, towelling dressing gown I was, as usual, creeping along the floor growling at him, with him growling back. Suddenly, I cornered him. Then, my teeth bared, I made to move closer to him. He suddenly flew through the air and buried his teeth in the towelling robe covering my shoulder, shaking the material furiously from side to side and hanging there. I was scared out of my wits. When he finally let go and fell to the floor, he looked up at me as much as to say: 'Don't you start on me again!' I knew he was a Yorkshire terrier, but as I've said, he'd have thought he was a Great Dane.

*   *   *

So, Anthea and I had moved from my unromantic Kensington flat into a lovely ground-floor apartment in Ascot Towers, just the other side of the racecourse in Ascot. One lovely thing about our new home was that, after we'd been there a couple of years, we were actually given a key to the racecourse grounds, which meant we could simply cross the road, go through a special gate, and walk the dogs, Bothwell and Monty, on the large open area ringed by the track, which also featured a small but tricky golf course.

Two years later, in 1975, we actually went to live on the golf course at Wentworth, which is still my home to this day. When we first came to see the house, I thought it was the ugliest monstrosity I had ever seen. Red-bricked, with three huge garages and awful 1930s metal windows, it looked like the back of a factory. 'Oh,' was my first reaction, 'I don't even want to go in.' But when I entered and saw the wonderful view from the back of the house, I did what most potential buyers do—started to make mental changes, thinking that if those windows were replaced and . . . and . . . Then, having checked with the estate agent and a builder that I *could* make alterations—could change the awful flat roof, which I loathed, and put on a traditional roof and build a huge en suite bedroom over the garages—I bought it.

Eighteen months later, when we had succeeded in getting the place into some kind of order, I was—as Anthea said at the time—in my 'seventh heaven, living at long last on a golf course'. But it was not just *a* golf course, it was *Wentworth*. I could remember driving on to the Wentworth estate when I was just in my twenties, and thinking, 'Fancy living *here*.'

A very sad thing happened, though, some time after we moved into the house. Monty—who had always been a bit of a wanderer, but a much meeker character than Bothwell!—was run over and killed at the bottom of our drive by a car that was cornering recklessly fast. Anthea was distraught and we decided to have a little tombstone erected for him in the garden. It is still there to this day.

CHAPTER TEN

'WHAT DO YOU DO FOR A LIVING?'

The new year of 1974 began well! Having once been reported as saying that I had an 'hour-glass stomach which sometimes caused me severe indigestion, a type of heartburn, especially during festive seasons' (which was an easy way of explaining my cup and spill condition!), I was asked to lend my name and mugshot to a medical ad for an antacid preparation! I wasn't the only member of the family in the newspapers that year. Debbie, aged nineteen, got a job as a 'bunny girl' in one of the nightclubs opened by Hugh Hefner of *Playboy* magazine fame; Julie, aged sixteen, went to Germany to make a series of education programmes; and Penny took the lease on a property in Hampstead to open a gift and card shop, all of which attracted a few column inches.

I joined Barry Clayman at the Management Agency and Music (MAM) for my one-man show. He represented, among others in the group, singers Tom Jones and Engelbert Humperdinck. Then, by February, to the delight of us all on *The Generation Game*, we learned that nineteen million viewers were watching the show. Not bad for a programme that Jim Moir had told me would be doing well if we achieved a six-million rating. In addition to the *Gen Game*, I also worked in Bunny's Place (no connection with Debbie), in Cleethorpes, Lancashire, where I had once shared an Empire Theatre dressing room with Duncan's Collies. Fortunately, this time there were no furry friends, not even bunnies, in my dressing room. But I did meet a chap called John Colebrook who, ten years previously, had sold me his BFE 9 number plate for my Rolls-Royce. Stomach problems or not, that summer I featured in a McCann-Erikson campaign for the relaunch of Stork margarine, by announcing the start of the promotion and appearing in the advertisements. The idea was to invite family members and four friends to nominate mothers who were in some way 'super'. Then I reappeared in a new series of ads interviewing the Supermums and presenting them with certificates. At the end of each commercial, I had to bite into a scone (which I *always* pronounce with an 'o') generously spread with Stork, look straight into camera and say those immortal words: 'Doesn't it spread well?' They had a bucket standing by for me to spit the rest of the scone into because, invariably, I'd have to do five or six takes on this. After about the third or fourth, my enjoyment was somewhat diminished. Even though Stork margarine is lovely, that amount of margarine in that space of time was a bit too much to take—literally. In fact, I haven't had a scone since!

On 16 November it was Royal Variety time again, starring among others, Telly Savalas, Michael Crawford, Harry Secombe, Count Basie, Dame Vera Lynn, with all the proceeds going as usual to charity. It was an enormous cast—350 in all. In fact, the facilities at the Palladium simply couldn't deal with it. A number of performers had to change into costumes at other London theatres and be brought to the Palladium by coach. And only a third of them, including the stars, could be presented to the Queen and Prince Philip. One reviewer had the cheek to say, 'Our overall impression is the *RVP* is now an attempt to revive a branch of show business which is long dead.' How can a show with all those big stars be as bad as that?

The year 1975, when I was forty-seven, was when I first began my one-man shows, starting with two nights at a big theatre, the Gaumont, Southampton. At the time I said, sounding braver than I felt, 'I'll take a *big* theatre for the debut because if the show works in a *really* big one, I know it will work in other places.' Thankfully it was a sell-out, with about two thousand in the audience, but on the night I was too nervous to count.

It can be a huge challenge to attempt a one-man show. One of the greats at it is Jackie Mason, the American comedian, and it was a show of his calibre I really wanted to do. But, of course, in my case, it would include a lot of music. Nevertheless, believe me, it is *very* demanding. Having worked out my first and second half, I jotted all the segments into a running order on a piece of paper for each half, so that I could see it all laid out in front of me. But what you can't know at the planning stage is whether the audience will stay with you for a second half. Will they become fed up, bored? Will they think, 'We've seen all this in the first half'? You can't help worrying that if you

294

do yet another piano number, they may say: 'Oh, not another one.' I honestly didn't know whether I was capable of doing a two-and-a-half-hour one-man show, or whether it would be a disaster. But I wanted to try, and I decided to take the risk.

Ideas for material in the show came from all sorts of places. One of our great exports to America is legendary Londoner, jazz pianist George Shearing. He has such a magical style that's all the more remarkable because he has been blind from birth. Regrettably I never met him, but I did base one of my one-man-show bits on him. One night I was listening to the radio in the car when I heard George playing a number called 'Nola'. *Yes,* I thought, excited, 'that's a piece for my one-man show. I could play it standing up at the piano, then dance to it, and finish by lying on the piano as if I was going to sleep.' I did and it was one of the most successful bits in the show. Bill Evans is also a name that means a lot to me because he had such a great influence on modern jazz. I will be a fan of his for ever. I actually heard him for the first time when I was walking home through Soho at about one o'clock in the morning. I can't remember exactly where this was, but I heard some jazz piano being played in a basement. It was such a wonderful sound that I just stopped outside and listened for about ten minutes. When I looked down the basement steps, there was a little blackboard that had the words 'Bill Evans tonight' chalked on it. He wasn't very well known in this country at the time, but I had heard of him and knew of his reputation as a master of chords and progressions. To see him performing in person was an opportunity I couldn't miss. So down the stairs and into the club I went, and there sitting at the piano was this very tall guy, about six-foot-four, wearing spectacles which kept slipping down as he played. Whenever they were ready to fall off the end of his nose, he'd flick a hand up from the keyboard, push them back on, and continue playing without missing a note. I saw him once more in LA, and it's a lovely memory I've always carried with me.

Even though my one-man show was very successful during its initial road tour, my agent Billy Marsh and everybody else still thought I was crazy to risk doing it at the New London Theatre. Nevertheless, I went ahead. Then, because it once again proved to be a huge sell-out triumph, this made it possible for me to do it at the best and most memorable place of all—the Palladium, my second home! My belief in its success was a 'gut reaction'. I could have been wrong, of course, but, having gone ahead against all advice and been proved right, it was *so* satisfying. I felt so smug— and I like a good smug!

I particularly remember the occasion at the New London Theatre. I'd done the show, and it had been a really wonderful night. The audience had been great all the way through and, after the musicians had left the stage, I said: 'Okay, if anybody's got a question they'd like to ask me, we can have a little talk-in.'

A fellow right in the front row, who had been absolutely marvellous all evening, laughing at all the gags, applauding louder and longer than anybody else, put up his hand. 'Yes, sir,' I said, 'what would you like to ask me?'

He said: '*What* do you do for a living?'

It was wonderful. After that, I often quoted his response at the end of my question time, and it always got a big laugh. Likewise, people who came to see the show for the second or third time—as they did!—would all shout: '*What* do you do for a living?' Such moments are godsent—perfect. But, then, spontaneity has always been a large part of my act. I have always preferred bits of a show to be left loose, not to be too rehearsed. That's also why I like taking questions at the end. I then finish, singing and playing that wonderful Jim Webb song 'Piano'. The spotlight fades and it's quite an effective ending.

In December, BBC Radio 4's *Woman's Hour* asked listeners to send in a postcard naming their prize 'Male Chauvinist Pig of the Year', stating their reasons. Guess who was nominated? Bruce Forsyth, because 'his wife Anthea is given so little to do on his TV show, *The Generation Game*'. They obviously didn't take into account that Anthea was already cooking, sewing, ironing, walking and looking after the dogs, and bringing me my slippers. How could we possibly ask her to do any more on the show?

*　　　*　　　*

I was soon recording the sixth series of the *Gen Game* and continuing to tour my one-man show. Despite my previous resolution to take things a bit more easy, I'd never known a schedule like it, never worked so hard in my life.

As I remember it, it was a truly frenetic seven-day week. And I was still doing cabaret, too. In May, I performed at the Wakefield Theatre Club,

Yorkshire, to an audience of a thousand. I had by now learned a great deal from my 'crumpet night' experience because I made sure no food was served and the bar was shut while I was on. In fact, in order to keep going, I'd drawn myself up a set of rules: not smoking at all, drinking little, taking vitamin and pollen tablets, and lemon and honey in my tea to protect my throat and chest. I had also learned that when I was in a stage show and doing a number of spots, not to keep a glass filled up with wine in the wings like I used to. One night when I was doing a lot of dashing on and off stage I'd totted it up and discovered I had drunk about three-quarters of a bottle. So I gave it up. I figure that if you're the only sober person in the theatre you've got a head start.

July saw the start of something that was to become a bit of a miniseries for me: there was an ITV spectacular called *Bring On the Girls*. This featured me chatting to the world-famous model Twiggy, who later became a musical performer, and dancing and singing with the very talented Lena Zavaroni to the number 'Be a Clown'—what a sweet little girl she was—performing with the group the Three Degrees, and doing a comedy sketch about being stuck in a lift with black-leather-clad Honor Blackman of the television series *The Avengers*. It evidently beat the BBC's coverage of the Montreal Olympics! It was also shown on American TV in September when a selection of Thames TV programmes were shown to New York audiences. As a result of the show's success, we were to do quite a few of these over the coming years.

There was more American excitement for me

when I was one of very few English artistes to appear as a guest on Jim Henson's brilliant creation, *The Muppet Show*. I was thrilled to be invited on to this US series because I wasn't really that well known in America and welcomed the opportunity to become more so. Jim told me that his team had seen me on British television and thought I would go down well with the Americans. I can honestly say that this was one of the most rewarding and enjoyable things I ever did. And I was so pleased when Lew Grade, having spotted the Muppets' potential, signed them up for the UK. Everybody was thrilled that the first UK series won a TV Oscar—the British Film and Television Academy Award for best light entertainment—and also a Golden Rose of Montreux Award.

When I arrived at Elstree in August 1976 for my first rehearsal, I was given a Muppet folder containing my script and everything I needed to know. I became very attached to this folder and used it for years afterwards. It turned out to be one of the weirdest rehearsals I ever did because the joy of working with the Muppets is that they seem so like real people, you stop thinking of them as puppets. As you'll recall, the programme was hosted by Kermit the Frog, so there was quite a bit of banter with him. And 'onstage' I had a bit of a tussle with two inquisitive gawky birds when I tried to sing 'All I Need Is a Girl', and I did a joke routine with Fozzie Bear. The finale was wonderful. I sat at the piano and sang with Miss Piggy whose cute little bottom was perched on the edge of the piano. We then sang a lovely number, 'Let There Be Love'. At the end of the day's filming I went to the workshop where all the

Muppets were hung up on pegs all round the room. It was such an eerie sight and so strange to see all those lovely faces now looking blankly at me from hooks when, just a few minutes earlier, they'd been full of 'life'. Somehow, when I left the room, I really felt sorry for them!

Given that it was August and the sun was shining, the great outdoors was calling me to golf, and in the company of singer Kenny Lynch, one of my closest friends. I love him and hate him. In fact, I *love* to hate him. And he loves to hate me. My happiest days with him were spent with another dear friend of ours, Leslie Vowles. Every year we used to go together to the Open Golf Championship and had the most wonderful time, most of which was spent aching with laughter. One summer we were dashing from the Open to a Pro-Celebrity that we had all been invited to play in at Gleneagles. We were in a hotel bedroom, packing our cases which included boxes of pastries we had bought as a treat earlier in the day. Suddenly Les, in his wonderful Dorset accent, piped up, 'Oi . . . 'Oo ate moi poi?' For the rest of the trip, this became a catch-phrase that we used many times. Also, because Leslie was so often in our company, people always assumed he was in show business, too. One day when Kenny and I were being asked for autographs, Les sidled up and said: 'Hey, people keep asking me for my autograph.' 'So give it to them,' we replied, 'they won't know. You look like Andy Pandy, just sign as Andy Pandy.' And he did!

In those days at Gleneagles, passes were not needed for anything. We just rolled up in a car and the people on the gate would allow us to park just round the corner right by the clubhouse. We used to play golf in the morning, watch the pros play in the afternoon, and enjoy the fact that in Scotland at that time of year it would be light until nearly eleven o'clock at night. On one occasion when I was there with Kenny, we played three rounds of golf in one day. We started after breakfast, had sandwiches for lunch, went out again, stopped for a light snack early evening and returned to the course, finishing on the eighteenth hole of the Queen's Course. When we teed off on the last hole it was getting quite dark, and I honestly don't know how we managed to finish the hole. By the time I joined Kenny on the green, it was pitch black. All I could see were the whites of his eyes! I told him this and we both burst into laughter.

Although everybody loves Kenny, he does have one fault—he is never on time for anything. After years of trying to get him into television's Pro-Celebrity Golf Series, Jimmy Tarbuck and I finally succeeded. 'When you play in this, Kenny,' I said, 'make sure you look smart.' When Kenny came down to breakfast on the day he was going to play, I noticed he was wearing a nice shirt and had nice creases in his trousers. Then I looked down and saw his shoes, a dirty brown pair, with scuff marks all over them. I told him his shoes looked dreadful. He said: 'I haven't got any on!' Of course he had, but that's his sense of humour. It made me laugh so much. Kenny could have been one of our top entertainers, but he just didn't get the breaks.

I was the only person to play in every series of the televised Celebrity Golf. I think this was mainly because I always made myself available. There were too many wonderful moments to mention them all, but possibly the funniest was the day when both James Hunt and Peter Cook took part. James had a beautiful Alsatian called Oscar, who accompanied him around the course for his morning match. At every tee and every green, the dog would patiently sit to one side, then follow his master on to the next.

After lunch, Peter Cook was playing. He duly approached the first tee. As he did so, we noticed that he was carrying a goldfish in a bowl, which he set down beside his clubs.

'What's all this, Peter?' asked Peter Alliss.

'Well,' he said, 'James Hunt was allowed to bring his dog along with him. The only pet I've got is my goldfish, and he just loves to come along with me when I play.'

And come along it did. After every shot, Peter picked the bowl up and walked to where his ball had landed, put it down, played his shot, then picked it up again and took it to his next shot—for all eighteen holes! It was one of the most hilarious pieces of comedy ever seen on a golf course. But that was Peter Cook: he had the most brilliant, inventive mind.

I don't like to name-drop, but look at this list of names for when the American team came over to play against the UK members at Gleneagles: Bing Crosby, Burt Lancaster, George C. Scott, Robert Stack, Phil Harris, Steve Forrest, Dick Martin, Jack Lemmon and Alan Shepard, the astronaut who took a golf ball to the moon and actually hit it while he was there. It was one of *the* most wonderful golf tournaments ever. Sean Connery was our captain, and, among others, we had James Hunt, Jackie Stewart, Max Bygraves, Henry

Cooper, Val Doonican and Jimmy Tarbuck in our team. What a crowd.

The first hole is about four hundred yards, and it goes uphill for the last hundred and fifty yards or so. On this occasion, the entire area was surrounded by people about twelve deep. They extended each side of the fairway up to the green and round the green. It was one of the most amazing golfing scenes I have ever seen, and somebody mentioned that they'd never seen such a turnout even for pro tournaments. I had the great pleasure of playing with Burt Lancaster. He was a charming man and we enjoyed playing together. Afterwards he said to me, 'If I can ever do anything for you, Bruce, or if you ever come over to the States, just let me know.' I never took him up on his offer, but I was silly not to. He would have been a wonderful guest on any show.

The day I played with the American crooner Bing Crosby, Bing turned on the heat when we got to the last few holes. He gave us a bit of a thrashing and won the game. He was such a keen golfer. He used to smoke this extra-long pipe which he put down on the grass before we played a shot. (*No*, I didn't tread on it. I'd learned my lesson with Eric Sykes.) I often wondered whether the position of the pipe helped to line him up for the direction in which he wanted to hit his shot. But I don't really think so. Would Bing do that to Brucie? How can I be so untrusting, so cynical? But, believe me, it *was* a very long pipe!

Jack Lemmon was a gentleman's gentleman who played every year for twenty-five years in the four-day Pebble Beach Pro-Am in the USA. The fact that in all that time he never made the cut to play in the last two days was always a topic for conversation in celebrity golfing circles. Every year the outcome of those opening days was more eagerly awaited than news of the pro who had actually won the tournament!

On another golfing night, there were about a dozen of us dining together in a really beautiful room at Gleneagles. Jimmy Tarbuck, in great form, was sitting next to Dick Martin's beautiful wife Dolly, who has a great sense of humour but a rather piercing laugh when she gets carried away. Jimmy was egging her on with his jokes and Dolly was laughing uproariously. As there were other people dining there and I could see one couple in particular glaring at our table, I was rather embarrassed and didn't join in. Eventually, as the couple got up to leave, the man strode over to me and, looking straight at me, said: 'You should be ashamed of yourself, making so much noise.' And he stomped out. I was speechless, shocked to be blamed for Jimmy and Dolly's raucous behaviour. I was the good one, but the one who was told off! But that's the sort of thing that always happens to me. Jimmy tells me he found the fellow later and gave him a right mouthful.

After the golf, there was the next round of recordings for *The Generation Game*. But there's something important I've not mentioned yet. During the past three years while I was doing the *Gen Game*, no matter where I was working, Michael Grade came to see me every year, trying to lure me away from the BBC and back to ITV. We always had a really good night together because Michael is one of the people who, having once been an agent and brought up in Billy Marsh's busy

304

office, knows about pros. He has a rapport with artists, knows (like Bill Cotton) how to talk to them. Given this, we always had plenty to discuss but, because the *Gen Game* was still doing so well, I always replied that I wasn't going to leave—and Michael always repeated that if I changed my mind, I could do anything I liked for ITV. 'If you *do* leave,' he always concluded, 'we'd make you *very* welcome, Bruce.' I hated refusing him, but I soldiered on.

In October, when the next season of the *Gen Game* was aired, Peter Fiddick of the *Guardian* described me as the 'most important man on TV'. It was very flattering but little did I know it was a quote that would come back to haunt me.

These were heady times—*The Generation Game* was regularly topping the ratings with 19–20 million viewers a week. Then, also in October, the *Sun* TV Awards voted me 'Top TV Personality'. But I was not feeling on top form. In November—and this was becoming an annual problem—I was ill with flu, doubtless because I had ignored my resolution to do less and was seriously overworking. In December, there was the Thames TV adaptation of the successful stage play *The Mating Game*, which had starred Sid James. As dear old Sid had died in April, I was asked to take over his role. It also starred Lionel's sister, Joyce Blair, who played the part of a beautiful widow who was always chasing my character around. When asked by a reporter what it was like to work with me, she said: 'I've known Bruce since I was fifteen—and we felt quite at home. At one point we had to exchange a big squelching kiss. I'd wanted to do that for thirty years.'

305

So 1976 was clearly a *busy-busy* time—and not a schedule that was conducive to my health or to my returning home to Anthea as often as I would have liked, especially as she had suffered the ordeal of two pregnancies ending in miscarriages. Then, to our delight, baby Charlotte was born on 22 December 1976. Then, incredibly, Anthea became pregnant again. Later in the year, while I was at a press conference in London, I got a message to dash to the Avenue Clinic where Anthea was in labour. Nine nerve-wracking hours later, on 7 November 1977, Louisa was born. I was now the proud father of five gorgeous daughters— three from my first marriage, two from my second. Oh, the stamina of the man!

The only cloud on the horizon was that, although I had insisted on a nanny, Anthea was enjoying motherhood so much, naturally she was travelling with me less and less. It might have been, as many people suggested at the time, perfectly understandable for me to have felt that there should be no children in our marriage—to have told Anthea: 'No, darling, I would rather not start another family.' But I am a Pisces—I always see the other person's point of view and, knowing how desperately Anthea wanted a baby, how *could* I disappoint her? In my view, motherhood is an important part of a woman's fulfilment—the woman's decision. If a woman wants a child so badly, is it not her right to have one? Nevertheless, I must be honest and admit that seeing so little of Anthea did in time place an additional strain on a marriage that my workload meant was already under some pressure.

The New Year of 1977 began with a one-man show in aid of the Prince of Wales's Prince's Trust at the Theatre Royal, Windsor: something most unexpected happened—just how I liked things to happen. I had been teasing an engaged couple unmercifully and subjecting them to my usual *Gen Game* banter. At the end of the show, Prince Charles came on stage to thank me and said, 'I'm glad I'm not engaged. Mind you, according to some of the things I read, *I am*—to somebody different every week!' He remained on stage with me for about ten minutes, and his comedic timing was very natural. I was more than impressed.

One of my Royal appearances was actually *at* Windsor Castle, in the ballroom. Seated in the centre of the audience, on two huge chairs, were the Queen Mother and Princess Margaret. These are always nervous occasions, but I strode on to the stage in my usual way, and said, 'What a thrill to be appearing here at Windsor Castle. Mind you, I've always liked your soup!' This got a little reaction, but the first part of my act was not really registering and Princess Margaret wasn't even looking at me. She was looking to the side. I then made a cut in my act and went into my golf routine, where I do an impression of four different golfers driving off on the first tee. The princess suddenly turned and, within seconds, was laughing and enjoying herself. What a relief! The press came out the next day, saying: 'Bruce Forsyth had Princess Margaret rocking backwards and forwards at his antics.' Good job it wasn't the Tower—I might have still been there!

In April—and nothing to do with fatherhood!—there was a *Bruce and More Girls* special. The *Sun*'s heading was 'It's girls galore again for Bruce'. This show featured three comedy actresses, all in their sixties—Thora Hird, Patricia Hayes, and Dandy Nichols—prancing around in leotards. Also on board was the lovely actress Lesley-Anne Down with whom I did a 1920s song-and-dance routine, the film star Nanette Newman, who is also a neighbour, and the singer Dana. This show was the first time that Dana had been able to burst back into song since a serious throat operation had threatened her career and forced a five-month lay-off. After the show, Dana said to the reporters, 'Everyone was fabulous to me and so understanding. I did a couple of duets with Bruce and he even spoke to me in whispers so I wouldn't feel embarrassed because, apart from tonight's singing, I still have to save my voice by speaking in whispers.' When Dana heard a playback of the show, she was delighted to find she sounded as she always had. Experts had said her voice might have changed completely as a result of the operation, and she'd evidently been worried she'd turn into an Eartha Kitt or perhaps a female Louis Armstrong. I bet at that time she didn't think she'd become a politician.

At the end of May, in aid of the Queen's Silver Jubilee Appeal, the BBC presented *The Royal Windsor Big Top Show* from Billy Smart's Circus at Home Park, Windsor, in the presence of the Queen and the Duke of Edinburgh. Bill Cotton had talked me into being the compère. And I must say this was the most difficult compère job I ever did. Apart from everything taking place in the round, the show which combined circus acts with variety acts presented us with so many problems. But it did turn out to be a very special show for television. I was given the honour of escorting the Queen to her seat, and they had to keep repeating the music in order to cover the length of the walk. She found this very amusing and, knowing how these things could happen, said, with a smile on her face, 'I don't think they wrote quite enough music, do you?' Of course, the producer and director were going crazy in the box. In addition to lots of wonderful circus artistes, Ronnie Corbett, Ronnie Barker, Les Dawson, Barry Humphries, Elton John, Olivia Newton John, Leo Sayer, Eric Sykes, and Mike Yarwood appeared in an action-packed line-up.

Very soon after that, I was escorting someone else. On 27 July, at London's Caxton Hall, I gave away in marriage my eldest daughter, nineteen-year-old Debbie, to singer-composer David Martin. All the sevens was the way that Debbie had wanted her wedding day, so we fixed the date to include as many lucky sevens as possible—the year 1977, the date the twenty-seventh, the reception timed to begin at seven minutes past seven, and seven people only in the pictures taken outside Caxton Hall. This lucky seven included the happily wedded couple, Julie, now a singer with the pop group Guys and Dolls, Jean Martin, the bridegroom's mother, Penny, the bride's mother, Laura, maid of honour, and proud dad, me.

In August, I had some more tremendous fun when Rita Moreno, who had won an Oscar for her performance in *West Side Story*, joined me for ITV's *The Entertainers* which went out during the

Bank Holiday. Rita, who sang 'I Like To Be In America' with such vivacity in the film, also danced incredibly well. So we were able to do some wonderful routines together, and had a great script from Barry Cryer. It was such a surprise for everyone to discover that Rita was also very good at comedy, and I made sure I used all her talents to great advantage. We sent up generations of movies, with spoofs of *Lullaby of Broadway*, *Tarzan and Jane*, and *Anthony and Cleopatra*. In another sketch, 'Sheik to Sheik', Rita played the silent-movie star Clara Bow and I played Rudolph Valentino. I also played 'Clair de Lune' at the piano—by 'De Brucie'!

Rita came from the rainforests of the Caribbean island of Puerto Rico, which her family had left to emigrate to America when she was a baby. I'd had another Puerto Rican encounter some years earlier, with the stage cast of *West Side Story*. When that electrifying musical came to London, the cast were invited to appear on *Sunday Night at the London Palladium*. But as it was a complicated show, it was transmitted from Her Majesty's Theatre. When I saw the rehearsal, I was thrilled by the dancing, the music, everything. I couldn't wait to see the whole show. The audience was in raptures by the end of the first act. London had never seen anything quite like it. Chita Rivera was superb. Dickie Valentine, who had actually started his career as a page and usher at Her Majesty's, was also on the TV show. Meeting some of the cast from *West Side Story* was my first contact with Puerto Ricans, and their life and culture. Their music and vivacity stole my heart away and, little did I know that one day, another Puerto Rican girl

310

would steal my heart and my hand in marriage . . .

I have had a very long association with Barry Cryer. We first met at the Windmill when he was doing a very funny act that finished with a hilarious impression of the adenoidal American, Jimmy 'Schnozzle' Durante. Since those days, Barry and I have done many shows together, especially 'Specials'. His great skill as a writer, and one that I cannot thank him enough for, is that he always succeeds in getting my true character into scripts and thinks up things that are totally 'me'. He did the same for Frankie Howerd. He is also a brilliant broadcaster, and very talented at giving speeches. To be so good at both writing and performing is a rare talent.

By 1977, after seven arduous years, I began to feel that I had given all I could to *The Generation Game*, that we were starting to run short of good games and beginning to repeat ones we had done a few years before. While thinking along these lines, I was offered the star role in a musical, *The Travelling Music Show*, which had music by Anthony Newley and Leslie Bricusse. It was, I felt, too good an opportunity to turn down. So I came to a decision which I anticipated would cause some shock and alarm in TV echelons, to leave what everyone thought of as my vehicle. In fact, I was only doing what I have always tried to do—to get out of something while it is still at the top. This is so much better than hanging around for a gradual fade, and then going down with a sinking ship. The announcement, of course, was followed by exactly what I had anticipated—plus a tremendous amount of press coverage.

CHAPTER ELEVEN

NO HARD FEELINGS

The Travelling Music Show, in which I was to play Fred Limelight, opened at the Billingham Forum, five miles down the road from Middlesbrough. A lovely 630-seater theatre, it's an excellent place to try out new productions. The show, produced by Hillard Elkins and directed by Burt Shevelove of *A Funny Thing Happened on the Way to the Forum* fame, was actually a *very* strange production. From day one, there was no script, no real plot worked out! It was more a question of 'How can we link all these wonderful Anthony Newley/Leslie Bricusse songs with a sort of thinnish storyline concerning Fred Limelight, an actor/artist/director who, with his wife, daughter, and two aspiring stars, attempts to stage a variety show and win the support of an eminent theatre-owner?' To propel the plot along (or, indeed, stand in for some sort of plot), his motley cast of characters faced a string of incredible hitches caused by the sudden disappearance of one of their leading ladies. But, in the great music hall tradition, the show went on and their efforts won the day. At least that was the idea. But, as one reviewer, Jane Sullivan, pointed out, the problem was fundamental. 'An invasion of starving termites could hardly have provided a more rickety, hollow structure,' she noted, but ended with: 'Bruce Forsyth doesn't so much carry the show on his back as toss and twirl it like a drum majorette. If he has ever charmed you on the box, beware: in the flesh his magnified skills may well defy all shortcomings and charm you into enjoying the whole evening.' Most of the reviewers couldn't then resist making cracks like 'Didn't it grow well' when referring to a moustache I had grown on a three-week holiday with Anthea in Barbados before beginning the rehearsals for the show. I've still got it! (The moustache, I mean.)

In March, the BBC showed a special that I'd pre-recorded with Michael Parkinson. Even before I arrived, I had been determined that we would do a top-hat-and-cane dance routine together. And, Michael, good chap that he is, was up for it. I think he really enjoyed putting tap shoes on, and making a noise with his feet instead of his mouth. Also that spring, 'Both Sides of Bruce', a double-record album produced by Warner Brothers, was released. The whole project was overseen by Derek Taylor, who had been the Beatles' press secretary for many years. I was really pleased with the result. The first part was a collection of eleven songs, and the second, my personal favourite, was a live recording of one of my London Palladium shows.

Amazingly, when we finished rehearsing *The Travelling Music Show* and opened in Billingham, it did quite well. Cheered by this, we then went to Brighton and the Palace Theatre, Manchester, where audiences loved it. Then on 28 March we did our first London performance at Her Majesty's Theatre in the Haymarket. Although the provincial reviews had been good, the opening-night London audience was very tough. They bucked up a bit in the second half but, by the end of the show, I was thinking: 'You *have* been a terrible audience!' Not surprisingly, we didn't get very good reviews that

313

night, but the paying public took the show for what it was—a good-hearted romp with lovely songs—and it did do reasonably well as a result, but not well enough to keep it open beyond late July, after a four-month run. I was particularly gutted because, had it truly been the hoped-for success, it would have gone to Broadway and given me my longed-for breakthrough in the USA.

The press, which had known since late April that Larry Grayson was to take over *The Generation Game* when it returned to BBC 1 in the autumn, kept mentioning the 'terrible gamble' I had taken in giving up the programme for the musical. Billy Marsh responded on my behalf by pointing out that, although I had enjoyed my time on the *Gen Game*, I had no regrets about leaving it. He then added that I'd been inundated with offers from the BBC and ITV since it was first announced that *The Travelling Music Show* was to close and, in fact, there was already a big new TV show planned for me in the autumn.

All this was true. The moment they knew *The Travelling Music Show* was to fold, Billy and Michael Grade had taken me out to lunch and shown me a format for a new ITV series called *Bruce Forsyth's Big Night*. At the time, I thought this was a good idea—and I still do. It was to be a two-hour live show, hosted by me, and would consist of some very good boy and girl dancers, audience-participation spots, 'Beat the Goalie'—a nationwide phone-in sports competition in which youngsters tried to score goals against top goalkeepers—comedy excerpts, and a big star guest. The projected budget for the twelve-part series was two million pounds.

On Saturdays in those days, both ITV and BBC ran sports programmes, *Grandstand* and *World of Sport*. And, after the latter finished, both channels transmitted a two-hour block of family entertainment. As these were before remote-control TV days, it was considered very important to have a good early-evening 'hook' for the programmes. *The Generation Game* was a good example of this—once people had settled into a channel, it was thought they were much less likely to get up out of their armchairs to change to another. And, thanks in part to the *Gen Game*, the BBC had dominated Saturday nights with what was considered a legendary schedule for a number of years. Now, with *Bruce Forsyth's Big Night*, ITV was determined to beat the Beeb at its own game.

But between the end of *The Travelling Music Show* and the beginning of my new TV series, there was to be a new drama. On 7 July, after an evening performance of the musical I had a sudden throat haemorrhage. This was not really surprising. Throughout the entire period of the musical I had been onstage for more than two hours for each performance. I knew I was straining my vocal chords, but carried on. When I went to see a throat specialist, he said: 'You must rest your voice, otherwise you might have to go for three months without talking.' Imagine that! I did what I was told and my understudy took my place onstage for a few days. I was then left in the same position as Dana, having to talk in whispers for days. Fortunately, this did the trick and I suffered no further problems. A welcome distraction from this fright arrived when a few weeks later I joined the hall of fame at Madame Tussaud's in the company of Glenda Jackson, Liza Minnelli and P.G. Wodehouse. 'Funny,' I thought when I saw my effigy, 'it's wearing a pair of my shoes and my Herbie Frogg suit!' It turned out that the Madame Tussaud's people had gone to my tailor and bought one of my 'signature' suits themselves. I would have sold them one!

One of the problems of *Bruce Forsyth's Big Night* was that, because LWT was so desperate to beat the BBC's ratings, it over-hyped the show. Quite frankly, short of a Second Coming on the first show, it was destined, however good it was, to be an anticlimax. So much of life is about expectancy, and when people's anticipation is raised sky-high, it's almost impossible—whatever you do and whoever the star guests are—to satisfy everybody.

But *Bruce Forsyth's Big Night* was a lovely show to host, and there *were* some phenomenal guest stars on it every week—Sammy Davis Jr, Elton John, Demis Roussos, Lulu, Jack Jones, Dolly Parton, Dolores Grey, Lena Zavarone, Karen Carpenter, Dudley Moore, and so on. These were all huge artists who performed during the last thirty minutes of the programme.

Bette Midler was the first. I didn't know much about this amazing lady when David Bell, the show's producer, and one of the best I've ever worked with, said: 'Let's get Bette Midler.'

'Who's she?' I asked.

'She's *good*. She's going to be one of the *biggest* stars in the world,' he replied.

He was always right, so why should I argue?

And, when Bette came over for a couple of weeks to appear on stage at the London Palladium, I was given a seat to go to see her Friday-night performance. By then, she had been booked to do the televised show with me the following week. I *loved* Bette's stage act. She did a lovely bit with motorized chairs, rather like wheelchairs, which girls, dressed like mermaids, drove around in. Lots of times during the show, Bette tumbled on to the floor and just continued to lie there on her back, saying risqué things like, '*This* is my favourite position.' It was all very comical. She also lay on the floor with the microphone and talked to the audience. 'This', I thought, 'is different.' I'd never seen a star lying on the floor talking to an audience before.

When, with the spotlights full on her, she was taking her bows at the end of the show, incidentally wearing black trousers that looked as if they had been sprayed on to her, she became aware of a commotion in the dress circle. Not quite sure what was going on, she waved the spotlights away, saying she couldn't see. Up in the dress circle there were a group of men—she had a very big gay following— who were holding up a banner that read, 'BETTE, SHOW US YOUR TITS'. People in the stalls couldn't see this and were calling out to Bette: '*Read it out . . . Read it out.*' So she did, then added: 'Oh, well . . . it *is* Friday night,' and pulled down her tank top. And there they were. In all my years in showbiz, I have never heard such a shocked laugh. When they say, 'The roof nearly caved in . . .' well, it nearly did. Bette then walked offstage, leaving the place in uproar. It was absolutely amazing.

I didn't go round to her dressing room that night because I knew she was going straight out. We didn't meet until the day we were doing the television show. Her agent, however, came to the script meeting to ask what we were planning to do with Bette. We explained this and that, then I came up with an idea. 'What I would *really* love to do,' I said, 'because she's always tumbling over during her act and lying there with her microphone, is *interview* her lying on the floor.' Everybody, including the agent, thought this was a wonderful idea. '*Oh, yes,*' he said. '*That* would be different.' Then, because good agents are always there to protect as well as promote their artists, he gave me a pleased smile and added: 'I think that's a great idea, Bruce.'

So, when Bette came on stage, I said all the usual introductory things, then added: 'Will you come over here?'

Bette saw the two plump pillows lying on the studio floor and said: 'What *are* we going to do?'

'I'd like to interview you lying down,' I explained.

'Oh?' she said. '*Really?* This *is* different.'

'Isn't this cosy?' I said, when we were in position.

'Marvellous,' she replied.

'Parkinson could *never* do this!' I added.

'Is that a disease?' she asked.

'Well . . . every Saturday night it *is* a sort of disease in this country!' I was able to reply through the laughter.

So we continued with this sort of chit-chat. And it was all great fun. Then, as arranged by the team, a girl entered the stage with a tray set for tea, which she put to the side of us. Leaning closer to Bette again, I said, 'Would you like to be Mother?'

It was obviously an English expression she hadn't come across. Looking at me as though I was being *very* suggestive, she replied, 'What does that mean? Does that mean you are going to be Father?' It was a lovely response and her bewildered reactions to everything I said became a string of double entendres. Then, at the end of the interview, because she was wearing these incredibly skintight trousers—*how* she got into them, I will never know—she was having trouble getting up. So, I got hold of her to help and, as I did so—the cameras still filming, of course—my hand slipped on to her bottom. 'Sorry,' I said, 'no *hard* feelings.' 'No *hard* feelings?' she repeated, before going into shocked laughter.

After we had left the stage, she said: 'By the way, Bruce, did you come and see my stage show?' 'Yes,' I said. 'I came on Big Friday.' 'Big Friday?' she queried, puzzled, and then falling in: 'Oh, *Big Friday.* My agent gave me *hell* about that. Oh . . . that was *really* bad . . . *really, really bad!*'

For me, the next lovely moment was that, as she was leaving her dressing room with her entourage—five or six in tow—they passed my dressing room. Bette came in to say goodbye again, and added: 'We're here for another couple of days, Bruce, can't we do something else? Isn't there another piece we could do together?' 'We're not taping again until the following week,' I explained. 'Oh,' she said, 'that *is* a shame! I'd have loved to do another piece with you.'

Other than on big cinema screens, I have never seen Bette from that day to this. Although I tried many times to get her on to my various shows, she

319

was never again available. She had, deservedly, become *mega*; had risen to superstar status. And when somebody's that mega, it's *very* difficult to get past their agent and get hold of them to do anything.

My mate Sammy Davis who, as everybody knows by now, had a glass eye, was also a guest on the *Big Night*. When he came on, we had a little jewellery chest ready for him to tuck away all his many rings. During my interview, as he got up to do something, one of the rings bounced from the table. 'Oh,' he said, with mock alarm, 'I thought that was my eye.' I, along with the audience, went completely to pieces. Then he did a Long John Silver voice, saying, 'Oh, my hearty . . . Oh, my hearty,' which broke us all up again. He was marvellous, all his antics were ad-libs. By the end, I knew it was one of the best shows we had ever done.

One day, David Bell suggested Russ Abbot as a guest. 'Russ who?' I asked. 'Russ Abbot, of the Black Abbots,' he said. Although I'd heard of the Abbots, I'd never actually seen them work. So when we met to rehearse a sketch about boy scouts, I must say I was a bit apprehensive. But this didn't last long—Russ proved to be so easy to work with. I was the straight man in the sketch, which I've never minded doing as long as I'm working with a good comic. And I found Russ to be an extremely funny man. In fact, he was so good we had to bring him back later in the series to do another spot. Shortly afterwards, he left the Black Abbots and went solo with his own series. Now he's a neighbour, and we often see him in our local Indian restaurant. I think he must have shares in the place—all the waiters call him Abbotswami!

All in all, *Bruce Forsyth's Big Night* was a good format—better, I think, than some that are on TV now. As a viewer I am so bored with seeing contestant after contestant featured on Saturday-night TV, from about six to eight o'clock. The contestants are now the stars. And, unless people can afford to go to a theatre, they can't see performers performing in the way we used to. Even in Puerto Rico, where I now have a home, there are variety-type shows that intermingle bands and singers with some performing. That's what I call *entertainment*!

Perhaps, in a bizarre way, I'm the one to blame! Maybe today's contestant-mentality TV is a legacy of *The Generation Game.* Certainly, one of the things people always marvelled at was how I could get others to do things without appearing to be too unkind when I took the mickey out of them. Alfred Marks once said to me: 'I could never get away with treating people the way *you* treat them, Bruce.' 'What do you mean?' I said, affronted. 'Well,' he replied, 'if I spoke to the people the way you do, I'd finish up with a black eye. But they just take it from you—let you get away with it.' They did—because they appreciated the funny side of me expressing my inner frustration when they were getting it all wrong. They loved statements like: 'You are not only ruining the show, you're *ruining my life*!'

One of my favourite expressions when a couple were up against another really bad couple was: 'Now *you* have a go—you've got *nothing* to beat.' Another, which became an incredibly popular catch-phrase that still follows me around the golf course today, was *'Good game . . . good game.'*

321

When I said this, it was usually because it was a terrible game and we needed some applause! This catch-phrase saved the moment so many times. I learned this art of sending people up in concert party, learned to study faces so I'd pick the right person. I never forced anybody, and always respected people who didn't want to come up on stage. I remember I particularly enjoyed getting a little girl to come up to talk about her pet dog. Anything could happen with this. 'Has any little girl got a dog at home?' A child would put up a hand and, when she came on stage, it would turn out to be a pet rabbit or a goldfish! The sad thing was that when word got around that I was doing this spot in a show, pushy mums would book seats close to the stage and force their poor daughters to sit through a two-hour show: 'You're going to go on stage with Bruce Forsyth,' they would say. 'Don't forget to tell him . . .' What they didn't understand was that such moments have to be spontaneous—off the cuff. On those occasions, I'd have to have a go at the mother to let the audience know *why* the child was there, because the poor little girl looked scared. 'Your mummy's brought you along specially to do this, hasn't she?' I would say to the child. 'Your mummy's a bit pushy, isn't she?' It would then take several minutes to get the child into the right mood to talk to me.

In the early days and during my Summer Season years, I used to give the children these rubber Bendy toy poodles which I got from a place in Ashford. In a week of twelve shows I needed a pretty good supply. Sometimes, these days, when I'm leaving a theatre, people come up to me and say, 'Oh . . . you gave me a toy poodle when I was a child.'

In the end, I suppose I have to say that, although by the time it finished *Bruce Forsyth's Big Night* was doing reasonably well, it proved to be a better idea in conception than it was in execution. People—including both the critics and the public—never seem to take into account that a television show needs time to settle down—something that is taken for granted where stage plays and musicals are concerned. For these, the performers have the luxury of three to five weeks of rehearsals, followed by an out-of-town pre-London run to knock off any rough edges. If only we in TV had that luxury and could also go on the road for a few weeks to get things right. But we don't. All through the series—fourteen shows in all—the newspapers were being pretty vitriolic in their criticisms. When you are faced with this type of thing, you either fight or crumble. I decided to fight, but the strain was enormous. We could not, it seemed, please them. Whoever—or whatever—we did on the show, they continued to slate it. Michael Grade took the blame, along with me, but every week the press tried to find something negative to report. I was very fortunate in having David Bell as my producer. He was wonderful throughout all this and I thanked God for him. If I had not had somebody as experienced as he was to work with, I think I would have folded under the strain. Eric Morecambe was also a great comfort. When asked by *TV Times* what sort of private man I was, Eric, who had known me since my Palladium days, replied: 'Bruce is probably the only entertainer I know who's virtually the same person off-stage as on. He is all verve, vitality, always talking, joking, quick off the mark, razor-sharp but with perfect control, always chasing round and getting the most out of every possible situation.'

In addition to the press, we also had some production problems. One of these was when Elton John was booked for the show. This particular recording began very badly because something was wrong with the piano track for his performance. I knew nothing about this until David came into my dressing room and said, 'Elton has just walked out of the studio.' 'My God,' I said, shocked. 'Where's he gone?' 'To the car park,' David replied. 'Why?' 'He says he can't work with the piano track because it's wrong and he has to over-dub it with *his* piano-playing.' Neither of us knew much about the technicalities of Elton's work, but we certainly knew we had a problem. 'What are we going to do?' I asked, concerned. 'We'll just have to find someone else in the next couple of days,' David replied, 'and record that item separately. Thank goodness it *is* a separate item—the climax of the show.' 'But . . . there's so little time,' I replied, anxiously. 'Let's do what we can tonight,' David said reassuringly, 'finish taping the show—and worry about that tomorrow.' 'Okay . . . fine,' I replied.

About half an hour later, there was another knock on my dressing-room door. And there was Elton. 'Hallo, Elton,' I said nervously. 'How are you?' 'All right,' he said, 'I just came back to apologize.' 'There's no need,' I reassured him. 'You're in the recording business, it's your livelihood, how you make your living. If the track's wrong, you can't just make do with it for tonight's show. Honestly, I understand—sympathize with you. I'm just disappointed we can't do the show.' 'You're such a trouper,' Elton said, 'I feel as though I'm letting you down.' 'You're not,' I replied. 'Don't worry about it. I *really* do understand.'

'What were you planning to do with me on the show?' he asked a moment later. 'I was going to ask you to teach me how to sing one of your songs— show me exactly how you do it—you know, going off the note and doing all sorts of different things with one word. I was going to sing it straight, but with you interrupting and teaching me.' 'That sounds fun,' he said. 'What else?' 'I wanted you to do that marvellous thing where you make up a song from the words on a studio admission ticket. I think that's brilliant.' 'I could do that easily,' Elton said, perking up. There was a long pause. 'Let's do it.' 'D'you mean it?' I asked. 'Yes,' he said. 'Come on—let's do it.' We did—and he was absolutely wonderful. The audience loved him. And Alyn Ainsworth, our musical director, was also his usual wonderful self. After all, Elton and I never rehearsed with Alyn or the twenty-five-piece orchestra before the show.

I never found out what Elton John did about the piano track, but I do know he somehow managed to get round the problem and agreed to play and sing live as well as performing with me. *He* was the real trouper. The story that came out in the press was that Elton had walked out on the show because he had had a row with me. Can you imagine what Elton John's fans must have thought about Bruce Forsyth?

Another occasion that presented us with a problem—but for very different reasons—was when the French singer Charles Aznavour was

325

booked to be on the show. The plan, when he came on, was that I would interview him, then we'd dance with two girls to his song, 'Dance in an Old-fashioned Way'. This was a comedy routine. The interview didn't go nearly as well as we hoped. I found I couldn't draw him out on anything. I don't know if he just didn't like me, or was worried I was going to go into my game-show-host mode and take the mickey out of him, but his answers to my questions were not very forthcoming! We concluded that the interview and the dance—in fact, his whole appearance—couldn't be used. I was only glad this item for the show wasn't being broadcast live.

Guests on talk shows always have the upper hand—if they don't answer the way you expect, or don't help you move things along, you're the one left carrying the can. When I'm the talk-show host, I tend to be subservient to the performer, try to help them, make them feel comfortable and at ease. My style when I'm interviewing is to forget about the cameras, just concentrate on the guest and do a show for the audience sitting there. If I want to bring the camera in for a moment to confide in the audience, that's a different matter. But, nine times out of ten, when I'm in a studio with a microphone and the spotlight on me or my guest, I simply forget what the cameraman is up to. In retrospect I wish I'd been a more aggressive interviewer on the Charles Aznavour occasion, and had a real go at him. Maybe then I'd have got a bit more out of him!

*　　　*　　　*

As well as slating *Bruce Forsyth's Big Night*, the newspapers also kept publishing rumours that my marriage to Anthea was in difficulties—that Anthea had been spotted in various clubs, dancing with other men, while I was away. I remember one particular reporter waiting for me as I walked to my dressing room, having just done an hour-and-a-half's live TV show. 'I hear', he said, 'that you and Anthea are splitting up.' It was the first I knew about it. But was it just another press rumour or not?

Looking back, I can see that much of the time when I was on a big professional 'high', I was also at my lowest ebb. This was true of my Palladium days, during the huge success of *Little Me*, and during *The Generation Game*. There was so much conflict in my personal life, I was never really able to enjoy the 'highs' because I knew the 'lows' were always lurking behind them. I know Ian, my business manager, would say that one of the realities about me is that, until the latter part of my life—the 1980s—I was always pretty ruthless about putting my professional life first. He used to joke that if he happened to drop dead before a show, I *would* be very sorry, but I'd give a damn good performance to compensate!

That, I suppose, is show business. But it's also a Pisces trait. On the whole, I was absolutely amazed that I was the kind of entertainer who could go on and, however low I felt, put my troubles behind me and concentrate on what I had to do and work well. I know some performers can't. But I could. For me, it was never even a matter of browbeating myself and saying: 'Come on, this has got to be good. The audience must have some fun tonight.' I simply saw

327

it as my job—and *would* be on the ball, quick on my feet. This is not something you can learn—you either can or can't do it. I was very lucky. There were many times when I would have been justified in saying, 'I'm so sorry, I can't work tonight, I'm just too upset,' but I never did. Some people might think this heartless—regard me as an unemotional person—but I've always been very aware that people have paid money to come and see me and that performing's like any other job. You are employed to deliver. I've always been so grateful that I've only ever had to cancel a performance through ill-health, and fortunately even those have been few and far between.

It's also a fact of life that divorce is expensive. When marriages go wrong, however low you may be feeling you have to work harder to cope with your responsibilities. Again, Ian is fond of saying that, if I had not been divorced, I would have been a billionaire. Certainly the end of my first marriage propelled me into the club circuit, working all hours in some really dreadful places for two or three years, before I was in a position to buy my home at Wentworth. But that's life, as many men know, after divorce.

Pisces, by the way, are far from being unemotional people; some astrologers claim we're the sexiest of all the star signs! Certainly, as a young Pisces I indulged in constant fantasies about the beautiful women I saw in films—Loretta Young, Gene Tierney, Ava Gardner, Cyd Charisse. I absolutely *adored* them. And, although I got married in my mid-twenties, I don't think I reached sexual maturity until my thirties. Ambition can take the place of everything—even sex. 'I want to be successful' is what drove me in my youth and throughout my twenties. I was always so busy rehearsing and practising new things that it left little time for anything else. Sex took second place. Only when I hit the Big Time, got the job at the Palladium, became 'the name', did I gain confidence not only in myself as a performer, but as a sexual being. Then, after being on that show for six weeks and seeing my name outside the Palladium as fourth top-of-the-bill in the pantomime, my libido grew, and I became sexually of age!

There have been times since, of course, when I regretted passing up some potentially splendid moments with some of the lovely girls I met— especially when I knew I could have pushed matters further. Invariably, though, I was already committed to somebody else. When I was with Ann Sidney, for example, I was doing loads of shows and, not surprisingly, there were endless opportunities. But I let them pass me by! Temptation, to use a golfing term, is par for the course in show business. If you are successful—and this is especially true if you are in the spotlight on the stage—women easily become enamoured, just as men do with female stars. There are, shall we say, opportunities that you wouldn't get in ordinary occupations—I guess it's one of the perks, and sometimes complications, of the job!

Having said that, as you grow older, there are also some embarrassing moments when you first go into a new show. Lovely, sexy, eighteen-year-old chorus girls in skintight leotards rush up to you . . . It's not unusual for one of them to say, 'Oh, Mr Forsyth, I'm so thrilled to be working with you.'

'Really, dear?' I reply, chuffed. But then they add something along the lines of, 'Yes—my mother worked with you years ago in Blackpool.' 'Keep your voice down, *dear. Keep your voice down,*' I whisper. Since I have been 'over the hill', as they say, this has happened too often. It doesn't exactly put me off my stride—but, for heaven's sake, I don't want all the girls to hear!

Anyway, enough of all that . . . *Bruce Forsyth's Big Night* marked the end of my public relations honeymoon with the press. It was as though it was the first thing I had done which did not meet with universal approval. Until then, throughout most of my career, I had been the 'most loved man in British television'. Suddenly, it seemed, I was the most hated. One month into my new series, I was particularly enraged by the *Sun* which, despite its readers having voted me the 'top TV personality' for the second year running, had just printed a series of personal attacks on me. The *Sun* TV Awards had taken place on 3 February at London's Hilton Hotel. As well as me receiving the 'top TV personality' award, Ronnie Corbett and Ronnie Barker had received the 'top comedy' award for *The Two Ronnies*, and Gemma Jones the 'top actress' award for her role in the series *The Duchess of Duke Street.* However, after the scurrilous articles were published, I decided to return my 1977 and 1978 awards.

At the end of the *Big Night* series, only one newspaper, the *Daily Mail*, commented on this viewing figure of fourteen million—all the others, including the *Sun*, had buried us weeks before. Then came the headlines, 'Bruce Is Axed' and 'ITV Show Flops'. I was so irate, so angry with the press

330

about these headlines that I decided—and this was a big decision for me—to do a two-minute slating of them on the show. I spoke to Billy Marsh, my agent, and said: 'I'm not going on tonight unless I'm allowed to do a two-minute bit on the press before the show starts.' 'I think, Bruce,' he said, 'that would be very unwise.' 'Well,' I said, 'tell Michael Grade I'm *definitely* not coming to the studio unless I can have my say.' In the end, Michael phoned me back to say: 'I agree with you, Bruce. The press is being *very* unfair. The show is coming together now—it's doing all right. The truth is we only booked you for thirteen shows, so you're *not* being axed. You *are* doing thirteen shows, and it isn't anything like the disaster they are saying it is. They've been having a go at you for a few weeks now, and it must be very difficult for you.'

It *was* difficult. In situations like this your back is against the wall. You are an easy target with little hope of reprisal. 'Okay,' I said. 'So I'll have my say at the beginning of the show.'

It was easy to include this because, at the start of the programme, I always chatted to—and took questions from—the audience. One of them—and this was not a 'plant'—asked me how I felt about all the bad publicity I had been receiving. So, speaking straight into camera, I told the audience and the viewers what the press had been up to and gave them a few facts about the show. I then said: 'I'm not just talking about myself here. I'm also talking about the ordinary man in the street. When they do something wrong—or if the newspapers think they have—they are persecuted. They're then ashamed to walk down the street, knowing that people are looking through their net curtains, pointing a finger at them.'

I then added—and, remember, this was well before all the really big Royal troubles began, and seems now almost like a premonition: 'Members of the Royal Family are the people I really feel sorry for. They can't answer back, can't contradict any statement that's made, or picture that's taken. And I think this is very wrong in our country. I can—so I'm a very lucky person. I just had to have these few moments to put matters straight, to alert you—the viewing public—to what is going on in our country today. The only thing you *can* believe when you look at a newspaper is . . . look at the top right-hand corner—*the date.*'

The following week there were literally two sackloads of mail from viewers saying: 'Bruce, you can't *even* believe the date. The papers often get that wrong, too'!

The press, of course, had an even bigger go at me after the show. Nobody before had ever looked straight into a television camera on a live entertainment programme and taken them to task. They had a field day—became even more vitriolic: 'How dare he? We made him—helped him . . .' They could not believe that anyone had given them a taste of their own medicine.

Strange as it may seem, I still have some good friends in the press—people I can trust. The others know *who*—and *what*—they are. But, historically speaking, this was probably the first 'build 'em up . . . knock 'em down' swing of the pendulum, which is so familiar to people now. It coincided with the time when the tabloids were engaged in a massive circulation war—a time when there were also lots of rumours about newspapers folding. Standards of journalism were dropping fast, and the whole ethos of public life was changing—being challenged.

As far as *Bruce Forsyth's Big Night*—and my angry outburst—is concerned, I must leave it to you to decide whether or not I did well.

CHAPTER TWELVE

DON'T LOOK BACK

Getting laughs is probably the most serious part of my one-man show. And this, believe me, is much more complex than it may appear. We hear a great deal about 'straight theatre', but most 'straight' actors are the first to admit that it's much tougher being in a comedy—knowing where the laughs *should* come, playing those scenes for all your worth, and 'riding high' for comical moments—than any other kind of play. You may be a very good dramatic actor, more than capable of getting an audience on your character's side, but succeeding in getting laughs in all the right places and sending people home happy and smiling at the end of a show, is really hard work. But this must never show. On the contrary, it should appear easy. I often analyse my performance, saying: 'I *should* have paused after that line,' or 'I didn't give that moment the emphasis I normally do.' I never stop diagnosing.

In my one-man shows, I can tell in the first five or so minutes what kind of audience I am facing— whether they are going to be a normal par-for-the-course lot, as easy as pie, or really tough and difficult. Personally, I prefer an audience that is not too boisterous at the start because, if it is, I may have to struggle to keep the pace at that level for a couple of hours. An audience that's *too* excited, *too* gee'd up about having come to see you, can prove to be the hardest to satisfy—may 'peak' too soon. Sometimes I feel like saying: 'Hold on . . . *Hold on*, ladies and gentlemen . . . We have over two hours to go!' An audience that's not quite so delirious, or takes the attitude, 'Okay, we're here . . . What are you going to do to entertain us?' can be coaxed—lifted up and up. It's a bit like fishing—you play them in, reel them out, let them know who's boss, who's in charge. By the end, they can be a *very* satisfying audience to work to.

This reminds me: I've never had what are called 'groupies' because I'm not that kind of performer! But, for years, I had a couple of ladies who were *always* seated up front wherever I was appearing. There were also some marvellous young guys in the Plymouth area, who formed the Bruce Forsyth Fan Club. I visited them one weekend when they were performing their version of one of my game shows. At the end of the evening, just as I was about to leave, they said: 'Wait a minute . . .' and sang the Tony Bennett song, 'It's Never Too Late', which I use as an opening for my one-man show. Now, this is not a well-known song—and I always sing it in an 'up' tempo rather than Tony's slow tempo—but the boys knew all the lyrics, got the change of tempo exactly right, and managed all the bits I had added to it. Some time later, when I was booked to do *An Audience With . . .* for LWT, I decided to sing this number as the opener and include all these young guys in the show. On the evening, I lined them all up behind me, then halfway through the song I stopped the orchestra, let them sing on their own, and then asked them to join me centre-stage. They were all wearing 'Bruce Forsyth' T-shirts. It was a lovely moment for them, for me—and for the show.

*   *   *

At the end of 1978, when the fourteen-week run of the troublesome *Bruce Forsyth's Big Night* finally came to an end, I decided to take a year out of the UK. Somehow, until then, I'd never really found the right vehicle to transport me to an international arena. 'Taking off with my one-man show', I thought, '*will* be a bit of a gamble, but I feel more than ready to explore foreign fields.' I could give this a shot by going first to New Zealand to fulfil a contract I'd signed eighteen months before, then on to the USA to pursue the 'American dream'— hopefully on Broadway and in Los Angeles.

So I flew to Auckland at the end of January and met up with my musical director, Don Hunt, to record a television special for TVNZ. Two weeks later we were joined by Ian and my drummer Freddie Adamson, a true Yorkshireman and one of the best big-band drummers of his generation. Rehearsals for what was to end up being the longest single tour of my one-man show then began in earnest with the New Zealand orchestra employed by promoter Chris Cambridge. Thanks to *The Generation Game* having been sold to New Zealand, I was as well known there as I was in the UK. Business on the tour was phenomenal, and a number of dates were even added to the schedule.

335

New Zealand is a beautiful country, and I saw almost all of it. From Auckland to Dunedin, Christchurch to Palmerston North, we seemed to go to every major city and a few not-so-major ones. While we were in Wellington, I even recorded a television commercial. It was a very happy time. Not surprisingly, selling shows out always makes everyone involved relaxed and, while we all worked really hard, Chris Cambridge was determined that we should also enjoy ourselves. So he set up a number of excursions and tourist-type activities for our days off.

I remember our visit to Rotorua particularly. Situated at the heart of the North Island, Rotorua is famous for its bubbling volcanic pools and boiling geysers. It's also a Maori cultural centre. I had one of the best massages of my life there, complete with hot spring water being sprayed on my back. It makes me tingle even now to think about it—not to mention that the masseuses were only wearing bikinis because of all the water spraying around. The only thing about the place I don't remember so fondly was the smell of sulphur—bad eggs! It was unbelievably strong, and actually I'm glad we only spent the one day there because it really got to my voice.

Talking of voices, Rod Stewart happened to be touring New Zealand at the same time as me, and we kept bumping into each other. After we'd checked into our hotel in Christchurch, Ian, who in those days had long hair and a beard, was mistaken for one of Rod's rock 'n' roll party and given their room list. He came up to me and said, 'Bruce, they've got eight suites and seventy double rooms. That makes our one suite and six doubles look pathetic.' My response was instant. 'Book some more rooms immediately!'

During that trip, I also had one of the longest birthdays of my life. I stayed in Auckland for about four weeks in all, and 'home' there was the White Heron, one of the best hotels—although, sadly, I think it's closed now. In addition to regular rooms, they had a number of chalet-style apartments, which were perfect for me: they felt more like flats than hotel rooms. I was delighted to discover that either side of me as neighbours were Brian Murphy and Yootha Joyce, who were in Auckland to perform a stage show of their hugely successful sitcom, *George and Mildred*. Both of them were great actors—far more so than you'd imagine from the series—and they were a pair of the most fun-loving people, with great senses of humour. When Yootha found out it was my birthday, she organized an impromptu get-together the night before. We sat by the pool at the White Heron under a starlit sky eating fish and chips—served with champagne—waiting for me to turn forty-seven.

The next day, my birthday proper, saw me on stage at the Auckland Town Hall. The audience sang me 'Happy Birthday', which was very touching, and then we went on to another celebration Chris Cambridge had organized at Auckland's then premiere—and possibly only—nightclub. If memory serves me right, I think it was called Diamond Lil's. Whatever, I can clearly remember that the cabaret was a drag act, and I ended up in bed exhausted at around four in the morning, and in absolutely no doubt that I'd had one hell of a birthday.

While the New Zealand tour was a great

experience, in June 1979 came the moment I'd been waiting for, the fulfilment of a lifetime's ambition. I arrived in the USA to put on my one-man show on Broadway at the fifteen-hundred-seat Winter Garden Theater. As I was only giving six performances, plus a preview on the Monday, this was an expensive big bite at the 'Big Apple'. But at least the pre-show advertising was impressive—a full page ad in the *New York Times*, featuring highly complimentary recommendations from Cary Grant, Neil Simon and Anthony Newley—and Sammy Davis Jr announcing he was 'flying in specially from California to introduce me for the first night'. There on Broadway, amid all the panache and buzz of New York and the glittering lights of Manhattan, I proved that I hadn't forgotten much since performing as a young man for the American Red Cross. It was obvious from the audience's response—and from some very good first-night reviews—that I still understood the American sense of humour.

The background negotiations for these shows, however, had not been so happy. Originally, Lord Delfont had agreed to back them but, for reasons never fully explained to me, he pulled the plug at the very last moment and withdrew his financial support. It was, to say the least, a nerve-racking situation. Fortunately, Michael Grade came to the rescue—at least in part. He commissioned a fly-on-the-wall documentary, with David Frost—not yet a Sir!—following me from my arrival in New York through the whole Broadway experience. The result was *Bruce Forsyth On Broadway*, which was transmitted on ITV in November. I put the fee I received from this towards the production costs of the Broadway run, and made up the shortfall from my own pocket.

Unbeknown to me at the time, the programme was to prove more than just a much-needed source of finance. It allowed the British public to see what really happened, albeit a few months later, in what was to be the most controversial episode of my professional career.

As will already be clear, since leaving *The Generation Game* in 1977 my relationship with the British press had become increasingly strained. Until then, I had always regarded dealing with them as part of my job. Sure, they can write reviews and articles about you that you don't like, but at the same time we all make sure we use the best from reviews to publicize our shows. Things, though, had changed. Too often, I was reading things about me personally and professionally which were simply untrue, completely made up, and rightly or wrongly, I was beginning to think they were deliberately out to get me. I had therefore decided not to bother with a press conference for the British press before my opening on Broadway. There was terrific interest in it with countless requests for interviews, and I was eventually persuaded by my agent, Billy Marsh, to bury the hatchet and see them. With hindsight, I don't know why I bothered.

By now there was a giant marquee above the Winter Garden Theater with a huge picture of myself—'Bruce Forsyth on Broadway'. I was thrilled—it was a dream come true, and I couldn't wait to get onstage and see if I could make an American audience enjoy my one-man show as much as a British one. I'll never forget waiting in the wings on that Monday night, half wondering what the hell I was doing there and half beside myself with excitement and anticipation. Within minutes of walking onstage, I knew it was going to be all right. The audience was fantastic and, apart from a few references in my act that I knew Americans wouldn't understand and had changed on my act, it was just like working the Palladium—I even got a standing ovation.

Tuesday was the official opening night. Sammy Davis Jr had flown in to introduce me and among many others Anthony Newley and Leslie Bricusse were there to give me moral support. It was another great evening and we left the theatre to go to the famous night-spot Sardi's, to sip some champagne and wait for the early editions of the New York newspapers to see what the critics had to say.

Clive Barnes of the *New York Post*, whose nickname was 'the butcher of Broadway', gave me one of the best reviews of my life. It started like this: 'Do you remember how many times you have been invited to a party you never expected to enjoy, but felt you ought, for some reason, to go anyway? I felt precisely that way about Bruce Forsyth's one-man show that opened at the Winter Garden Theater. It was, in the event, funny, lovely, heart-warming, terrific—pick your adjectives. It was simply a happy evening in the theatre. I expected much less. Bruce Forsyth is a lanky, cheerful British performer who does almost something of almost everything. In Britain he is the equivalent of our Johnny Carson—the indisputable Number One superstar. A TV idol. Here he is unknown . . . The man amuses and charms. He is only scheduled here in New York for a week. Go, take a look at him.'

There were other good ones too, as well as some penned by people who'd obviously hated me. For example, one paper said, 'He would have been a riot at a neighbour's wedding but not on Broadway.' Naturally, it would have been great if all the reviews were as good as Clive Barnes's, but one thing you learn early in show business is that you can't please all the people all the time. To come to New York and break even with the critics was more than good enough from my point of view.

Because New York is five hours behind the UK, the first people at home to know about how the show had gone read about it in the London evening newspapers—in those days there was both the *Evening News* and the *Evening Standard.* In a strange way, they summed the situation up fairly accurately—one said, 'Bruce wows Broadway' and the other, 'Bruce flops on Broadway'. Much later, someone sent me a photograph of two news-stands with these conflicting messages side by side. It amuses me to this day.

However, I was far from amused at how the following day's national newspapers chose to report what had happened. They seized on all the worst reviews and portrayed my American venture as a complete disaster. I even received a call from a reporter from one of the major broadsheets to apologize for his article. He explained that he had filed what he considered to be a balanced report, but was told by his editor that as all the other papers were saying I was a failure, he had to rewrite his piece to stay in line! It was a very strange time. People in New York were ringing to congratulate me, and people from London were ringing to sympathize, and ask if I was all right. I don't pretend to understand why this happened. I sometimes suspect that the British press doesn't like someone to be *too* successful. And in the years since then I've watched how they seem to love to build someone up, only to knock them down.

For years afterwards, almost every article about me, even if it was complimentary, seemed to start, 'Bruce Forsyth, who flopped on Broadway . . .' and it never ceased to irritate me. When I did the one-man show at the London Palladium the following year, I devoted the centre two pages of the programme to 'Some Reviews You Might Not Have Heard About', printing all the marvellous American reviews I'd received and which no one had seen fit to report. In some respects this might have been seen as adding fuel to the fire, but by then I had decided I wasn't going to talk to the British press—about anything! It was an embargo that lasted almost ten years, and my life was no worse for it.

While the PR effects of Broadway were unfortunate, the real tragedy was that I was only billed to perform there for one week on Broadway and, what's more, only able to *finance* one week. In that short time, word of mouth combined with the good reviews meant that box office trends were very healthy. If I could have hung on for another two weeks or more, I would have been a much bigger 'hit'. The other thing I lacked was someone—as the Americans say—to 'kick ass'. And 'kicking ass', as they are *so* fond of telling you, is an essential part of life in New York.

On a lighter note, when I was deciding which songs to sing on Broadway, I toyed with two that featured New York in the title. One was a big hit at the time, called 'New York' by Gerard Kenny, the other a relatively unknown song called 'New York, New York' which had been the title song for a movie by the same name starring Liza Minnelli and Robert De Niro. A few weeks before I flew to New York, Leslie Bricusse had taken me to see Juliette Bora perform in Los Angeles and she had included this number in her set. I thought it was great and decided to close the first half of my show with it. It went down really well, and the two people whom I had employed to produce the Broadway show on my behalf, Lee Gruber and Shelley Gross, told me how much they liked it. As it happened, Lee and Shelley were Frank Sinatra's East Coast promoters and about nine months later he released his version. Why didn't they ask *me* to record it?!

Anyway, I had taken the gamble on Broadway and, even though I knew it would entail financial loss for me, I believed—given the chance—I could have a wide international appeal. Even in London, people from all over the world were always saying: 'We understand your humour—enjoy your acts so much.' In the end, though, because I did not go to Broadway for a longer run, things did not turn out the way I had hoped. I discovered you can't appear there for just one week and expect great things to happen. That might be how it's portrayed in Hollywood musicals but, in reality, things just do not happen in that way. Also, unlike the music business, where singers and groups can make a record in a UK studio and then send it off in the post to America, and be 'made' if it lands in the right hands, performers like me have to meet the challenge of performing 'live' in the actual country.

Even so, many British entertainers—once they have become as big as they can on home ground—invest in exploratory work to try out their 'wings' there. But very few succeed.

One of our biggest showbiz 'exports' was Benny Hill. An enormous number of his shows—despite the fact that they were considered too risqué for the US family-entertainment market—were bought by an American production company, which cut his series of hour-long programmes into half-hour shows and scheduled these at post-watershed times against the News on rival channels. Their investment proved to be very sound. After a few weeks, Benny's shows beat all the other channels' ratings. The US's home-spun comedians went mad, hardly able to believe that Benny was getting away with so many innuendoes, not to mention all the half-naked girls cavorting around. '*We*', they kept exclaiming in despair, 'would *never* have been allowed to make shows like that years ago. In those days, our production companies still regarded the so-called average American viewer as very prudish about both films and television.' Benny, however—despite the bizarre fact that he always refused to work 'live' on TV—was not only tolerated, but also a phenomenal success.

*   *   *

I'd better tell you that leading up to and throughout this period in the USA, my personal life was in the rock-bottom doldrums. Sadly, Anthea and I had indeed drifted apart. We were just not feeling the 'vibes' any more—you could say that the romance had disappeared from our marriage. We had to admit to each other—and to the rest of the world, which was keenly watching—that it was all over. The extraordinary thing, though, about our decision to separate—and our eventual divorce—was that Anthea and I were both so easy-going, so civilized with each other, about it all. We even agreed, as part of our divorce settlement, to do some articles for the *Sun* newspaper, which ran in 1979. This, we felt, would be the best way to counteract all other press speculation and rumours about why our marriage had failed and ended. We also agreed that we would each look at each other's articles before they were published, to ensure that they were okay from both our points of view.

What I told the paper was that there wasn't really a single incident that sparked off the end of the marriage. It wasn't as though there was another man in Anthea's life who caused the split, or another woman in mine. For love to work, my feeling is that both partners have to go halves—there needs to be an equal amount of loving from each person at the same time. But this isn't easy, by any means. And I think that if you get the balance wrong—if one person starts to give short measure, or indeed too much—you can be heading for failure before you know it. What Anthea said was that she thought we loved each other differently. 'For a woman, love is her whole life, whereas for a man it's only part of his life,' she said, adding: 'Perhaps women have to love in this way so that they can totally love children.'

I believed that our trouble was that both of us had actually begun to give each other *less* than half. Once this happened, before too long, we were drifting apart. The final break actually came after my return from New Zealand, when I was invited to Tobago in the West Indies to play in a charity golf match. I'd asked Anthea to bring our two little girls along with her, but she didn't want to come at all. 'I felt I couldn't keep taking the two babies on and off planes just to be with him,' she told the paper in response to the question why she hadn't come along on the New Zealand, American and West Indies trips. 'Maybe that was wrong of me . . .'

Whatever the case, when I came home from that last trip, we knew it was all over. We'd only seen each other for a matter of a few weeks out of almost twelve months. Separate bedrooms and separate lives soon followed. As I told the *Sun*: 'After a period away from each other, you know instinctively, just by looking into each other's eyes, whether you have missed one another. I knew Anthea hadn't missed me as a husband. And I knew I hadn't missed her as a wife.'

There weren't any big fights, then or before. Anthea's philosophy was that it is always better to get your problems out into the open and talk them through. We didn't even argue much. But in hindsight, our day-to-day communication skills probably weren't the best, despite this goal of discussing difficult things together. And to be honest, we'd never really taken our different backgrounds, habits and career paths into consideration.

When I met Anthea, I had known little apart from show business, in one form or another, since the age of fourteen. If I'd been a nine-to-five man, we could well have stayed married—things would have been completely different. This could have

346

made things work from Anthea's perspective—she talked in her part of the *Sun* articles about having simply wanted a home, babies and to sit there happily with her man. But as the *Sun* noted, a leopard cannot change its spots overnight. So, while at the beginning Anthea had lovingly travelled everywhere with me, supporting me, patiently waiting alone in hotel lounges or theatre dressing rooms, once we were married and had established a life together, all that lost something of its magic. 'At times I desperately needed her by my side,' I noted, 'just as she yearned for someone to be with her when I was away. But then I can understand this. Hanging around while your partner does a night's work is not my idea of fun either.' Interestingly, Anthea put this another way. She called herself 'over-possessive', saying that at the start she actually wanted me to herself the whole time. She said she wasn't even that keen on socializing, as she wanted to hang on to what she called 'that one hundred per cent feeling'.

What happened during the run of *The Travelling Music Show* is pretty indicative of the pattern we were to get into. It was a marathon of a show, with me on stage for practically the whole two and a half hours. Afterwards, I'd need to relax, come down from that 'high' which every performer knows about. What I most wanted to do was let off steam over a meal out with Anthea, catching her up with everything that had gone during that night's performance. But on most occasions Anthea, who of course had probably had a busy day with the children or with her own activities, would actually stay away from the theatre and head off to bed rather than wait around as I entertained friends in my dressing room. My profession had made me used to odd hours, whereas a late night for Anthea usually meant a couple of days resting up afterwards. So I'd usually find myself driving home to Wentworth by myself, and getting there at any time up to one o'clock, where supper would be left waiting for me in the kitchen. 'I would creep upstairs like a burglar, anxious not to wake her,' I told the *Sun*.

In Anthea's 'side' of the story in these articles, she confirmed this. 'I have spent the loneliest years of my life since I've known Bruce,' she said, 'yet much of this is really my own fault . . . I didn't realize when I first fell in love with him that there would be this great problem with his profession, that eventually show business would become the third party in our marriage.'

'But,' I added, 'show business must take only part of the blame. Anthea and I also reached a stage where we discovered that the things we once enjoyed doing together, we no longer did. I loved to go the theatre. Anthea was not that keen. Anthea is also not a great party-goer, so the invitations we accepted became fewer and fewer . . . There were occasions, of course, when I would want to play a round of golf, and Anthea had other plans in mind. But this is inevitable. There are conflicts of interest in any marriage.'

Anthea even confessed to what she actually called 'a terrible fault'. She called herself 'far too possessive and anti-social'. She said that her possessiveness didn't have anything to do with what she called my 'supposed Casanova image', and denied in response to the interviewer's questioning that I had a roving eye beyond any normal man's response to a pretty girl. But after being there for the children, she said that I seemed to be basically away, whether it was for work or to play golf.

Another ingredient in the break-up was the string of challenges my career was facing. After all, in one twelve-month period, we went through *The Travelling Music Show* being taken off after just four months, the mixed response to *Bruce Forsyth's Big Night*, and the Broadway debut that was called a flop at home while a significant part of the hyper-critical New York press gave it rave reviews. And that's without mentioning all the 'personal attacks, wild rumours and plain untruths' that I would have been happy to list for the *Sun*'s readers. I'd got to a point where I was fairly thick-skinned and would bounce back from criticism, but even run-of-the-mill press jibes were getting very tough for Anthea. Any other sort of marital difficulty aside, that's an additional pressure you suffer from in a high-profile marriage, one that most people don't have to bear.

The way we formally put it was that 'the two of us publicly separated, deciding that, unless someone came into our lives, we would have a two-year separation, and then divorce on the grounds that our marriage had irretrievably broken down'. But it was very important for me to add that I felt terrible for the children. I absolutely adored—and now more than ever!—Charlotte and Louisa, and there was absolutely no question of regretting having them, for either of us. I said then that I wanted 'to see as much of them as I can in the future', and I'm fortunate that I have been able to, and I still love having them around me.

As far as practical arrangements went, once we

divorced Anthea decided that if I would buy another house for her and the girls nearer Virginia Water, I would keep the house at Wentworth. Her reasoning was that I had lost one home already, when my marriage to Penny was over. As I said to the paper, this was just one of the signs that although we had fallen out of love, Anthea and I hadn't lost our fondness or respect for each other. For her part, Anthea said: 'Now it's all over, I don't feel unwanted because I know Bruce loves me and I love him. I know I will always love him and I hope he will me. But that chemical in-love thing has gone . . . I want Charlotte and Louisa to think their daddy is wonderful. Which he is. I'm hoping in the future that their daddy and I will be great friends . . .'

All the other newspapers which, for many months past, had been publishing those wild rumours about Anthea being seen dancing here, there and everywhere while I was away, and predicting the end of our six-year marriage, were only given a two-paragraph statement from our solicitors. This said: 'We have been instructed by our clients to state that they have formally decided to separate upon the most amicable terms. No further statement will be made by either party, or on their behalf.' This did not prevent the press, of course, continuing to publish speculative stories from July 1979 onwards. And, needless to say, they dug out and rehashed everything they could find from cuttings and other dubious sources, on every woman who had ever fallen in love with me—or me with them—from my early youth upwards. Some of the rehashed stories were true, some were better than fiction. I will not embarrass the ladies—

showbiz singers and dancers I had worked with at one time or another—by re-naming them in this book. Let me just say, I was often on my own, often unattached—but show business is show business!

One final bizarre event leading up to the divorce from Anthea is that, because everything remained so amicable between us, Anthea wanted to use the same settlement lawyer as me! I had to talk her out of this—literally force her to use another lawyer. The fact that she wanted to *does*—and I think readers will agree—say much about us and all the happy times we had shared together.

Ian Wilson has also reminded me of a time when, after we had first separated, a newspaper offered Anthea £40,000 to do an article, and Anthea asked Ian if I would mind him going along to discuss the deal. At the meeting, Ian said to the journalist: 'The first thing we must do is list what Anthea is and is not prepared to talk about.' Over the next hour, the paper's offer of £40,000 was reduced to £3,500, because Anthea kept saying: 'Oh, *no*, dear, I couldn't possibly talk about that . . .' and 'Oh, no, dear, I'd never talk about Bruce in that way.' The paper's anticipated story then changed from 'All the dirt about my life with Bruce Forsyth' to 'Well . . . we really love each other very much'! Anthea is always very amusingly hoity-toity when she gets all protective. The poor newspaper journalist obviously did not know what he had let himself in for.

I'm delighted to close this chapter of my life by saying that, to this day, Anthea and I are great friends—two once-married people who speak to each other on a regular basis. Also that our lovely daughters, Charlotte and Louise—now well and

351

truly grown up—remain a very special and essential part of my life. Given how busy we all are, we still manage to meet as often as most extended families; and I'm always particularly thrilled to see how wonderfully well all my children get on with each other. This may not be what some members of the press would like to hear, but it's true!

Of course, the unexpected still happens. When in April 2001 Kirsty Gallagher was offered the chance to be the new hostess on the current version of *The Generation Game*, one newspaper published an 'exclusive' saying that she had actually taken the job—which was in fact completely untrue. As ever, the other newspapers scrabbled to get articles together to follow up the 'exclusive'. A number of them thought it would be interesting to approach former hostesses for their comment. Anthea hardly ever talks to the press, but the *Daily Mail* managed to get through to her. And what started as 'giving a comment' turned into a two- to three-hour interview, which I think was quite a silly thing to have done, because out of it was bound to come an article that focused on the very old story of our marriage.

Under a headline that declared '. . . BRUCE WAS THE ONE WHO WAS UNFAITHFUL', the two-page article did include some nice bits, but went over the top in a number of areas. Indeed, in my opinion it actually inferred that Wilnelia had been the reason for the break-up of my marriage to Anthea—and because of the way it was written up, that Anthea had taken the blame. She was quoted as saying that she had admitted adultery to save my career. Nothing could have been further from the truth, as Anthea knew. And let alone the reading public, I did not want our daughters thinking that Wilnelia had broken up my marriage to their mother. Anthea and I had publicly announced our separation in the summer of 1979, yet Wilnelia and I didn't even meet until November 1980. How, fourteen months later, could she possibly have been the cause of our divorce? In fact, Anthea admitted adultery in March 1981 because she and her new boyfriend Freddie wanted to marry quickly.

I was stunned when I read that interview with Anthea. It was the Saturday after the Easter holiday. Charlotte and Louisa came round that afternoon telling me that Anthea was in a terrible state about the whole thing—and that, to add insult to injury, she believed the headline the paper had used were not even her own words. She had been shown the article before it went to press, but she was on her way back to Spain, where she has a home, and hadn't had time to read it carefully enough. I later saw the copy, and she was right, the actual words used in the headline were not in the article at all. Whoever came up with it might be a first-class journalist but, I'd like to add, I think he's a first-class something else, too.

Needless to say, I was extremely angry about the whole thing. When Anthea called me from Spain, in tears and apologizing for all the trouble it had caused Wilnelia and me, I had to tell her that it had been an extremely unwise move of hers to talk to a journalist in that way after all our previous experiences. And I had to tell her that I was more than annoyed. But as our association has been so good for the past twenty years—and very importantly, for the sake of our daughters—I forgave her. As far as our family is concerned, it's now forgotten.

*   *   *

Having the papers delve into your family affairs is incredibly upsetting, especially when you go to great lengths to keep relationships straightforward and positive even if your family is 'extended' over several marriages. Julie, my daughter from my first marriage to Penny, once felt she had to 'put the record straight' about my two broken marriages—to her mother and to Anthea, the story of which was still current. From the best of intentions—love of me—Julie was responding to comments Penny was reported to have made about me and our relationship in a *Daily Mirror* series entitled 'The Real Forsyth Saga'. The series read as a vitriolic kiss 'n' tell attack, obviously timed to complement the now topical news stories about the end of my marriage to Anthea.

To whet readers' appetites, the pieces were introduced thus: 'Day One of the heartbreak behind a comic's smile'. You can imagine how things only went downhill from there. Claiming that 'one woman knows only too well the other side of Bruce Forsyth the star', it painted a picture of Penny helping me become one of Britain's highest-paid performers, then watching as 'her once idyllic marriage' ran on to 'the show-business rocks' when I 'walked out' to marry Anthea. As ever, the truth was probably more interesting than this piece of fiction. The first article continued with a story set on Christmas Day, 1971—which was when Anthea finally made up her mind about whether she wanted to be with Louis or me. Part of the story that follows is true—that it was Christmas, and that Anthea phoned me. But as for the rest . . .

The article is so ridiculously over the top I'll have to quote some of it: 'Penny Forsyth walked into her kitchen and picked up a carving knife which, a few hours earlier, she had used to slice the Christmas turkey. "I said to myself there's only one way to end this and that's to kill him," she recalls. The dramatic scene called for the intervention of an action man like James Bond. As if on cue, Sean Connery—one of the Forsyths' Christmas Day guests—strode into the kitchen and grabbed the would-be murder weapon . . .' According to the story, Anthea ('Bruce's glamour stooge from BBC TV's *Generation Game*') had been calling all day. Supposedly, Penny and I were reconciled for the holidays—which was a complete nonsense. In fact, I'd only gone over for the day, to be with the girls and their mother. Sean, as a family friend, was also a guest.

The article claimed that after lunch 'the phone calls began', as I watched television upstairs with Sean (the Ali–Frazier fight was on), and that eventually Penny had steamed into the room where we were, to say: 'Pick up that phone, Bruce, and talk to that stupid girl and then get out of here and out of our lives.' When I did speak to Anthea, I'd supposedly started to take down the address of where she was staying in a diary Penny had been given for Christmas. Evidently, Penny had grabbed it and hit me over the head with it. At which point Sean had taken a fiver from his wallet for me to write the address on that instead! It was then that Penny went downstairs to get the carving knife . . .

355

If she had, no wonder I packed and went out 'through the front door for the last time' as the story had it, driving off in my maroon and silver Rolls-Royce.

The rest of the article was as ridiculous and distorted. The knife bit didn't happen. Hitting me over the head wasn't true. Really, the whole thing was pure fabrication from beginning to end, and very hurtful. 'He was a naughty boy with the ladies even before then, but he was far nicer about it before success and fame came along,' ran one section in Penny's 'own words'. Apparently before long 'everyone was an Anthea—young, pretty, leggy girls' who fell about for me. If only! But one bit did at least make me laugh. Apparently, each time I left 'home', I sent for my piano. The paper had Penny saying: 'the Steinway people came to move that themselves and the last time they called to collect it I had stuffed all his press cuttings inside. One of the movers looked at the piano and said: "Mrs Forsyth, if your husband leaves you again, he can fetch his own grand piano. This is the last time."' The strange thing about this was that I didn't live anywhere big enough to put a grand piano!

I later learned from Penny that she had originally been approached by the journalist Chris Hutchins for an article to run in one of the women's magazines. She was offered a reasonable sum to be one of three ex-wives who would talk about life after divorce from a famous spouse. She thought this was quite harmless and the money would come in handy. She was invited to lunch in Hampstead to talk to Mr Hutchins, and the champagne flowed. More champagne accompanied a follow-up visit he had with her in Whitstable, where she lived.

A copy of the article was sent to Penny before it was published, and she was terribly upset about the way it read. She crossed out the parts she wanted removed and signed each page. But she also learned that the article was going to be bigger than expected, and was even going to run in a national newspaper. It turned out she didn't actually get copy approval—the piece was going to press as is. Penny was so upset she phoned a solicitor and tried to get the piece injuncted, but it was too late. It all happened very quickly.

Julie—obviously deeply distressed by some of the things that Hutchins had extracted from Penny—answered back in the *News of the World*, under the banner headline, 'Mum shouldn't have said those dreadful things about Daddy.' 'When I read what my mother said about the way my father was supposed to behave, I just broke down and cried,' she told the *News of the World* reporter. 'My mother made him sound like a tyrant who was having affairs all over the place. And that we lived in some kind of prison camp with Dad strutting around like a mad colonel issuing orders. But that's crazy. The bit "Bruce Forsyth only lives for Bruce Forsyth" is a lie. Like everyone else in his crazy business he wants to see his name in lights—is still ambitious. But being a star doesn't mean everything to him. He's not arrogant and selfish or on some kind of ego trip. I admire him so much. He has always been a very gentle and undemanding personality at home. I've never seen him lose his temper. Not once. And that's amazing.'

I was, of course—what father wouldn't be!—

deeply touched by Julie coming to my defence. Today, as I write this book, I'm delighted to say that, since those awful days, all Penny's and Julie's differences have been reconciled—and that my first wife and I are now good friends again, too.

I did meet Chris Hutchins at a function some time after this, and took him to one side. I don't think he will bother me again.

*   *   *

After Anthea and I were divorced—and I was once again unattached—there were a number of occasions when the press's interest in me made my life a misery. During this period I sometimes went out for an evening with girls or 'stars' who were appearing in my shows. On one of these jaunts—incidentally, an innocent fun-night out that on this particular occasion included me as the host, Ian Wilson, the *Play Your Cards Right* hostesses and the male assistant, John Melaney—we went to Stringfellows, in London's St Martin's Lane. Just before we were due to leave the nightclub, one of the girls discovered that there were some photographers lurking, cameras at the ready, outside the front entrance. 'You'd better be careful, Bruce,' she warned. 'One of them has just been heard to say: "Which of the girls is Forsyth with?" Why don't we see if there's another way out of here?' Such moments—and there were too many of them—are not exactly conducive to relaxing between bouts of hard work.

On another evening, when I was in Stringfellows, a pretty Malaysian girl approached me to ask if she could have her photograph taken with me. I said:

358

'I'm sorry, but we didn't come here together. And I have to be *very* careful, you see.' 'Oh!' she said, obviously disappointed. 'All right. But can I talk to you for a few minutes?' 'Yes,' I said, still doubtful. 'Your show, *Play Your Cards Right,* is *very* popular in Malaysia,' she began. 'In fact, I'm responsible for sending the videos out there every week. I've got two or three tape machines, you see, which I use to copy them, and then I send them to my husband who sells them.'

She was so open about her 'piracy', I was speechless. But, then, if we showbiz people knew just how much piracy goes on, we'd all be in despair. Piracy's a *very* profitable business. The only investment that's required is a couple of television sets and video machines. The trouble is that none of the bona fide producers or 'stars' receive any of the rewards. It turned out that this pretty girl—who admitted she was making a lucrative income out of *Play Your Cards Right*—only wanted her photograph taken with me, so she could send it on to her husband to be placed on sale next to the videos.

Another so-called 'photographic opportunity' arose just after Anthea and I had agreed to end our marriage. Returning from Spain, where I'd been staying with Jimmy Hill and his family, I was met at Heathrow by Ian Wilson and Paul Whitlock, my driver of many years. Ian had phoned ahead to say that the press would most certainly be at the airport waiting for me. As I sat on the plane bracing myself, it occurred to me that they would be wanting to photograph a Bruce Forsyth who had a distressed look on his face. I decided not to give them what they wanted: if I could manage a big grin, that would ruin their story. But if I had to open my mouth to give a comment, I'd lose the grin, and they'd get their shot. So I decided to make out that I couldn't actually speak—that I'd lost my voice. That way, I could just point at my throat and keep grinning. When the first journalist approached me, with four photographers in tow, and started asking questions I made sure I didn't relax that grin for a second. And as a result, there wasn't a single photograph of me getting off the plane in the papers the next day. One of my better ideas!

However, our car was followed from the airport by a number of journalists. When we reached my home at Wentworth, all of them stopped at the bottom of the drive except for one who had the tenacity to follow us up to the top. As we reached my gates, Paul stopped the car and Ian got out to 'have words'. The conversation was brief and ended with Ian punching our unwelcome guest—a *Daily Express* photographer—and manhandling him into the bushes and throwing his camera down the drive. The other journalists, who had parked in the road below in their usual positions (these were times when anyone coming into or out of my home would pass anything up to thirty journalists and photographers) and were awaiting news, heard the fracas and began to rush up the drive on foot to see what was happening. Ian got me out of the car and we hurried into the house.

By now, one extremely upset photographer has extracted himself from the rhododendrons. Screaming abuse, he ran towards us and went to strike Ian on the back of his head with his camera. Paul was having none of this. A stocky and powerful man who looked like a rugby prop forward or club bouncer and had previously worked as a coach driver, he was no stranger to this sort of situation—and he finished the job that Ian had started. Inside the house, I telephoned the police and by the time they arrived, the photographer had already filed a complaint. Fortunately, the police took the view that, given the laws of trespass, both Ian and Paul had used reasonable force to protect my property, and they decided not to press charges. However, it was the first and only time that Ian got a name check on ITN's *News at Ten*!

On yet another occasion, when I was being driven home, I wanted to stop and buy a couple of toys for my two daughters. I went into a local shop, but the paparazzi, who were still on the story about the break-up of my marriage, were following me everywhere in cars. I tore in and out of the shop, then speeded on to the house. Having arrived and entered the dining room to greet Anthea and our daughters, I saw two of the paparazzi guys crawling commando-style—flat on their bellies—up our lawn. I instantly phoned the local police, saying: 'I *can't* bear it. I'm *not* going to have them coming into my garden, trying to get pictures of me, my wife, and my children. You had better get here right now or all hell is going to break loose at Wentworth. And, if something conclusive isn't sorted today, I'm going to get some really vicious guard dogs, plus anything else that's necessary to protect us. These people are *not* coming on to my property—invading our privacy. I am *not* going to have my wife and daughters threatened.' '*Please*, Mr Forsyth,' the policeman at the receiving end of this tirade replied, 'don't do anything foolish. I know you're *very* angry, but we will be there *very* soon.'

To this day, I believe your face and your body are *personal* property—and your children are *sacrosanct*. Where invasion of privacy is concerned, the press should be governed more strictly. And they should certainly be made to ask permission before taking photographs.

*   *   *

While on the subject of fame and getting recognized, I must now—for light relief!—tell you the following true story—and one that was printed in the *Reader's Digest*, no less. A friend and I had hailed a London taxi. I gave the driver instructions, while my companion got into the back. 'Just a minute, I *know* the face. Who are you?' demanded the cabbie. 'I'm Bruce Forsyth,' I replied. 'If you're Bruce Forsyth,' chuckled the driver. 'I'm James Bond.' 'No, you *can't* be, because *I am*,' said my companion. For it was none other than Sean!

I've never had much trouble with the police but, on one occasion, when I was driving through London's Regent's Park, I very nearly did. Being in rather a hurry, I was driving too fast and was stopped by the police. Now, in those days—long before speed cameras—they used to set a police 'speed trap', which meant that two policemen would suddenly step out from hiding and raise their hands to stop any car that was breaking the speed limit, and say: 'Sir, you have just been timed over the last two or three hundred yards [whatever it was] and the police officer now running towards us will tell you the speed that you were doing.' As I looked in my wing mirror, I could see him approaching my car. When he arrived, he said: 'It is my duty to inform you, sir, that the speed you were going was . . . *OH, BRUCE* . . .', in such an apologetic tone. This, of course, started all the other policemen laughing. But I still got a warning!

My *professional* action-packed end of 1979 saw another trip abroad. In November I took my one-man show to the Huntingdon Hartford, a major Hollywood venue, now called the Doolittle Theater. Whether I would be the kind of success I hoped to be when I faced up to the next of my lifetime's ambitions, appearing as a relatively 'unknown' in Hollywood, I had no way of knowing. What I *did* know was that Hollywood's British colony would be out in force: Christopher Lee, Dudley Moore, Anthony Newley, Sally Ann Howes, Juliet Mills, Vidal Sassoon, Patrick MacNee, and Sabrina (the spectacularly well-endowed 'sweater girl' star who had emigrated from London some years ago). What a star-studded line-up to face!

Cary Grant was also there. He had first seen me in pantomime in Bristol years before and once, when Anthea and I were in Hollywood, he had taken us and our daughters to the Hollywood racetrack of which he was a director. The children loved it and we all had a wonderful day. I was also thrilled to learn that Donald O'Connor, a fantastic dancer and one of my great favourites in so many ways, came to see the show. So while I was in Las Vegas, I also took the opportunity to see him performing in *his* show. He was so charming. He mentioned to his audience that I was present and told them how much he had enjoyed *my* show. Afterwards, he invited me to dinner at his home one evening, adding that, as everybody was in the habit of eating early in Los Angeles, could I arrive at seven thirty? As I always like to be on time, I turned up on the dot. Donald opened the door, very formally dressed in black tie and tuxedo. For a moment I froze. Although I was smartly turned out, I was not formally dressed. Looking me over, Donald said: 'Oh . . . Didn't I tell you, it's a formal dinner.' He then managed to retain his dismayed expression for quite a while, before breaking into one of his lovely smiles. It was a joke! When I went into the house, I discovered he'd greeted his other guests in the same way. For a moment, though, he'd certainly had me fooled. I also remember Red Buttons, a very popular clown-like American comedian whom I'd never met before, coming up to me and saying: 'Let me know if there's anything I can do to help you while you're in LA.' 'This is one occasion', I thought, 'when I might need all the help I can get!'

Despite all my nervousness—and, believe me, *I was nervous*—my one-man shows there were a complete sell-out. As I was waiting to go on that first night, my face somewhat strained and pale under the funny-man make-up, I remember turning to Ian at the side of the stage and saying: '*What* am I doing this for . . .? *Why* am I putting myself out on a limb again?' But the moment I launched myself on to the stage I found out why. As I walked on, I felt the warmth. 'This feels good,' I thought.

As I've doubtless mentioned before, I can always tell what an audience is going to be like. People don't just sit there, and applaud and laugh—they

364

create an atmosphere, give off vibrations. These can be slightly hostile, very ordinary, or something that gives you a little extra—helps get the old adrenalin pumping even more, gives you what you need for being on really top form. That's what I felt in the Huntingdon Hartford. It was marvellous. In the first few minutes of chatting to the audience, I got some wonderfully good laughs. And, throughout the entire show, they were fantastic to perform to. It proved something that I had always believed, that my brand of entertainment doesn't have national boundaries.

Afterwards—after the standing ovation—when the performance was finished, I was elated. I felt just like anybody feels who's received something they've wanted for a very long time. I felt a sense of achievement. And *that* last feeling was something I had not felt for a very long time. Then, because I knew I had a lot of personal and show-business friends out there, I could hardly wait to get my make-up off and go to the after-show party to hear *their* reactions. Once there, I was totally overwhelmed when this VIP 'audience' broke into another round of applause, and then lined up to kiss me, shake my hand, and tell me what a marvellous performance I had given. Cary Grant, I remember, was the first in the sea of amazingly well-known faces to grab me. Then, having spoken to everybody in the line, which included Gene Barry, Cyd Charisse and Barbara Eden, I walked around the room for two spectacular hours talking to everyone else present. Finally, I sunk down in a corner of the room with a glass of champagne and orange juice. I don't doubt for one moment that— along with all the lipstick traces—a sense of achievement was written all over my face. I couldn't even begin to guess how many times I'd been kissed and had my hand nearly shaken free from my wrist. Let me just say I felt absolutely great! Once again a 'high', but I was on my own.

The next night—the last performance of my two-night stand—brought more of the same. I could hardly believe what was happening. Once again more stars, including Dick and Dolly Martin, Howard Keel, Steve Forest and his brother, Dana Andrews, Robert Stack and his wife Rosemary, turned up for the show. Two nights, such as these, were more than enough to have me floating on air—and *I was*, even before the critics produced rave reviews for my 'stage debuts in film city' in, for example, the *Los Angeles Times*.

All of these events, of course, remained largely unreported by the British press. With a couple of exceptions, journalists back home were still too busy having a field day with the breakdown of my marriage—and were still digging up as many cuttings as they could find on my past romances. As far as my professional life was concerned, they had lost interest.

All in all, the Los Angeles appearances were the realization of a dream—just the sort of heady tonic I needed to distract me from the unrelenting UK press interest in my personal life. I did not, though, escape from this altogether in LA. While I was there, Hugh Hefner, who built his empire on *Playboy* magazine, threw a wonderful party in Hollywood to celebrate twenty-five successful years in publishing it. I went along with Patrick Curtis, once married to the stunning Raquel Welch, and an English singer, Juliette Bora, who had made her home in California. I refused to answer any reporters' questions. 'I am', I tried to explain, 'supposed to be here to meet friends and enjoy myself at a wonderful party. Isn't that what you're supposed to do at parties?' But it was hopeless.

*   *   *

One day, while still in LA, staying at the Westwood Marquis, in Westwood Village, I decided to have an hour in the sun. Suntan cream at the ready, I looked up and, to my astonishment, saw Benny Hill standing there on a very hot day in what I can only describe as a typical English businessman's mackintosh—but by no means as smart as a Burberry! He also had on a very strange-looking hat and was carrying a brown-paper carrier bag with all his things stuffed in it. I couldn't believe it—thought for a moment I was watching the start of one of his sketches. 'Benny,' I said, taken aback, 'what are you doing here?' 'How are you, Bruce?' he replied, completely unfazed by my presence. 'I was asked to come over for a couple of meetings. I'm only here for a very short while.' After a pause, he added: 'Bruce, you come here quite often, don't you? Have you got any useful phone numbers for me?' Not quite sure what kind of telephone numbers he was after, I said cautiously, 'Not really, Benny.' 'That's a shame,' he replied. 'They might have been useful.'

I then learned that he was there to negotiate working in Las Vegas, was being offered $300,000 a week, but had turned down the work. 'Live performances', he explained—as he always did on such occasions—'are *not* my thing'. Now, if I'd

367

been given this chance to perform 'live' in Las Vegas, I would have jumped at the opportunity—would have done as many shows as were offered. I *love* performing 'live'—enjoy that so much more than pre-recorded television—but Benny only enjoyed thinking up his scripts, going off to write them, then getting into a TV studio to do his 'thing'. He was so lucky. The Americans were screaming for more and more of his TV shows and when, back in the UK, he started to produce half-hour scripts to meet this need, the network never stopped repeating them—even after his death. To this day, when I go to Puerto Rico, Americans—knowing I'm English—come up to me and say: 'We *loved* your Benny Hill, you know. Your Benny Hill was *such* a funny guy.'

The tragic thing is that, after all the millions Benny made for UK television, he lost his show. It broke his heart. We subsequently heard that the show had ended because Benny was no longer considered PC—politically correct—was still using women as sex objects on his shows. I, for one, will *never* understand *why* television companies ignore their silent-majority audiences who are only too happy to watch such programmes, and pay instead so much attention to a few hundred vocal people who are obsessed with PC nonsense. What harm, for example, does the 'Miss World' contest do? Yet there's a minority that claims it's most harmful. But it's a contest that gives so much pleasure to both the entrants and the audiences. The winner is given a wonderful, unique opportunity in life—and all the other contestants get to go somewhere really lovely for a week. Thereafter, all of them are 'celebrities' in their own country. What's wrong with that? Also let me add that millions of pounds have gone to children's charities because of 'Miss World'. Political correctness is a fashionable killjoy. And Benny, I believe, was a casualty of this wave.

Speaking of Benny has jogged another happy LA memory. Comedy, as I implied at the beginning of this chapter, is a very serious business to get right. And comedy on a record is, believe me, even more difficult. One of the all-time masters of this art is the great American comic Bob Newhart. I just love his record about Sir Walter Raleigh explaining the discovery of tobacco and what it was used for. And I was thrilled to meet Bob and play some golf with him at the Las Vegas International Golf Club. Tony Newley's drummer, a croupier, and Jack Jones were also present, walking around with us while we played. At a short hole, Bob hit a very nice shot that bounced a little before the pin and then finished about seven feet from the other side of the hole. I was the next to play and my ball bounced just in front of the hole and then dropped right into it. *Well!* We all went crazy and Jack Jones, who is usually a very laid-back guy, jumped six feet into the air. *What a shot!* So, having got a hole in one, I had to buy a round of drinks for everybody in the clubhouse. In that club, however, nothing was paid for in cash. Everything was paid for in coupons. So Bob, as the member, had to pay for my drinks. Wasn't that nice of him? A hole in one, but no hole in my wallet!

By chance, while relaxing one morning in Los Angeles, I had watched a half-hour game show called *Card Sharks*. In this show, contestants were invited to choose playing cards from a giant pack and to guess whether or not the next card dealt would be higher or lower. When they guessed correctly, they were rewarded with substantial prizes. It was the kind of show that viewers loved to see me doing. 'This', I thought, sitting up, suddenly animated, 'would make a really excellent show for UK TV—and I'm sure I could persuade David Bell [by then Controller of Entertainment at LWT] to buy the rights.' For me, this would be perfect timing. Having been out of the UK for the best part of a year, I was feeling ready to take on a new TV challenge on my home turf.

Card Sharks, called a 'strip show' in America because it was 'stripped in' five times a week between other programmes, was being shown on American TV during the same period as another excellent game show, *Family Feud*. The rights to both, I discovered, were owned by Goodson & Todman. By coincidence, one morning, when I was breakfasting in the lovely L'Ermitage hotel in Beverly Hills, I bumped into Paul Talbot, who was in charge of their overseas market.

'How extraordinary,' I said, 'I was going to phone you later. I think your *Card Sharks* would make an excellent game show for the UK. But—having said that—now that I've also seen *Family Feud*, I think I prefer that one.' 'Oh, hard luck,' Paul replied. 'The rights to *Family Feud* are no longer available. Bob Monkhouse bought those last week.' Disappointed to have missed this game by a whisker, I added: 'I'd still like to consider *Card Sharks*.'

After I'd parted from Paul, I immediately phoned Ian, saying: 'Please find out if Bob has seen *Card Sharks*, and—if so—ask him if he would consider swapping his rights in *Family Feud* for this

370

game.' 'Sorry, Bruce,' Ian phoned back to say, 'Bob is not interested in any kind of a swap.' So . . . I decided to go ahead with *Card Sharks.*

While at a meeting with Goodson & Todman in their offices, they asked me if I would be using the same format for the game in the UK. 'I intend to start the show off with single contestants,' I replied. 'But then I'd like to change the format and use couples. That, I think, would be even more interesting—not only in how they react to the prize money, but how they react to each other. Which of them, for example, will turn out to be the dominant partner, saying "Come on—let's go for it"?' Proof that this was an excellent idea was later confirmed, not only by the success of *Card Sharks*, which we rechristened *Play Your Cards Right* for the UK, but by the *Who Wants to be a Millionaire?* 'couples' specials. But I've never claimed a royalty!

Although I would have loved to have had the kind of success Benny Hill had in America and continued to work there for much longer, I never seriously thought of leaving the UK until after my marriage to Anthea fell apart. But because so much seemed to have gone wrong, both in my personal life and my UK career, I did seriously consider going to live in the USA for at least a couple of years. In the end, though, because I only had sufficient capital to meet my current financial commitments—the Wentworth house, the children and the pending divorce settlement with Anthea—I returned to the UK.

The main reason *why* I would have liked to have been a great success in America is that *if*, following my one-man shows in New York and Los Angeles, I had become a really big name there, I would have earned enough to set up my own production company. Having done this, I would have achieved another lifetime's ambition producing all kinds of shows, from light entertainment to dramas and documentaries. Performers such as Johnny Carson and Mary Tyler Moore did this in America, but UK artistes of my generation were never given the chance to form these sort of companies or, even more important, ever been encouraged to become heads of production companies.

This, I think, is a great pity because artistes in a position to represent other artistes have a very different attitude. I *really* would have loved to have made mega American dollars, and put these into running a company for the good of UK television. I'm not suggesting that I had aspirations to be a mogul, sitting on top of a huge financial empire. I'm simply saying that, as a performer, I'm absolutely convinced I would have known how to treat performers. And, by no means the least consideration, I think I could have advised them on how to handle their public image better than I did.

CHAPTER THIRTEEN

A GOOD HAND

People are fond of saying their 'New Year came in with a bang'. Mine *really* did—a *bang* and a *whimper.* And neither—unfortunately for me—was champagne-induced! Six days into January 1980, just after I had returned from Spain to the UK, an unscheduled 'drama' occurred on stage at the

Fulcrum Theatre, Slough, during a performance of my one-man show. This 'drama', which resulted in my being unable to be as energetic as usual, also nearly put paid to my next engagement at the Fairfield Halls, Croydon, South London. What happened in Slough?

At the sound check in the afternoon, I noticed that the stage was very slippery and that tap-dancing on it at the end of the show would be like dancing on glass. I asked the stage manager to ensure that it was scrubbed before the show and, later in the day, was assured that this had been done. All went well during the performance until, as I was walking off the side of the stage, my feet suddenly disappeared from beneath me, my legs went up in the air, and I did a spectacular clown-like tumble, and landed on my right wrist. The trouble is that the audience always thinks this sort of thing is part of the act. Holding my broken wrist, I tried to explain what had happened, but they just laughed. I had no way of knowing if I could finish the show as planned, singing at the piano, but I decided to try. To my amazement, although my wrist hurt like hell, I got through it. When I arrived at the hospital, I was told it was definitely fractured and would be in plaster for six weeks.

Wrist in plaster, a few days later, I did the show in Croydon. Given that this and the show at Slough were my first appearances on a British stage in more than a year, and that there had been so much bad press in the interim, it was really gratifying that both nights were sell-outs. I might have fallen out with the British press but the public, at least my public, were as giving and as enthusiastic as ever. I was touched. At Croydon, the theatre manager told me he had overheard a member of the audience tell the journalist sitting next to her, 'Don't you dare print anything nasty. You've given our Bruce a very bad time of late. Give him a break now.' The pun, I was assured, was entirely unintentional!

I really did these two shows in order to warm myself up for a brand new television series, *Play Your Cards Right*, the UK version of the game show *Card Sharks* that I had discovered in Los Angeles. While still in the States, I had arranged to meet David Bell, LWT's Head of Light Entertainment, and, just as I had hoped, he and his boss, Michael Grade, agreed that the card game looked like a tailor-made 'winner' both for me and the UK market. Four gorgeous girls—Jo Thomas, Natalie Shaw, Yvonne Younger and Denny Kemp—were booked as the show's hostesses, together with John Melaney as our new male assistant. No one actually told me at the time that this was to counter criticisms of not being politically correct.

No longer a 'stripped show', the UK format for *Play Your Cards Right* had been revamped as a once-a-week programme, scheduled for prime-time TV from 1 February onwards. The main 'revamp' problem had been timing. Theoretically, each game could be over in three or four minutes if the contestants got all the cards right, or could go on interminably if they did not. In the American-style 'stripped show' this had not mattered because, when a game ended halfway through or overran, the players had simply been asked to come back the next day. For our format, however, we had to complete each game within one show. Apart from that, the content was the same. An outsize pack of cards was cut and five cards placed on a board for each pair of contestants who then had to guess whether the next card turned over would be higher or lower. I always did a run-down of the rules for the contestants after my opening remarks and before asking the questions (which always began 'We asked a hundred married men/single women in their twenties/female strippers/male pigeon-fanciers' or whatever) that decided which couple would go first at each round. They probably explain as well as anything else that I could say, how the game worked:

> The object of the game is to work your way across the board by predicting whether each of the cards is higher or lower than the preceding one. The first one to turn over the last card correctly will win the game—and a Brucie Bonus. [This to a great roar from the audience— as ever on game shows I'd hosted, there were 'Brucie Bonuses' to be picked up at different stages along the way.] All our questions are based on a poll of over a hundred people, and all our polls are genuine. Did you cut the cards? [The contestants did this before the show, and the studio audience witnessed it.] Good luck to you all.

There were lots of other little rules, but the turning over of the cards could be very dramatic, not only for the contestants, but also for the studio audience and the people at home, which made it the ideal show to play along with.

There was also always the famous introduction

to my wonderful assistants:

> I'm the leader of the pack
> which makes me such a lucky jack.
> And here they are, they're so appealing,
> OK, dollies, do your dealing!

As PC came and went, this was reworked a few times. As I have said, early on we tried out the interestingly innovative idea of counteracting any 'non-PC' charges by also including a male model. But for a period in the nineties we weren't even allowed to call the girl hostesses 'dolly dealers'. By the middle of that decade, however, everyone said, 'Oh, blow the PC merchants! Let's call them dolly dealers again!'

Catch-phrases came thick and fast on this show. If two cards were the same—different suits, of course—I'd always say, 'You don't get anything for a pair.' *'Not in this game,'* the audience would reply. It became such a famous line that it inspired a joke, which went as follows: 'I was at home the other night and there was a knock at the door. I opened it, and standing there was this beautiful girl with a raincoat on. She then threw off her coat and there she was, topless! I said, "What's all this about?" She said, "I'm a Page Three girl, and my editor sent me here to ask you if I'd get anything for a pair." I said, "Look, dear, Brucie Bonuses are not that easy to come by!"'

Another rule was that contestants could 'freeze' their cards, which stopped their opponents taking advantage of them. Often, instead of 'freeze', they'd say 'stick'. I would get very annoyed. 'Stick?' I'd say. 'What do you think this is, pontoon? You've taken all the class out of the show.'

Following advance publicity for the series, I was criticized because *Play Your Cards Right* was an American format. I didn't understand why this was so important, but as I thought about it, I realized just how few British-devised game shows had been successful. At the time, British television was rightfully praised as being the best in the world, and I fully agreed with that. But as far as game shows were concerned, we weren't very good at devising them. *The Generation Game* was imported from Holland, and other old favourites such as *What's My Line?* and *This Is Your Life* were bought from America. This was to continue on through the eighties. *Family Fortunes, Sale of the Century* and *Wheel of Fortune* were all American; *You Bet!*, German, *3-2-1*, Spanish—the list goes on. Mind you, things have changed now. Big international hits like *Who Wants to Be a Millionaire?* and *The Weakest Link* mean that we are now, at last, getting into the game-show business!

Anyway . . . before I go any further into what was to become series after series of *Play Your Cards Right*—a 'trump' card for both me and LWT's ratings—I need to mention two more personal-life dramas that occurred towards the beginning of the New Year. The first was a High Court case on 28 January, involving my daughter, Julie. The second was tabloid publicity for a 'tell-all' autobiography that was 'about to be written' by Ann Sidney, my 1960s 'Miss World' girlfriend. But, first things first.

By now, Julie, aged twenty-one, had become the youngest singer in a pop group called Guys and Dolls, which had shot to fame with its version of the song 'There's a Whole Lot of Loving'. Having achieved 'overnight success' by selling over a million copies of their record, the group, having parted from its original management team, was now in the High Court. Once there, instead of a whole lot of loving, there was a whole lot of feuding going on! Former managers Ammo Productions were claiming £12,000 in commission which they claimed was owed to them when the group 'repudiated its agreement'. Guys and Dolls was cross-claiming £3,418 which they said was due to them in record sales. They were also counter-suing, claiming mismanagement. Ammo Productions had made a production deal with Magnet Records (Lord Levy's old label), and had given the group 2 per cent between the six of them. The group had also had to pay recording costs. The group's million-seller song, the court was told, had been written by Ammo directors Chris Arnold, Geoff Morrow and David Martin. And David Martin, who was Julie's brother-in-law—married to her sister Debbie—had sung the lyrics on the 'dummy recording'. As, after this, the Ammo directors had felt they had a potential 'hit'—and the pop market was ready for a new group of good-looking personable people—Guys and Dolls had been formed and Julie had sung the song.

How, I know readers must be wondering, did Julie find herself in court on the opposite side to her sister's husband? To answer this, I must backtrack to a row that had occurred between Julie and Debbie and their two partners, Dominic and David. This had arisen five years before the court case, during the time when Guys and Dolls was first up and running, and David was the record producer who held a large stake in the group's best-selling record. After a series of differences of opinions concerning business matters, the girls and their partners had fallen out and refused to speak to each other.

Five years is a distressingly long time for two of one's lovely daughters and their partners to be at loggerheads, even if they did all manage to meet at family gatherings without ever firing a cross word. The brilliant thing about the last day of the court case—which, incidentally, was settled out of court, with both sides agreeing to pay legal costs of around £10,000 each—was that they all made it up and family peace was restored. As Debbie said: 'It was all rather embarrassing with David and myself on one side and Julie and Dominic on the other. Then, while we were in court for the last time, we suddenly realized how stupid we were all being.'

There was also some more good news at this time. Julie was pregnant—and phoned me to say: 'Dad, you're going to be grandfather in August.' Dominic and she had also decided to get married as soon as his divorce came through. I was so happy that they were going to make an honest grandfather out of me!

But the other personal drama of 1980 was less fortunate. The year had begun with a succession of stories that Anthea had split up with her current boyfriend, car-dealer Lawrence Matz, and that we were back together again. Neither story was true, any more than the rumour that she was about to join me on television in *Play Your Cards Right.* Then, in March it was reported that Ann Sidney was 'engaged in a behind-the-scenes deal to write her memoirs' supposedly worth up to £100,000— even more of a considerable sum then than it is now. It would be, the *Daily Mirror* informed its readers, 'a remarkable tale of glamour, tears and torment . . . the story of a Miss World'. Ann, who the papers pointed out, had been 'twice married' since those days was quoted as saying: 'I'm going to tell all in the book . . . I've had romances with many leading entertainers, including Bruce Forsyth. I see nothing wrong in writing about him . . .'

As it happened, there was so much press coverage about what the book would contain that the book itself was not written. For me, there was little comfort in this. The press had already ensured that anything that might have been said was already being said in their columns. Two decades since that 1960s love affair, when I was thirty-eight years old, all the minute detail— whether accurate or not—was once again dredged up as sensational breakfast-time reading for millions of their readers. And all this was happening just four weeks after my new television series, *Play Your Cards Right*, had first been beamed into those same homes. What an extraordinary coincidence!

*   *   *

For the first series of *Play Your Cards Right*, we had the problem of me appearing on television with my right hand in plaster. But, somehow, despite the plaster cast, I had just enough movement in my fingers to turn over the cards with my right hand and hold the microphone in my left. We also overcame the problem of needing to complete each game within one show by devising fill-in card games that I could play with the audience. Then, from the second series onwards, the plan was for me to do six- to eight-minute interviews with the contestants. This proved to be a bit of a sod's-law plan, however, because whenever I had a really 'good-for-loads-of-laughs' couple on the show, the game would either overrun, meaning the interview would have to be cut to ribbons, or, sure as eggs are eggs, would have to be cut out altogether. In the early days of the show, we were also restricted to prizes not exceeding the value of a Mini car—about four thousand pounds. In the nineties, however, the contestants were allowed to win a car worth about sixteen thousand pounds, plus another four to five thousand pounds on top. This meant they could walk away with about twenty thousand pounds—a lot of money.

During one series, a woman wrote to a newspaper asking why I always showed the male partner of the winning couple to the driving seat— wasn't this sexist? Well, if I'm going out with my wife, *I* take *her* out—*I* drive the car. I want her to have a good time. So for the show, I always felt it was only the gentlemanly thing to open the passenger door for the lady, and make sure she was seated comfortably. Just to check, I asked the women in the studio audience one night, don't you like being driven when your boyfriend or husband takes you out? 'Yes,' they all shouted, 'but we always have to drive him home when he's drunk!' I was gobsmacked. For once, I didn't know what to say. But what people never noticed was that while the keys of the car were given to the man, I'd always given the woman the prize-money cheque . . .

In the first series of the show we had single

381

contestants. One man from Birmingham did *everything* wrong. If the card that had just been turned over was a five or a six, he chose 'lower' for the next one, and if it were a ten or a jack he'd say 'higher', with no regard for the laws of probability. But he still managed to win the game, and even went on to the prize round, where he won the car! I said to later audiences, 'We had a fellow on the show who did everything wrong and still won a car—luckiest fellow in the world. The last I heard of him, he got run over by a bus!'

After I'd totalled up the value of the winnings, I'd say goodbye to everyone, including the losers (with whom I'd always have a drink upstairs afterwards). I'd say, 'Well, it could still be a big night—if you play your cards right. Good-night!' The winners always managed to do so well even if they didn't get the car that the show always ended on an upbeat note.

By the way, Bob Monkhouse's *Family Feud*—rechristened *Family Fortunes* for British TV—proved to be a great show in which Bob was an excellent compère. The good news, from my point of view, is that once the format of *Play Your Cards Right* was adapted for couples, it gave it another dimension and worked so well. I was very pleased I hadn't made the swap with Bob. *Play Your Cards Right* was a perfect vehicle for me.

ITV's Michael Grade also paid me very handsomely for this series—possibly because he was sorry I had taken such a lot of flak for one of his ideas, *Bruce Forsyth's Big Night*. I do understand, though, that taking the flak is all part and parcel of being the star of a series. After all, the star gets the plaudits when other people's ideas

382

work . . . so the star should also be prepared to take the 'stick' when things go wrong. For twenty years now television had been, by far, my biggest source of income. I earned more money, for example, for a single episode of *The Generation Game* than for any of my two-hour one-man shows. And, by the eighties, I would have had to do five or six one-man shows to equal the fee from one transmission of *Play Your Cards Right.* I really do consider myself incredibly lucky to have found my way into a business that throws money at you for what most of the time you love doing! If I'd been born a billionaire, I would probably have paid those who paid me to *let* me perform! But, just in case I become a billionaire, I intend to keep this under my hat . . .

*   *   *

The 1980s, like most decades, were a mixed bag for people in all realms of life. And 'realm' is an apt word to use here! The Prince of Wales married Lady Diana Spencer in July 1981; Prince William and Prince Harry were born in June 1982 and September 1984; and Prince Andrew married Sarah Ferguson in July 1986. It was not all jollity, though, for our nation. There were riots in Brixton, followed by riots in other cities; unemployment reached three million; the Falklands War began; the 'Irish troubles' continued, and there were miners, dockers and nurses strikes. There were also some really appalling disasters—a passenger ferry sank in Zeebruge, there was a fire at London's King's Cross Station, the Hillsborough football stadium collapsed. In the entertainment world, rock star Bob Geldof formed Band Aid to raise money for the famine victims in Ethiopia and, in 1985, Live Aid raised forty million pounds for the same cause. Peter Sellers, a man we all loved and recognized for his unique comic gifts and his Inspector Clouseau character in the *Pink Panther* films, died at the age of fifty-four. And the much-loved Eric Morecambe died of a heart attack. Oh, yes, and Channel Four ran into trouble, only a month after it began transmission, for using 'bad language', creating 'political bias' and introducing other 'undesirable qualities' into our home viewing. Whatever one's own problems, thinking back on decades certainly puts one's own life into perspective.

*　　　*　　　*

In March 1980 my television show, *Bruce Forsyth's Big Night*, returned to the screen for a ninety-minute Easter special. Produced by David Bell, directed by Bruce Gowers, and shown on Good Friday, the music was again provided by the Alyn Ainsworth Orchestra. In this show, among other things, I introduced 'All Star Secrets'. In this quiz game, a question about a celebrity's past indiscretion was put to a panel and members of the audience for them to identify the red-faced culprit concerned. Example: 'Who got completely tiddly while making a TV ad?' Answer: Joan Collins. The panel for this game's debut consisted of good-sport Joan herself, former ITN newscaster Reginald Bosanquet, actresses Carol Charming and Susan George, and comedian Jimmy Tarbuck. Also appearing in the show was actress-dancer Juliet

Prowse, who had flown all the way from Los Angeles just to appear with me.

When the producer, director, and I were discussing what we should do, I suggested a routine that I had done in pantomime. 'Eight of the girl dancers with Juliet', I said, 'could do a "stripping" routine, ending with all of them gathered around Juliet. She would then be revealed posing only in her bra and panties, then exit. At this point, eight of the group's boy dancers, plus me, could come on stage, clad in football scarves, flat caps, mackintoshes and hobnailed boots. Having finished their strip, they would then gather around me and I would be revealed posing in a pair of long johns and a vest, with a hot-water bottle on my rear. I think this would be a good bit for television.' They both agreed.

At the dress rehearsal, all the girls did their bit, then Juliet—to an audible gasp from everybody present—was exposed wearing the briefest of G-strings ever created and with the teeniest of diamantés placed over her nipples. Confronted by one of the most beautiful bodies ever created, none of us could believe our eyes. And glued to this vision, all the chaps and the cameras started to steam up. She was just overwhelmingly lovely.

After the rehearsal David Bell, the show's producer, rushed round to my room, saying: 'You've got to tell her . . . She simply cannot do *that* on the show.' 'All right,' I replied, trying not to smile. '*All right* . . . I'll go and see her.' Having knocked on Juliet's dressing-room door, I said: 'You can't do "The Stripper" number like that.' 'Oh . . .?' she said. 'I thought that's what you wanted.' 'It's not that I don't want it,' I said. 'It's

385

not the time nor the place for it. And . . . for the reveal, could you *possibly* wear something that'll cover you up just a bit more.' She just threw her head back and laughed. I think she did the dress rehearsal like that just to shock us. Anyway, 'The Stripper' was a big success—and ITV didn't lose its licence.

In writing this story up, practically every journalist mentioned that 'Juliet, an ex-fiancée of Frank Sinatra, boasted the longest and most shapely legs in show business'. She did. And I had made absolutely sure she used every inch of them in my Easter show! 'Bruce clearly gets a kick out of her,' one wrote. 'But he'd better watch his step!' I did.

The reviews for the show were generally favourable, but it was the start of a time when most comments about me, even if they were complimentary, were always prefaced by a 'despite'—'despite the marital and professional ups and downs of Bruce Forsyth's past year . . .' And so on . . . I still had friends, though. One lady, Irene Feldman from Maida Vale, penned the following to the *Evening Standard*'s letter page: 'I must disagree with the view of Peter McKay in his summing up of *Bruce Forsyth's Big Night*. I am sure many people will agree when I say that Bruce's show was superior to most British TV shows and a good deal more polished than the norm. Apart from Carol Channing hamming it up (which I thought the only flaw), it was thoroughly enjoyable. I would also like to comment that we can't as a nation all of a sudden be hypersensitive about racially based humour. Race and religion has always been the foundation of British humour and, as long as it is taken in good part by all concerned, there is absolutely no harm in it. Jewish jokes seem perfectly acceptable but not "Black" jokes. How ridiculous!'

As I've already mentioned, despite our differences Anthea and I were still great friends. However, if we were sighted together, an 'Anthea and Bruce keep us guessing' headline would invariably appear. What amazed me most, however, was to read one day that 'just after a year of separation from Anthea', I was about to be 'reconciled with Penny'! And all because Penny and I, who had by now put much of the hurt behind us—and, remember, had three daughters—had been spotted spending a relaxing few hours together in Spain. This was a happy-hour—maybe a two or three happy-hour time that was subsequently written up by Pat Tracey in the *Sunday People* as me 'playing my cards right with Penny in the intimate atmosphere of a cosy bar' in Marbella. She then posed the question: 'Are Bruce and Penny falling in love again?' What were we *really* up to? Given that *I* was present, I can actually answer this question! We were enjoying some time together, catching up on each other's life and talking fondly about our children.

Anyway, enough of all that. But if one downside of showbiz fame is as much interest in performers' personal lives as in our professional lives, so is the world not knowing the reality of much of the workaday lives many of us lead! Showbiz—the smell of the greasepaint and the roar of the crowd—may seem glamorous to people outside the business, but audiences would be astonished if, for instance, they saw the kind of dressing rooms we sometimes have to put up with. And this applies even to those who reach 'star' status. Both in the West End of London and in the provinces, dressing-rooms are usually awful, uncomfortable, dowdy places that are nearly always in need of a coat of paint. The only way we can cope is to create our own comforts, like taking along some brightly coloured towels to hang up for a bit of cheer. I still find it strange that managements expect us to cope in such unwelcoming conditions. They're often also badly lit, which is a great hazard when you're doing your own make-up, as I do for my one-man shows. When I first came into the business, colleagues used to say, 'Use some five and nine'! What this meant was a stick of Number Five Leichner for general use all over your face, and Number Nine Leichner to highlight your cheekbones. Then you'd use a brown or black pencil for your eyebrows, and finish with an eyeliner along the rim of your eyelids. These days, I use Lancôme for my face. I no longer highlight my cheekbones, but always do my eyebrows because they are a strange shape and rather sparse at the ends. For television appearances, of course, you have a make-up person who does this for you. And they all get overtime for doing *my* face!

The first time I was made up for television was at the Shepherd's Bush Empire in the fifties. The girl put so much white under my eyes that, when the show was transmitted, it made them look very small. I've never allowed anybody to do that again! From then on, I also discovered that if I made my eyebrows thicker, these would frame my eyes and make them appear larger. I've never used make-up on my hands because that would make them greasy and be disastrous for playing the piano. In the old days, I also used to buy Leichner Make-Up Remover, which came in a big pot with a blue lid. I'd smear this all over my face and get myself into a terrible mess when wiping it all off with a cloth. It really was a case of 'the smell of the greasepaint', which stayed with you for hours. Nowadays, we just wash make-up off or use a tube of cream and tissues.

Without a doubt, the worst dressing room I have ever had was at a Returned Servicemen's League club in Australia, when I had to use the men's toilets. But the *best* dressing room—in TV or theatre—was the one Bruce Gyngell created for me at Yorkshire Television. When I went to Leeds to tape the first series of *Bruce's Price is Right*, Bruce was there to greet me. He said they were so pleased that I'd agreed to come up to Leeds and do the shows that the least they could do was give me a comfortable dressing room. He led me up to what can only be described as a suite. It had a large lounge with a settee and two armchairs, a big television set with satellite television and a video recorder, a coffee machine and a kettle for tea, swing doors into a make-up area, and even a bedroom. Plus a shower that you could get at least six people into—not that I've ever tried! Bruce Gyngell was Managing Director of Yorkshire Television from May 1995 until September 1997. Sadly, he passed away on 7 September 2000. I will always remember his kindness, and all-round great showbiz attitude.

When I was at the Palladium I had a brilliant tailor called Robbie Stanford—the one I was with when I bumped into Richard Harris. But when the

Italian ready-made suits came in, I could go into any London store or shop and buy them 'off the peg'. One day, when I was about forty-five, I went into Jaeger, and said I would like a jacket. The assistant eyed me up and down, and then came back, saying, 'Here's one you might like to try, sir. It's a young man's fitting.' 'If it fits me,' I said. 'I'll have it.' It did—and I was so pleased that the label inside read, 'Young man's fitting'. I told everybody this each time I wore it. Which just goes to show that when you're in your forties, you worry more about your age and figure than when you're in your seventies! Since those days, I haven't had anything made for me. My dear friend Ian Brill owned an exclusive men's wear shop in Leeds and he was always marvellous when I was doing shows in London and on TV. He would come up with a selection for me to try on. I've enjoyed his company so much over the years. We always used to go to the golf championships together in Scotland, and we had such fun riffling through his stall which sold all the wonderful checked, baggy, flared golf trousers and tight-fitting shirts that were worn in the old days.

I have never liked people coming round to my dressing room before a show, not because they're such horrible places, but because I like to use the time to focus my mind. I also hate being spoken to when I'm waiting at the side of a stage to go on. If somebody does come up to me and says something like, 'Oh, Bruce, I heard a good one today . . .', I interrupt and reply, 'Sorry, I'm not being rude, but I need to gather my wits. It won't take long.' To avoid moments like this, I often walk up and down until Ian Wilson says: 'It's all right, Bruce. They're ready'—meaning the front of the house is seated. 'Good luck for tonight.' Then I do my little hop and go on.

How I feel when I come off depends, of course, on how I think I've performed. If it's been a good show there is no better feeling and I stay on a high for two or three hours. If not, I don't need the critics, I criticize myself. I've always done this, because I want everything to be spot on. It doesn't matter how many things have gone well, the bits I remember and brood over are the things that have not. Either way, high or low, I like ten minutes alone in my dressing room after a show. And then, however tired I am, I sign autographs, see friends or people who have asked to meet me, and then have a drink and something to eat before going back to a hotel or home to bed.

Like most people in our business, I am also superstitious. When I left the Windmill all those years ago, the girls gave me a little plastic sailor, with an inscription on his back that read 'HMS Windmill'. To this day, he is my lucky mascot. Whenever I'm doing a show, even though his arms are now loose and threatening to fall off, I put him, still in his sailor's cap, in my make-up bag and always make sure he is standing up before I leave the dressing room and when I come back.

Green for me, as it is for lots of people, is an unlucky colour. I used to love wine gums, but I never ate the green ones; and I never bought a green car. I also go crazy if somebody puts a hat on the bed; and get very upset if I see a single magpie. Some idiot once told me that if, when I saw one by itself, I said, 'Good morning, General,' this would dispel their curse. And, idiot that I am, I always do.

My son JJ, however, loves them because his favourite football team, Newcastle, which wears black-and-white striped shirts, are called the Magpies. Likewise, if I see anybody knitting in the studio or theatre during rehearsals, I have to get somebody to ask them to stop. This is partly because some showbiz bod once rushed off stage, tripped, and got a waiting person's knitting needle stuck in their eye, but also because knitting always reminds me of the French Revolution, and the awful women who used to sit knitting outside the Bastille while people were being guillotined! I think it originates from them.

I have my mother to thank for three more superstitions. She always used to get very cross if anybody put new shoes on the table, opened an umbrella indoors or walked under a ladder. I know some of the superstitions are stupid, but some are based on good sense. 'Bless you', for instance, originated with the spreading of germs during the Great Plague. The theatrical profession, I know, is more superstitious than most. In the 1960s and 1970s, the girl dancers—don't ask me why!—used to say 'Chuckers' before going on stage. Of course, that's nothing to compare with the whole *language*—nothing to do with superstition—the gays made up, the *palari*, that nobody else could understand. One of my friends at the Windmill was a homosexual and a very amusing man. He used to speak in gay palari, and one of his sentences went like this: 'Who's the bona palone with the bona ecaf and the bona lallies?' 'Bona' meant beautiful or good, 'ecaf' was 'face', spelled backwards, and 'lallies' meant legs.

$$* \qquad * \qquad *$$

The start of a new real-life generation game for me began on 6 August 1980. Julie gave birth to her first child, a baby boy named Luke. 'Luke's got Dad's chin,' she told the papers, 'but that never did Dad any harm, did it?' Then, sounding very much like a 'chip off the old block', she added: 'Thank goodness Luke arrived on time. I have a Guys and Dolls gig on 1 September at the Pavilion, Great Yarmouth. But I'm not worried about taking the baby along . . . Mum told me that when Debbie and I were babies we all travelled around in a caravan with her and Dad, and we were absolutely fine.'

On 21 September there was yet another big and happy event—a 'Let's play it again, Sam'! I teamed up with my old pal, Sammy Davis Jr—'the only man in the world', the *TV Times* pointed out, 'who could make Forsyth shut up, sit up and watch in rapt admiration'. The *Sammy and Bruce* spectacular was originally called *Bruce and Sammy*. But I telephoned LWT executives and insisted on the order of our names being changed around. 'He's an American superstar,' I said. 'You *can't* bill his name after mine.' They did what I asked.

By now, Sammy and I, having first met in 1960, had known each other for twenty years. And before the *Sammy and Bruce* show Don Hunt, my musical director, and I spent two wonderful weeks in Atlantic City, where Sammy was appearing, working out the song-and-dance and comedy routines, and then talking them over with Sammy. Don, by the way, is not just a musical director and pianist—he's a very dear friend. We first got together when I was having a bit of a crisis because

393

my pianist had left me to work with somebody else. A friend at Danny la Rue's club suggested that Don would be the perfect person for me—and she was so right. Don and I got on wonderfully well straight away. When I found out he was also a brilliant jazz keyboard player, I was even more delighted. Our first working engagement together was at The Talk of the Town—not really the place to try out somebody you had only just met, but we worked together so well. During the show, Don came on wearing huge dark glasses and dressed as a hippy in a long coat with fur all round its hem. And he was wonderful in the jazz number 'Lucrecia McEvil' from an album by the famous Blood, Sweat and Tears group. Throughout the years, Don has also been so good at doing comedy bits with me in my one-man show, especially when he retaliates against my bullying and ends up with the audience on his side. This is always a lovely moment. The audience really turns on me because they are so sorry for Don! He has a great personality and a wonderful sense of humour. I am only sorry that, in the last few years since I have eased up on the work side, we haven't worked together as often as we used to in the past. But . . . we have so many good memories. As well as the cabaret, Don worked with me on the last few Sundays of *Sunday Night at the London Palladium*, was in charge of the orchestra for my series of *The Generation Game*, and appeared with me in Summer Season Shows for many years. But, as I said above, he's always been a very true friend.

On one particular occasion in Atlantic City, after Don and I had spent three solid days working on an eight-minute medley—a lot of songs—we phoned

Sammy's minder and said we were ready to rehearse this with Sammy. 'Hold on a minute,' he replied, and we could hear him passing our message on to Sammy and Sammy replying: 'Okay . . . Ask Bruce if three o'clock will suit him?' 'Fine,' I said when the chap relayed the message to us. 'We'll see Sammy three o'clock tomorrow.' '*No*,' he replied. 'Three o'clock tonight.' We couldn't believe it. We knew Sammy was working until one o'clock in the morning, then had to have something to eat and a couple of drinks . . . But that's when the meeting took place. Having been working flat out for three days, Don and I were in a terrible state—certainly in no mood to go through an eight-minute medley at that hour in the morning. But Sammy was livelier than a cricket. It was all worth it. *Sammy and Bruce* proved to be *the* show of my life—the best I've ever been involved with.

One surprise in the show was the appearance of Anthea. It was Sammy's idea. 'Wouldn't it be lovely', he said, 'if I got Altovise [his wife] to take you off and Anthea to take me off—without causing any trouble between us.' When I told Anthea, who was still living in our Wentworth home, what Sammy had suggested, she thought this was a marvellous idea. After the show we all had a drink together. Then Anthea went off on her way, and I went off on mine. Having done a show like that, it was such a peculiar experience to part and go our separate ways. Even Sammy was amazed by this.

Anthea's actual walk on- and offstage had only occupied a few seconds of an hour's show— seconds that didn't even include one of her twirls— but the press, of course, loved it, claiming the next day that Sammy was responsible for 'bringing us back together again'!

The rapport between Sammy and me was just incredible. It's so marvellous when you're with someone you really respect and can bounce off. At the end of the *Sammy and Bruce* spectacular, when we were both going off the studio floor doing a kicking step, I put my arm around him. And I was shocked. He was so thin, I could feel all his bones. How, I wondered, can such a tiny frame produce that wonderfully deep, resonant voice? His slenderness was all the more extraordinary because he absolutely adored cooking. The kitchen in his lovely house in Los Angeles was in the middle of the garden—almost a separate little house—and he was always happy to cook anything for anybody. But, only on very rare occasions did I see him tuck into a meal and really eat anything.

People were always talking and writing about Sammy's drink problem, saying that he had been warned so many times that the alcohol would kill him. I have to admit that when we rehearsed he was never without a tall glass of what looked like diluted Ribena, but was Dubonnet and soda. I remember early on going up in a lift with him and Shirley Rhodes—his tour manager—and Shirley saying angrily: 'Sammy, I've told so many times . . . That stuff will kill you.' I thought she was joking at first, but she was deadly serious and Sammy knew that she was right. So, even in those days, drink was a great problem. Sammy, I felt, was rather like all those dear old ladies who say: 'Yes, dear, I'll just have another sherry!' without realizing that most fortified wine, which is about eighteen per cent proof, goes straight into the bloodstream. The higher the proof, the longer it takes to get into the bloodstream. A large Scotch, for example, doesn't take effect for about forty-five minutes, but a sherry—or in Sammy's case a Dubonnet—goes straight in, as do some beers. That's why dear old ladies who go to sherry parties can hardly walk when they leave. And they wonder why! I must now mention Shirley's husband, George Rhodes. He was Sammy's conductor—and such a wonderful, sweet person. He and Sammy did some superb things together.

Sammy was so showbiz—I loved him and everything he did. I remember being in Paris on one occasion with Matt Monro and a couple of other guys, and we went to see Sammy's one-man show at the Olympia. Because he was worried that the French audience would not understand him singing in English, he cut the show to the bone—didn't include any parts where he would be speaking for too long—which, sometimes, he did! I had also seen Sammy in some wonderful cabaret appearances in Los Angeles, Las Vegas and Atlantic City, but his performance that night in Paris was superb—the best performance I ever saw him do.

That was also the first time I saw him do his gun routine. For this, he strapped on two six-shooters, stood there a moment, did an extraordinarily quick draw, spun the gun and fired it. He was as good as any cowboy star in a Western, must have practised for hours. I envied Sammy an awful lot. He was so talented and came from a country where show business was always more to the fore than in the UK. In America there were twice as many great performers whom he could watch and gain wonderful experience from, and then work with over the years in so many different theatres, clubs and locations. He even grew up on the road in show business, was with his father's and uncle's trio, had all those childhood years in which to gain experience. What wouldn't I have given for that! Just being backstage, seeing all that went on, would have spurred me along; and I could have learned so much more, while still young, about what it takes to be a performer. In showbiz, you never stop learning. I will always envy Sammy's early days in the business.

I rounded off the year with a stint of my one-man show at the London Palladium from the thirteenth to the nineteenth of October. It was lovely to be back there again. I know I've gone on a bit about my one-man show already in this book, but being on that stage with just an orchestra behind you, knowing that at the end of the show the audience isn't applauding the scenery or the plot or the other members of the cast, is a feeling that one will never know unless you experience it for yourself. It's a one-on-one atmosphere that is so difficult to explain. But I suppose you could say that it's the highest of highs. And now I was doing it at the theatre that had given me my biggest break, where everything got started for me. After one of the shows, my darling sister Maisie came backstage and told me that ticket touts outside were even offering seats at vastly inflated prices. I hope they had a good night too!

I had hardly had time to enjoy the success of *Sammy and Bruce* and my week at the London Palladium before another revelation about my private life hit the news-stands—even if it was twenty years old! On 26 October, the *Sunday People* published a full-page feature article entitled 'Kathy Kirby's own heartbreak story', accompanied by a photograph of me. Kathy, who I had not seen since the sixties, said, between the lines of her life story: 'I often wonder, at this stage, if I would have been in the same mess today if I had married Bruce Forsyth. I could have done. He was the one real love that I have ever known . . .' Well, we did have a secret affair—secret by mutual consent. It was in the early sixties, and although Penny and I had acknowledged our marriage was in less than good shape, there was no need to cause her or the girls upset. We used to rendezvous in Kathy's flat in Grosvenor Square after we'd both finished work.

The article ended: 'It was the saddest moment of my life as I turned my back on Bruce . . . he has always proved a gentleman and the kind of husband that a woman can rely upon. I myself was never lucky enough to meet a man like him again . . .' Curiously Kathy's really big hit record at the time of our affair was 'Secret Love', a number which, some years before, had been a tremendous hit for Doris Day. Kathy had a rich quality to her voice and sang this song so well. She was a soft person who had a Marilyn Monroe quality about her.

In her article, she also said: 'Once I had been making a fortune. But most of that had been gambled away by my manager and lover, Bert Ambrose, the "thirties bandleader".' If that is true, it is very sad indeed. Kathy was a big earner who need never have ended up in such desperate financial circumstances. Professionally, Ambrose had been one of the classiest of the 'society' bandleaders. His name on a programme indicated that the event was a top-notch affair. But female stars have always been vulnerable—have always found it very difficult to find a man who will not only be a good manager but also a good partner or husband. This has happened to so many over the years—Doris Day and Judy Garland are just a couple of examples. I am so sad that Kathy fell on such hard times. But that's the other side of the business we are in.

So, after a year packed full to the brim with professional engagements, including by now a second series of *Play Your Cards Right*, I was back in the news for all the wrong reasons. All the hard-won good reviews under 1980 headlines, such as 'Joker Brucie comes up with a trump', 'Brucie's big trump card', 'The Joker turns up again', were eclipsed by my personal life from two decades before. I went home, gritted my teeth, and poured myself a larger-than-usual Jack Daniels.

CHAPTER FOURTEEN

JUST WHEN YOU'RE NOT EXPECTING IT

What I haven't yet mentioned is that, just after I returned from my one-man shows at the Huntingdon Hartford Theater, Los Angeles, I was asked to be a judge at the 1980 'Miss World' contest. Tempted!—but very busy with my shows and recording *Play Your Cards Right*—I said: 'Whether or not I can do this will depend on how much time I would need to be involved.' 'Certainly for the pre-judging on the Wednesday and the judging on the Thursday at the Royal Albert Hall,' the organizer replied. 'Oh, dear,' I said, 'I couldn't possibly manage two days. But thank you for asking me . . . Perhaps another year?' 'What a pity,' the organizer replied, 'we so much wanted you to be one of the judges.' She then phoned back the next day, saying: 'Could you manage just the Thursday, at about two o'clock.' 'Yes, that'll be fine,' I said.

This is why, on 11 November 1980, I was on my way to the Royal Albert Hall, Kensington, looking forward to a different kind of working day. And there, gathered already when I arrived, were all but one of the other judges. A few minutes later, the absent member arrived, carrying a very large black bag. *'Good heavens,'* I thought, stunned. *'Who is she? She looks like a South American princess. She's absolutely gorgeous!'*

Then, as this unknown, incredibly elegant lady bent down, pulling out what looked like make-up gear from her bag, all I could see was the back of her head and her wonderful long black hair. When she straightened up again and turned round, I sneaked a second look. This proved to be even more impressive than the first! Her 'cappuccino' skin was absolutely flawless, she had enormous dark, limpid eyes, lovely wide mouth, perfectly proportioned face, and her curvaceous body was every woman's dream come true! I was besotted— couldn't take my eyes off her, could hardly wait for the moment when the beauty pageant would begin and the announcer would introduce all the judges, one by one. I would then find out what she was called and where she was from. 'But my goodness,' I thought, 'I might not know her name, but I *do*

401

know she's absolutely beautiful—one of the *loveliest* women I've ever seen.'

Before the pageant started, the contestants came in for a little interview with the judges and to answer some of our questions. Rather satisfyingly—given that I was hoping to impress a certain lady—I received the biggest laugh when it came to 'Miss Turkey's' turn. I said: 'Tell me, "Miss Turkey" . . . something I've always wanted to know . . . What *do* people in your country eat for Christmas dinner?' 'Turkey,' she replied innocently. Casting a sidelong glance along the row, I could see my gorgeous person laughing and thinking, 'Who *is* this man?'

As bad luck would have it, throughout the actual beauty pageant, 'Miss World's' founder, Eric Morley, sat in the middle of the judges. I was not pleased! This meant I was sitting on his left, separated from *THE* lady who was sitting on his right. Although Eric left his seat from time to time to deal with administrative matters, there was no opportunity to sort out her name. All I could do was exchange the occasional glance and comment, and look forward to the judges' names being announced. But when the announcer *did* finally go down the line, naming all the judges, I couldn't make any sense of what he said. It sounded something like Wilneliamercedi. What I *did* catch and, given her stunning looks, was not at all surprised to hear, was that she was 'Miss World 1975'; and that she came from Puerto Rico. Was Wilneliamercedi, I was left wondering, a first name?—a second name?—or a first-and-second name rolled into one?

Later in the day, after I had at last established

that her name was Wilnelia Merced, I made sure I arrived early for the dinner and dance held after each year's contest. Confronted by two large tables—one already nearly full—I stood trying to figure out which table my 'Miss World' was most likely to sit at. Standing around, though, proved to be rather hazardous. All the other judges kept saying: 'Where are you going to sit, Bruce?' and I had to keep replying: 'Please don't worry about me—I'm looking for someone!' To avoid the possibility of being put at the wrong table, I went up and down in the lift a few times. Then, *at last*, I was rewarded with Wilnelia's arrival. But—and this was a body blow—she was in the company of a suave, good-looking, oriental man. All I could do was look on as he, lucky man, sat down beside her. '*That*', I thought dismally, 'is *that.*' But never one to give up at a first hurdle, I sat down at the same table, carefully choosing a chair opposite her so that we would at least have some eye-to-eye contact! Now, as I write this, I can see how *manipulative* I was. But, given the happy outcome of that day, I don't care! As I had hoped, I was able from time to time to get her attention, and a few of her winning smiles.

After dinner, the music began and people started to dance. During this, the current crop of 'Miss World' contestants—and some of the other guests—came up to ask me for my autograph or a photograph. I was more than happy to oblige. I wanted Wilnelia to notice all these goings-on so that my kudos would go up and she would realize I was a 'somebody'! Then, just as I finished signing, I realized that all the other judges had left the table and that Wilnelia was now sitting there alone. 'How very strange!' I thought, as I crossed over to her. 'Excuse me,' I said, 'would your boyfriend be very annoyed if I asked you for a dance?' 'No,' she replied. 'He's *not* my boyfriend—he's a dear Chinese friend from Paris who's just gone to look for Miss Hong Kong.' 'What a stroke of luck,' I said. 'I hope he's caught a slow boat to China.' Gratifyingly, she laughed. And then, when I added: '*Would* you like to dance?' she even more gratifyingly replied: 'I'd love to.' So we danced . . . And danced . . . And danced . . . And, between steps, Wilnelia kept saying to me: 'I *can't* believe you are English, you dance *so* well, just like a Latin!'

The really exciting thing about dancing with somebody you are very attracted to is the 'electricity' that passes through your body from theirs! It is a wonderful chemistry. You either dance with a partner who feels like a plank of wood, or with somebody whose body just melts into yours. The latter doesn't happen often, but when it does it's *very* special—you feel like one person. And that's how we felt. Having started to dance, we just couldn't bear to stop—we continued for at least two hours, totally oblivious of all the other people in the room. As far as we were concerned we could have been in a tiny bistro alongside a jukebox.

Wilnelia, I quickly discovered, as well as being outrageously beautiful, is highly intelligent, totally unspoiled by her good looks and a delight to be with. Between the beginning and end of each dance, we stayed close to each other, talking about anything and everything. I learned that this was only the second time that Wilnelia Merced had

404

been to England. The first time, as the announcer had proudly mentioned, was when, aged seventeen, she was crowned 'Miss World'. All this time spent together did not go unnoticed. Lots of people—I learned later from a friend—were watching and saying: 'Look at those two . . . They've hardly left the floor *and* have never stopped talking since they met!' They were obviously wondering what I was now up to . . .

When the dancing finally came to an end, Wilnelia and I returned to the table where she introduced me to her friend, Jonathan Luk. 'This', I thought, feeling suddenly bereft, 'is "Cinderella" time. Soon—*too soon*—I will have to say goodnight to her.' I had already made up my mind not to be 'pushy', to play it 'cool' and be a 'proper English gentleman'. I didn't want her to think I was predatory. I'd never been *that*, and I certainly didn't want to spoil my chances by her thinking I might be. At least she had liked me enough to give me the telephone number of her hotel, and the number of her dearest friend, Teresa, who had been her chaperone when she was in London in 1975. Outside the Royal Albert Hall, having hailed a taxi for her and Jonathan, I kissed her hand. '*Thank you*', I said, 'for the *most* wonderful evening of my life. I do hope we can meet again before you leave London.' I was not spinning a line, I was totally sincere—completely captivated by her. Much later on, Wilnelia told me she had found me 'very courteous and gentlemanly' that night, and so different from the men she had met during her modelling work in New York.

Over the next couple of days, I was rehearsing for a Royal Variety Show and staying in London at the Royal Garden Hotel. I kept telephoning Wilnelia, wanting to take her out to dinner, but she was not an easy person to get hold of. Then, when I did succeed in speaking to her, she had already made arrangements to go out with some friends. Later in the evening, however, while I was resignedly lying in bed watching a football match, she phoned me back. 'Jonathan, Teresa, and I', she said, 'would like to go to Stringfellows. Could you possibly get us in?' (Stringfellows was *THE* club to go to then.) 'I could if I came with you,' I replied, ever quick on my toes. 'Oh, *really*? Would you like to do that?' 'I'd *love* to,' I said. 'I'd *love* to. Where are you?' Although the hotel she named was close by, she and her friends were *very* surprised by my speed of arrival. So was I! I had had to abandon my bed, get dressed, and get over there. It was probably one of my fastest quick changes.

Between glasses of champagne at Stringfellows, Wilnelia and I continued where we had left off—and danced the night away. Inevitably—and luckily in the circumstances—there were people present who recognized me and asked for autographs. Once again, I didn't mind! At the end of the evening, I repeated what I had said outside the Royal Albert Hall—that I would love to see her again before she left London. And, this time, I invited her to have dinner with me the next evening. But again, however, she had already made arrangements to meet friends—quite a few of them. 'Why not', I said, 'bring them all over to my hotel. We could have some drinks, then all go out to dinner together in Chelsea.' To my delight, she agreed.

By the next day, however, most of Wilnelia's

Puerto Rican companions had decided that what they most wanted to do was go to the theatre, another had cancelled because she had a headache, and Jonathan had already made plans of his own. Wilnelia, I learned later, was extremely embarrassed at finding herself suddenly on her own for the evening. And, when Jonathan drove her over to my hotel, she tried very hard to persuade him to come in with her and remain for the dinner in Chelsea. 'Oh, you'll be all right,' he kept reassuring her. 'Bruce is a gentleman, a very nice man.' And, suddenly, there she was, unaccompanied, in my hotel, feeling very nervous and even more embarrassed when she saw the bottles of champagne I had organized for the drinks party. I, of course, was thrilled! It was the first opportunity I had had to be completely alone with her.

As she had already noticed that people— including waiters in the club and restaurant and passers-by in the street—recognized me and kept coming up for my autograph or to take a photograph, I began by telling her about my career. Having done that, I moved on to the more tricky subject—my personal life. I explained that, although I had been married twice and had five daughters, I was now unattached. The difficult bit was when I had to add that, although Anthea and I were legally separated, our divorce had not yet been finalized and, for the time being, my ex-wife and I were still living in the same house in Surrey. I was right to be concerned. Wilnelia was very uneasy about this, and I soon discovered that one of her friends had warned her that I was still married, had 'a bit of a reputation', and that she would be *very* unwise to become involved with me.

Over dinner, Wilnelia then told me about her life. Born and brought up in Caguas near the Puerto Rican capital of San Juan, she had enjoyed her schooldays, was always tall for her age, growing up to be 5ft 9in, and encouraged by her mother to go on to modelling school. She had felt very honoured to be chosen to represent Puerto Rico in the 'Miss World' competition and had loved her subsequent year as 'Miss World'. Beauty contests, she explained, were called 'pageants' in Puerto Rico because her island had very close links with America. Puerto Ricans, like most Latin people, she also told me, were very family-orientated and, in addition to her mother, Delia, her father Enrique, and her brother Kiko, she had masses of aunts, uncles, and cousins. After modelling school, she had gone to work in New York. Her construction manager dad, who had been divorced from her mother since Wilnelia was eight years old, was very concerned that her success had come too soon. Then, when she was asked to do a TV commercial, wearing a bikini, he was really worried. 'Because I was still so young, I had to write to my parents for permission,' she told me. 'My father is very religious and was really anxious. I completely understood his point of view. Even at thirteen, I looked like an eighteen-year-old. But he knew I was never a "wild" child. And, fortunately, when he saw the commercial he was happy because it was very tastefully done.

'Coming to England,' she added, 'was really daunting. But it was like a fantasy—so many castles and palaces, so much royal history. At the beginning of the contest, I was more than happy to

408

be just "Miss Puerto Rico" who had reached the final fifteen in the contest. So, when I actually won the crown, it was just all too incredible for words.' She was now, I learned, a fashion model for Dior and other top designers.

What I haven't mentioned yet is that, although I had not immediately recognized her during the judging at the Royal Albert Hall, I had actually seen her momentous 'Miss World 1975' parade on TV. Like all red-blooded Englishmen, I *love* watching the 'Miss World' contests, even if I have not placed a bet on the likely winner. And, in 1975, I had returned home from work just in time to see Wilnelia, looking absolutely fantastic, as she paraded up and down in a striped swimming costume, wearing the 'Miss World' sash and crown. 'She's *lovely*,' I said to myself. And, unfortunately, the show ended.

None of this, of course, meant very much to me at the time. I didn't know Wilnelia; didn't even know where Puerto Rico was! But what I did know by the end of our first evening alone was that I could not see enough of her. As I kissed her gently goodnight on both cheeks, I asked her if she would have lunch with me the next day. She did. And from then on, I continued to invite her out every day until she returned to New York. On our last evening together, I remember walking hand in hand with her all over London, then sitting in the car until about three o'clock in the morning, talking . . . and talking. Very reluctant to say goodbye, I said: 'There's a slight chance that I'll be coming to Miami for a few days' charity work. If I do, can I call you and, perhaps, come and see you in New York on my way back to London?' 'I would like that,' she replied.

After that evening, the beginning of what was to be a two-year clandestine transatlantic romance, I kept very closely in touch with her by telephone.

For this foolishly romantic fellow, both the rehearsals and the Royal Variety Show itself on 17 November were a very welcome distraction. Always a glittering gala that turned out a galaxy of stars, the show was an even more special occasion than usual. Not only were we celebrating the Queen Mother's eightieth birthday, but the seventieth birthday of my second home, the world's number-one theatre—the London Palladium. Lined up on the royal side were the Queen, her birthday-girl mother, and HRH Prince Charles. In a gesture of genuine warmth and affection, the world of entertainment rallied to make the night a star-studded celebration. Lined up on our side— too many to list all the names here—were Chesney Allen, Arthur Askey, Sammy Davis Jr, Charlie Drake, Roy Hudd, Danny Kaye, Grace Kennedy, Cleo Laine, Peggy Lee, Tommy Trinder, Harry Worth, Larry Hagman, June Whitfield—and, of course, me. Somehow, I managed to keep my mind on the job, and the evening turned out to be exactly what it had promised to be, a memorable double-birthday celebration.

The morning after this show, I left for Florida to appear in the charity gala I had mentioned to Wilnelia, organized by Mike Winters of the British double act Mike and Bernie Winters. But it proved to be a disaster—a complete a waste of my time. I was supposed to do my one-man act during the second half of the evening, but the so-called 'rich' members of the audience—about half the number present—left after the cocktail party reception in the interval. I was then supposed to work at another Miami venue. But, when I went to see the exhibition area where I was supposed to perform, the conditions were so appalling I said to the organizers: 'I can't *possibly* work here,' and, breaking the rule of a lifetime, cancelled my appearance.

It completely lacked any atmosphere whatsoever. And, as I said at the time, the only way I could have worked there, the sort of huge place where prize fights are held, was with Muhammad Ali, having a fight. As Ian Wilson also commented, had I tried to perform in such a cavernous hall, it would have been like trying to put on an intimate comedy show at Olympia or Earls Court.

So, having walked out of the show, which was meant to be the highlight of a festival thanking the 250,000 British tourists who had visited the resort that year, I now had four free days. That evening I telephoned Wilnelia and said, 'I'm planning to come to New York. Is there any chance of seeing you? Will I be in the way? Are you involved with anybody? If you don't want to see me, I'll quite understand. But, if you do, *please* don't think I'm expecting anything else . . . I'd just love to spend some more time with you—go to a show, go out for dinner. I can come for a couple of days. But, of course, I'll understand if you're too busy or would rather I didn't.' When I finally finished rattling on in this way, Wilnelia said: 'I do have a couple of fashion shows to do. But I'd like to see you. When are you coming?' It was then that I realized her upbringing was very different to mine. She had had a very strict Catholic education, and although she had travelled extensively she had not had a serious relationship.

When I arrived in New York, it was on a day when Wilnelia was involved in not one but *four* fashion shows, followed by a launch party. She was so busy running from place to place, she had had nothing to eat. Not surprisingly, by the time she met up with me, she was feeling really ill. When I suggested going out to dinner, she said: 'I'm *so* sorry, Bruce, I feel awful. I couldn't possibly eat anything!' Having suggested that she should have a rest in my room, I told her I was going to call a doctor. As a result of all this, she decided I was a *very* kind man who really knew how to look after people. Then, when I called a taxi and accompanied her back to her apartment, she made up her mind, however busy she was the next day, to call me and make up for our non-eventful evening. She did! The next night I had the pleasure of taking her to a superb restaurant, then on to a jazz club. And once again, we had a really wonderful time together.

I then flew back to Miami. I was a happy man. Although the trip had been most unsatisfactory from a professional point of view, I was glad I had made the journey. Personally it had been a hit—I'd got to know much more about Wilnelia. And when I returned to London, I continued to keep in daily touch with her by phone.

*   *   *

Among the events that the Variety Club of Great Britain organizes are tributes to entertainers for their services to show business. I always look forward to these enormously because they give me the chance to applaud my fellow entertainers and renew old friendships. Such was my experience when we met to celebrate songwriter Sammy Cahn's fifty years as one of the music business's top writers. Sammy, in wonderful form, sang some of his much loved songs 'Tender Trap', 'It's Magic', 'Time after Time' and 'Day by Day', but parodied each of them with very funny lines. Michael Parkinson, Tim Rice and Benny Green paid tributes to him. And, in turn, Sammy thanked Paul and Linda McCartney, Joan and Jackie Collins, and me for making the lunch possible. A satisfyingly large cheque was then presented to the Metropolitan Police Commissioner, Sir David McNee, for the children's section of the police dependants' fund. Then off we all went, already looking forward to the next tribute.

Just before Christmas, there was another showbiz event. A *Night of 100 Stars* spectacular, performed in the presence of Princess Margaret, was screened on ITV to mark the fiftieth anniversary of the actors' union Equity. Terry Wogan was the host, and among the stars he introduced were Stewart Granger, Honor Blackman, Richard Harris, Ian Ogilvy, Rula Lenska, Susannah York, Dennis Waterman, Lulu— and me. Lulu and I had worked together many times before and, on this occasion, we greatly enjoyed singing a parody of 'You Gotta Have Heart', staged by Robert Nesbitt and choreographed by Irving Davies and Brian Rogers. It was lovely to meet up again with so many old friends.

When Wilnelia told me she was going to Puerto

Rico for Christmas, I asked if I could come too, so we could see each other on her home ground. But her life, like mine, was not that simple. Having achieved so much, she was a celebrity on the island—far too well known in old San Juan to be seen in the company of an Englishman, thirty years older than herself. So . . . after Christmas— hopefully very early in January!—we decided to meet elsewhere. 'Perhaps I could come to England?' Wilnelia said. 'That could prove difficult for me!' I replied, thinking of my own problems with the press. 'Why don't we both look at a map and choose somewhere in the Caribbean that's reasonably close to Puerto Rico?'

So, off we both went to get a map before returning to our telephone conversation. 'Antigua sounds possible,' I said. 'It's only an hour's flight from Puerto Rico.' The chief problem, as Wilnelia then explained, was that she'd only just returned from New York to visit her family. How could she justify such a brief 'Hallo—here I am' before saying 'Goodbye—I have to go . . .' without her mother and everybody else becoming suspicious? What she needed was a really good excuse to leave the island. Only then could she keep everybody happy. 'How about me telling everyone I have to go to Antigua for a fashion show?' she suggested. 'That's a brilliant idea,' I replied. Then, as an 'alibi' for me, we decided—what a surprise—to look for a hotel by a golf course! When Wilnelia phoned me back to say the best hotel seemed to be the Runaway Hotel, I fell about laughing. 'What are you laughing at?' she asked. 'The Runaway Hotel!' I replied.

There were two further problems, which neither

414

of us had anticipated. The first was that there was only one flight a week from Puerto Rico to Antigua; the second—unknown to me until Wilnelia eventually arrived in Antigua—was that, in order to pacify her mother, she had to agree to a chaperone. This meant travelling in the company of Osvaldo, a friend of the family, who was known to be very good at looking after her when she was journeying to new places alone. Osvaldo—who, incidentally, had also designed Wilnelia's clothes for the 'Miss World' contest—presented one major problem. He was—he is a bit better now— renowned for being late for everything. The almost inevitable result was that when he and Wilnelia arrived at the San Juan Airport check-in, the *only* plane to Antigua that week had taken off. Wilnelia was left thinking, 'If I go back home, I won't, having missed the fashion show, have a reason to leave again.'

So . . . she stayed at the airport and set about finding an alternative way to get to Antigua. This was not easy. The *only* way was to fly to St Thomas, then to Martinique, then from Martinique to Antigua. A nightmare journey. But she decided to go ahead with it. Her problems, however, were not over. When she and Osvaldo arrived in St Thomas, which is only a half-hour flight from San Juan, the next departure to Martinique had been cancelled. Each time she phoned me in Antigua to update me on yet another change of plan, I was left thinking, 'What's going on? Is she giving me the runaround? Am I getting the treatment? *AND* . . . what's all this about Oz-somebody-or-another being a chaperone?'

To make matters worse, the Runaway Hotel

didn't have telephones in its rooms. Believe me, it was no fun staying at the Runaway being given the runaround! Each time Wilnelia phoned, I had to make a mad dash to the lobby, a hundred yards away, where it was impossible to have a private conversation. All I could do was continue to think, 'What *is* going on here?' and then remain seated by a palm tree outside my room—a Jack Daniels on hand—ready for the next call. Three days later—three *days* from the time Wilnelia had left home—she succeeded in getting a flight from Martinique, just one hour's flying time away.

Waiting at the airport for her—still feeling somewhat ruffled—I saw her coming down the gangway, dressed in an absolutely lovely white dress and matching hat. *But*, alongside her, was this amazingly good-looking guy. They looked like a *really lovely* couple. 'What's this?' I thought, taken aback. 'I *am* being taken for a ride!' Even before this moment, I had been feeling embarrassed. The only car I had been able to rent was an absolutely *awful* rust bucket, minus a carpet of any description. Now, to add to my penniless beachcomber image, here was Wilnelia looking absolutely fantastic in the company of an elegant, suave, smooth, handsome man. Great!

Having introduced me to her Adonis, Wilnelia then immediately reassured me about their exact family-friend relationship. Still feeling a trifle edgy—but mainly now about the car!—I at least knew that nothing other than a journey from hell had been going on. At the Runaway Hotel, we spent our remaining three days there being as discreet as possible. I must say the chambermaids got very confused. As much as they tried, they

416

couldn't work out who she was with!

Our troubles, though, were far from over. When we decided to go out for the evening to the biggest hotel in Antigua, we discovered that the English cricket team, along with the UK press covering the tour, had just checked in! It was hardly an ideal romantic situation. Given that the newshounds were present, I couldn't even risk dancing with Wilnelia. Not wanting her to miss out on all the fun, and knowing how much she loved dancing, I had to sit at the table, watching her out of the corner of my eye dancing with Osvaldo. Then, I had to seem not to mind that there was a golf-pro present who had taken quite a fancy to her and wanted to dance with her all evening. I was in no position to say, 'Oi—sling your hook . . .' or 'Keep your hands off her'! Wilnelia, only too happy to be able to dance and have some fun, was enjoying the funny side of all this. I, a person who *also* loves to dance, was not finding it so amusing, was for much of the time beside myself with frustration. Fortunately, a lady tennis coach arrived on the dance floor. From then on, I could at least exercise my feet.

Perhaps, given this entire Antigua fiasco, it was rather surprising that Wilnelia decided that she *did* want me to visit her one day soon in Puerto Rico. She would, she said, book me into a hotel, show me the beautiful Caribbean island where she had grown up . . . *And* introduce me to her mother as 'the man I love'. There couldn't have been a better or more romantic ending to our time together on Antigua.

*   *   *

417

In February, when I was doing cabaret in one of my favourite places, The Talk of the Town, for a month, before going off on a tour of Australia, my daughter Julie came round to see me at rehearsals with her six-month-old son Luke. He had started touring with Julie and her husband when he was two weeks old. Since then he had been to another six countries with their group Guys and Dolls. Looking at him, I thought fondly, 'I bet he's on his way to a career in show business.' He was, but more on that later. In late February, there were more fun and games for me on another *Parkinson* show, which I always enjoyed.

In between all this, Wilnelia and I spent the best part of the year travelling to and from each other in New York and different parts of Europe. On one occasion we arranged to meet in Madrid, but finished up booking into different hotels! Ours was a truly globe-trotting love affair. And, in addition to all these wonderful times together, our letters whizzed to and fro, and our telephone bills rose to astronomical heights. Too often we were separated by our work. And, what's more, I was still going through the process of finalizing my divorce from Anthea. For most of this time I had no option but to play it 'cool'. I so much wanted Winnie to feel that our relationship was based on trust; that there was no collar and leash. I'd never been the kind of person who phones up places and says, 'Is so-and-so there?' just to check on their partner's activities, and I was determined not to become that kind of person now. I wanted her to know that I am only 'Latin' when I dance!

Nevertheless, on the phone to her in New

York—about midnight UK time, eight o'clock in the evening there—I would ask casually: 'Are you going anywhere tonight?' 'Yes. I'm going to a party with a few friends,' she would reply. 'Oh, *good*,' I'd reply. 'Have a *lovely* time'. But . . . I would be thinking: 'Oh, God, I can't bear it . . . It's *only* eight o'clock over there. *Who's* she going out with?' I never let on, though, made myself sound *so* relaxed, *so* very English, *so* cool. 'I'll phone you tomorrow. Have a nice time tonight,' I'd add, just before I put the phone down. Then I'd run around shouting, *'She's going out!—She's going out!'* Here I am—midnight in London! . . . and *she's going out! And who with?'* The next evening, however, I'd say: 'Did you have a nice time, darling? Was it *fun*?' Later, Wilnelia told me she appreciated all this. She had had more than enough of possessive people in the past. So we continued, phone call after phone call, letter after letter, backwards and forwards across the Atlantic. During this time— and right up to today—the Dionne Warwick number 'I'll Never Love This Way Again' became 'our song' because I associated it with wonderful memories of my first meeting and dances with Winnie. Dionne, whom I have worked with many times, is a singer most associated with songs by Bacharach and David. Our song is not by them but, in my opinion, it's one of Dionne's best! Ever since Winnie and I met, whenever I hear it on the car radio, I get all sentimental and drift off into happy memories.

But, separated as we so often were, I had to do other things to console myself. Golf, nobody will be surprised to hear, played a large part in my 1981 diary. This started at the beginning of the year

419

when a prankster—long after the official closing date had passed—put forward my name to be elected as a member of the Wentworth Golf Club's committee, and then let it be known that I had been turned down! That's the kind of thing that happens to you when you're a celebrity; you never know what's lurking in the undergrowth. Still, there were other nice things in store. In July the first 'Bruce Forsyth Pro-Am Charity Classic' was held at Moor Park, sponsored by Chef & Brewer Ltd, in aid of charities for the disabled. I invited *all* my golfing friends—Terry Wogan, Eddie Large of the Little and Large duo, Bernard Cribbins, James Hunt, Sean Connery, Ian Botham, Dickie Henderson, and the golfing pros included Nick Faldo, Bernard Gallagher, Greg Norman and Neil Coles. Speaking to the *TV Times*'s sports writer Mark Andrews, I said, and again this will not surprise anybody: 'If I wasn't an entertainer, I'd have loved to be a professional golfer, provided I was good enough to be in the top ten or twelve in the world. I wouldn't want to be anything in life unless it was at world-class level.' My Pisces character was obviously very much on form that day! Then, in September, on a day when we teed off to rain bucketing down at seven forty-five in the morning, it was the Bob Hope British Classic. Fortunately, by lunchtime the sun was shining on the pros. Unfortunately, I didn't start the day too well. I left home without my clubs and had to borrow a set from the pro's shop.

*   *   *

I've already mentioned my devotion to my
420

Steinway piano—and all my wives will certainly testify to that! An unexpected pleasure occurred in March 1981 when I was asked to appear in a documentary about Bob Glazebrook, Steinway's senior concert technician at that time. Bob's job was to look after about a hundred grand pianos scattered throughout the country, and he knew off by heart every piano by its sound and serial number. He was also responsible for the top-quality pianos reserved for people like Claudio Arrau, Emil Gilels and Clifford Curzon. Appearing in the programme were Howard Shelley, Alfred Brendel, Abbey Simon, Vladimir Ashkenazy, Peter Frankl—and me! To be in that kind of company was a great honour.

Also in March, there was another Variety Club tribute lunch at the Savoy, attended by a very large gathering of personalities. Supporting charity events has always been a very important part of show business. It's our way of helping to encourage people in need from all different walks of life. This time we were celebrating Frankie Howerd's thirty-five years in show business. The Queen Mother sent Frankie a telegram expressing her good wishes, and there were tributes and praise from me, Sheila Hancock, J.B. Priestley, Arthur Askey, Dickie Henderson—and Cilla Black sang 'Happy Birthday' to him. Other guests included Tom Courtenay, Terry Scott, June Whitfield, Tommy Trinder, John Thaw, and Harry Worth. I remember dear old Frankie saying that he was surprised to be in show business at all, even more surprised to have survived for that length of time, and still constantly surprised every time a show actually got put on. He then quoted Maurice Chevalier who always claimed he had his farewell speech ready every time he went on stage, just in case the audience didn't like him. Everybody in our business sympathized with that!

In June there was an evening of jolly good fun at the London Palladium when Louis Benjamin, managing director of Moss Empires, the Palladium's holding company, and producer of *Barnum*, starring Michael Crawford, gave a party and turned the theatre into a three-ring circus. On the menu was some really delicious meat and potato pie, bubble and squeak, hot dogs, and cockles and mussels, and Kenny Lynch and I kept going back for second helpings. Danny La Rue was there and we got to talking about his club and the skits that he and Ronnie Corbett used to do together—what a team they were. These were stand-up pieces and, in particular, I remembered a hilarious one about Napoleon and Josephine. Danny La Rue's club had become *the* place to go to in London. Whether or not you had already seen the floor show, if you were wanting a late meal, a nightcap or a cup of coffee, it would always be, 'Oh, let's go to Danny's.' So many pros would be there, and it never mattered if you turned up halfway through the cabaret. One of the show-stoppers was when Annie, Ronnie Corbett's wife, came out to do a number. It was always a 'belter' that was received with a huge ovation.

There were a couple of golfing occasions when Sean Connery made me—and some other golfers— do what I call 'grin-and-bear its'. I saw a lot of Sean in the 1960s to 1980s, and we had some really wonderful times together. We particularly enjoyed our games of golf with Jimmy Tarbuck, Eric Sykes,

Ronnie Carroll, and Glen Mason. The first grin-and-bear-it was when I was playing a four-ball with Sean. It was absolutely teeming down with rain and we were sheltering in a bunker under our umbrellas. Two minutes later, when there was still no let-up in the downpour, Sean, becoming impatient, said, 'Come on, let's keep moving. *Come on. Come on.* Follow me.' 'Hold on, Sean,' I replied. 'We're not making a war film.' But Sean simply grimaced and punched me on the arm. War or no war, rain or no rain, golf was always a matter of life and death to him. He certainly wasn't going to be defeated by a few sploshes of water, even if they were almost the size our golf balls.

The second grin-and-bear-it relates to Sean's fame as Ian Fleming's James Bond. As well as being a member of the Stage Golfing Society, I was also a member then of Moor Park which has two beautiful courses. The clubhouse is a magnificent mansion, built for Cardinal Wolsey in the sixteenth century. When you arrive at the course and go through the entrance, the road curves and descends down the hill to the parking area. So, from the clubhouse you can see cars arriving. The reason I mention this is because I had made the mistake of telling two friends that I had invited Sean over to have a game with me. They, of course, had told somebody else, and very soon the entire membership of the golf club knew Sean was coming. Having created a huge stir as 007 in the film *Dr No*, which had featured thrilling special effects, including the magnificent Aston Martin DB5 car, there was a tremendous sense of anticipation and excitement. Everybody was buzzing with the thought that 'James Bond' would arrive in the car! To make matters worse, Sean was late—completely out of character for him when a game of golf was involved. In fact, most golfers are very punctual, generally arrive before they are due to play so that they can hit a few balls or have a cup of coffee.

Anyway, there we all were gathered round the first tee, with our golf bags and clubs at the ready, and other members hovering behind us for their tee-off moment. Suddenly, we heard this noise coming over the hill—a couple of incredibly loud backfires, followed by what sounded like a series of bangs. The car came over the brow of the hill and there, instead of the Aston Martin DB5 that everyone had been looking forward to, was this clapped-out ancient Mk 10 Jaguar. Its paintwork was a drab battleship grey that had certainly known much better days, and now left a great deal to be desired. Chug-chug-chug it was going all the way, coughing up the worst bronchial engine sounds we had ever heard. Finally, to the great relief of us all, it drew to a halt and Sean climbed out—obviously not a happy man. Now, when he's in a temper, I find him very funny because his prominent eyebrows become even more prominent. But this time his eyes were blazing with fury, too. 'I've just been stopped by the police,' he announced. 'The silly buggers didn't think my car was roadworthy. They made me late for the game.' 'Really!' I said, trying not to look at the car. 'What on earth made them think that, Sean!'

All the other golfers who had watched and waited for 'James Bond' were now thoroughly deflated and sniggering about Sean's inauspicious arrival. But once Sean had recovered from his unrighteous indignation, we had a good game. Material things never seemed to matter much to him. I remember going to see him in the early seventies after his marriage to the actress Diane Cilento had come to an end. He was living on his own in a flat off London's Marylebone Road. His accommodation was in the basement, and all he had was a bed and bedside locker, a phone and a book on the floor. 'Well,' he said by way of explanation, 'I haven't decided where I'm going to live next and, when I think about it, all I *really* need is a bed, a phone and a book to read.' He meant it.

Talking of bad moods has reminded me that Ian Wilson sometimes jokes about me being in a bad mood before going onstage. This, I might add, occasionally helps to get my adrenalin running and results in me working better, especially when I'm feeling overworked or tired. One occasion I got really wound up was in 1964 when I was in Bournemouth and Eric Winston's band was also on the bill. The show was simply not coming down to time and was generally causing a lot of aggravation. 'If you do this and this,' I said, impatiently, 'and cut time here, we won't be in such a terrible mess.' But no one took any notice of me. Previous experience had taught me that the only way to get anything done in show business, when you know you're in the right, is to go to the manager—either the touring manager or the show's manager, representing the company you're working for. This is what I did on this occasion, using what I have always called my 'ultimate sanction'. 'There will be no show tonight, unless the timing is altered—*starting now*. I will *not* walk on that stage tonight if this is not done. If the show goes ahead the way it's been going, I won't be in it. Let me know your answer before four o'clock—by which time I *should* be getting ready to come to the theatre.' Things got sorted pretty quickly after that display of my ultimate sanctionship. I had my answer by four, and the show went ahead with me in it.

* * *

The third series of *Play Your Cards Right* came back to the screen in October 1981 with Dolly Dealers, Gillian Elvins, Lesley Anderson, Natalie Shaw, and Denny Kemp. Our male host, John Melaney, who displayed the prizes and handed out the consolation prizes, made the prize comment: 'I enjoy doing the programme—it's just like being Santa Claus!'

Just as UK producers buy TV programmes from America, so American producers search among ours for new material. I was not really surprised, therefore, when Beryl Vertue, then deputy chairman of the American Robert Stigwood group, acquired the format rights of *The Generation Game* from the BBC. Plans were then made for me to go to the US in November to make a pilot, taped in front of a live audience. This version of *The Generation Game* was going to be called *A Piece of Cake*, and, in order for the pilot to go through an assessment and marketing procedure, it was to be shown to an audience in a preview theatre on Sunset Boulevard. If it was considered a success, it was then to be shown in January 1982, or the autumn of that year. But, by now—and readers will know why—although I'm always very enthusiastic, I don't count my chickens until they're hatched! I

426

was wise not to. The American ABC network, having wrecked the original format of the programme by cutting it to thirty minutes and not allowing me to have fun with the contestants in case I helped one couple more than the other, turned down the pilot for *A Piece of Cake*, and *The Generation Game* never came to fruition in the USA.

As soon as I was free again, I used whatever spare time I had flying to and from clandestine meetings with Wilnelia. On one occasion, when she was modelling in Venezuela, I also tried to join her there. But, once again, we were thwarted by airline flights being delayed, then cancelled. On another occasion when Wilnelia was in London, we went on a Thanksgiving holiday together, staying in a friend's apartment in Miami. This was the first time Wilnelia had cooked turkey and I remember her calling her mother at least eight times for instructions. 'What do I do now?' she kept asking. But the dinner was perfect. Wilnelia had bought a beautiful dress to mark the occasion; and the two of us sat snugly together at a corner of a dining-room table that was designed to seat eighteen.

When the time came for us to leave London Heathrow for this trip, I enlisted the help of an agent friend, Michael Black, a wonderful character and the brother of Don Black who had written musicals with Andrew Lloyd Webber and the lyrics for a number of Oscar-winning songs. As Michael was going to Miami to check out a venue for one of my one-man shows, I said, 'Would you do me a favour? The lovely girl who's been staying with me in London is coming with me to Miami for Thanksgiving. But I can't risk us being seen checking in together at the airport. Could you possibly keep a lookout for her arriving at departures, and make sure she gets on the plane okay?' 'Of course,' Michael said, his usual obliging self. 'No problem. What does she look like?' All I said was: 'You'll know.' And when he saw Wilnelia getting out of the taxi, he could hardly believe that *he* was the lucky man who would be escorting such an exquisitely beautiful woman to the plane. He *loved* every moment of being with her, *loved* seeing all the other passengers turn their heads as she floated past. I had to remind him that I was going to sit next to her. He didn't stop talking about her for days afterwards. I completely understood! I, for one, had *never* forgotten the impact of seeing Wilnelia for the first time; how totally enamoured I had been by the vision of that lovely face, framed by all that gorgeous long black hair. And, since that first day, when I so quickly discovered that her beauty is so much more than skin-deep, I'm *never* surprised when other people—both men and women—are amazed at how unspoiled she is; how lovely and sensitive she is in character; how intelligent and enjoyable she is to be around; and how easy she is to talk to and get along with. From that first day, I knew *I* wanted to be the lucky man who would first win her heart, then the rest of her in marriage.

*　　　*　　　*

In early December I was preoccupied with *Bruce Meets the Girls* for ITV. It was lovely to have the chance to put some light entertainment back into TV, and this one-hour special was exactly the right vehicle to do this. Among the lovelies on the programme were Diane Keen, Anita Harris, Ruth Madoc, and two of my home-grown ones, my daughters Julie and Laura. By then Laura had joined Julie and Dominic in their group Guys and Dolls. When the idea to invite the two of them on to the programme was first mooted, I had to admit that, after only a few gigs abroad, Laura was showing some real potential as a singer and Julie was a true pro. Although there was not a great deal I could teach Julie, I did give some advice to Laura. 'Wait for the laughs,' I said. 'Hang on for the laughs.' And during the rehearsals, I held her arms and gave a little squeeze as a cue. Afterwards, she said, 'That was marvellous, Daddy. It's given me much more confidence. I'm not such a little girl any more.' She certainly wasn't. In fact, both she and Julie did a great show.

The writers for this were Dick Hills, Barry Cryer, David Renwick, Andrew Marshall, and Garry Chambers. On this occasion, Lionel Blair was the ideas man and the choreography was done by the very talented Nigel Lythgoe—now (in)famous for his *Pop Stars* judging! It was directed by Keith Beckett, who was also responsible for the last one I'd made, in 1976. Later, on 21 December, the same director and writers, with the addition of Eric Merriman, teamed up with me again for another hour of laughter and glamour in *Nice to See You!*, along with Harry H. Corbett, Faith Brown, Marti Webb, Lionel Blair, Katie Randall, Alison Bell, and Andre Reid. We had some good fun with this. It was supposed to be set in my flat, along with the stars as my 'staff', and a thirty-piece orchestra. But because there was an industrial dispute which

429

played havoc with the schedule, Keith filmed it in one day as a live show.

By 5 December, Larry Grayson and his hostess, the Scottish folksinger Isla St Clair, who had had a good run hosting *The Generation Game*, had announced that the time had come when they both felt they needed to do something else, and that they were quitting the programme. Their last edition was to be recorded on 17 December. I could understand only too well how they felt, and wondered who the BBC would approach. The *Gen Game*'s ratings had recently slumped against *Game for a Laugh*, which starred, among others, Matthew Kelly, Henry Kelly, Jeremy Beadle and Sarah Kennedy, who have gone on to do all sorts of marvellous things.

When I returned to London, after those blissful Thanksgiving days in Miami, I went to see my daughters Louisa and Charlotte. And I was absolutely thrilled for Anthea when she told me she had met a man called Freddie Hoffman in a little eatery in the Wentworth area. 'We hit it off together wonderfully well straight away,' Anthea explained. 'And he has now invited me and the children to spend Christmas with him and his parents at a hotel they run in Berkshire. Do you mind?' 'No, of course not,' I said.

Not only was Anthea so much happier, it was clear that both of us could now move on with our lives. I couldn't wait to get home and phone Wilnelia, so we could make arrangements to spend Christmas and the New Year together. 'Jonathan', Wilnelia told me (her friend whom I had now met several times since the 'Miss World' judging), 'is also going to be around at Christmas. And, as you both share such a wonderful sense of humour, that'll be lovely. We'll spend most of the time laughing.'

It all sounded perfect. I went out immediately and bought Wilnelia a present, a 'W'-shaped diamond brooch.

As we were still trying to keep our love affair 'under wraps', I decided to stay with Jonathan in the Granada Apartments at San Juan. Once again, there were no telephones in the rooms, and Jonathan spent much of our time there together teasing me about the receptionist, a particularly plain woman called Adele, whom, he claimed, was making up excuses to call me to the lobby, because she had the 'hots' for me! 'Do me a favour!' I kept replying.

While I was in Puerto Rico, sharing the Christmas and New Year festivities with Wilnelia, I was in for a very happy time—and some pleasant surprises. Among the latter was Delia—Wilnelia's mother—who was absolutely charming to me, and never once mentioned the difference between Wilnelia's age and mine, even though she herself was younger than me! She just seemed happy to accept that I was truly in love with her lovely daughter. We all had a marvellous time—and it was the best New Year's Eve ever. 'If I could have dreamed up a perfect beginning to 1982,' I remember thinking, 'this would be *IT*.' And the year ahead—the second of my courtship of Wilnelia—could not have looked more promising.

The island of Puerto Rico itself, the smallest and easternmost of the Greater Antilles in the Caribbean, with its gaily painted Spanish colonial architecture, has dozens of unspoiled white-sand

431

beaches and jagged coral outcroppings, and is encircled by crystal-clear lagoons and the bluest-of-blue sea and sky. It also has vast coconut groves, tropical trees, rare exotic flora and fauna, and a mountainous region that's home to rainforests and small mysterious caverns. With this wealth of natural wonders, it was—and still is—one of the most beautifully romantic, idyllic places I've ever visited. I was already looking forward to my next visit when I would meet Wilnelia's father and other members of her family.

During the period when I had been at a rock-bottom low—and even toying with the idea of leaving the UK for a couple of years—I had not planned to keep the house on at Wentworth. But, when *Play Your Cards Right* and Wilnelia came along, I decided to remain there. I knew Wilnelia was the love of my life; someone I could be with twenty-four hours a day without even looking for an excuse to go out and play golf! This didn't mean that we would live in each other's pockets and risk smothering each other. Simply that if Wilnelia wanted to visit her family and friends in Puerto Rico when I wasn't free, or if I wanted to go away for a week's Open Golf Championship, which might be boring for her, we'd say: 'Fine.' And then just fit in with each other's plans. In this way, we'd have a lovely, trusting relationship, unspoiled by jealousy and possessiveness which both of us loathed.

My New Year's resolution was already on hand that year. Whatever happened in the fixture in my professional life, I wouldn't make the same mistakes again; would not allow work to create too many separations and cause rifts and marital problems. I would, I resolved, always ensure there was time for us. And that's one resolution which, to this day, I've lived by.

CHAPTER FIFTEEN

A NEW LIFE

By the time Wilnelia entered my life, I had met many, many beautiful women—perhaps too many—and I was only too aware that beauty could bring its own problems. Some exceptionally good-looking women are ruined from the age of fifteen or sixteen, can so easily become spoiled, hard and manipulative, using their looks to get things they would probably be better off without! But, from our very first meeting, Wilnelia was never like that. I was constantly amazed that she was not only one of the *most* beautiful women I had ever met, she was also one of the *nicest*. The very first thing I noticed when she came to England in 1982 to spend the summer with me was that all my friends liked her. Suspicious to begin with, assuming that somebody as beautiful as Wilnelia was bound to think a lot of herself, they were always sidling up to me and exclaiming: 'Bruce! She's *so* nice . . . *So* calm . . . *So* full of consideration for others. She's just a *lovely, lovely* woman.' '*Yes!*' I would reply. 'That's why I was so attracted to her.'

I had been so looking forward to Wilnelia coming to England but, before she arrived, I was my usual busy-busy self. The New Year began with golf when BBC television transmitted the recorded games for the previous year's Marley Trophy. Peter Alliss commentated and talked to the players, Lee Trevino, George C. Scott, making his first appearance, and me. George played very badly in his first match—perhaps because this was the first time he'd played in a televised game. He made up for it, though, in the second game, when he played just like Tiger Woods! There was no stopping him then, as I found out to my cost when he gave me a resounding beating. Golf is like that—one day you play well, the next day badly.

On the actual gala evening there had been a grand dinner which went on till the early hours of the morning. The next day, one of the night porters told us that, having come across George C. Scott lying in the middle of the floor of the VIP hospitality room, he went over, shook George, and said: 'Mr Scott, it's three o'clock in the morning.' 'Get me a taxi,' George replied, opening one eye. 'Get me a taxi right away . . .' When the taxi arrived, the porter shook George again and told him the taxi was outside. 'Right,' George said, 'okay,' struggling up and walking out to the taxi, still wearing his tuxedo. 'What shall I do with your clubs and your clothes?' the porter asked. Leaning out of the taxi window, George growled: *'Burn 'em.'* And the taxi drove off. This story, of course, went all round the hotel, and we heard later that one of his celebrity friends packed up his golf clubs and clothes and took them back to the USA.

On the work front, 1982 began with the next series of *Play Your Cards Right*, with the addition of two new Dolly Dealers, Gillian Duxbury and Camilla Blair. Camilla also appeared on my hour-long ITV special show *Forsyth's Follies* in 1983. In

February, while I was doing my one-man show at the Fairfield Halls, Croydon, my daughter Debbie started her own record company, DEB, with the first single release, 'I'm Not Really Me Without You', sung by her husband David and Madeleine Bell. In March, my divorce from Anthea was finalized; and on 26 April in Maidenhead Anthea married Freddie Hoffman. This, though, was kept a secret and not public knowledge until 14 June. In May, Terry Wogan began his new career as a BBC TV chat-show host and invited me as his special guest on the very first night along with Paula Yates and Nigel Rees. I didn't have any trouble persuading Terry to join me in a dance routine, and it turned out that, while he had been compèring all those *Come Dancing* shows, he'd learned a bit about shuffling his feet, too. I was then very sad to hear of the death of my friend Harry H. Corbett, who had made such a great success of his role in *Steptoe and Son*. Many people don't know that Harry started his acting career playing mainly classical roles. In June, we held a benefit performance for his family at London's Adelphi Theatre, and, among so many who contributed to its success, were Ray Galton and Alan Simpson who wrote the scripts for *Steptoe*, Roy Hudd, Christopher Timothy, Bert Weedon, Los Zafiros and Legs and Co. Also in June, *my* Pro-Am Charity Golf Classic was held at Moor Park. Tony Jacklin was there, along with Mark Thatcher, Seve Ballesteros, and Bernhard Langer who won the trophy.

So, I was far from idle in the weeks before Wilnelia arrived for our first time together in Chelsea, London. And I was not idle when she settled in. My workload recording the next series of *Play Your Cards Right* was pretty heavy for the first six weeks of her visit. But this proved not to be a problem. Knowing how much she loved cooking, I said: 'Would you like me to arrange a cookery course for you at the Cordon Bleu School in Marylebone High Street?' 'Oh, yes!' she said, smiling. 'I'd *love* that, Bruce. I've always wanted to be a Cordon Bleu.' So, in the mornings, on my way to the recording studios, Paul (my driver) and I would drop her off at the school, just off London's Wigmore Street. Then every afternoon when I went to collect her, she would come out carrying all the bits and pieces she'd been cooking. Paul and I would sit munching away on these in the car. Throughout that entire period, we were both so full we hardly ever ate a 'proper' dinner.

I didn't propose to Wilnelia in Chelsea. I was biding my time for the right romantic setting. This arrived six weeks later, when she came with me to Turnberry where I was invited to play in yet another golfing TV series. Then, on a moonlit night, at the end of a perfect day, I went down on my knees on the balcony—I *really* did, without a single creak!—and asked her in the time-honoured way to marry me. I also reassured her that, if she did marry me, I would always want her to feel free. 'There'd be no need for you to worry about work,' I kept saying. 'If there's anything you've always wanted to do, but never had the chance . . . you could do it. You can do anything you want to do . . .' Then, because I was only too aware that becoming the third 'Mrs Forsyth' would mean a dramatic change in her life, that she would be giving up so much to be with me, and would also become part of my extraordinary 'extended family', which included five daughters—two almost the same age as her—I added: 'Don't answer at once, darling . . . Think about what I'm asking . . . Think about everything this will mean. It's a *huge* decision—a much bigger one for you than it is for me.' 'I've *already* thought about it,' she replied, hugging me. 'And I know the answer . . . Know how I feel. Know it's the right decision for me. I've never been in love before . . . but I *am* now with you. I know there's a difference in our age, but even if our marriage lasts for only a few years, I'm too happy to care at this moment. *I love you.* The answer is "*yes*".'

She then said that she would want us to have children. I said: 'Of course, darling.' I didn't even ask how many.

Okay! So perhaps it does all sound very Mills & Boon. But that's how it was. That's how we felt about each other. And *I* was the happiest man alive and determined to ensure that, from that moment on, she would be the happiest woman.

One meeting that Wilnelia and I were anxious about was the one with my five daughters, especially as Debbie was older than her! It was, we felt, a rather tricky situation. But we needn't have worried. All the girls took to Wilnelia at once—and she took to them. I can honestly say that, over the years, Wilnelia has brought the family closer together. You can only imagine how relieved and lucky I felt.

Wilnelia then decided she didn't want to get married in Puerto Rico because of the huge amount of attention it would create there; and because there was not a big enough hotel for her to invite half the island to the wedding reception! I, for the first reason, didn't want to get married in the UK. Where then, could we hold our wedding? As I was booked to go to Australia in May 1983 for a 'down-under' series of *Play Your Cards Right*, we decided that was far enough away from both our 'fields' to get married. My next problem, apart from where to get married, was the honeymoon— how can you take a Caribbean girl to the Caribbean?

While we were at Turnberry, where all those years ago, in 1943, my brother John had been killed in a low-altitude RAF training exercise, I also played with Seve Ballesteros against Sir Douglas Bader and Lee Trevino. Douglas, despite losing both his legs in a flying accident in 1931, overcame his terrible disability and returned to active service in 1939 to command the first RAF Canadian Fighter Squadron. A Second World War hero, he was mentioned three times in despatches, and was awarded the DSO and DFC, the Légion d'honneur and the Croix de Guerre. Now seventy-two, displaying his usual agility, he had almost completed the nine-hole match when he began to experience chest pains. We called for a doctor who, of course, suggested the game should be abandoned. However, as Douglas and Lee were so far ahead of Seve and me, we gave Douglas and Lee the game. Fortunately, all was well. Douglas recovered. He came down to dinner that night as if he had just walked out of a health farm.

When I played in August at the Finchley Golf Club, North London, Wilnelia and I were photographed laughing and joking together. So, in no time at all, the heading in the *Daily Express* was

'Nice to see her . . . but who, Bruce?' Of course, after a bit of detective work, they quickly put two and two together and came up with Wilnelia's name. From then on our clandestine love affair was public property, and we were followed and photographed wherever we went. I was so glad I had already asked Wilnelia to marry me. I know she wouldn't have lived with me otherwise.

*   *   *

One day—not long after Wilnelia and I had become engaged—I was driving home when I realized I needed petrol. When this occurs—to avoid being mobbed!—I always look for a garage that isn't too busy. Wasn't it lovely in the old days when you could drive up to a petrol pump, and remain seated in the car while an attendant put the petrol in, checked the oil, cleaned the windows, and so on. This was such a luxury—and something we all took for granted until, almost overnight it seemed, those days were gone, replaced by the so-called progress of 'Serve your bloody self'.

Anyway, on this occasion, having spotted a garage with nobody in it, I thought, 'Good—I'll pull in here.' I was halfway through filling up when I saw a seventy-odd-seater coach drawing in. As the passengers started to get out, I turned round to face the pump so that I could stand with my back to everyone and remain inconspicuous. But as I closed the petrol cap, I saw a woman standing by the bonnet of my car looking at me. 'It *is* you, isn't it?' she said. 'Yes,' I agreed. 'It is.' 'Bruce Forsyth.' 'Yes, dear—I'll give you five points for that.' 'Oh, yes . . . I've seen you a lot over the years. You're

439

conceited, aren't you?' 'Well . . .' I said, taken aback. 'I've had a few things said to me over the years, but *conceited* . . . Nobody's ever come up, looked me in the eye, and told me I'm *conceited.*' 'But you *are,*' she said. 'You sing, dance, play the piano—do so many things.'

What she was trying to say, I suddenly realized, was that I was *versatile!* But, because I did so many things—and showed other people what I could do—*that* to her mind was conceited. 'Yes, dear,' I said. 'I *know* what you mean. I am *very, very* conceited.'

And long may I remain so, I thought, as I went in and paid my bill.

Another hazard of being a face that is instantly recognized is when people have had a few drinks too many. Some of them are then either a little belligerent . . . or downright nasty. Unless you are *very* careful, and smile all the time and remain pleasant, they can very easily go from being pleased to see you to the opposite extreme. It really is a bit of a minefield—and you can find yourself walking a very fine line. Particularly dicey problem areas are crowded bars, so I don't go to pubs any more. Normally, though, if you are in a theatre bar during an interval, people simply smile at you. They appreciate that, like them, you have come to see a show. In the main, you have a lot of fun ad-libbing with people who come up and make a remark, and ninety-nine per cent of the time they're very nice and it's fine.

A stock moment I'm frequently subjected to occurred again the other day in Waitrose. A woman was taking a *very* long time to make up her mind about what she wanted when she suddenly turned round and saw I was waiting behind her. Looking hard at me, she said: 'Oh . . . it's *so* lovely to see you—and you look *so much younger* than you do on television.' 'Oh, do I? You must have a *very old* set,' is my stock reply. Maybe if she bought a *new* one, I'd look even younger!

I also often meet people who recognize me, but can't quite place me or my name. Recently, when I went into a shop, the staff realized straight away I was a familiar face, and when I went to pay kept saying, Mr . . .? Mr . . .?, needing some help with my name. They often feel embarrassed, but they shouldn't. We all watch so much television these days, it's so easy to get names and faces muddled. I always sympathize with people who are trying to remember who I am—I sometimes have trouble with that myself!

Quite recently I called into the video shop in Sunningdale. A boy, aged about twelve, was waiting at the counter, but the manager turned to serve me. 'No,' I said, 'serve the boy. He was here first.' The boy looked at me very intently, looked away, then looked at me again. 'Hallo, son,' I said, 'you all right? Are you trying to work out who I am?' 'Yes,' he said, 'I'm not quite sure.' 'Well,' I said, 'I'm here getting a video, too. Try to think of my name and, if you can't place it by the time we're paying, I'll tell you when we're leaving.'

So we got our videos and I said to him, 'Have you remembered yet?' 'No,' he said, 'I still can't place you.' 'Bruce . . .', I said, helpfully. He shook his head: 'No.' 'I'll give you £5 if you can remember my name,' I said. 'You're not', he said instantly, brightening up, *'Bruce Willis*?' As that star's face flashed before my eyes, it was difficult not to fall

441

about laughing. 'No, I'm *not* Bruce Willis,' I said, 'and you're *not* getting your £5.' But I suppose it *was* flattering!

There was also a time when Wilnelia and I were in Marbella with Louisa and Charlotte, who were then quite young. We were sitting in a café, waiting for our lunch, when I noticed another guy sitting further to our right talking to the Spanish owner and indicating me. About ten minutes later the guy got up, looked over at me, said, 'Goodbye,' and that was that. When we got up to pay the bill, however, the owner of the café, said: 'Oh, Mr Forsyth, can I have your autograph?' I was about to sign when he added cheerfully: 'I've read all your books, you know.' 'Oh, really?' I said, twigging that the guy must have said 'Forsyth', and he thought he meant Frederick Forsyth. But, to keep him happy, I wrote Frederick Forsyth, and said mischievously: 'I'm glad you like my books. The next one is all about Marbella and the rest of the Costa del Sol. It's a story about the Mafia and is full of the intrigue and loving that goes on here. And when it's finished, I'll send you a copy.' 'Oh, thank you, Mr Forsyth,' he said. It was not until some years later at a party given by Sir David Frost, a wonderful annual event with guests from the media, show business, politicians and writers, that I met Frederick Forsyth. I went over and told him the Marbella story. 'Bruce,' he said, 'that's nothing. Someone's always coming over to me at literary functions or when I'm in a bar, saying, "What's it like being married to a Miss World?"'

Wilnelia and I always enjoy going to David and Carina Frost's parties. They are always one of the special nights of the year because we always bump

442

into people we haven't seen for ages. Carina is a lovely lady, and I have always had a tremendously high regard for David's interviewing techniques and his longevity on television. No matter who he is dealing with, whether it is politicians, celebrities, or people in the arts, he always asks the right questions and has a wonderful knack of putting everybody at their ease and into the right frame of mind. This is much more of an art than is commonly realized. Years ago—I won't mention the name—there was an interviewer who, having asked a question, would leave his chat-show guests stranded because he was thinking of the next question he was going to ask. It is so off-putting being with somebody like that. David has never fallen into that trap. He remains completely focused on both the question and the answer.

As far as the pros, cons, and the hazards of being a celebrity are concerned, it's difficult to choose between the various nationalities. The Americans, for example, don't seem to go in for autographs in the way the British do. And it's amazing, considering how long I've been around, how much mail and how many requests for photographs and autographs I still get from all over the place.

*　　　*　　　*

In October, to my great delight, I became a grandfather again. This time it was Debbie and David's turn, and they had a daughter whom they named Josie. David, who composed 'Can't Smile Without You' for Barry Manilow, wrote a song called 'Josie' to celebrate the birth of the baby. Members of our globe-trotting family came back to

England to share in their happiness. I returned from Spain where I was having a short break, Penny (Debbie's mother) returned from her home in Spain, Julie arrived from Holland, and Laura and David's mother, Jean, came from America.

In November my golfing mate, Jimmy Tarbuck, was signed by LWT to compère a new version of *Sunday Night at the London Palladium*, which was to be called *Live at Her Majesty's* and to be broadcast from Her Majesty's Theatre in the New Year. There must have been quite a tussle going on behind the scenes because the BBC had wanted Jimmy to take over *The Generation Game* from its previous host, Larry Grayson. But even Jimmy could not manage to be in two places at the same time!

At Christmas Wilnelia and I went to Puerto Rico again so I could meet the rest of her family— including her father's fifteen brothers and sisters and their children. Wilnelia then told her father and everybody else present that she was in love with me. And, as she had never been in love with anybody before, they all realized she was very serious. She also told them—what I had told her— that, as well as being in love with her, I'd fallen in love with Puerto Rico and, in particular, being me, with its magnificent golf course at Dorado. After Antigua's golf course, which I can only describe as fourth-rate, I'd not really known what to expect of the Hyatt Regency Course at Dorado Beach. But its two courses, east and west, designed by Robert Trent Jones Sr—and all through the 1990s the site of the Senior PGA Tournament of Champions— was absolutely first-rate. One of the best in the world. I was absolutely over the moon, playing there. We also became very good friends of the golf professional Junior Colon and his wife Gladys, and love spending New Year's Eve with them and their family.

We then celebrated with a party for about two hundred guests. This proved to be such a perfect celebration in such a perfect setting that I kept trying to persuade Wilnelia to marry me there and then! She resisted. It was also, at the risk of sounding sexist, what I can only describe as a woman's engagement party. All the ladies, knowing that Wilnelia would be leaving the island to marry me, kept crying. We really should have arranged hankies, as well as napkins, for all the guests. We decided to get married in New York. This was where Wilnelia had spent the last three years of her life working, and where I had become a regular commuter since first meeting her. And we did not need confetti.

On *the* day—15 January 1983—it was snowing heavily in Manhattan. The night before, not allowed, of course, to stay with the bride, I was exiled to what turned out to be a hotel three blocks away. The next morning, while Wilnelia was enjoying herself at breakfast and making all the usual bridal preparations, I breakfasted alone and then trudged through the sludge to await the Big Moment in the Helmsley Palace Hotel, decorated with flowers. The overnight exile and the trudge was more than worth it. I was about to be married to the woman I loved. And, true to form, when she arrived, Wilnelia was the most beautiful bride ever, wearing a long, white, off-the-shoulder dress. And Jonathan Luk, who'd known about us from the beginning, was our best man.

After the ceremony—witnessed by my daughter Laura, and attended by about forty-five family and friends, we all moved into a small banqueting room of the Helmsley Palace Hotel. Despite trying to keep all our plans secret—and believing we had succeeded—one persistent journalist had spent days chasing Wilnelia all over New York, badgering her—and members of her family—for photographs and interviews. Then, thanks to him, other reporters got on to the story. The fact is, however secretive and organized you try to be, it is impossible to avoid such 'leaks' and 'leeches'. As far as 'names'—or the 'rich'—are concerned, every hotel, every well-known restaurant and nightclub, even every television studio and theatre, has moles who phone the press and say: 'So-and-so has just walked in with so-and-so', or: 'Somebody here is doing you know what with you know who.' You are at the mercy of a mole Mafia that's impossible to control. Even when you know or suspect *who* the 'tipsters' are, there's nothing you can do to stop them selling a story. And some restaurants and hotels connive with all this, lap up the free publicity when their establishment gets a mention in the tabloids. In the end, you can only wait for the inevitable . . . bite the bullet when it comes.

That's how it was on our wedding day. The cat was well and truly out of the bag. There were half a dozen members of the press in the hotel, plus a news camera. Resigned to the inevitable—and knowing we would be given no peace until we surrendered—I decided to invite them all in for a glass of champagne, give one quick group interview, and then send them on their way. Only then would Wilnelia and I be allowed to rejoin our guests and enjoy the rest of the day.

At least, after our wedding day, Wilnelia and I succeeded in having an intrusion-free honeymoon at the Hyatt Regency in Maui, Hawaii, for two weeks. There's a long line of hotels on the beach, with a bus service that runs all the way along these, picking people up and dropping them off. The only honeymoon embarrassment we suffered there was when we were sitting on one of these empty buses going to another hotel. The driver said: 'I'm used to having happy couples on board, but you two seem especially happy.' 'We're on our honeymoon,' we laughed, caught off guard. 'On your *honeymoooon . . .* On your *honeymoooooon . . .*', he kept repeating cheekily, loving every moment of it. Then, on our return, we were unlucky enough to get the same driver who, by this time, had about forty other passengers on board. All went well until it was our stop. Then he suddenly yelled at the top of his voice: 'Okay, you two *honeymooooooners*, off you get . . .', and the whole busload fell about and pointed at us. We ran into the hotel, and had a good, embarrassed laugh ourselves. Looking back at the honeymoon, it was perfect.

We then went on to Auckland, New Zealand where I was booked to do a chocolate commercial. But, because a sixty-mile-an-hour wind was blowing non-stop, we couldn't leave the hotel very often. Then there was some unexpected work-permit problems for the *Play Your Cards Right* trip to Australia. I was furious with Australian Equity stepping in and recommending that the Australian Employment Department turn down my work-permit request because 'too many British variety stars had been hogging telly time in Australia'.

447

'How dare they make me feel so unwelcome,' I thought, 'when so many Aussies have been allowed to enter the UK to become big stars?' But, in my heart of hearts, I was also rather relieved. If I had signed the contract and the show had proved to be the success it was in Britain, I would have had to keep going there. And that would have interrupted my lovely life at home with Wilnelia.

Anyway, as the weather in Auckland was so awful and I couldn't go to Australia as planned, we decided to continue our honeymoon for another two months. And we planned the trip to include Hong Kong, Rome, and Marbella before returning home. We celebrated Valentine's Day, my birthday, the Chinese New Year and our wedding anniversary, which we celebrated on the fifteenth of *every* month, in Hong Kong. Talk about fireworks! Nobody has ever, I promise, seen a proper fireworks display until they see them ignited en masse from boats in Hong Kong harbour. It was a fantastic, breathtaking, unbelievably exciting display. Then, as Anthea and the children were now living with Freddie, we returned to Wentworth. 'Shall we sell this house and buy another in the area?' I asked Wilnelia. After some thought, she decided that, even though one of Anthea's coats was still hanging in the cloakroom—something a woman would notice!— she was happy to stay where we were. She also said: 'You are the one with the memories in this house. If they do not bother you, they do not bother me.' Since then, during all the years that have followed, Wilnelia has turned it into her house with all her ideas and tastes.

Wilnelia's English, she would be the first to

admit, was not very good when we first met, but it gets better by the day. As it is not her first language, she naturally still comes out with some lovely ones. For example, when planning a trip for some Puerto Rican friends who were coming to stay, she said: 'They can go on the Hoover to France.' I said, 'The what?' She said, 'The Hoover.' I could just see them crossing the Channel on vacuum-cleaners! I couldn't resist teasing her. Then, because I moan a lot, she got her own back. Having become a fan of *One Foot in the Grave*, she said: 'You're a bit of a Victor Meldrew, aren't you, but for all that I still love you.' At least Wilnelia spoke English. Heaven knows how we would have managed if she was like me. Despite all the help I've been given, I've hardly—and this still applies today—mastered a word of Spanish. And, given that we bought a second home in Puerto Rico, I would have been wise to do so!

The first place Wilnelia found was just outside the capital, San Juan, and she phoned me to say: 'It has the most marvellous view over parkland.' 'It might have a wonderful view *today*,' I said, always so British about 'abroad'! 'But *will* it have a view of a new tower block *tomorrow*?' 'The land', my ever-patient Wilnelia replied, 'is protected, Bruce. It can never be built on.' We bought it.

Then, about five years ago, I was given the chance to live on another golf course. Dorado Beach is still our home in Puerto Rico and it's one of the most beautiful spots in the Caribbean. Situated on the northern shores of the island, it is secluded but has wonderful views of the course, the sea, and lots of the little native *coqui* frogs sing us to sleep at night. We stay there for four blissful months every year. It was not always so restful and romantic, though. While it was being built, everything that could go wrong, did go wrong. I was happy enough playing the best golf ever. But Wilnelia was coping with builders who connected wrong pipes together, resulting in a spout of boiling hot water every time we flushed the loo.

By then, in the Caribbean, where the local people only have eyes for Wilnelia who is their one-and-only 'Miss World', an honour they will never forget, I was getting used to being called 'Señor Mundo'—Spanish for 'Mr World'. And knew, if I'd ever been daft enough to run down a street hollering: *'Encantada de verte . . . de verte encantada'*—'Nice to see you . . . to see you, nice'—nobody would have turned a hair or recognized me. Likewise, in Britain, Wilnelia—who had known nothing about me or my career when we first met—was getting used to people coming up, greeting me warmly, and calling out catch-phrases. Also, when we were first married, and she was in the room while I was answering the phone, saying 'All right, my love. All right?' and 'Hallo, my darling,' she was very curious about who all these mysterious 'loves' and 'darlings' were. It was weeks before she realized I was a bit of a 'lovey' who called everyone 'love' and 'darling'.

Back in the UK, between learning to sculpt and paint, Wilnelia—who could have been a first-class interior designer if she had wanted—worked wonders on our Wentworth house. Never one to be outdone, I had my moments, too. One day I stood in the drive, which only had one drive-in and no separate drive-out, wondering how much land we had to the left where there was nothing but trees

450

and rhododendrons. Having walked to what I believed to be the boundary of our land, I couldn't believe the amount of wasted space that was there. As we wanted a tennis court, I phoned up a guy and asked him to come and have a look. He disappeared among the trees and bushes for about three hours, then came and knocked on the door. 'Mr Forsyth,' he said, looking pleased with himself. 'Come and have a look. There's more than enough room for the tennis court. I've placed four poles with a flag on top where it can be. And you've actually got enough space left over as well for the second driveway your wife mentioned.' 'Amazing!' I said, never having had the time before to focus on such matters. A few days later, armed with bulldozers and diggers, our man disappeared behind the bushes again and it all started to happen.

I was rather pleased with myself—feeling, in my own small way, that I was following in the footsteps of my great-great-great-grandfather, William Forsyth, a landscaper, who had lived between 1737 and 1804. I only knew what he did because Penny—who by now had forgiven me for the awful days when she'd threatened to write a book about our turbulent marriage, entitled *Darling, Your Dinner's in the Dustbin*—had been busy researching the Forsyth genealogy. Thanks to our being friends again, Penny had told me that my great-great-great-grandfather was George III's head gardener at Kensington Palace. And, as a founder member of the Royal Horticultural Society, he had been rewarded for his life's toil by having the Forsythia shrub named after him. He'd also pioneered a cattle-dung poultice for damaged oak trees.

451

At the start of her researches, Penny, who mistakenly thought that the Queen Mother lived at Kensington Palace, had written to her there for help. Despite not living there, the Queen Mother sent back an encouraging letter. Penny, surprised to get a reply at all, was thrilled to receive such a charming response. Other distant relations then informed us that William had also landscaped part of the grounds of the White House in America. Perhaps, I thought proudly, this is why, given a free moment between work and golf, I love looking out of a window, or standing in the garden, playing at 'landscaping'. That, though, is as far as gardening goes for me. Getting my hands dirty is another matter. That, unlike my talented relative, I leave to others—especially Wilnelia, who particularly loves water features and gardening.

When we were having an indoor swimming-pool installed, a large statue—which I can only describe as a Grecian lady—was delivered to the house. She was supposed to stand on a plinth but, when this was attempted, her head touched the ceiling! So I said to the four guys who had brought her: 'I'll make a deal with you. If you carry her down to the bottom of the garden to where there is a space between some shrubs, and place a few pieces of left-over balustrade behind her . . . If she looks really nice there, I'll buy her. If not, you'll have to carry her all the way back up the steep slope and put her back on the truck.' 'You're driving a hard bargain, Mr Forsyth,' the head guy said, knowing she weighed a ton, 'but we'll do it.'

Fortunately for them—and us—she looked lovely. I approved, Wilnelia approved, and I'm sure if he'd been present my great-great-great-grandfather would have approved. There are certain times in the summer when a shaft of sunlight comes through the trees and literally spotlights the statue's head and shoulders. It is so theatrical. She looks like Shirley Bassey going into her closing number! She also, at times, looks like a guardian angel—and, goodness knows, we all need one of those!

We then decided to sell my pied-à-terre in Chelsea. This—I had long ago discovered, whenever I was working in London and staying there—had a very small, hostile foldaway bed that had the alarming habit of leaping out and, once you were on board, threatening to leap back into its recess! What we needed was a bigger apartment in town, with a less dangerous-to-life-and-limb bed! I also had a few other requirements: 'Whatever you do, Wilnelia,' I said, 'find us a flat with all the vital shops and restaurants nearby. I don't want to get a taxi every time I go out to buy anything!' So Wilnelia found this apartment, practically next door to every shop we might need when in Chelsea. She then rang me to say: 'It's perfect, Bruce—in brilliant shape—we can just move in. We don't need to do a thing, darling . . .' I should have known better! It is *NOW* perfect, but only since we have renovated it to Wilnelia's high interior-design standards: had the fireplace ripped out and replaced with a Louis XV version, the decor redone, and a wall-size mural added. It's amazing. Why is she always right?!

*   *   *

In April 1985, Thames TV asked me to take over

the late Leonard Rossiter's role in a spin-off from the comedy series *Tripper's Day.* Leonard, who was a household favourite and one of mine for his roles in *Rising Damp* and *The Fall and Rise of Reginald Perrin*, had died the previous year, aged fifty-seven. It was an interesting challenge to play Leonard's role as a crazy supermarket manager, wrestling with really difficult staff and awkward customers. Re-titled *Slinger's Day,* I approved the scripts for a six-part series and we went into production. It was my first and, to date, only sitcom, and I enjoyed doing it. Thames requested a second series, which we did the following year. I was even offered a third series, but by then my eye was on another format . . .

This was an idea called *Hollywood or Bust,* a show in which I assumed the role of a film director auditioning members of the studio audience to play famous film actors and enact a scene from a famous movie. For example, we'd get four would-be Vivien Leighs and Clark Gables out of the audience, choose two of them and then get them to perform a scene from *Gone With the Wind*—under my direction. It was an entertaining idea and, but for some contractual problems over the format, would have benefited from a second series to perfect.

But it was during this period that I finally got what I had once been so anxious to achieve: the chance to do a series on American television. I went off to Los Angeles to record sixty-five half-hour programmes of *Hot Streak,* a word-guessing game for two teams—five women playing against five men. Each contestant wore headphones and, having guessed the subject matter, for example ice cream, had somehow to convey this to the next team member. No miming clues or repeat words were allowed—and the penalty for breaking these rules was disqualification. The prize was ten thousand dollars. The series went very well and was a different way of working for me as we would tape five shows in one day. The only problem was that the men kept winning which, given that this was a daytime show, with mainly women viewers, wasn't ideal!

A much bigger problem was that the ABC network, for whom we were making the show, was in complete turmoil. As *Hot Streak* aired on US television, not only was the head of ABC fired, the head of daytime television was fired along with most of that department. It prompted David Letterman, host of one of America's biggest late-night talk shows, to joke, 'ABC are in such confusion that they are going to start re-runs of the news.' I hasten to add that although all this had nothing to do with *Hot Streak*, it did mean that almost everything that these guys had been responsible for was axed by the new regime. *Hot Streak*, which had had precious little chance to establish itself, was no exception.

Had something like this happened a few years earlier, I would have been devastated. As it was, I was disappointed, of course, but it wasn't the end of the world. We were just unlucky with the timing and all the network politics. Life with Wilnelia was making me much more relaxed, and I had a new series of *Play Your Cards Right*, still a Top-Twenty ratings show, to look forward to. As far as *Hot Streak* is concerned, few people in the UK have ever heard about it. So if you are ever in a pub quiz or the like and are asked who was the first English person to host a game show on American television, trust me, Anne Robinson is the wrong answer!!

However, all good things have to come to an end. After nine hugely successful years of *Play Your Cards Right*, the powers that be decided to rest it. However, I had a replacement show lined up. Julie and Dominic had seen a show in Holland that they thought would be good for me, and so Ian and I went over to Hilversum in the Netherlands to look at it. In fact, the show was not Dutch but devised by a German company. We acquired the UK rights and sold them on to London Weekend Television. Thus *You Bet!* was born.

We taped a pilot at the London Studios but it didn't look very good—the studio itself was too small for the show. We went on to make the series at Shepperton. This was long before 'big' shows like *Gladiators* hit the screens, and was the first time in the UK a television game show had been made on this scale. The format was quite simple: a member of the public would claim that they could complete a seemingly impossible challenge and a celebrity panel would then bet on whether they could or not. While the winning celebrity would win a lot of money for a charity of his or her choice, if a celebrity was wrong they had to do an unpleasant forfeit. Many of the challenges were spectacular—involving motorbikes, mechanical diggers and the like—which was why we had to have a big, big stage.

You Bet! was a Saturday night ratings success, and the first time I had been on Saturday night television since *Big Night*. I did three series, assisted in all of them by Ellis Ward, but despite the show's huge viewing figures, I realized it wasn't really for me. Don't get me wrong, it was a great show and continued successfully for many years afterwards in the capable hands of Matthew Kelly. However, I personally felt it didn't allow me to have much fun. For the first time in my life, I was more often than not simply a presenter, not an entertainer, and I missed the opportunity of having a real laugh with people.

While I don't regret doing *You Bet!*, I do wish that I had not done quite so many game shows. I've only fully realized this in the last few years and, in television terms, it's my only true career regret. To my mind, I am what I was when I first came into the business: an all-round performer. Yes, the game shows have been—and still are—very profitable, and people do love them. But I *wish* I had held out for more musical entertainment shows, more 'specials' or some other kind of specially tailored for me light-entertainment series for ITV or BBC. I should have done this in the 1970s when I was at the height of my powers to pick and choose; should have said: 'I'll do one series of a game show, followed by an entertainment series.' They would have let me then. If I had done this, these shows would still be put out as family-entertainment repeats at Christmas and other times.

I did, of course, do some really good 'specials', but by no means enough. The problem with *The Generation Game* was that it was such a successful show, with such phenomenal ratings, I got carried along on the tide to do ever more similar programmes, when I should have swum against it.

This, now, is a deep regret because, unless the public sees you performing often in a light-entertainment series, they cease to think of you as an all-round entertainer. These days, if a man or woman in the street was asked: 'Who's Bruce Forsyth?' they'd reply: 'He's a game-show host.' But I was far from being *just* that when I first appeared at the London Palladium. I would love to go back in time to put this right. This kind of typecasting is so much worse in Britain than it is in America. Over there, Las Vegas comedians and other cabaret artistes are often also seen in TV series and playing 'bit' parts in movies and so on. Here, once you are pigeon-holed, you're stuck. Your dancing shoes are set in concrete! So, apart from doing my one-man shows during the past twenty years, I've had to put many of my talents on hold.

One of the cuttings in my file that has always amused me is 'Schlockwatch' by John Hind, who wrote in *The Listener*:

> I have recently been wondering . . . Is it *healthy*—in 1988—to still possess a videotape containing seven *Play Your Cards Right*, recorded way back in 1980? Is it sound to spend at least five minutes per waking day wallowing in the catch-phrases, chin and music-hall calisthenics of these ancient LWT moments? That is not all. As a fully paid-up Forsyth-ologist I would also admit to owning *Bruce and The Girls* and *Slinger's Day*, assorted sacred Forsyth TV interviews, *plus* a soundtape of Bruce's double album, *Both*

Sides of Bruce—The Singer/TV Entertainer! More than this, however, I will not admit to, other than in the company of a fully certified psychoanalyst. But Bruce Forsyth makes me laugh, and—as Freud himself would admit—that can't be a bad thing. Most of what passes for televisual light entertainment bores me to sickness, and I can't handle [he mentioned two well-known names here, but I don't want to be disloyal to them] unless I have a crucifix to hand. But Mr Forsyth-Johnson (as he is listed in *Who's Who*) is, I feel, a whole different kettle of comic qualities. The Edmonton Enigma, as I call him, is a pro, a wag, a shoe-shuffe, a journeyman, a soulful singer, and, in his finest moments, almost a latterday surrealist. His face, meanwhile, falls little short of Oliver Hardy's in the humour stakes. Forsyth is a master of the quick-change. One second he's 'one of the lads', the next a jester, then he's a fall guy, then Mr Hospitality, then a piss-taker, then—to top the top—a sincere man pining a love song about his piano (despite confused laughs from the audience). 'Seems like it always comes down to this', he croons, 'Me swinging my piano stool, while you sit there grinning like a fool!' Forsyth's performance is schizophrenic, and TV desperately needs schizophrenic presenters. The enjoyment of watching him is in paying attention to, and

> attempting to figure out, that bizarre and multifarious blend of professional and psychological ingredients which make up 'the Man' before us—on stage, screen and golf course.

On reading that again, I am still trying to figure that out myself!

*   *   *

In February 1986, Wilnelia sat down beside me in our Wentworth home and told me some wonderful news. She was pregnant. While I was smiling about this, she added that she was absolutely convinced we were going to have a son. 'I don't mind,' I said. 'I really don't mind *what* sex the baby is as long as you're all right. I just think it's wonderful news. *Wonderful!*'

When Wilnelia was four months pregnant, she went for a scan. 'Would you like to know the sex of the baby?' the scan-operator asked while I was in the room. 'No,' Wilnelia replied on the instant. 'I still have five months of pregnancy to go. I don't want to feel disappointed if you tell me it's a girl. My husband already has five daughters. So, for now, I'd rather not know.'

We then heard the woman, who was still looking at the scan on the machine, say: 'Oh, look, she's turning round.' In the lift, I said to Wilnelia: 'I'm so sorry you heard that, darling. *Please* don't be too disappointed—I'm not.' 'So . . .' Wilnelia sighed, 'we are going to have a baby girl . . . But I promise you, darling, she'll be one of the most beautiful girls in the world.' I did not doubt that.

Later on—after her eight-month scan—Wilnelia was in for a surprise. Having once again told the technician that I already had five daughters and she was soon to give birth to another one, the technician said: 'Hm? Then I know you'll be a very happy woman if I tell you what the sex of your baby *really* is!'

One month later, on 10 November 1986, our son Jonathan Joseph was born. And this time, having raced to Wilnelia's side from rehearsals for *Slinger's Day*, I was present for the birth. I was very nervous—more nervous than I'd ever been in my life—but so pleased Wilnelia wanted me to be with her, so thrilled that she was pleased I was there. I had no idea what to expect—what man does?

One of the most extraordinary things about Wilnelia's labour and our son's eventual birth was the number of people waiting in her room in the Portland Clinic. It was all so 'un-British'! Worse, they were having an impromptu champagne party. I could hardly believe it. 'Why?' I kept asking myself. 'Why are they drinking champagne already?' But that's because I am English; and was foolishly concerned in a typically English way about what the clinic staff were thinking. However, neither I nor the gynaecologist, Criton Pavlou, could quite believe that people were partying in Wilnelia's room. 'I know . . . *I know*,' I kept repeating helplessly. 'But what can I do? That's how Latin people are—they're far more family-oriented than we will ever be. This is how they express their love.'

In the labour room, I was simply amazed at the physical struggle and strain, the mental and emotional concentration that giving birth entails.

461

'It must be', I kept thinking, 'absolutely exhausting for Wilnelia and every other woman. And all I can do is stand here, mop her brow, hold her hand, say little things—and give her all the love, support, and comfort I can.' Then everything started to happen so fast. One moment our baby was in Wilnelia's womb, the next he was in the world—in her arms, in my arms. Meanwhile, almost before my eyes it seemed, Wilnelia had changed from huge bump to normal size. It was all—and there is no other word to describe it—miraculous.

Some newborn babies have a 'Where am I? What is this place? Who's that?' almost startled expression in their eyes. But, right from the first moment, our son was very laid back with a remarkably focused look in his eyes. When he finally entered the world, we were overjoyed. But then I realized there was something missing! The usual baby sound effect. 'He hasn't cried . . . *He hasn't cried*,' I said anxiously to the matron. 'Don't worry. He will,' she reassured me. 'Just wait until we bathe him, you'll hear him then.' But we didn't. The matron came back and said: 'Well . . . I can't believe he didn't cry. He's obviously a very contented baby.' 'He is,' I thought. 'He's half Puerto Rican—an island boy. Of course, he loves water.' I then remembered reading in *The Guinness Book of Records* that Puerto Ricans, because they do not worry as much as most people, live for a very long time. And Wilnelia had once said to me: 'Bruce, I want you to become like a Puerto Rican and live for ever.' Looking down at our tiny contented newborn baby, I thought: 'That's what I want for you, son.'

All my five lovely daughters, of course, fell in

love with their only brother the moment they set eyes on him. While Debbie was present with her husband and my two little grandchildren, Josie and Jeremy, I caught the two children standing on tiptoes to peep at the new arrival in his cot. 'Hold on, everybody,' I said, struck by a sudden thought. 'Do you realize Josie and Jeremy are looking at their uncle?' Everybody laughed, but I was right. My grandchildren were looking at their uncle. They, of course, were too young to understand, couldn't take it in, were obviously puzzled, thinking: 'How can *that* baby possibly be our uncle?'

'It's a shame,' I added. 'He's too small to be able to do all the things that uncles usually do . . . You know, give you lots of money . . . lots of presents.' Having noted all their uncle's soft baby toys, they looked totally unconcerned.

Another lovely moment was that, although we had called our son Jonathan Joseph Enrique, thinking this a reasonably uncommon name in the UK, one of Wilnelia's uncles was quick to point out when we took our six-week-old baby to Puerto Rico that his first two names would be translated as Juan José—two of the commonest boy's names on the island! We settled for calling him 'JJ'—a nickname that's remained until this day.

There was a new direction in my life, and my beautiful wife and brand-new baby son were a very important part of it. I had changed. I was feeling far more relaxed and easy-going. There was a time when, if I'd been asked to name the most important things in my life, the word 'work' would have taken the top five places. It had to be that way if I was to stay at the top. After all, it's far too competitive, too cut-throat and too tough a business to go into half-heartedly. But when I met Wilnelia, I realized that my life seemed to be all work, I always seemed to be signed up for about eighteen months in advance. However, when I started to take some time off I wasn't bored, I was really enjoying myself. There were so many other things to do.

Even before JJ was born, I was spending much more time at home and was now looking forward to even more time there in future. I no longer needed work to turn me on; no longer needed to see my name up in lights to make me feel good. I would still enjoy working, but it was no longer everything—my wife and the little fellow were more important. With my five daughters, I had only been half a dad because I was away so much. In the circumstances I'd been very lucky that we were so close to each other as they got older. But now I wanted to cut back on work and do fewer television appearances. The death of people like Eric Morecambe, Tommy Cooper, and Leonard Rossiter had made me realize that I didn't want people standing at my memorial service saying he was a great performer, so sad he was only fifty-eight years old.

Then I was so touched when Wilnelia, holding our new baby son in her arms, said, 'I couldn't be happier, Bruce. I have more than most people have in their entire lives. All I know is that you're the only man in the world I want to be with.'

I felt exactly the same about her. Work was no more the be and end all of my existence, and life had never been more brilliant.

464

CHAPTER SIXTEEN

THE REGENERATION GAME

I will never forget our first New Year's Eve in Puerto Rico, six weeks after JJ was born. Wilnelia and I didn't want to go out anywhere to celebrate. We just couldn't bear to leave JJ, and we wanted to see the New Year in with him. Luckily, the Hilton Hotel, which was right opposite Wilnelia's mother's San Juan apartment, had the most wonderful firework display. So we opened a bottle of champagne and stood on the terrace, watching this with JJ. It was a perfect beginning to 1987. There was, however, a JJ hitch when we decided to go on a week's second honeymoon in Antigua. Wilnelia had organized everything beautifully for her mother Delia to look after the baby, but she was still very anxious about leaving him and kept saying, 'Will he be okay?' as though her mother had never had a baby. And when we arrived in Antigua, Wilnelia felt as if she had left her right hand behind. Every time she saw a mother with a baby, she started to cry, and telephoned her mother, asking: 'Is he okay? Is he crying? Does he have enough milk?' It was a disaster. We had only been in Antigua for three days, but Wilnelia was so unhappy, so upset, we had to cancel the rest of the week, return to Puerto Rico and actually finish our second honeymoon with JJ. I should have known that it was far too soon to leave him.

Although I had never succeeded in getting my own chat show off the ground, in March 1987 I was made an offer I couldn't resist. The BBC asked me to host Terry Wogan's show while Terry was on holiday. Derek Jameson did the first week, and when I joined the programme I had the pleasure of interviewing the newscaster Moira Stuart, Debbie Owen (wife of Lord David) and Judy Steele (married to Sir David). As I had always anticipated, I loved doing a chat show and thoroughly enjoyed sitting in Terry's chair. As this was my first stint as a talk-show host, I hoped it would prove to those in charge that I could do the job. But, unfortunately, further offers did not flood in. I was still pigeon-holed as a game-show host. As Bill Cotton said: 'It's not that Bruce isn't good at other things, it's that he's so bloody marvellous at game shows.'

In January 1988, while Wilnelia and I were on holiday in Spain, there was a wonderful evening in store for me that I knew absolutely nothing about. Although I had repeatedly told Wilnelia that I didn't want to do anything special for my sixtieth birthday, she had already planned a surprise birthday party for me. On the night before my birthday, she said innocently: 'Darling, I bumped into some of our friends in Marbella this morning, and said we would meet them for a drink tomorrow night.' 'Oh, no,' I said, dismayed. 'You know I don't want a fuss, don't want to go out.' 'Just for half an hour,' she said. When I got to the place, it was crammed full with family and friends who had flown in, and were now shouting, *'Surprise!'*, *'Surprise!'* I was stunned. Unknown to me, they had all secretly rehearsed in London, had even recorded a special birthday tape. The trouble they had gone to was so moving. Wilnelia and members of my close family then walked on to the stage, dressed in Spanish costumes, and sang all these specially written lyrics. It was the night of nights—very special. Knowing my kids had never seen me drunk, I decided to give them a surprise as well. Having had a couple of Jack Daniels, I ordered a few more, emptied these discreetly in plant pots, and began to act the part. 'You're always saying you've never seen me drunk,' I kept repeating in a slurred voice, staggering about. 'But now you know what it's like to have a drunken father.' I loved acting this role, pretending to be legless—and was so convincing, even Wilnelia was frightened I might fall down the stairs. After a while, I stood up very straight and owned up, saying: 'Well, that's enough of all that. I'd love a cup of tea.' I'd given a performance worthy of an Oscar, fooled them all! Well, one surprise deserves another!

Ronnie Corbett and I hosted the 1988 Royal Variety Performance together in the presence of the Queen Mother. I will never forget her saying after the show, 'What a *lovely* couple you are'! Neither Ronnie nor I were quite sure how we should take this! But we settled for being a lovely couple—'Tiny and Tall', rather than 'Little and Large'! Ronnie is one of those people who can always make me laugh the moment I set eyes on him, not because he's pint-size, but because I only have to look at his face and I'm a goner. We have worked together many times and have enjoyed every moment. What I admire about him is that he is as meticulous about his performances as he is about the way he dresses. When we rehearse we always do everything at full throttle, and invariably work side by side as though we are actually onstage. We both like to know exactly what we are going to do, and never take the attitude 'It'll be all right on the night'. But this has never meant that we can't be spontaneous and have lots of fun with our acts.

We also did a Christmas special together for the BBC that year. But when we were rehearsing in November, there was a big disappointment in store for us. Marcus Mortimer, the producer, came into the rehearsal room, stood looking at Ronnie and me, then said, obviously upset: 'I don't know how to tell you this.' 'What's wrong?' we asked, alarmed. 'I've just had the schedules,' he replied. 'And we are to follow Lenny Henry who's on at ten o'clock on Boxing Night.' We could not believe it. This meant two family entertainment shows, back-to-back, out of prime-time family viewing. Can you imagine how we felt during the last week's rehearsal, knowing that we were doing a Christmas show that was going out at eleven o'clock at night? It was *so* discouraging. It was not as if the programme-planners had seen our show and said: 'We don't think much of that.' They had scheduled it in a graveyard slot even before we had got as far as the studio and recorded it.

For one Royal Variety Show I did a sketch with a soprano, Ruth Welting, who performed at the Metropolitan Opera House, New York. While our show was in the planning stages, I was told that she would make a great guest for it. She was currently singing in *The Barber of Seville* at the Hollywood Bowl, had a wonderful voice, and a very attractive figure and personality. I phoned the stage door of the Hollywood Bowl and was surprised but delighted to be put straight through to her. I explained that I was coming to the US to hear her

468

sing and could I have a coffee with her afterwards so I could tell her about the Royal Variety Show I was hosting? She could easily have thought I was some kind of nut, but she didn't. When I saw her performance, I thought she was simply marvellous. Afterwards, I made my proposal: 'Would you be prepared to come to England for the Royal Variety Show,' I asked, 'and do a comedy sketch with me? The way it's been set up, I'm supposed to be your lover. I'll be dressed in a powdered wig and a period costume. You will sing an aria first, then I'll walk on. After you have explained to me what the opera is all about, we'd then do the sketch together.' 'I'd love to,' she said. I was so pleased. If anybody had come to the stage door after a show and asked me to do something like this, I would have thought, 'Who is this lunatic?' Our sketch proved to be one of the highlights of the evening.

All performers get very nervous before Royal Variety Shows. We could, though, always rely on Tommy Cooper to ease the tension and make us all laugh. I don't think Tommy ever fully appreciated just how funny he was, and nobody loved to laugh as much as he did. He always had to have his prop man Ronnie with him at the Palladium because he never knew where anything was. Once when I was watching him checking his props, I noticed he hadn't got any eyebrows. I told him this, and he said, 'Haven't I? No wonder I get made up so quickly.' But that, of course, was why he always seemed to have a vacant look on his face. Seeing him in his dressing room or in the corridors before a show was hilarious. He was always wandering about in long baggy underpants that came almost to his knees, and wearing suspenders to hold up his short socks. His feet were enormous, size 13B. He just loved people, loved company. Whenever you arrived at clubs after he'd been performing there, the stage managers would be full of him. 'Tommy', they would say, 'stayed with a group of us after the show until five or six in the morning. We never stopped laughing.' There were also several occasions when I bumped into him outside Hamleys' toy shop, in London's Regent Street, where he'd been looking for a toy he could turn into a joke.

*   *   *

In 1989, long before this autobiography was a twinkle in my eye, I wrote another book, *Golf . . . is it only a game?*, published by Sackville Books. In it, I included the following letter—a pathetic libel from two of my friends. Written on the Gleneagles Hotel's headed notepaper, it said:

> We, the undersigned, being of sound mind and body, do hereby solemnly swear and declare that Mr Bruce Forsyth is, in our opinion, the most proficient celebrity at the game of golf that we have so far encountered during our stay at this Pub.
>
> Signed
> WITHOUT PREJUDICE,
> Mr Lee Trevino and Mr Severiano Ballesteros

Pub! Well, never mind all that. I'll gloss over the fact that the writers were obviously not of sound or sober mind at the time—and, while suffering from temporary amnesia, had obviously forgotten I had a single-figure handicap at the time! I must own up, however, to some odd encounters—and embarrassing moments—on the course. Perhaps the oddest was when I was playing the water hole in Palm Springs. This is a short hole, over the water and you have about a 140-yard carry before you get to the green. It's quite a tricky hole. All my three partners had played, so I got all set up, addressed the ball, took the club back. I was at the top of my swing when . . . a frogman came out of the water! I mean he shot out of the water like a killer whale. I nearly had a heart attack. My club went flying and my three friends were in hysterics. That was just typical of my luck, but then, as anybody who sets foot on a course knows, all golfers are always just an inch from perfection. Another odd occasion was when I was playing with Telly Savalas, of *Kojak* fame, in the Charity Golf Tournament at the RAC Golf Club. I had always thought the lollipop was a TV gimmick. But to my amazement, halfway through the round, Telly pulled a lollipop out of his golf bag and stuck it in his mouth before he played his next shot—a wicked slice. 'It's your own fault, Telly,' I said. *'That's* where your lollipop was pointing!'

My lovely Wilnelia accounted for two embarrassing moments—both, I hasten to add, before she knew as much about the game as she does now. The first was in Florida, when I asked her to ride in a buggy with me so that she could see what golf was all about. I wasn't playing well that day and was just primed to hit what I hoped would be a first-class rescue shot. At that precise moment, Wilnelia called out: *'Come on, Brucie baby.'* I just wish I had a keepsake picture of the look I gave her as the ball disappeared into the trees. The second occasion was in Spain. I was playing in a competition and I couldn't find the ball in the rough. Quite a few people were trying to help, including Wilnelia. All of a sudden I heard her shout, *'I've found it, Bruce. I've found it!'* I was *thrilled*—until I turned round. There she was triumphantly holding the ball, waving it above her head. That moment earned me a two-shot penalty.

My *most* embarrassing moment, however, was at Finchley Golf Club when I was playing with Brian Barnes. There had been a lot of rain so the ground was very soft. I had to play off a sloping fairway, but still thought I could play a 3-wood. The ball was below my feet. I took my stance and made a swing which felt quite good. I then looked down the fairway, but Brian shouted, 'The ball's still there, Bruce.' *'Where?'* I called back. On further investigation, I found it buried deep in the turf, right by my feet. It had gone straight through the wet, soggy ground and been covered by the grass. Things, I am delighted to report, have gone reasonably well since then. However, once asked to comment on my swing, Brian Barnes said, 'With a swing like that he'll *always* make a good dancer.' Would I demean myself by replying to that?

Seve Ballesteros, co-author of the above letter, is one of my favourite golfers. His touch, his short game, particularly around the green, and the way he can get himself out of trouble makes him one of the greatest golfers ever. We have played together a number of times over the years, and we actually won a pro-am tournament together. I say 'we', but it was actually a team of three amateurs and I was one of them. When I was writing my golf book, which was very pictorial, I included lots of photos of the pros doing things with me, or demonstrating different situations. I thought of a good one for Seve. The idea was for me to lie down on the ground, holding a golf tee between my teeth, with the golf ball on the tee, and for Seve to be pictured at the top of his swing coming down. The caption would then be 'Always have confidence in your pro-am partner'! As we were about to shoot the picture, Seve said, 'Wouldn't it be better if I lay on the ground, with the golf tee between my teeth, and you swung the club?' 'Well,' I said, 'I didn't like to ask you . . .' 'But it would be much funnier,' he said. So that's what we did. He really is a delightful man, with a good sense of humour.

Lee Trevino is another guy who's a lot of fun. I once played with him and Seve in a pro-celebrity game at Gleneagles. They were a wonderful team. I think Lee more than anybody enjoys putting amateurs right. He just loves sorting everybody out. On one occasion, his caddy, Willie Aitcheson, phoned me when Lee was going to be my partner at a big pro-am game in Scotland. 'Bruce,' he said, 'when you play with Lee on Sunday, could my son possibly caddy for you? He'd love to be with us, and it'll be a family occasion.' On the day, this very nice lad put the bag on the trolley and off we all set to have a lovely time. We'd been playing for a couple of hours when we came to a short hole surrounded by onlookers. Now, when you see a green surrounded by people, four to six bodies deep, you still have to go for the target, but it can be terrifying. The others played off successfully but, unfortunately, my 6-iron went a bit to the left and, instead of the ball going on to the green, it went into the crowd. Naturally, I was very upset and hoped that nobody had been injured. It was not until I went into the clubhouse after the game that I heard my ball had unfortunately hit a young girl on the head, and she was being treated for a terrific bump. Who was it? It was Willie Aitcheson's daughter. He had said it would be a 'family occasion', and it was! His son had caddied for me and I had hit his daughter on the head with a ball. Horrible though this was, it was also funny and we couldn't help but laugh about it later. The trouble is, onlookers do not realize how lethal golf balls can be, and it's a wonder there are not more serious injuries.

When I used to go to golf events at Wentworth or Sunningdale as a young man, my favourite golfers were Peter Alliss, Dave Thomas, Max Faulkner, and Neil Coles. I would always look to see what part of the course they were on and go and watch whoever was nearest. Having admired players like these, it was quite something for me to meet them when I hit the Big Time. Peter Alliss and his wife Jackie are now among my dearest friends. When I first got to know Peter, we often used to sit in the clubhouse having a drink, talking about our troubles. We are both Pisces and a little oversensitive, but we were able give each other some comfort and a bit of hope when we were going through similar personal experiences. Peter was always a great player, but a bit suspect, as he freely admits, with his putting in the early years. Personally, I don't think he was as bad a putter as he thought, but he decided to go into commentating which, of course, he is marvellous at. Whenever I am in Puerto Rico and he is commentating for American television I feel homesick. But I love to listen to him. He has such a wonderful, fertile brain and always has a comical remark up his sleeve. He has commented at Wentworth so many times, and if somebody happens to slice a ball he says: 'That one could have landed in Bruce Forsyth's garden. Bruce is always out there with his field glasses and a bucket, hoping that'll happen.' He and Jackie have two sons and a daughter, and I was so touched when they asked me to be their eldest son Simon's godfather. They're very special people.

*   *   *

The new series of *You Bet!*, with Ellis Ward as my hostess, began in mid-February 1990 and continued until mid-April. As before, all the stars proved to be good sports when presented with their various challenges—no doubt because they were used to facing much worse in their everyday lives. During this series our guests included Duncan Goodhew, Sharon Davies, Barry McGuigan, Bobby Davro, Bob Champion, Jan Leeming, Leslie Crowther, Trevor Brooking, and Tessa Sanderson. As I had decided to leave the show at the end of March to host the BBC's new game show *Takeover Bid* and later in the year *The Generation Game*, it was announced that Matthew Kelly would be taking over as the host for the next series. This was good news for Matthew, veteran of *Game for a Laugh*. According to the newspapers, he had recently had to sell his family home to pay a big tax demand. Doubtless it would have been even better news if he'd heard about his change of fortune before he moved!

In May I was very sad to hear that Max Wall had died. He was the last of our music-hall greats, a man whose career was the toast of variety. I had a tremendous admiration for him. As well as being a brilliant stand-up comic, he was a performer who had embraced Shakespeare and Samuel Beckett plays, and appeared in soap operas such as *Coronation Street* and *Emmerdale*. Two other showbiz men I had great respect for died in October—Alyn Ainsworth and David Bell, with whom I had so enjoyed working at Scottish Television and LWT. Alyn and I had also shared a long, happy partnership. He had arranged the music and conducted the orchestra for many of the shows I presented. Shortly before his death, he was preparing a special gala tribute to David with whom he had worked over a twelve-year period after David became Controller of Entertainment at LWT. Alyn's driving ambition was to be the best and to work with the best. He was a real pro. At the end of the month I appeared as part of *The Night of 100 Stars*, the tribute he had been working on for David, at the London Palladium. So in a way, it became a tribute to both of them. It was a truly memorable evening that ended with a eulogy spoken with true grace by David Frost.

Takeover Bid, the new BBC game produced by David Taylor with me as its host came to the screen in May. Claire Sutton, who assisted me, had the wonderful ability to laugh at herself—something I always appreciate in people. Her eyes were very unusual—one was blue, the other green. But both were equally lovely. About this time, the *Birmingham Evening Mail*'s TV editor, Graham

476

Young, was busy comparing game shows, awarding points out of a hundred to their hosts. Bob Monkhouse received seventy-five, I received seventy-six. A few days later, the *Sun* ran a similar feature. This time Bob scored forty points, I scored thirty-eight. You win some, lose some! Nevertheless, in April 1991, I was quite relieved to leave *Takeover Bid* after the second series. It was all right as game shows go, but not going great guns. Its formula was very simple. As a variation on the usual theme, the contestants were given the prizes at the beginning of the show and then had to battle to take them from one another! Now, if they had been competing for prizes worth up to five thousand pounds, plus maybe a car at the end, this would have been exciting, but the prizes that were offered were not big enough, and of course in those days the BBC couldn't give big prizes away.

*   *   *

In September 1990, Britain woke up to headlines that put paid to a well-kept secret: Regeneration Game for Bruce' and 'A generation on, and still in the game'. The cat was out of the bag! Yes, *The Generation Game* was back. Some time before, Jim Moir, BBC's Head of Light Entertainment, had invited me and Billy Marsh to lunch. But he'd waited until we reached the coffee stage before saying: 'Bruce, what about coming back to do *The Generation Game*?' 'Good heavens,' I replied, taken aback. 'That's the last thing I was expecting, Jim. It's thirteen years since I did that.' But, having recovered from the initial shock, I said, 'Let me think about it for a couple of days.' This was my usual strategy when presented with something new. Even if I immediately think it's a good idea, I always take stock for a couple of days. I learned very early on that it's too easy to agree to something over lunch, when you have probably had a drink or two. But that's not the wisest way to make career choices.

'Well, mind you do think about it,' Jim replied, 'because I'm really keen to revive it.' He said this in a way that made me realize that if I didn't do it, somebody else would.

Over the next few days I watched some of the old *Gen Game* tapes in a completely unbiased way. They still made me laugh. It was really funny watching people being put in at the deep end, trying to do what the professionals had done. 'This is a good programme—this is funny,' I kept saying to myself. But I was still unsure whether I wanted to turn the clock back; wasn't sure that this would be sufficiently creatively satisfying. What I really wanted to do was something different—anything other than another game show. But Billy Marsh was all for the idea. And the more I discussed it with him, the more enthusiastic I became. One great plus was that David Taylor was to head the new team. He'd been a young assistant on the seventies' shows. This meant I wouldn't be starting from scratch with an entirely new crew who didn't understand the inner workings of the show. So in the end I said to Billy, 'Okay. Let's get back to Jim, and suggest a further talk.'

At the next discussion, Jim surprised me by saying, 'Even though the little plays were very popular before, I don't think we should include them in this series. This is the nineties. The show needs to have a much faster pace.' 'But we don't need to do them three times, the way we did before—one with the professionals and twice with the amateurs,' I said. 'We needn't use professionals. We can tell the contestants what they have to play, then put them straight in with their spoken lines coming up on camera. That way would be much faster and we could still get some fun out of them.' 'Okay,' Jim said. 'But I'm still a bit worried. Don't let's include one until the fourth show.'

Even though I have to admit that Jim is often right and I am wrong, I always like to try to prove him wrong! It's a game I play with him. We did as he suggested, only included one little play after the first month, but they proved to be so popular we had to continue with them. Jim is a great character, one of the people who always makes me laugh. Although he never wanted to be a comedian, he could have been a very good one. He has the brain of a comic. Apparently, when I wasn't around, he used to do an impression of me. For this, I'm told, he would use catch-phrases that I never actually used on the shows, but was prone to using during rehearsals—'Print it, print it . . .' I would say if an item was good enough for the show, or 'That's a bit Mother Goose, isn't it?' if it was too old-fashioned.

I always had the highest regard for Bill Cotton, too. He did a wonderful job at the BBC. I have always been grateful to him for taking me under his wing at a rather low ebb in my career and trusting me with *The Generation Game*. This proved to be one of the most popular shows ever transmitted on British television, and Bill placed it in my hands. He's my kind of show business, and the spirit of his

'Wakey-Wakey' band-leader father, Billy Cotton. To just talk to Bill and get his views on what is going on in television today is marvellously enlightening. I regard him and his lovely wife Kate as two of my very dearest friends—friends with whom I can always take up where we left off.

For the new series of the *Gen Game*, the hostess was the brilliant dancer, singer and actress, Rosemarie Ford, who had been a lead dancer in Andrew Lloyd Webber's musical, *Cats*. The dancing, in fact, was better in this series than any we had ever done before. Rosie was absolutely wonderful and a joy to work with. During the course of the series we found another great dancer—Wilnelia Merced Forsyth! This way we were able to include Latin American dances. I even wrote a merengue number for the show, which Rosemarie Ford and Wilnelia performed together with a guy we called Paco. His name was actually Richard Calkin and he came from the East End of London! That number was so popular that we then included a mambo, and several other Latin dancing sequences that featured Wilnelia and Rosemarie. There again, my lovely wife dances like a pro, and many people thought that she'd been a professional dancer all her life. She could have been. After just one day in the rehearsal room, she said, 'Okay, that's fine, darling, I'll come along for the show.' 'No,' I said, 'you have to rehearse again tomorrow.' 'But we've done it,' she said. 'No,' I repeated, 'we have do it again tomorrow, and then the next day, and then you will have to come in for the dress rehearsal.' She couldn't believe it. Dancing is just another of her many talents. She's so versatile, she could have made a career of many things—could easily have been an interior designer, a painter, a sculptor, a dancer, a tennis or a golf pro. In golf, she has one of the most natural swings I've ever seen. A few weeks after I first met her, I took her to a driving range. Now, when people swing a golf club for the first dozen or so times, they do not usually hit the ball. But there was Wilnelia hitting ball after ball. She was so coordinated, she only missed one! But she never bothers to play. If she had, two or three times a week, she'd be a single-figure handicap by now. The fact that she's so talented in so many ways is a handicap in itself. If she focused on one thing, she'd put others to shame!

Anyway, *The Generation Game* came back on to the screen with a bang. Since we had last done it, there was another generation that had grown up and was ready for a show like that. We were thrilled with the ratings. It was all very lovely and the reviews were good. One review that made me laugh was when Sean Macaulay wrote in *Punch*, 'Giving Bruce Forsyth a game show without the chance to do a turn is like taking a terrier on heat to Crufts and not letting her loose.'

Well, *really!* Not quite the analogy I'd have chosen!

*   *   *

In March, after an absence of ten years, I returned with enormous pleasure to my favourite theatre, the London Palladium, to launch my one-man show for six nights, and a BBC video compiled from these shows, *Bruce Forsyth—Live at the London Palladium*, was released. The enthusiasm

481

of the first-night audience, and the standing ovation, was almost overwhelming—just wonderful. Looking back at the cuttings the *Evening Standard*'s critic, Milton Shulman, managed both to praise me and whittle me down to size: 'To expect to fill one of the largest theatres in London for an entire evening with only oneself and a nineteen-piece band certainly requires *chutzpah*. *Chutzpah* is a Yiddish word meaning brazen effrontery or unabashed gall. It is the quality demonstrated by the man who, having killed his mother and father, asks for the mercy of the court because he is an orphan . . .! False modesty is an essential part of Bruce Forsyth's act—"I've had such a nice day. I've been counting my jokes"—intermingled with mock insults such as accusing a man in the stalls for not laughing. "I know it's an old joke. What's new? Look at your suit!" There is no doubt that he is a master of the art of audience participation.'

It was around this time that my fellow comedians Frank Carson, Peter Cook, Frankie Howerd, Ronnie Corbett and I did a Panama cigar commercial. Most people, I know, think the cash rolls in for us performers every time a commercial is shown, but that's not always the case. In this particular instance, we all accepted a flat one-off fee. The idea for the commercial was that we should all refuse the cigar; that it should kick off with Mel Smith jumping out of a cab saying, 'No, thank you.' When it was my turn, however, I was filmed at Wentworth putting my golf bag in the boot of my Rolls-Royce and, saying: 'Oh, yes. Lovely, thank you.' Off screen, Griff Rhys Jones was then heard to say: 'Panama cigars are not for comedians.' I had the last word, though. Looking offended, I turned to camera and proclaimed, 'I'm not a comedian, I'm an entertainer.'

I was very sorry to hear that Alan Tarrant, a producer with whom I had worked on *The Generation Game*, had died at the age of sixty-six. During the 1960s, Alan had produced and directed most of ATV's top light-entertainment shows. Shortly afterwards I was further saddened when my old pal Bernie Winters, aged fifty-eight, died in May. A tribute, in aid of cancer research, was held for him at the London Palladium and we had a wonderful line-up of comics to celebrate his life— Bob Monkhouse, Jimmy Tarbuck, Les Dawson, Leslie Crowther, Bobby Davro, Mike Reid, and I were just some of those present.

On April Fool's Day—no reflection on the show!—audiences were able to watch *Forsyth's Show* on BBC 1. In this I introduced Kenneth Connor, and sung with Shirley Bassey and José Carreras. José, who was such a nice, down-to-earth, immensely professional man, gave me a hilarious singing lesson. I also did a sketch with Linda Lusardi, danced with Rosemarie Ford and played the piano. I'd been suffering from laryngitis throughout the rehearsals, and only managed to perform by not speaking at all when I wasn't working. This meant I was the butt of many jokes in the show, but it was such good fun. And also very gratifying when the Television and Radio Industries Club named me as 'Top BBC Personality'.

I'm not too sure whether being included in the *Oxford Dictionary of Modern Quotations* is a mark of 'having arrived' either, but when I was told that three of my catch-phrases had been listed in it, I looked it up and found that 'I'm in charge', 'Nice to see you . . . to see you, nice', and 'Didn't she do well?' were in the book. 'Nice to see you . . . to see you, nice', though, had been wrongly attributed to *The Generation Game* instead of the *Bruce Forsyth Show* that I did for ABC TV in the late sixties. Nevertheless, despite the editor's error, I was pleased to be ranked alongside literary giants such as Oscar Wilde and George Bernard Shaw. In June there was a shock for Wilnelia and me. Our two King Charles spaniels, Tessa, aged eight, and her son Dakin, aged four, adored by us and everybody who met them, were stolen from the grounds of our house at Wentworth. They were abducted during the final day of the Volvo PGA Golf Championship, and we think the thieves must have used the crowds as cover. We were totally devastated and, to this day, can hardly bear to think what happened to them.

One of the things I really liked about the *Gen Game* was the unexpected one-off, a gift to someone like me. We had included a 'Tarzan' play in which one of the male contestants wore—under his leopard skin cover-up—a pair of flimsy, flesh-coloured Y-fronts. When I pushed him into a pool of water to wrestle with an inflated plastic crocodile, his Y-fronts, having become wet, left very little to the imagination! Barbara Windsor was judging this contest and cheekily awarded his team an extra point. I didn't have the faintest idea what would be seen . . . Would I do anything so outrageous!

In November, I was amazed to hear that students at Manchester Polytechnic had decided to change the name of their student union

484

headquarters from Winnie Mandela to Bruce Forsyth because they thought the place should be named after someone light-hearted rather than political. I could only say that I was very flattered but, if they were going to name a building after me, they'd better check the foundations! In the end, they didn't have to—the polytechnic's authorities refused permission for the change of name. I bet they're sorry now! I was just as amused when a taxi driver wrote to a newspaper telling this story: 'My taxi was stuck in a traffic jam. I was about to apologize to my passenger when he said: "Don't worry," and leapt out and directed cars until the jam was sorted out. Not so surprising really . . . the passenger was Bruce Forsyth.'

Never having given up on the idea of my own chat show—and spurred on by having sat in for Terry Wogan when he was on holiday—I approached the BBC again, suggesting a totally different kind of talk show, *Bruce's Guest Night*. I didn't want my celebrities to simply sit on a sofa and make polite conversation. I wanted to create an atmosphere in which the guests performed as well as talked, and include some interaction between me and the studio audience. People always take this in good part. Mind you, I have to watch my step with professionals—I can't take the same liberties with them that I take with the public! I hoped this approach would get us away from the over-slick trendy school of light entertainment, and I was thrilled when the BBC did agree to me doing a couple of series of *Bruce's Guest Night*. This was the realization of an ambition. The first programme was shown in April 1992. My guest stars for the six programmes included Cliff

Richard, Rita Rudner, Pat Cash, Peter Cook, Leslie Grantham, Jack Dee, Jim Davidson, Bea Arthur, Frank Carson, Wet Wet Wet, and Bobby Davro.

As I'd anticipated, the show really sparkled when I did what I do best, fooling around and sparring with members of the audience. I remember one old dear putting up her hand to ask Cliff Richard a question: 'How do you stay so young-looking when you're the same age as me?' she said. 'How dare you ask Cliff such a cheeky question,' I answered. 'How old are you?' 'I'm eighty-one,' she replied. 'Well,' I said, eying her up and down. 'I've got a question for you. How do *you* manage to keep so old-looking?' The audience loved moments like this, and I was thrilled when I won an award for *Bruce's Guest Night* at the British Comedy Awards, held every Christmas, and was nominated for Top BBC Entertainment Presenter for this series. At the very least, I thought these accolades would clinch the deal for another series, but the BBC was still agonizing about whether it was the right kind of show for it to do at that time. When it did finally decide to recommission the series, it all proved to be a great disappointment for me, and *Bruce's Guest Night* was not a ratings success for its second year running. It suffered the same fate, I think, that was dogging Terry Wogan and Jonathan Ross—a lack of really big-name guests. Nevertheless, during the new series, we still managed to include some really impressive stars: Jim Tavare, Ruthie Henshaw, Bobby Davro, k d lang, Jack Jones, Jimmy Tarbuck, Cliff Richard and Lisa Stansfield.

Like me, Frankie Howerd was a Pisces and,

although Pisces have a habit of putting on a great show of bravado and are larger than life on stage, it is all an act. Underneath we are quite shy, sensitive people who are easily hurt. When I heard in April 1992 that Frankie was ill, I went to visit him at his home and took him a box of chocolates. 'Thank goodness you bought chocolates, Bruce,' he said. 'When I woke up and saw all these flowers, I thought I was in a funeral parlour!' When I was leaving, he said, 'The next time you come, can I tape a special interview with you for radio or TV, thanking all the people who've written to me and sent cards and flowers?' 'Of course,' I said. I was so happy that he'd asked me to do this. But when I returned from a short break in Spain, I learned that Frankie had died a few days after I visited him. More than four hundred guests went to his memorial service in July at St Martin-in-the-Fields, Trafalgar Square. It was wonderful to see so many remembering him with such love and affection. True to his life, it was an occasion for more titters than tears. Cilla Black told us how Frankie had invited himself to Sunday lunch with her and Bobby every week, and how she had always cooked him roast lamb until he said: 'Can't you cook anything else, Cilla?' June Whitfield and I read the lessons, and I remember saying, 'As I go back to my seat, I will hear Frankie's voice whispering in my ear, "Wasn't that dreadful?"' At the end of a song, just as I was about to get up to give my tribute, somebody started to applaud. I said, 'Yes, come on—*applaud*. Why not? Frankie would love that.' And the rest of the service in St Martin-in-the-Fields was like being in a variety theatre.

In May, Wentworth was besieged when HRH the

Duchess of York—Sarah Ferguson—rented a property on the estate, but the residents and local shopkeepers were more than capable of closing ranks and taking all this in their stride. Wilnelia and Sarah became great friends, and Sarah visited us in Puerto Rico. This came about because in 1994 Wilnelia established and became the president of the Wilnelia Merced Forsyth Foundation, devoted to helping children with critical health problems in Puerto Rico. As Wilnelia said at the time, 'When I was elected "Miss World" it was a dream that came true for me very early in life and it gave me the opportunity to be a kind of ambassador for my country around the world. We live in a world of the haves and have nots, and this is my way of saying thank you for so much happiness in my life—and for my son JJ's health.' When Wilnelia was helping to organize a royal gala for the charity, she invited the Duchess of York to visit Puerto Rico. Sarah came, and was absolutely fantastic. She met the eighty underprivileged and handicapped children, and talked to each one of them individually. She was so loving and warm and totally sincere. It was a wonderful occasion for the children, for Puerto Rico, which has a population of only three and a half million, and for Wilnelia and me.

*   *   *

The new fifteen-part series of *The Generation Game* that was screened on BBC 1 from September to December began with a compilation from the previous year's series. Once again, I had the lovely Rosemarie Ford as my hostess. She was

488

such an asset to the show. Eight thousand couples had written in to volunteer their services. The researchers selected nearly a thousand to interview, then chose sixty couples. I particularly remember Mike Taylor, one of the husbands, mentioning that he'd received a telephone call from his mother on his wedding night. 'What's she called?' I asked. 'Bertha,' he replied. I couldn't resist saying: 'Bertha Control?' It was also in this series that a female contestant called Nicky Colbourne walked away with a husband-to-be. Every day for a year her boyfriend had asked her to marry him, but Nicky had always said 'No'. By the time she came on the programme, however, she'd had a change of heart. She asked me if it would be all right for her to ask her boyfriend to marry her during the *Gen Game*? When Nicky came on stage, I played along with this, asking her if she had a boyfriend and, when the spotlight swung round to where he was sitting, the guy was overcome with blushes. I then went down on one knee, while Nicky asked him to marry her. 'Yes,' he replied! And Rosemarie and I sent them champagne for their wedding day.

The year ended on a high note for me with a New Year's Eve BBC special marking my fifty years in show business. Michael Parkinson did the honours and, as we sat in clubby, high-backed chairs, either side of a baronial fireplace, we chatted about my career and watched excerpts from my TV programmes. In August there had been a dinner at London's Dorchester Hotel. To make the occasion my family and lots of my friends—Ronnie Corbett, Sir Harry Secombe, Roy Castle, Peter Alliss, Jimmy Tarbuck, and Michael Parkinson—were there to celebrate with me. Every table in the dining room was labelled with the name of a theatre I had worked at and, as I visited each of the tables, I told an anecdote about my appearances there. JJ had a starring role. At the end of the dinner he had been primed to present me with a lovely model of a silver piano that had been specially commissioned by my daughters. JJ managed his star role beautifully, but I was rather anxious throughout that he'd miss his cue! He was only five years old. It was a wonderful night, but the subsequent television screening was ruined by being cut to the bone in the editing room, and having its transmission date changed three times. Then, to make matters worse, it was shown after eleven o'clock at night when most people are in bed! There was yet another disappointment when the BBC Christmas schedules placed the new series of *The Generation Game* against *Coronation Street*. I was becoming seriously fed up with the Corporation.

I was very intrigued when I heard that bookmakers William Hill were taking bets on me receiving a knighthood in the New Year Honours List. Apparently Hills had included me in their novelty bets for 1994, expecting the odd fiver, but punters in various parts of the country had started to lay out sums of a hundred to two hundred pounds. Beginning to think they might lose up to eighty-four thousand pounds if I did receive a knighthood, they were apparently alarmed! I could have reassured them—comics, unless they are of the calibre of my old mate, Harry Secombe, don't usually get knighted. But, just for a moment, I did think Sir Bruce had a nice ring to it!

Another mate, Roy Castle, whom I had first met

490

when we were both about to hit the Big Time as up-and-coming wonder-boys in the TV show *The New Look*, died in August 1994. Roy, a great friend, was someone who had always impressed me in so many different versatile ways. He was a fantastically talented man—comedian, musician, singer, and dancer. Put Roy on a stage and he could turn his hand to anything. The year before he died we danced together on my *Guest Night*, and he sang and played his trumpet. Also featuring in the show was his talented son, Ben, playing tenor sax. He is now a band leader, composer and arranger. I'm sure Roy would be very proud of his achievements, as I know Fiona, Roy's wife, certainly must be. In the last couple of years, while Roy was coping with cancer, Roy proved that he was very courageous, as was Fiona. But I was so shocked when the BBC transmitted the tribute show to him at four-thirty in the afternoon. It was an insult to his memory: it should have been shown at prime time. He was always the most underrated performer in the country.

There were, then, a number of reasons why I decided to leave the BBC and return to LWT, but not least was that every time I started to record a new series of *The Generation Game*, I started to get the flu. I would then have to complete the last two months of the show while I was recovering, never an easy thing to do. I've always been scared of the flu because, when I get it, it always goes to my chest, and there is always the fear of it becoming pneumonia. I started to think, 'Do I really want to risk my health in this way every year?' Since meeting Wilnelia, I had so much to live for—had never been happier. 'Why am I killing myself doing this?' I kept asking myself. 'Especially when so many lovely people I have known and worked with have already died prematurely.' The more I thought about it, the more I began to feel it was not worth killing myself for. Another problem was that, as well as being the *Gen Game*'s host, I was also half producing the show with David Taylor. David and I were both so meticulous. We studied every game for its potential, chucked out anything we didn't think was good enough, and embellished things we felt could be marvellous. But, in order to achieve what I wanted to achieve, I was overworking again. It was five heavy days a week. By the weekend I was so tired I didn't want to go out. Wilnelia and I might invite a couple of friends to dinner on Saturdays, but that was it. On Sundays I wouldn't do a thing because I was too aware I'd be back in the studio on Monday. On Tuesdays we would tape the show, then on Wednesdays and Thursdays I would work at home on choosing the contestants for the following week. On Fridays I'd be in the rehearsal rooms, getting the games or little plays right, and rehearsing the dance routines.

So, after five more years of this schedule, I really felt as if I was doing something I had promised myself I would never do again—overtaxing my energy—and that it was time to take serious stock. By then, I had done seven years of the *Gen Game* in the seventies, plus another five years, making a total of twelve years in all. Also, once again, I was feeling as if I was doing the same old things, and that we were back to reviving old games.

Although the show was still doing well from the ratings point of view, I decided to call it a day and leave. When I told the powers-that-be at the BBC, they were worried that I might say something on camera during the last show of the series that would give the impression the programme was gone for ever. But this was far from the case. I was planning to say something like: 'I'm leaving the show simply because I feel it is the right time for me to leave. But this doesn't mean the end of *The Generation Game*. It will probably go on for many years. I just want to say how marvellous it has been to be with you, and that I shall miss you all.' The BBC, however, still remained concerned that I might say something damaging or controversial.

Like everybody else who finally takes a decision that needs to be taken, I felt greatly relieved. But I also knew that I'd miss David and the team.

CHAPTER SEVENTEEN

WHAT TANGLED WEBS WE WEAVE

Having decided to leave *The Generation Game*, I started considering other things I could do. Marcus Plantin, ITV's network scheduler, had been interested for some time in reviving *Play Your Cards Right*. I liked this idea. It had always been a very popular show and, when it was taken off in the late eighties, I felt it had been brought to an end long before it should have been. Greg Dyke had recently joined LWT and Alan Boyd was Controller of Entertainment. To this day, I don't know what happened. But I do know that *3-2-1*, *The Price Is Right* and *Play Your Cards Right* were all cancelled at the same time.

I loved *Play Your Cards Right*. It was a fun show to do—I never knew what was going to happen next. The schedule would also be much easier than the *Gen Game*, and would give me plenty of time off. As the BBC was still being non-committal about whether or not it would commission more *Bruce's Guest Night*, the show *I really* wanted to continue with, I thought, 'Okay, I'll sign the ITV contract.' This offered me two fifteen-week runs of *Play Your Cards Right*, beginning in March 1994, plus two variety specials. The schedule would be better for my health and would also leave me free to go on trips with Wilnelia for the rest of the year. Perfect! My existing BBC contract committed me to hosting the final series of *The Generation Game*, which was due to commence transmission at the beginning of December 1994. Having honoured this commitment, I made sure the press would be aware of my reasons for leaving the BBC by having my say at LWT's press launch for *Play Your Cards Right* in March. I attacked my former network for not paying enough attention to light entertainment and for treating me so badly in its schedules. I made it clear that the last straw had been the switching of *The Generation Game* from Christmas Day to Christmas Eve. 'It was wonderful working at the BBC in the days of Bill Cotton and Michael Grade,' I concluded.

Before leaving the *Gen Game* and after the first series of the new *Play Your Cards Right*, I was offered a TV show called *Raise the Roof*, a spin-off of the classic American TV show *Twenty-one* upon which Robert Redford had based his film *Quiz Show*. This film was about a young professor who had been exposed for cheating—for already

494

knowing all the questions before answering them on a TV game show. The original name for *Raise the Roof* was *Twenty-one*, but Yorkshire Television decided to change the title and offer the winner a house. I was never really enthusiastic about this show because it had a question-and-answer format that did not allow me to get among the contestants and make it more entertaining. Interestingly, when a US network bought the rights of *Who Wants to Be a Millionaire?* for American TV, another US network revived *Twenty-one* to compete with it, but it never took off. Although *Who Wants to Be a Millionaire?* has proved to be a universally popular show, with an excellent format, I don't think—if I had been asked, which I wasn't—that I would have wanted to host more than a couple of series of this because it's another question-and-answer format.

Now, I am ready to tell the world the secrets of my youthfulness! While Wilnelia and I were in Puerto Rico for my next sabbatical, my mother-in-law Delia decided to take me in hand and regenerate me! She gave me a book, *The Fountain of Youth*, by Peter Kelder, first published in 1939 as *Tibetan Secrets of Youth and Vitality*, and told me to be sure to read it. Perhaps she was trying to tell me something! If so, I'm so glad she did. From then on, I was convinced I owed my new health and fitness to the priceless knowledge Peter Kelder had gleaned from Tibetan monks—men and women— who look half their ages, even in their dotage. Before breakfast, I now do a fifteen-minute Tibetan workout, which mainly consists of stretching exercises that really wake you up and make you feel good. For another exercise, you spin round and round on the spot like a dancer or whirling dervish. I now do this twenty-one times. The other four exercises—the monks call these rites—involve leg-raising and stretching which relax stiff muscles and joints. After the exercises, I always have porridge with raisins, soya milk and fructose sugar. I don't smoke and, since a wine-poisoning incident twenty years ago, drink little alcohol. I actually try to keep a measuring 'stick' inside me and rarely go over the top. I make sure I eat lots of fruit and vegetables, and I take a couple of garlic tablets every day. Garlic is good for the chest and I reckon it kills just about everything else nasty as well. Occasionally, I also go on a spate of vitamin supplements. There you are, that's my fountain of youth—and I hope it doesn't run dry!

Also while I was in Puerto Rico—feeling, thanks to my mother-in-law, a new man—another game show entered my life. I was flicking through channels when I came across *The Price Is Right*. This game show, which had been on American TV for about twenty-five successful years, had also been hosted some years back in the UK by Leslie Crowther. In America, it was hosted by Bob Barker of CBS for an hour every morning at eleven o'clock. But now, a new young fellow was presenting it in a half-hour evening format. Knowing that ITV's Marcus Plantin was always looking for half-hour shows, I thought, 'Yes, *of course!* The second half of *The Price Is Right* is an exact repeat of the first, so it can be sliced right down the middle and make a very successful half-hour format.' I telephoned Ian to ask him to check out who owned the rights and to establish if anybody had taken up an option on these. 'If ITV is still looking for half-hour formats,' I added, 'we could talk to Marcus about this one and perhaps make a pilot for a possible autumn series.' When Ian came back to me and said that, although Central Television had taken up the option, this had now lapsed, I was delighted. I knew Yorkshire Television still had a vacant slot because the arrangements for *Raise the Roof* had not been finalized. 'Let's acquire it,' I said, 'and see if Marcus is interested.' The next thing I knew was that Yorkshire Television was dead keen on the idea and wanted me to return in April for some pre-publicity for its new seventeen-week series in the autumn, *Bruce's Price Is Right.* The only question was with regard to the hostess, in what had become PC-obsessed times. I had already anticipated that this problem would come up at the meeting, and I was spot on. 'The problem of *The Price Is Right*', they said, 'is that in the American show they have three girls posing with the prizes.' 'I see no harm in that,' I replied, 'but I'm not going to argue about it. What we can do is have three girls, plus a male model, showing the prizes. Then the men sitting at home can enjoy watching the girls, and the women can say, "Isn't that chap on *The Price Is Right* a hunk?" This might create a bit of competition for me with the lady viewers, but I don't mind! And it will at least shut up the minority groups.' So it was that along with Kimberley Correll, Emma Steadman and Emma Noble—later succeeded by Leah Cristensen—that we were joined by Simon Peete.

What a palaver! But the powers-that-be were very happy, and that was that. I was looking forward to the series, and the chance to work again with Bill Morton, who had directed the later series of *The Generation Game*, and producer Howard Huntridge, who has been so much fun to work with. (And that's all I'm going to say about him!) By the end of May we had finished filming the seventeen shows, and the rest is history. *The Price Is Right* has been on our screens ever since. It's a show I really enjoy, and of course, it has given rise to its own catch-phrases. I've also been able to work in the best crowd-pleasing bits of some of my other shows. For instance, if somebody loses a round, I often say 'Oh, wasn't that a *shame.*' The audience invariably choruses back, 'Shame!' And every now and then, I can drop in 'all right, my loves?' which is what I used to say on *The Generation Game* after a game had been explained to the couples, to check that they'd understood. At the end of the show I still do what a lot of people say was one of their favourite bits of *Play Your Cards Right*, when I tot up the prizewinners' earnings. It's even more dramatic for *Price is Right* because there are so many more prizes they can win. It looks as though I am doing the most complicated piece of recall and mental arithmetic, but of course I've got a big board in front of me, which the camera doesn't show, listing everything that's been won and what it's worth. But I always raise my eyes heavenwards, hand to forehead, as if thinking *very* hard, until I finally come up with the magic total. I think viewers probably know what's up—I usually can't resist a grin!

So, in the end, having gone away not really bothered about where my next week's work was coming from, I finished up with two series on ITV, *Play Your Cards Right* and *Price Is Right*. Both these could be done in a very short part of the year, and leave the remainder for me to enjoy myself; to be able to go to Puerto Rico, and spend more time with my wife and my son. It was wonderful, gave me a lifestyle where I was not having to push myself too hard. In fact, although for the last seven years I have been on television thirty-four weeks every year I have not really exerted myself since I left *The Generation Game* in 1995. Naturally, people who see me on TV all the time think I am still working every hour that God has given me, but I have more time off now than I've ever had in my life. It suits me. I couldn't be happier.

Taping two shows a day for both the *Play Your Cards Right* and *Price Is Right* series has meant that I've had to get the studio audiences in on the act, to make out that in fact the second show they are watching that day is actually a different week. After we've shuffled them around a bit, so that you can't recognize the same faces at the front of the crowd, I always tell them, 'You're such a lovely audience—so much better than last week's!' Then I slag them off, telling them how dreadful the 'last lot' has been! Audiences love being in on a joke like this—and the viewer at home, aware something funny is going on, is left figuring it all out.

In December 1996 I was in trouble along with two other naughty boys, my friends Jimmy Tarbuck and Kenny Lynch. Having brought out a Christmas single, 'Winter Wonderland', with a spoof cover in which we called ourselves 'The Three Fivers', we were being threatened with a court action by the Three Tenors, Luciano Pavarotti, Placido Domingo, and José Carreras. Unfortunately the Three Tenors and their record company, Tenor Trademarks, failed to see our record as a joke,

499

thought that we had 'vulgarized' and 'injured' the tenors' reputations, and were seeking damages and a court injunction for us to change the sleeve. Oh dear! As Kenny said at the time: 'If people mistake us for them then I worry for their eyesight, not to mention their hearing!' Personally, I'd always fancied myself as a bit of an opera singer and thought I sounded remarkably like Pavarotti. But, luckily for us all, it all proved to be a hiccup in our prestigious careers!

Like most of the world, I was absolutely stunned in August 1997 when I heard that Princess Diana had died in a Paris car crash. Wilnelia, who was in Puerto Rico, phoned me at about five o'clock in the morning. 'I thought I should tell you straightaway,' she said. 'It's on the midnight news bulletins here. The reports are coming from the American news services.' I turned on the television and stayed in the bedroom for four hours, flicking from channel to channel, watching the tragedy unfold. It was a monumental shock—I couldn't take it in. When the early accounts mentioned the paparazzi chasing the car after it had left the Paris Ritz with the Princess and Dodi Al Fayed on board, I knew that everybody in show business who had ever been in a car trying to get away from the press would have a special understanding of the dreadful events that followed. They would also have been thinking how easily they could have met the same fate. In circumstances where you are trying to escape from relentless press attention, you do take chances—whether you are driving yourself or being driven. You have only one thought—to shake them off. And, to do this, you do break the speed limit and risk your life. But even show-business people could not fully appreciate how appalling life must have been for Princess Diana. She was never shown any mercy, was hounded every time she set foot out of the door. Whatever anybody else had suffered at the hands of the paparazzi, it must have been a thousand times worse for her. It was heartbreaking, unbelievable—a shock that rippled around the entire world.

The year 1998, when I celebrated my seventieth birthday, began in a very special way with birthday celebrations that went on for two months! The fun and games started with a huge party for family and friends at the Wentworth Golf Club, and continued until March when I also celebrated forty years since my first appearance on *Sunday Night at the London Palladium*. To mark these two anniversaries, I presented my one-man show at the Palladium for five days. Then on the Sunday we did a live special of *SNAP*. It was a truly lovely double anniversary, and I enjoyed it all immensely. It was wonderful to have Diana Ross as my top-of-the-bill. I hadn't actually met her before, but had always admired her. I was introduced to her during the rehearsals. But then, at the end of the show after she had been watching it on a monitor in her dressing room, she asked her agent to bring me in so that she could say how much she had enjoyed my work. I was touched. She was a genuinely warm-hearted person, who gave a wonderful performance on the show. We included a song and dance routine from *Saturday Night Fever*, had the original Tiller Girls, bless 'em, on board, and Emma Noble, who later married John Major's son, a Russian acrobat, an Irish comedian, Frank Carson, Ronnie Corbett and lots of other lovely acts. Every time I arrived at the

Palladium or left it, passers-by kept calling out, 'Happy birthday, Bruce. Happy birthday.' I couldn't have been a happier man, especially as Wilnelia and I were then off to a golfing tournament in Spain.

This holiday began with a lovely surprise that was to end a few weeks later in heartbreak for Wilnelia and me. Wilnelia was over the moon when she told me she had just bought a pregnancy-test kit and that the result was positive. We were expecting our second baby. We were both so thrilled. Ever since JJ was a toddler, we had been hoping to give him a brother or sister. We could hardly believe our good luck, thought it was a miracle. But, just after we returned to London, things began to go seriously wrong. Wilnelia was in pain and finding it very difficult to digest food. When she had a scan, it was the worst possible news. She was suffering from an ectopic pregnancy: the baby was developing in one of her Fallopian tubes instead of the womb. This is a very dangerous, potentially life-threatening condition which needs an immediate operation. We were heartbroken to lose our baby, but so grateful Wilnelia had survived such a dreadful, traumatic experience. She was also disappointed at not being able to go to the 'Miss World' contest in the Seychelles, especially as she had worked so hard to arrange for the singer Ricky Martin to appear in the show. But thank goodness it had happened before she went on the trip. To help us cope with the emotional aftermath, we went on holiday with JJ to Puerto Rico for Christmas. Wilnelia was so brave. She said, 'I will never forget the baby, will always have a scar to remind me, but I'm so lucky to have you and JJ.' We remained on the island until I had to return to England in April to record the next series of *The Price Is Right.*

The year was now going very nicely, and I was both stunned and delighted when it was announced that I was to receive an OBE in the Queen's Birthday Honours. I was so glad that it wasn't posthumous, and I did hope the Queen wouldn't say 'Lower, lower,' when I bowed! The actual week of the investiture, though, turned out to be no laughing matter—one of the worst weeks of my life. At the beginning of the week, Wilnelia was going downstairs to our laundry room when she slipped and hurt her back. During the last ten years or so, she had often needed acupuncture and physiotherapy for back pain, but this time the acupuncturist told her that the fall had damaged one of her discs and that there wasn't much he could do to help. On the day of the investiture I said: 'Darling, please don't come, you are in too much pain.' But Wilnelia would not put herself first and rest up—she so wanted to be with me. JJ and my daughter Debbie, who had drawn the last of the permitted three passes from a hat, also came along. Getting in and out of the car was agony for Wilnelia, and so was sitting on the ballroom chairs for two hours at the Palace while all the awards were being presented. For me it was a wonderful honour to receive the OBE, but I would gladly have handed it back if the Queen could have made Wilnelia's back better. When presenting me with the award, the Queen said: 'You have made us laugh for a long time now, and it is very important for people to laugh.' 'Yes, Your Majesty,' I replied. 'It has been a *long* time.' It was a nice moment because the Queen, who is just a couple of years older than I am, smiled as if to say, 'Probably for as long as I have been doing this job!'

After the photographs in Buckingham Palace's quadrangle, we went off to meet Julie, Laura, Charlotte, and Louisa at the Dorchester Hotel, Park Lane, for lunch, so that we could all share this special day. When we got there I arranged for Wilnelia to lie down for half an hour to rest her back, which did help a little. The lunch was lovely, but I was very aware that Wilnelia was still in pain. When we finally arrived home, Wilnelia, having been seen by our local GP, Michael Loxton, had to be taken to hospital by ambulance for a scan. The specialist then confirmed that it was a disc problem and that Wilnelia needed an operation right away. The day following the operation, which took about two hours, Wilnelia was allowed to get up, but was told not to sit down for more than ten minutes at a time. She could either walk, stand or go back to bed. This remained the case for about eight weeks—throughout August and September— during which time Wilnelia, confined to our Wentworth house, did all her exercises and gradually became more mobile. Her back since then has been marvellous, even though she doesn't do the exercises as often as she should!

In September we had another cause for celebration. The *Radio Times* conducted its Seventy-fifth Anniversary Readers' Poll, and I was voted the 'best TV entertainer'. Then, in December, amid much controversy in the media, Chile's General Pinochet came to live at Wentworth while the Government considered demands to extradite him. Once again, the estate was besieged by the press. Then, at the end of a year when I had been awarded an OBE and the 'best TV entertainer' accolade, I was in for yet another surprise. I was presented with a Lifetime Achievement Award by the wonderful singer Liza Minnelli at the December Comedy Awards. The fact that Liza had come all the way from America just to present me with this was a true 'cherry on the cake'. The other 'cherry' was that the Comedy Awards always attracts a very young audience and, having seen some clips from the *Sammy and Bruce Show*, they gave me a standing ovation when I went up to receive the award.

Lew Grade, who had once run ATV, one of the biggest television companies, and who also owned Moss Empires Theatres, which included the London Palladium, the Coliseum and the Theatre Royal, Drury Lane, died on 13 December. 'Show business', I thought sadly, 'will never be quite the same again.' I was, however, comforted by the thought that his nephew Michael, another of my favourite people, would continue to carry his showbiz torch. It was Michael who had persuaded me to leave the BBC at the end of the seventies and go back to ITV. The only trouble was that he kept doing a disappearing act! When I went back to LWT, he went off to America, then when I returned to the BBC, he came back to the UK and was in charge of Channel Four. It still grieves me that after *Bruce Forsyth's Big Night*, we never really managed to work closely together again. He was great to talk to and, whenever we met, we always shared lots of in-jokes about the business and enjoyed chatting in a variety/agents/artistes sort of way. I always liked and admired him and, having read his autobiography *It Seemed Like a Good Idea at the Time*, I was sorry that he had had to take so many bad knocks at the BBC. But he has come through all of these with a great sense of purpose. We could certainly do with lots more Lew and Michael Grades in the entertainment business today.

When the Variety Club honoured Jackie Mason in 2000, I had the great pleasure of introducing him. Jackie is one of my favourite comedians. We go all the way back to my earliest days at the Palladium when he also performed there regularly. For the lunch I thought up a piece based on these early appearances when he was only allocated about six minutes onstage. When he was presenting his act to Val Parnell and Charlie Henry, he'd always walk on, do a very funny six-minute routine, and then say in his wonderfully warm, thick, Jewish accent: 'Or you can have dis one'—and he'd do another six-minute routine. In the end he'd do at least three routines, then he'd say, 'Well, you can have either de foist, de second or de thoid. Or, you can have half de foist with half de second, or half de second with half de thoid, or half de thoid and half de foist or . . . But for this money, all you're going to get is six minutes.' I can still see his face! I had elongated the piece and it went down really well.

On one occasion, when I hadn't seen Jackie for many years, Wilnelia and I went round to his dressing room after his London show. He was in great form, couldn't believe that this beautiful woman was married to me. 'You're married to him?' he kept saying, in shock. 'A goil wid your looks, settled for this? This outdated poison? You

506

shouldn't be seen dead wid him. You should be seen wid somebody like me!' Wilnelia adored him, loved the remarks he always made thereafter about Puerto Rico. She just curls up and laughs at this man. He, in return, loves to tease her. When we went to his show that night, we sat next to four Jewish ladies who were obviously great fans, rocking backwards and forwards in their seats, absolutely adoring him. Near the end of the first half, though, he went into a routine about Jewish women. 'Have you noticed', he said, 'that Jewish women never admit dey are Jewish? They are either Italians, Greeks, Brazilians, Venezuelans, but never Jewish. Have you noticed this?' And he then made some very caustic remarks about Jewish women. Suddenly the four sitting next to us stopped laughing and their faces turned to stone. 'Oh, my goodness,' I thought. 'What has he done? He's gone too far.' And I immediately started to worry about how all the other Jewish women in the audience were reacting. Finally, to my great relief, he got off the subject and started a new theme. Within minutes the ladies sitting next to us started tittering and, before we knew where we were, they were laughing their heads off again, rocking backwards and forwards, and absolutely loving him. It was simply wonderful how, having managed to upset them, he got them back. But that is the mark of a great performer; that is the art of a wonderful comic. He will always be one of my all-time favourites.

Being able to laugh at ourselves, whatever creed or race we are, is wonderfully healing and therapeutic. And being able to see the funny side of things is a marvellous coping mechanism for overcoming setbacks. But this, I have to admit, is not always easy these days. There are so many irritating, annoying, everyday things to catch us out, so many things that do not happen when people say they will. Today, for example, I had one of those days when everything seemed to go wrong. Having been lucky enough to find a parking meter in Chelsea, parked the car, found the right money and got out, it turned out to be a meter that would not accept coins because it was jammed; having gone shopping with JJ, I then had to walk from one end of Harrods to the other and then back again trying to get the batteries changed for my pocket computer. Remembering, while on this trek, that on a previous occasion Wilnelia had seen a compact, decorated with her sign of the zodiac, and said to me, 'Look, darling, there's the Libra one. It's translucent and the prettiest of them all,' I decided to buy it for her. 'I'm sorry, sir,' the young lady assistant said, 'we've only got them in gold and beige. But I'll try to track down the one you want.' Four telephone calls later, I was beginning to get impatient. 'Look,' I said, 'I'll come back in twenty minutes when you have sorted this out.' JJ and I then went off to get a sandwich. But as we passed the sushi bar, JJ said he would rather have that. 'Give him as much as he likes,' I said to the waiter, 'but no alcohol—no champagne, no brandy!' Having settled JJ in, I then went off for my favourite Parma ham sandwich. I've had this a million times there and it's always delicious. Today, however, it was so salty I couldn't even eat it. So I asked the sympathetic waiter to bring me something else. 'As long as it isn't chicken,' I added. 'I've had so much chicken recently I'm beginning to walk like one!' So he brought me pasta—the last thing I wanted to eat at eleven o'clock in the morning! By then I was thinking, 'The parking meter, my pocket computer, the compact, my salty sandwich, my unwanted pasta. What next?' At that moment JJ returned from his sushi snack. 'That cost twenty-six pounds, Dad,' he said! What next? Ah, yes, the compact. 'Sorry, sir, it's discontinued.' At that point, I did begin to see the funny side of it all—and at least the retelling of it has made me laugh!

Life these days, with so much information technology—computers and everything—may seem simple. But it's not. I hate automated switchboards, which reel out so many options that you are left totally bewildered and sent round in giddy circles. 'Oh, to hell with it,' I think. 'I'll write a letter!' And what you can't say to a computer is: 'That's more information than I need right now!' or 'I don't actually want to do that, thank you very much . . . Can't I just do so and so?' I find it all so frustrating. I seem to wait longer and longer for answers. I want to go back to the days when we had really helpful telephone operators who talked to you and not get all those awful taped choices, and to shop in places where the bill and the money was sent round in little tubes on overhead wires! It was so exciting watching these go to and from the cashier and back again to the shop assistant! In many respects, instead of going forwards, I think we've gone backwards. I hope, though, I will always continue to see the funny side of everyday situations. But I can't promise! Oh, what you young people missed.

I also hope I will never lose sight of how lucky I really am. Compared to many, my everyday irritations and frustrations are minor hiccups. And nothing helps more to keep this in perspective than charity work. For obvious reasons, my role in this seems to be mainly concerned with celebrity golf tournaments, especially my own for SPARKS which raises money for a number of children's charities. In the last four years or so, we have raised about £200,000 for charity. The Variety Club and the Variety Club Golfing Society's charity events to raise money to buy Sunshine coaches are also something I support as often as possible. Recently, I also compèred a charity auction at the Natural History Museum for the European Children's Trust, including all the forgotten people of the Yugoslavian conflicts. Although the Natural History Museum is a huge place, this event could not have gone better. It was amazing how the organizers transformed the entrance hall into a charity gala dinner, especially as there is an absolutely huge dinosaur standing in the middle. The acoustics were terrible, but I remember saying: 'This is the first time I've ever appeared facing a dinosaur's jacksy.' But it was more than worthwhile. We raised a great deal of money for a very worthy cause that night.

For example, in the summer I could play in a different golf tournament for charity practically every day. But these golf days can take anything up to ten hours if I have to drive there and back. There are so many worthy causes, so many requests that, at times, just answering the mail is a full-time job. I try to ration it out because I know that if I don't I will be overwhelmed. Begging letters can also be a problem, and my secretary checks these out. It's amazing how often they prove to be cons, with no connection whatsoever to what the person is claiming he or she is doing or wants to do. I once had a request for money from somebody who needed help to further their career. Having obliged, I was flooded with similar requests. Obviously, the person I had sent money to had told all his friends! You have to be so careful because once people think you are an easy touch, so many others climb on the bandwagon. I would have to work day and night just to keep up with it all.

One of the most amusing things I was ever asked to do for charity was to design a golf car, not a golf buggy for playing golf, but an ideal car for when one is gridlocked in London's traffic. This would be put on display at the Motor Show in Birmingham to raise awareness for the motor industry's charity, BEN. So, I decided to redesign one of those stretch limos that take up nearly a whole street. I arranged for grass to be growing on top of its roof, with a golf pin and hole set at one end. Then if you were stationary for any length of time, you could just climb up on to the roof and practise your putting while you were waiting. I'm sorry to say it was never put into production!

Something that succeeded in curtailing both my golfing activities and playing the piano for nearly a year was an operation I had on my left hand to remove some small lumps, which were running in a line from my little finger to my wrist. This condition is called Dupuytren's contracture. According to Michael Loxton, my GP, who over the years has become a great friend along with his wife Mary, this condition is named after the surgeon who operated on Napoleon's favourite carriage driver. A carriage driver holds the horses' reins through his fingers and, like any repetitive strain injury, this action can cause the fingers to lock. Having driven hundreds of miles, especially in Russia where it was freezing cold, the driver's fingers were in a really bad way. Fond of his driver, Napoleon asked Dupuytren, his surgeon, if he could do anything for the man and the surgeon performed the operation. One night, when I was doing a show, I told this story. Afterwards, when I was changing in my dressing room, which happened to be near one of the exits through which people were still leaving, I heard these two old dears chatting to each other. 'Shame about Bruce's hand, isn't it?' one of them said. 'Yes,' the other replied. 'But what was he doing driving Napoleon's carriage?'!

Unable to play golf or the piano, I had to find something else to do. For instance, I spent more time listening to music. My musical tastes spread across a wide range. In addition to big bands and jazz, I enjoy a lot of classical music. Some of this, in fact, has great similarities with jazz, has some jazzy little riffs. Another of my favourites is Puerto Rican music which, with its South American influence, is so rhythmical. Wilnelia was one of the presenters of a two-hour TV show, a tribute to one of their famous composers, Bobby Copo. In this, she also danced and introduced ten or twelve of the island's best solo singers. This show was sponsored by the Banco Popular—one of the biggest banks on the island—which took over all three of the local channels for this particular night. Although, when I saw the show, I didn't understand a single word of the songs, I loved the rhythm of all the different types of Latin-American music, the bolero, the salsa, the bossanova. It was really quite something. I hadn't expected to enjoy listening to songs I couldn't understand, but it was amazing! Why can't we do something like this in Britain?

On the other hand, I do try to avoid steel bands. I find them unmelodious. I can appreciate that the musicians are very clever to be able to play on such 'instruments', and that they must practise very hard and rehearse together a great deal, but my ears simply won't take it. Hillbilly music is another no-go for me. I can't stand it. The amazing thing is that the top people who play this in the USA earn billions of dollars.

But I'm a sucker for old movies on TV. There are some films I can't watch often enough, especially when they feature my screen idols—Fred Astaire, Gene Kelly, George Murphy, Donald O'Conner, Bing Crosby, and Frank Sinatra. I also love the actor Spencer Tracey, but I was very surprised when reading Katharine Hepburn's autobiography to learn that, although he was a very loveable person, he was also a very strange man who was given to terrible bouts of drunkenness and going on 'benders' for two or three days at a time. Other favourites are Gregory Peck, Cary Grant, George C. Scott, Burt Lancaster, Jack Lemmon, Walter Matthau, and John Wayne. Once, when I was in the restaurant of London's White Elephant Club, a great haunt of US film stars, John Wayne was there. He wasn't roaring drunk by any means, but had obviously had a few drinks, and was going round all the tables saying 'hallo' to everybody. He was such a big, strong, tall man, I was grateful he was in such a jovial mood. Looking up at him, I thought how awful it would have been if the drink

513

had had the opposite effect and made him hostile. He'd have cleared the White Elephant in true Western style in two seconds!

I also love the classic actors, John Gielgud, Laurence Olivier, Ralph Richardson and Alec Guinness. Their performances are absolutely riveting to watch. I adored Loretta Young, Betty Grable, Rita Hayworth, Gene Tierney, Vera Ellen, Eleanor Powell, Anne Miller, Mitzi Gaynor, Cyd Charisse, and Marilyn Monroe. They were all superb actresses and dancers, and so gorgeous to look at. One of the reasons I love watching old movies as often as I can is that the acting, the script writing, the thought behind each line, the dialogue are all so superb. I'd like a bit more of that today, and not so much action.

Tony Newley was another talent I admired. Sadly he died in 1999. He told me once that he didn't really like performing. What he loved best was writing songs and working with Leslie Bricusse. They wrote some lovely songs together. Two of my many favourites are 'Who Can I Turn To?' and 'Going to Build a Mountain'. I knew Leslie better than Tony because I used to stay with him quite often in Los Angeles. Despite what Tony said about himself, he was, in my view, a great performer. He did some wonderfully successful seasons at the Desert Inn Hotel, Las Vegas, where he had a sort of steam bath built in his dressing room to clear his nasal passages after a show. This was a wise move. Although Las Vegas is a big city, it's in the desert, and when you're performing there you can get 'desert throat', a dryness which quickly develops into a form of laryngitis. In Las Vegas, Tony was usually on the bill with Juliet Prowse.

Nobody worked harder than she did with an act that was on twice-nightly, seven days a week, for a month at a time. She was great. For health reasons, she always told her dancers and fellow performers to eat Japanese food which she considered the healthiest and most nutritious diet. And I agree with her—we just love Japanese food.

Talking of favourites—two of our friends are Lesley and Bernard Gallagher. Bernard captained the Ryder Cup team so successfully. We have known each other for many years, live near each other, and have always followed the progress of each other's children. They have one son, Jamie, and two daughters, Kirsty and Laura. Kirsty is making quite a name for herself on television. Bernie once did me the great honour of asking me to be the cabaret act at The Belfry for the Ryder Cup in England. It was a wonderful night—the kind of occasion I am always very nervous before because it is a different kind of audience: the two teams, plus everybody else involved in golf. For the finish, I asked some of the seniors of the golfing world to come up on stage and do a top-hat-and-stick routine with me. They were such good sports. The whole evening went very well.

Two years later, Bernie also arranged for Wilnelia and me to go to the Ryder Cup at Oakhill, America. We were there for the opening ceremony for which there were two huge banks of seating, one for the American fans, the other for the Europeans. When Wilnelia and I walked out to take our seats, there was quite a stir among the Europeans and I could see all the Americans turning round and saying to each other: 'Who are this couple?' In the USA people always think

515

Wilnelia is a film star and I'm her agent or her coach! They just can't work it out. I'll never get used to it. It was a very exciting week, and when Europe actually won the cup the atmosphere was absolutely electric. It's the equivalent to the World Cup Final in golfing terms. After the game, we were walking round the clubhouse when Kirsty Gallagher, who was helping her father, saw us and invited us into the team's celebration. Being a keen golfer, HRH Prince Andrew was there. Lesley asked me to go out on to the balcony and say hallo to the crowd who were mostly British fans. When I did, the ovation I received nearly knocked me off my feet. Somebody started singing to the tune of 'Guantanamara':

> One Brucie Forsyth
> There's only one Brucie Forsyth
> One Brucie Foooor-syth . . .
> There's only one Brucie Forysth!

And the crowd sang the name of anyone who stepped out on the balcony like this, even the caddies. Well, when you get five thousand people joining in and chanting that—it's a tremendous moment. I felt as though I had won the cup myself. Thank you, Bernie! Oh yes—then I noticed a girl with a microphone waving to me to come and talk to her—I thought it could be NBC, CBS, ABC, CNN or one of the other big American networks. She then said to me, 'Will you say a few words for GMTV?' I was still glad to, bless her.

*   *   *

516

But enough of all that—back to professional matters. In June 1999, things took a serious turn for the worse when I leant that the provisional studio dates for the forthcoming series of *Play Your Cards Right* had been cancelled. I have to say I had by then already prepared myself for the fact that another series was becoming very unlikely, but I never thought I would find out the way I did, via the press as opposed to being formally notified by my employers. Conversations about a new series had started some ten months before and despite initial positive feedback, the fact it was taking so long to reach an answer had already led me to think the worst. It was difficult to understand why—the last series of the show had done so well in the ratings. However, as I later gathered, ITV was changing its scheduling policy and, with *Emmerdale* due to air five nights a week, some fifty half-hour slots previously occupied mostly by game shows were going to have to go. And *Play Your Cards Right* was to be one of the first casualties.

The way things worked out was messy, to say the least. The press got wind of the fact that *Play Your Cards Right* might not return, but this was denied by ITV Network who stated that no decision had been made. In the end, while the *Sun* agreed not to run the story—which they had been on to for some time (their headline was apparently going to be 'Nice to Axe You to Axe You . . .'), the *Sunday People* jumped the gun with a front page declaring 'Brucie Axed! He's Too Old says ITV'. All this happened the day before Ian Wilson and my agent, Jan Kennedy, were due to meet with David Liddiment of ITV to resolve my future with the network.

Unsurprisingly, this was a stormy meeting. But the upshot was an extension of the deal for my other ITV series, *Bruce's Price Is Right*, and the offer of six one-hour variety specials. As far as *Play Your Cards Right* was concerned, the official position remained that no decision had yet been made, and given that my existing contract had been extended, I was persuaded to conduct subsequent interviews accordingly, downplaying the *Play Your Cards Right* situation. The papers were full of my new multi-million pound ITV deal—and the *Sunday People* was quick to claim credit for saving my career! However, deep down I was upset at the way in which a format that I had discovered myself in the USA, and had served me and ITV so well over two decades, was no longer valued. I guess the romantic in me wanted to believe it might yet be recommissioned, while the realist in me knew damn well that it had been axed. The frustration and hurt underlying this was eventually to surface!

With the exception of the Royal Variety Performance, after years of no variety series on television at all, Channel 5's *Big Stage* had done surprisingly well in the ratings. I can only assume that its success must have alerted both ITV and the BBC to the fact that perhaps the notion of variety on television wasn't dead after all. Certainly, the first half of 2000 saw not one but three variety series—mine, another season of *Big Stage*, and a series on BBC1 hosted by Jim Davidson from the Cambridge Theatre. Talk about buses—none for ages and then three suddenly come along at once! But, as ever, we went straight back to no buses at all: none of these three series was to reappear the following year.

Contrary to what some people thought, I was not desperate to get myself involved in a variety show. Indeed, I was surprised that ITV suggested it in the first place. The one-off live *Sunday Night at the London Palladium* two years earlier had been a wonderful night, but I remembered how hard it was to find acts, even for one show, who were true 'down-front' performers, the stuff of which variety depends. I also had no interest in doing the series in a television studio; if we were going to do it, it needed to be somewhere special. Fortunately, somewhere special, somewhere very special, became available. Just as we had managed to squeeze in between *Oliver!* closing and *Saturday Night Fever* opening in 1998, Ian Wilson, who was in regular contact with David Kinsey of Stoll Moss Theatres (now the Really Useful Theatre Company) told me we might be able to get back into the Palladium between the end of *Saturday Night Fever* and the opening of *The King and I*. When this firmed up, I became truly excited about the idea for the first time. The only negative was that we had to record all six shows in two weeks.

This brief window inevitably proved a problem. Doing so many shows in such a short period meant a punishing schedule, and that I couldn't do as many bits of 'business' with guests as I would have liked; there simply wasn't enough time to rehearse. The other problem, as I had suspected, was the availability of artistes. Over any two-week period, only so many big names are available. While we had some great people on the series, it was a real struggle to book bills that were truly memorable. However, the biggest disappointment was that instead of it being *Sunday Night at the London*

Palladium, the show had to be called *Tonight at the London Palladium* because it was to be scheduled not on Sunday, as I had originally imagined, but on Friday nights at eight o'clock. In the end, the final show of the series did end up on a Sunday evening and, interestingly, while the five shows on Friday nights did fine in the ratings, this last show did best of all. For me, Sunday night was always its most natural home.

By now, I was lacking faith in ITV and the way in which I perceived I was being treated. In the previous year, only eleven out of seventeen *Bruce's Price Is Right* were shown. I wrote to David Liddiment about this, and he responded with an apology, explaining that there had been an error in the planning department. With these and the new series I had recorded, they now had twenty-three shows. My understanding was that this would mean an extended run across and beyond Christmas. So I was more than surprised when they began transmitting them in August! It was the first time in my long career that a series of mine had ever been shown in the summer months. Next, without warning, episodes of the series were shown two, even three times in a week. Finally, and least welcome of all, the show was scheduled at 5.20 p.m. on Saturday evening—another first, in that up until that moment no series of mine had ever been scheduled out of prime time. It had been put in a 'death slot': at that time on a Saturday, the boys are only just coming back in from football, the men are often out, maybe having a drink with friends, and the women are not back from shopping, or are cooking the evening meal.

Convinced I was being 'phased out', I decided I

had had enough. I called a press conference for a select group of some of the finest and most experienced journalists I knew, to explain my position. 'I will honour my contract to host one more year of *The Price Is Right*,' I said, 'then I will axe *myself*!' After two hours or more at the Dorchester Hotel giving vent to my feelings and frustration—complete with graphs showing the ratings and audience share for *Play Your Cards Right* and *The Price Is Right* over the previous two years—the resultant coverage was highly critical of ITV, and David Liddiment in particular. To be completely honest, like having a toublesome tooth extracted, I felt much better afterwards, relieved that I had got all this off my chest—and had little or no concern for the consequent hurt and discomfort I had caused David. I honestly didn't care how many bridges I had burned.

Time is a great healer and it's strange how sometimes people can cross even burnt-out bridges! Thoughout his spell as Network Scheduler, David, even when pressed by my manager or agent, always stated that there was a place for me on ITV as long as I wanted it. When I had my go at him, he maintained this position even though it would have been so easy for him to retaliate. While I cannot pretend to understand some of the scheduling decisions that prompted my outburst, I nevertheless respected the quiet dignity that David maintained throughout.

As I've said, there was an awful lot of press comment about it all. But it was something my old friend Barry Cryer said in the *Daily Mail* that proved most prophetic:

Bruce is not one to be broken on any wheel. He's no angel. He can be difficult to work with—brilliant people often are. He's a perfectionist and can spot somebody not doing their job a mile off. But the atmosphere he creates is phenomenal. When he left the BBC in 1977, where he had been king of the hill with *The Generation Game*, it seemed as if television's Titanic had met the iceberg. But as with all heavyweight champions, he came through and the critics retreated. I don't think the public ever forsook him. This powerhouse is not without a sense of humour about himself and has an acute self-awareness. He once informed me, with glee, that a tabloid had printed two lists based on readers' votes: one the most popular performers on TV; the other the most unpopular. 'I was on both,' he beamed. 'That's success.' Bruce was always the virtuoso of the catch-phrase. May I present him with a new one from the unlikely lips of Arnold Schwarzenegger in *The Terminator*—'I'll be back.' And he will.

But never mind all that—on to an unexpected meeting. For a number of years, Nasty-But-Nice Nigel Lythgoe, head of light entertainment at London Weekend Television, has held a small Christmas lunch for artistes with whom they were working. I was seldom able to attend as I had normally already flown to Puerto Rico for my Christmas break. Indeed, until Wilnelia picked up a bug and we postponed our flight for a few days, this was going to be the case again. I rang up to say I could make it after all and thought no more of it. The day before, however, Ian called. Someone at London Weekend had quietly let slip that one of the other invitees to this select gathering was none other than David Liddiment. They wanted to know if this would be a problem for me. I thought about it and sent the message back that I saw no reason why either of us shouldn't go; we could always sit at opposite ends of the table! Nevertheless, as I walked into the restaurant the following day, I was feeling slightly apprehensive. As it happened, meeting David face to face was much less uncomfortable than one might have imagined and in fact we ended up having a lengthy and very good-humoured chat.

During the first couple of months of 2001, there was conciliatory correspondence and conversations between myself, my representatives and various members of the ITV hierarchy. ITV Chairman Lesley Hill, in particular, was very gracious. As I have already mentioned, being a Pisces I am quick to hatch conspiracy theories. I had become convinced that all the things that I have already mentioned were connected, part of a plot to phase me out. However, it was beginning to get hard to reconcile this view with the increasingly positive overtures from ITV, particularly after the criticisms I had voiced so publicly. Maybe, just maybe, I had got it wrong.

If anyone had suggested when I began writing this book that some five months later I would be having lunch with David Liddiment to discuss an extension of my contract with ITV, I would have doubted their sanity. This, however, is exactly what took place on my return from Puerto Rico in April. It was a magnanimous move on David's part and brought to an end a difficult and regrettable period for both of us.

To be completely honest, I still do not understand why some of the things in the previous two years happened the way they did. What I got wrong was the way I interpreted them. I had found it increasingly hard and eventually impossible to reconcile being valued by ITV on the one hand and scheduled in a way that I felt was uncaring on the other. I guess I had failed to appreciate the complexity and subtlety of modern-day scheduling. You have to remember that when I started in television there was only one channel—what is now BBC 1—and by the time I got my big break in 1958, just two—BBC 1 and ITV. Nowadays, there are hundreds of channels and nothing like as many 'safe' slots in which to schedule television programmes as there used to be. It has become an extremely complicated business that I do not pretend to understand; all I do appreciate a bit better now is how intricate and difficult a job someone like David has to do. Whether so many more television channels means better television is another matter. That's up to the viewers to judge. While there might technically be more choice, I do worry sometimes if the cake isn't being sliced a little bit too thin!

Anyway, I am grateful that I have the opportunity to do something that I enjoy and has been part of my life for so many years, a little longer. I'm also grateful that, thanks to ITV, my career in television is not to end on a sour note. I suspect some people won't believe me when I say that I have never wanted to continue working just for the sake of it, but it's true. I have had a fantastic career and sometimes I honestly can't believe that it has lasted as long as it has. Back in the fifties, as I neared my thirtieth birthday and before I got the break on *Sunday Night at the London Palladium*, I was genuinely prepared to quit rather than become one of the embittered 'nearly' men that I had met so often on my travels. Similarly, nothing to me is sadder than a performer, however successful or famous they might have once been, who lives in the past and clings to former glories. Believe me, when people no longer want to see what I do or when I feel I can't deliver what I was once capable of, I won't need anyone to tell me to pack it in. I'll be on the golf course long before that. But until then, who knows?

EPILOGUE

Over the years, so much has been written about me by other people that at times I've begun to wonder just who I am. So who am I? I wouldn't say I'm cool. I wouldn't say I'm calm. I wouldn't say I'm collected. But I am a much more relaxed person than anybody seeing me on stage or TV might think. The showbiz Bruce is an enlargement of me. I couldn't be that person all the time. He'd drive me crazy. I have to tuck him away and just bring him out when he's needed. When I'm working he has to be there. When I'm not working—or when I come home after a hard day's work or golf—I think nothing of going to bed for a couple of hours at six o'clock before getting up again for dinner. As others have said, 'being horizontal is my favourite position'!

I can, of course, get tense, annoyed, and irritable when I'm working. I can't stand incompetence. As Bill Cotton once said of me: 'Bruce is a perfectionist. He likes things to be right. He is immaculate in his appearance and he wants his work to be immaculate. I wouldn't say he has a bad temper, but he doesn't suffer fools gladly.' I don't get annoyed if someone who is *trying* makes a mistake. That's a different matter. If somebody knows they've messed up and says sorry that, too, is a different matter. But 'sorry' these days is a rarely used word. Personally, I've always made a point of using it. If I make a mistake in a studio, I say sorry to everybody on the studio floor; when I mess up, I go to the producer or director and apologize.

526

Looking back, I suppose I can be cool, calm and collected!

When one thing after another goes against me, I do get irritated. But, funnily enough, the irritation often produces a funny line. I come up with something that sums up the situation and I make myself laugh. On the whole, I'm a pretty 'up' person most of the time. A lot of showbiz people have to be on the TV or stage all the time to make them tick. If they're not, they feel lost or get bored. But not me. I go off to Puerto Rico with my lovely wife for three to four months every year and the time never drags for me. I *never* get bored. I love to read, I love to watch TV, and I love going out and discovering new restaurants. Then when I return to the UK in May to work I enjoy it all the more because I've have had such a lovely long break.

One personal regret is that I wish I had been a more pushy character. I don't mean this in a nasty way, but in a business sense. Once upon a time I had a great deal of power in television and I wish I had used some of this during the middle years to further more of my own ambitions; wish I had ensured I met more of the 'right people' and moved more often in the 'right circles', as so many people do in show business. My tendency is to be somebody who stays on the outside, not manipulating myself into situations or making arrangements to 'bump into people'. I now think all this was a mistake. There were so many stars I could have done so much more with. I should have been more upfront and involved in directing how my career should go instead of waiting in the wings for everything to come to me. But it was not in my nature to push myself, to make myself be seen in all the right places at the right time. If I had been blessed with a different kind of temperament, I could probably have done even more things I would have been very proud of.

I don't have that many friends, but then I don't need many to make my life tick. The ones I have are very close friends with whom I can always take up where we left off. That's how I like friendship to be.

I'm not a very religious person, but I do have certain spiritual beliefs. I do believe there is something waiting for us beyond this world. Like most people, I do pray, especially at times of trouble, and I have no doubt that there is a God and Jesus. But I can't go along with what has happened to religion and all the troubles and strife and wars that have been fought in its name. It disturbs me that religion has had such a negative effect on the world. I just wish we all loved the one God, or at least didn't make such a song and dance about worshipping in so many different ways. Then we would all be so much happier and all the troubles would die away.

Speaking of spiritual matters has reminded me of something very strange that happened to me one day when I was in Puerto Rico. I had just returned from playing golf and, as I opened the patio doors and went inside, there was this lovely little white heron, unique to the area, lying dead on the floor. 'How strange,' I thought. 'How could this little creature have died here?' It didn't seem to make sense. I then noticed that the answering machine was bleeping. There was a message asking me to get in touch with my niece, Barbara, because Maisie, my sister, had been taken very ill. I telephoned at once, and was told that Maisie had had a heart attack and was in intensive care. I was so afraid that, for me, this would be a repeat of what had happened with my mother and father, that I would not get home in time to be with Maisie, but I did. We booked the first flight out of Puerto Rico and when Wilnelia and I arrived at the hospital, Maisie, although in a confused state of mind, was still alive. She had the same questioning look in her eyes that I had noticed in my mother's after she had had a stroke. Maisie knew that Wilnelia and I had come back specially to see her, but she couldn't quite fathom out why we were there. I was so relieved that we were. Being with her meant so much to me.

During the week that followed she regained her memory, and we were able to have many conversations. I was able to say all the things that I had not been able to say to my parents. A couple of days before she died, although she was on morphine, she knew we were all standing around the bed. Her daughters Barbie and Lynn and her son Terry were there, not forgetting Chris, Barbara's husband, who had been so good to her over the years. In fact, we were all there. Maisie had always had a lovely sense of humour and retained it to the end, making light of everything, saying to us all: 'This is more like a party.' She was wonderful. And I was able to reassure her and say: 'Don't worry, Maisie. We will be with you until the end.' And we were. And, although I had never directly experienced the death of somebody close to me before, somehow I was able to find a strength I never knew I had to comfort Barbie, Lynn and Terry.

Although Maisie was ten years older than me, we had always been very close. The only time we ever fell out was when her friend Tony Fisher sold the photographs he had taken at my wedding to Anthea. He courted her for years, but when he finally asked her to marry him, Maisie said: 'No. Ten or fifteen years ago, I would have jumped at it, but not now. I have my own life.' Apart from that awful period, Maisie and I were always a real brother and sister. We loved each other very much. She was always so thrilled with everything I did; always wanted to be there. Whenever I did a television series, she would get a group of about fifty people together, hire a coach and come for an evening.

During the last eighteen months of her life, because she needed care and attention, she was looked after in a lovely nursing home called Lynwood. It was run by BEN, the motor trades charity—the garage business having always been our family's 'trade'—and she was very happy there. During this time, we managed to see more of each other than in many previous years and shared so many lovely moments laughing together. Like my parents, whom we both loved so very much, she was a Salvationist, as was her husband Tom. She was also a member of the Enfield Rotary Club for which she did a lot of charity work. I'm so glad we shared those extra times together and so glad we were together to the last. I've never forgotten how wonderful she was to me when I was a child and how she bore the brunt of my dreadful behaviour as the 'baby of the family'. I think she thought I had improved with age.

Of all my daughters, Laura, my youngest from

my marriage to Penny, is the one I saw the least when she was a child because she was so young when I moved out of The Paddocks at Totteridge. Because they were older, I was always able to take Debbie and Julie, my other two daughters by Penny, out at the weekends. Missing Laura's childhood has always been one of my biggest regrets, and I have often told her this. She has only really got to know me since she was grown up, but we have established a very close relationship now. She's a wonderful character, with a very good head for business. She was a BBC props buyer for a while, but is now in the middle of a new business venture which I so hope works out for her. She really is a darling. She should have furthered her singing career—she really has got a good voice. When she was going through a difficult patch, she came to stay with us in Puerto Rico and had a wonderful time. We became closer to each other then than ever before. She has a lovely sense of humour and I feel I have a daughter who is also a friend who can come to me with anything, and I can tell her anything.

Debbie, my first daughter, has always been introverted, the kind of person who keeps troubles to herself. I'm so very pleased that in her second marriage, to Richard, she has found a happiness she has not known for many years. Funnily enough, he had a crush on her when he was a teenager. I do wish, though, that she had confided in me more in the past. She's a wonderful and caring mother and she has a very calm attitude to life, which makes it easy for me to say that she deserves the best.

When I was informed that I'd been awarded the OBE, you are told that you are only allowed three people to accompany you. Wilnelia was going to come, of course, and also JJ. But there was only one way to choose who had the other place: all the other names would have to go into a hat. As I have said, of the five daughters, I drew Debbie's name. All she could say was, 'The rest of them will never believe it!'

I always enjoy my girls coming to see me. A few years ago, Debbie and Laura called to say they were popping over for a cup of tea. Laura started to tell me about how she'd broken up with her boyfriend, finishing in tears. Then Debbie told me that they were going to have to move out of their beautiful house near the golf course in Berkshire—more tears. There I was with my arms around them both, trying to console them with tea and daddy sympathy. It's the only time I wished I'd had all sons—because we could just have gone down to the local pub, had a drink and played darts!

I did say to the girls that it was a pity they couldn't type, because I needed a secretary. Debbie reminded me that she had indeed done a Lucy Clayton course and helped me out in the past—I'd been boss and dad, a dual role! Then again, JJ has surprised me with his typing skills while I've been writing this book. He's taken dictation from me like a pro. 'Your typing's terrific,' I said. 'You see, Dad,' he replied, 'all that time I spend on the computer playing games and surfing the Internet *is* worthwhile—my keyboard skills have even helped you!' No comment.

Julie, as I have mentioned before in this book, is married to Dominic Grant, whom she first met when she was fifteen years old when they were both members of the pop group Guys and Dolls. They are now very well known in Holland as the singing duo the Grants, and have a string of hit records, top-selling albums, platinum and gold albums, gold discs, and this and that behind them. They really are big stars over there and have worked very hard for their position in show business. I'm very proud of them. I will never forget the time when I went to see them when they were on the bill at the Palladium. While we were having a drink after the show, they told me that they were in love and were going to live together. I, of course, was very concerned. Dominic was still married to his childhood sweetheart at that time and Julie was only eighteen. I was so afraid she was making a mistake that she would regret later. But I didn't lay the law down, didn't want to risk driving her away by saying, 'You're too young. You can't do this.' I'm so glad I didn't, because their marriage has more than passed the test of time and they are blissfully happy together.

In 1988, to my great joy, Julie wrote a song called 'Go', which was sung by Scott Fitzgerald representing Britain in the Eurovision Song Contest. Her song failed to win by just one point. I was *so* upset. Scott Fitzgerald was a big star in Holland, who had worked for ten years in Rotterdam, but he was not awarded a single point by the Dutch, and Yugoslavia, which was the last country to vote, didn't give the song a point either. Julie's song was pipped by Celine Dion singing for Switzerland. I couldn't conceal my disappointment with the Yugoslav vote. The show had been so exciting, and I was convinced that Julie's song would walk it; that no way could she possibly lose. I'd had many knocks in my own career, but Julie's bad luck in the Eurovision was even harder for me to bear. When you love someone as much as I love her, you hate to see them lose by such a narrow margin. Julie, though, was wonderful: 'If you're going to lose by one point, it's the best way,' she said. 'If it had been by two, it wouldn't have been the same at all.' She was also more sorry for Scott than for herself. I remained devastated. I don't think I have ever been so 'up' about something and then so deflated by the lack of one vote. When the last vote was cast, the UK cameras captured a shot of me with an expression of total disbelief written all over my face.

I didn't actually meet Celine Dion until a couple of years ago when I was asked to host the National Lottery and she was the guest star. I worked out a bit of dialogue that Celine and I could do. I wanted to refer to the Eurovision Song Contest in a fun kind of way, making it clear that, as Julie's father, I didn't blame Celine in any way for winning. But when I arrived at the BBC studio, the producer met me saying that Celine Dion didn't want to take part in any dialogue at all with me. I was disappointed. She's an exceptionally good singer, who I'm sure would have made it with or without the Eurovision Song Contest, but some stars do not like to look back on their initial breakthroughs. Certainly in the UK, that was the event that brought Celine to Britain's attention. Anyway, even though she didn't want to talk to me, I still got my remarks in. When Celine had finished singing her number, I shouted after her as she left the stage, 'Oh, Celine, that was so wonderful. By the way, my love, I don't blame you for the Eurovision Song Contest when my daughter nearly won, but lost by one point. I didn't

blame you at all, my dear. It was Yugoslavia!'
When you're hosting a show you can always put the
score right like that!

What I still find difficult to understand about
Julie and Dominic's singing is that people love
country music, yet it is so rarely promoted in the
UK. Our DJs seem to play all the American stuff,
like Dolly Parton, but not our home-grown singers.
I'm sure there is a market for country, but it's
simply not given a chance. We only seem to have
one theme—pop, pop and more pop. Nothing else
gets a proper look in. I think this is because the
music business is run by just a few people who keep
it precisely the way they want it. But that's up to
them.

Now for Charlotte and Louisa, my two daughters
by Anthea—who herself is now happily remarried.
Charlotte, the eldest, is a teacher at a local
Catholic school. This was quite a difficult school
to get a position at and she is very happy there,
teaching seven-to-eight-year-olds. I remember
giving her tap-dancing lessons when she was about
four, and she was so quick in picking up steps. But
she only ever had one ambition, to be a teacher.
And what could be more worthwhile? She loves her
work, has a real vocation for it, and I'm a very
proud daddy. Her life is going along nicely and she
feels fulfilled. She and Louisa live together not far
from us at Wentworth. They often come to see us
at weekends to play tennis and we all enjoy going
out together for a meal. They're lovely girls.

I have clear memories of both Charlotte and
Louisa's graduation from college. Charlotte was
only allowed tickets for two people to attend hers,
so Anthea and I went together and we all had tea

together afterwards at the Carlton Towers Hotel. It was a very special occasion for all of us. Louisa was allowed four tickets for hers, so Anthea, her partner David, Wilnelia, and I were all able to go and we had lunch together beforehand in a hotel in Southampton.

Having chosen media studies at university, Louisa, a very tall elegant young lady, is now working for Sky TV. I don't think she has quite found her niche yet, but she wants to do something in television or films, possibly some presenting later on. Whatever she settles into, I'm sure she will go from strength to strength and find what she is looking for. Something else I remember well is how Charlotte and Louisa used to come to rehearsals for the second edition of *The Generation Game* as often as they could, and would be our 'stand-in' contestants. They really loved it and Jeff Thacker, who staged the games, was always very kind to them.

I am so lucky with all my five daughters. I love them all so dearly, would not trade one of them. I'm so proud of them. One of the best days of the year for me is Father's Day when they all come over with presents and spoil me rotten. They really do. I'm not allowed to lift a finger, and they are all just so lovely to be with. Wilnelia adores them, understands each of them, knows all their individual characters and likes and dislikes. She gets on wonderfully well with all of them. And they love her. I'm so lucky it is like this.

JJ, my only son, is now fourteen, and all my daughters adore him. He's much too handsome, I'm often told, for his own good! He could, like his mummy, be a natural at golf, and I am delighted he has a gift for music. He's learning the piano and the tenor sax, and has just added a bass guitar to his collection. He also has a good singing voice. All of which I'm thrilled about. Neither I nor Wilnelia would have any qualms if he wanted to follow in my footsteps and go into show business. This would be his decision and his decision alone. It can be a very cruel business, but then it can also be marvellous, too. It's really too soon to know what JJ will make of his life, but I have no doubt that he'll make an excellent job of whatever he decides to do. When I was going to a party where Steven Spielberg was launching a very worthy Jewish charity, JJ said: 'Daddy, will you please get Steven Spielberg's autograph for me?' So, to please him, I lined up with everybody else and, to excuse myself, told Spielberg it was for my son. After he'd signed, I added: 'I feel I must tell you, my son particularly asked for your autograph because he wants to take it to school and sell it.' 'He sounds a good businessman,' Spielberg replied.

I do honestly regret not being a younger father for JJ. I'd love to have been able to pick him up and throw him around the way dads do with their kids, and been able to play physical sports with him more. I do take him on the golf course with me when he wants to come—which isn't very often. But he will take his own time to find out what he wants to do.

Two other characters complete our household. Although I once had a dog called Rusty, whom I adored, another Rusty has crept into my life—a ginger cat. The end of his tail looks like it's been dipped in white paint. He's got something of a split personality: one minute he's lying in the sun

537

daydreaming, but if he notices you creeping towards him he'll crouch on the grass like a tiger, almost winding himself up inside like a clockwork toy. When he reaches the point where he can't contain himself any longer, he'll leap in the air and charge at your legs. If you try and stroke him during one of his more insane moments, he'll grab at your arms. But this is all part of the daily routine of this crazed feline. JJ chose him, taking his apparent shyness at face value. How wrong he was!

Cora is our housekeeper. She is from the Philippines, and is famous in the neighbourhood for her homemade spring rolls—which are indeed delicious! She is a little dynamo and can turn her hand to anything. What with my wife from Puerto Rico, my housekeeper from the Philippines and my Spanish gardeners, I sometimes don't know what country I'm in!

I now have four grandchildren: Luke and Sophie from Julie and Dominic; and Josie and Jeremy, Debbie's children.

Luke, who was born on 3 August 1980, is now on the threshold of stardom in pop music. Once when I went to Holland to see his parents' show, all of a sudden this guy burst on to the stage with a guitar, jumping up and down on the rostrum, and making a phenomenal noise. I suddenly realized it was Luke. This was such a shock because he had always been such an introverted child who only ever got demonstratively excited about Michael Jackson. I was so flabbergasted at the transformation in him that Wilnelia had to say: 'Close your mouth, darling'! Luke and his group have now been signed up in Holland for a five-record deal and brought out their first album. I am so thrilled for him. In the summer of 2000, when I returned to England from Puerto Rico, Julie told me that Luke had got a gig at the Rock Garden Café, Covent Garden, and would love me to come and hear him. 'I'll be there,' I said. When I arrived, I was taken down steps into the depths of the café where Julie and other members of the family were waiting to gather around me because they didn't want anybody to come up and disturb me during the gig. The group had just started to play, and there was Luke, the lead singer, up there with three other guys, doing his thing, and everybody was loving it. At the end of the set, while we were all standing there clapping and saying, 'Great,' this huge guy—about four feet wide—walked across the floor right at me. 'Oh God,' I thought. ' 'Allo, Bruce,' he said in his very cockney accent. 'I didn't know you were into 'eavy metal.' 'Well, I'm not really,' I replied. 'I'm more into light aluminium.' 'Well, it's good to see you in a place like this,' he laughed. 'It's great—really cool, man.' 'Yeah, cool, man,' I said.

When Luke took me upstairs to say goodbye, he said: 'What do you think, Grandad?' 'Well, Luke,' I said, 'I've got to be honest with you, this kind of music will never find a real home in my heart, because I grew up in a different age, and my kind of music is at the other end of the street, a good block away. But what I *can* appreciate is your dedication, the way your beat stays together all the time, and the wonderful rhythm it has. You lads must have rehearsed very hard to get such a professional sound. So, in that respect, I appreciate what you're doing one hundred per cent. And I wish you and the group all the luck in the world.'

Just before Luke became interested in heavy

metal he was quite into jazz and would say: 'Grandad, tell me what this is all about.' For one of his birthdays, I bought him a couple of Stephane Grappelli and Django Rheinhardt CDs, saying: 'You might like some of this stuff, Luke—not all of it, perhaps, but some of it.' I was very pleased when he came back, saying: 'I really relate to some of it, Grandad. I'm really into it.' Then, when he visited us for Thanksgiving, and brought his guitar with him, he named a few pieces of music. 'I don't know any of those,' I said. 'Well,' said Luke, 'can you play a twelve-bar blues in E flat?' That was more like it. We did a session together for the family. He was really good. I'm hoping, of course, that he will grow even more into the sort of music I play, so that we can play together more often. Then if JJ keeps on with his tenor sax, practising more than he does at the moment!, we might all be able to play together.

Last New Year's Eve, I played on my Yamaha Clavinova, a wonderful keyboard that enables you to be every instrument in the orchestra. I'm hoping to do a CD with it. When Luke was sitting beside me, I could feel him working out why I go from that chord to this chord. I'm so glad he appreciates the mysteries involved in chord sequences and what goes into a certain type of jazz. Later on in life, he may get even more into it, which would mean so much to me. He definitely has the feeling for it and, like everything else in life, if you have the feeling for something you are more likely to delve further. 'Stay with it, Luke,' I say. 'Next time I'm in Harrods, I'm going to look out some more jazz CDs for you.'

Sophie, Luke's sister and our youngest grandchild, is a cute little madam. Both she and

Luke have grown up in show business. And Sophie certainly knows what it's like to stand at the side of the stage when Mummy and Daddy are performing, and is occasionally allowed to take a bow at the end of a performance. She has a lovely little voice, and we sometimes coax her to sing for us. At Thanksgiving, all the men had to leave the room, except for me, so that I could play 'The Black Hills of Dakota', which she sings in harmony with Julie. I'm sure as she grows older, we will hear more of her singing voice. She has what I call 'attitude'—sounds much more grown-up than she is, and comes out with rather old-fashioned statements that are far beyond her years. Now aged nine, she talks like a thirty-year-old. She's absolutely adorable, very self-assured, and we all love her. Apart from all this, she is an accomplished horsewoman and rides practically every day.

My granddaughter Josie, born on 1 October 1982, is a beautiful girl with a lovely manner. I remember phoning her from Puerto Rico with my phone card, which means I have to dial thirty-nine digits to get through. She answered and said, 'Can you phone back, Grandad. I'm talking to someone.' I kid her about this and her slight Dorset accent. Where she got this, I do not know. To more serious stuff, she finished her A-levels in art and photography with A-grades in each, and one of her ceramic pieces won first prize in not only 2000's West London Independent Schools Association art and craft competition, but also the national one. I went along to see her A-level work before the examiners and was very impressed, so I wasn't at all surprised by her results—although of course I am

541

biased! She is now taking a 'year out' to think about what to do next: besides art and photography she is interested in special effects make-up, and is also a talented singer and songwriter! She really is a marvellous girl as well as multi-talented, and I'm sure she'll have a wonderful future.

My grandson Jeremy, born on 13 July 1984, said to me the other day: 'I hope you are going to give me a chapter in your book, Grandad.' He had just been informed that he was one of only eight boys from all the public schools in Britain chosen to play golf on the East Coast of America for three weeks in April 2001. Proud grandad that I am, let me quote from his letter of invitation: 'The field for selection this year was very strong indeed and it is a great accolade for you. Your golfing talent, your generous contribution to a team and your soundness as an ambassador for your school and country in this tour to the United States are most convincing.'

I started him off with golf. I showed him how to grip the club and hit a few balls, and used to take him to the short course at Wentworth. When he started having proper lessons, the teacher asked him if anyone had given him some tips. 'Yes, my grandad,' he replied. The teacher said: 'He did a good job,' which pleased me immensely. He's a three handicap already, which is quite amazing, and it's still going down. How can he be sixteen years of age and be a three handicap? I've been playing for over fifty years and I'm a twelve handicap. Sometimes life just isn't fair! He really has a wonderful swing and so much potential. To have achieved the East Coast of America trip is fantastic. I'm so proud of him and his progress in the game. I hope his dedication is justly rewarded.

* * *

Looking back, there are three really big moments of my career that I so enjoy reflecting on. The first has to be my opening night hosting *Sunday Night at the London Palladium* in 1958, the kind of break that all artistes dream about happening and, for me, it did. That was absolutely wonderful—something I will never ever forget. My only regret is that there were no videotapes then because I would love to watch some of those programmes again. The next biggie has to be the opening night of *Little Me*, which was sensational. There were so many show-stopping numbers in that musical; so many wonderful moments, not only for me but for the rest of the cast, too. And the ovations and reviews were terrific, memorably wonderful. The third has to be doing my one-man shows, a big achievement for me and, although I did these in many places, the most memorable, of course, was the Palladium, my all-time favourite theatre. Performing it there meant so much to me. Just a minute, there will have to be *four* big moments. How could I leave out the *Sammy and Bruce* show?

As far as showbiz is concerned, I would like to be remembered as an all-round entertainer rather than a game-show host who launched a thousand catch-phrases. As a human being, I would like to be remembered as a person who always saw both sides of every argument; somebody who lived up to my Pisces symbol that shows fishes swimming in two different directions. I would also like to be remembered as fair-minded—but as somebody with whom people couldn't take liberties. Whenever I have thought I was being treated unfairly, or when there's a wrong to be righted, I have always had the strength to stand up to be counted. I am straight with people and never go behind their back. I don't like being forced into situations, I like to make up my own mind. I know I can sometimes be wrong and, unlike some people, I will always admit this and say sorry if I am. Then if there is anything I can do to put matters right, I will. If I have inadvertently said something that has been misconstrued, I will put it right with the person rather than delegate it or sweep it under the carpet.

Whatever mistakes I have made in my life, I have always tried to live by certain principles— what people call a code. I've tried to be a loving but reasonably strict father with all my children. This is more difficult today because times and family life have changed so much and many children are, in my opinion, spoiled from an early age. I try not to let JJ get away with too much, try to impress upon him that he is blessed with health and wealth, lives in a lovely home and, although he is very privileged to go to a wonderful public school, many people have a hard time, just as I did in the early days of my career. I also try to help him to appreciate that he has had a truly wonderful upbringing, with an exceptional mother who is beautiful in every sense of the word. Wilnelia is so good with him, and I so want him to appreciate how special a mother she is.

Although I have been married three times, I am good friends with my ex-wives and have remained close to all our daughters. I'm proud of that. I hope I have been a good dad to them, even though I didn't see as much of them as I would have liked during their early lives. At least, since then, they know that I am here for them and that they can always come to me. Above all, I would like them and JJ to remember me as a man who tried to be a good dad, a man who knew how to give and receive affection—and who was demonstrative in a way that few people are in showing his love. And romantic, which I am and have always been!

Since I met Wilnelia, which is twenty years ago now, although I have been on television thirty-four weeks a year, my workload has only been three weeks in Leeds where *The Price Is Right is* recorded, and about six weeks for the other shows. So I am talking about ten weeks' work that covers several months' appearance on television. Which is just perfect! Wilnelia and I have the rest of the year to be together. She's given me a real sense of peace. She was worth waiting for.

I'll end this book as I started it, on the first line of a song: 'I'll never love this way again'!

APPENDIX

For golfers only—everyone else can just skip these pages.

● FORSYTH

BRUCE

Jack Nicklaus Esq.   10th May, 1989

Dear Jack,

I've had the pleasure of playing with many, many famous golfers including:

Bernhard Langer	Lee Trevino
Seve Ballesteros	Sandy Lyle
Greg Norman	Tom Watson
Nick Faldo	Ian Woosnam
Gary Player	Arnold Palmer
Peter Alliss	Bobby Locke
Harold Henning	Bob Charles
Mark O'Meara	Jerry Pate
Johnny Miller	Tom Weiskopf
Ben Crenshaw	Craig Stadler
Ray Floyd	Tony Jacklin
Rodger Davis	Mark McNulty

The fact I've never had the honour of walking some fairways with you, and playing beside you, makes my golfing life incomplete.

Should you be in the Wentworth area anytime soon, please come and be my guest for the day.

Yours sincerely,

Bruce Forsyth

P.S. I've just thought of a few more, Jack:

Clive Clark; Michael King; John O'Leary; Mark James; Paul Way;
Sam Torrance; David J. Russell; Howard Clark; Christy O'Connor;
Bernard Gallacher; Dave Thomas; Brian Barnes; Neil Coles; Jack
Newton; Eamonn D'Arcy; Ronan Rafferty; Chi Chi Rodriguez; Doug
Sanders; Tommy Horton; John Jacobs; Manuel Pinero; Ian Mosey;
Larry Nelson; John Davies; Bruce Critchley; Peter McEvoy; Peter
Townsend; David A. Russell; Antonio Garrido; David Feherty;
Gordon J. Brand; Max Faulkner; Guy Wolstenholme; Manuel Calero;
Jose-Maria Olazabal; Vicente Fernandex; Gordon Brand Jnr; Fuzzy
Zoeller; Hugh Baiocchi.

Jack Nicklaus

May 30, 1989

Dear Bruce:

Thank you for your letter. You know, I've been hearing Greg and Ben and Lee and a lot of the other guys talk about the great experience they had playing golf with Bruce Forsyth. Now, I enjoy a good time just as much as the next guy, and I was beginning to wonder why you never invited me!

Actually, my schedule is usually pretty tight, but if I'm in the Wentworth area, I will do my best to give you a call. I just hope my game is up to yours!

Best regards,